God's Legacy of Love~Jesus

By

Grace Newheart Love

ISBN: 1-4033-4330-6 (e-book)
ISBN: 1-4033-4331-4 (Paperback)

This book is printed on acid free paper.

1stBooks – rev. 03/18/04

Dedication

I wish to dedicate this devotional to Almighty God our Father, His only Son Jesus our Savior, and His Holy Spirit. It was by the power of the Holy Spirit that these writings have come…Of myself, it would have been impossible…The Power of God makes all the difference in our lives, when He proposes to do a work, and we are obedient… … …   *GNL*

Lord, I renounce my desire for human praise;
For the approval of my peers;
The need for public recognition…
I deliberately put these aside today,
Content to hear You whisper
"Well done, My faithful servant."
Anonymous

All monies received from the sale of this book is for charitable endeavors.

Introduction

I refer to the pages in this devotional as "writings"...The first writing came while having a telephone conversation with my dearest friend, DWR*. During this conversation, I said something and she said I must write a poem about those thoughts. I told her I had never been able to write a poem in all my life. She kept insisting; I kept refusing. Finally she said "Promise me you will put these thoughts down on paper as soon as we hang up."

I promised and went to my typewriter. As soon as I put my fingers on the keyboard my fingers flew and in a few minutes I had filled the 8 1/2 x 11 page! I pulled the page out and was amazed to read it! I rushed to the phone and shared it with her. The Lord generously entitled this first writing "Your Gift," (Jan. 2nd). It is about the gift of LIFE which Almighty God gives each of us so lovingly...That was the first of over 600 writings.

As our Lord continued bringing them forth, I could see that they continually reflected praise, thanksgiving and gratitude to Him...They were filled with messages to us to try to understand His LOVE and also His Forgiveness for us...Several of the writings had actual circumstances surrounding them...Many of them have been encouraging, especially to those who did not know much about Jesus Christ as Savior...God has used them in amazing ways to bring miracles about...

DWR and I had another dear sister through Jesus - CAP. She is now with our dear Jesus in her Heavenly Home. As the writings came and I would share them with these two loving Christians they encouraged me to continue to listen to the Lord. CAP was the first one to speak about making a daily devotional. She would always ask me what number I had just finished (I always numbered them). When I would tell her, she would get so excited and tell me that the time was getting closer to publication!

My Pastor RWB was the first person to talk about having them printed as I had well over 400 at the time. He suggested putting a Scripture with each writing. Thank You Pastor, for your encouragement...

---

*(Initials are used rather than names)

I felt that I needed someone deeply experienced in the Lord, and in the Scriptures, to critique the writings. A dear lady, SHO, suggested several ladies' names, and one of those ladies recommended MS. I spoke to her on the phone. We agreed to pray for a month to see if the Lord was calling her to be connected with me in preparing the writings for publication. Without reading any of them MS called and said that the Lord had put on her heart to become part of this work. When she first read some of the writings, she suggested putting a Scripture on each of them. Immediately I told her that it was a confirmation from the Lord! It confirmed Pastor RWB's suggestion of putting a Scripture on each writing. MS has been faithfully working with me for over four years. Without her help this book could not have been accomplished.

My son, JCC, has been a tremendous help in preparing the manuscript for this devotional. Another of my very dear friends, MCF, has been very supportive of these writings since I met her over six years ago. I am so grateful to the countless others who have been supportive to me over the years. Thank You, dear Lord Jesus, for bringing to me those You knew would be encouragers.

My name will not be connected with this devotional. Many years ago the Lord let me know that my name was not to be used. He gave me the pen name "Grace Love".

Some years later while in the hospital due to a heart problem, a dear friend, NRM, called me and told me that God was going to give me a new heart. While I was in the hospital records indicated that there was an unexplainable change in my heart! Just as NRM had said, God gave me a new heart! The August 15th writing called A New Heart! tells this story. Years later, God inserted "Newheart" into my pen name and it is now Grace Newheart Love.

May you be encouraged to listen to the Lord and obey whatever He may tell you to do…As our dear Savior said in John 15:9 – "When you obey me you are living in my love, just as I obey my Father and live in his love." May we all continue to live in His love… … …

GNL

NOTES TO THE READER

Upon rereading these writings, I am continually aware of the constancy of exclaiming to God our Father and Jesus His Son, my thankfulness to them! Gratitude seems to be one of the themes throughout the devotional. His Forgiveness and unconditional LOVE continually flow through. This is so that we understand how deep His special LOVE is for each one of us. He also desires us to show our love and gratitude to Him...

There has been a long span of time between the first writing and the latest one. The Lord was teaching me as the years passed by. The writing "Guiding Light" on March 23rd reflects this, along with several others.

Dear reader, though these words came to me, I strongly feel that these same words can be for you also. If you desire to do so, please take them as if you personally are experiencing them.

The word LOVE is capitalized when it refers to God's LOVE because it is so much greater than we can grasp! The word LIFE is also capitalized, for it is a precious gift from God. In specific writings other words may also be capitalized or printed in bold for emphasis.

Only once did the Holy Spirit bring forth a sequence of writings. This started with Palm Sunday, the Sunday before Easter. He began a series of writings about Our Lord. These were as follows: My Lord's Feet, My Lord's Face, My Lord's Hands, My Lord's Body, My Lord's Blood, Our Crucified Lord, Rest in Peace, Lord, and Glory, Alleluia! These along with other writings for special days are included in the back of the book. These are listed in the section "Special Days"; see page 468

On some of the writings you will notice words which are in quotes and in script. These are the words the Lord spoke so specifically to me that it was almost audible. His direct words to me are difficult to explain and it was necessary for them to be given special emphasis.

The majority of the Scriptures quoted are from the Living Bible. If any other version has been used, it is indicated in parenthesis after the Bible reference.

"WOW" can stand for several ways of describing God! It can stand for Without Words – for there are no words to adequately describe Him! It can also stand for Wonder of Wonders, which our awesome God surely is… He is also a Worker of Wonders!

Where an exclamation point is used, it is a reminder to be excited about what the Lord is accomplishing! At the end of many sentences there are three dots…These are to encourage you to pause and meditate about what was just expressed…

*Important Note – Message about Salvation on page 467.

January

The New Year   Jan 1

Matthew 5:14-16

"You are the world's light—a city on a hill, glowing in the night for all to see. Don't hide your light! Let it shine for all; let your good deeds glow for all to see, so that they will praise your heavenly Father."

"I give you a new year... This is a new beginning for you, and you, and you... Heartaches are to be left behind – gratitude should be the desire of your heart... You have been given so much: the gift of Life, the gift of Myself... Look around you, all around you. Seek out reasons to be grateful for you have been given so much.

The past is the past and is to be forgotten. Only you can make a difference in the decisions you make... Will they be positive or negative? Dwell on these thoughts, dear hearts... Time is fleeting."

Yes Lord, time is slipping away—there is no stopping it...What can we do to make it more meaningful, Lord? What MUST I do, dear Jesus, to be in Your will?

Can you, who are reading this, or I, make a difference in this messed up world? Yes, we can...But do we want to? That is the question...

The world has been darkened by man's sin and corruption...Yet in this darkness we CAN make a difference! You showed me this, Lord, when I was in a completely darkened room. When I turned the dimmer switch on ever so gradually, a tiny bit of light made a difference in that darkened room. As I turned the dimmer switch up more and more, the room took on such radiance that I was almost blinded! You showed me that we can be light-bearers in the darkness of this world.

Are we content to be as we were one year ago? Are we content to be just stuck there? Are we willing to grow and become workers in Your mighty harvest in the world?

Dear Lord, we can be that light if we allow You to shine through us...The more we empty ourselves the more there is room inside to radiate You, dear Jesus...

We each can be a light in this world – *"Time is fleeting"*... ... ...

Your Gift   Jan 2

2nd Corinthians 9:15

Thank God for his Son – his Gift too wonderful for words.

Dear sweet Jesus, You made us. You gave us all that we are and all that we have. Without You we are hopelessly lost and alone...

When You made us, You wrapped each and every one of us, ever so gently, in layers of very thin wrappings, like tissue paper, protecting a very special and delicate gift.

Then, in our growth, we start to add to these layers ourselves, adding one layer after another, until we are pitifully lost inside! It is our way of thinking we are protecting ourselves from the hurts of this world...

As life continues, we get so involved with ourselves, we forget that we are a gift from You. We forget that in order to enjoy this gift, it is necessary to share this gift of Life with others, and above all, with You.

The only way we can do this is to yield to Your Holy Spirit. He can perform this very delicate, but necessary, operation by having us share with others the joys and praises You deserve, by praying openly to You, not just in the privacy of our own hearts...

Each time You give us courage, and enable us to pray and to sing out Your praises and express our love for You, Your Spirit begins to remove these wrappings.

Only after He removes all these coverings which divide us from You, can You really look at us again, purely and honestly. Then You will see Your precious gift of Life and Your added bonus, LOVE, flowing through us, because of Jesus Christ.

It is only in opening our hearts to You before the whole, wide world, that we are able to stand before You and feel that in some way, we have returned to You a small portion of the gifts You have given us!

Thank You, sweet Jesus, our Lord, especially for the greatest gift of all, YOU! We praise You and glorify You and will love You always... ... ...

"The Greatest Of These Is Love" **Jan 3**

1st Corinthians13:13

There are three things that remain—faith, hope, and love—and the greatest of these is love.

"...And the greatest of these is love." Yes, Father, the greatest gift of all is love...Unfortunately, it is often the most misunderstood of all Your gifts, too, Lord. If only we could all love like You Love us! You Love us when we are weak, strong-willed, indifferent to You, selfish, unkind, and so many more unpleasant ways in which we behave...

Yet when we love, especially those around us, we expect them to be worthy of our love! We forget that You Love us when we are so unlovable! We feel that others should appreciate the love, which we have for them. Sometimes they don't return this feeling of "love" like we think they should. Our feelings get hurt; our love for them begins to falter...The more we think about it, the more we come to the conclusion that they do not love us, so perhaps we should stop loving them to some degree...

It's easy to love those who are lovable; the real test is to love those around us who become unlovable to us! That's the hard part of love! That's the time when we come to better understand what love is all about! That's the time when we have to look deep within our hearts and examine the real meaning of love.

Is it a giving-taking thing? Is it just taking, just giving? You give me some love, I'll give you some! We hear it on the radio and TV, on tapes and CD's, and everywhere we go - love. Yet so very few really understand what love is all about...

Love is giving of oneself for the sake of another. It is a pure act of giving without any strings attached...Love is never thinking there will be some personal gain from it. It is the hardest thing to do, to learn with our selfish natures. It is the thing we have to continually work at every day, every hour, every minute.

Dear Lord, it is impossible without You to guide us, each and every moment of our waking hours! We can try, but until we put our weak selves into Your hands, we are going to continue getting bogged down in our human selfishness! We beg You to help us with this, dear

Father! We want to be able to love like You Love us, to be filled with Your Love - Your Divine Love! We want to be able to love everyone we come in contact with, because of Your undying Love for us!

Please keep near us, dear Lord, and remind us of Your example – CALVARY... ... ...

Don't Worry!   Jan 4

Philippians 4:6

Don't worry about anything; instead, pray about everything; tell God your needs and don't forget to thank him for his answers.

Colossians 3:1,2

Since you became alive again, so to speak, when Christ arose from the dead, now set your sites on the rich treasures and joys of heaven where he sits beside God in the place of honor and power. Let heaven fill your thoughts; don't spend your time worrying about things down here.

Please Lord, teach us to accept one day at a time. Teach us not to worry about tomorrow...Teach us to keep ever in our minds, the joy of Easter, the joy of rebirth, and the joy of hope! As we get through today, keeping our minds on You and the wonderful promises You have made to us about Heaven we will keep our hearts open to You...When our hearts are open, You will fill them!

Sometimes we forget, dear Lord, and try to fill our hearts ourselves. Then we find ourselves bogged down and before we know it, we are dragging along...Remind us, Father if we look upwards, our thoughts can only dwell on what is pleasing to You. Suddenly our hearts empty themselves of our littleness and You are then able to fill us with the true joy of knowing and loving You!

Lord, what wasted hours we have spent worrying in our lives! Nothing was ever accomplished by it. We only ended up by losing sleep and sometimes our tempers! Some of us are worriers by nature. We are not happy unless we have something to worry about! Lord Jesus, we'll have to work overtime with You about this. We really don't want to worry, but then we find ourselves doing it again the first time things don't seem to go our way!

Perhaps that's the clue right there, Jesus, - when things don't seem to go our way! Perhaps it's because we haven't learned that important lesson yet, Lord...

We have to learn to turn our lives over to You. We have to step aside and say:

"Please, Father I've tried to make a go of my life, but all I do is end up worrying about this and that, and then there's that, and oh, I can't forget about this. See, Lord, how I am? I need You; I want You, Lord. I love You; I trust You. Take over my life for me...Whatever You decide to do with me will be OK with me...I know You do love me. I know You know what is best for me...I know You love my loved ones too. I know I can turn over my loved ones to You and You will care for them, protect them. So here I am... I offer up my prayers to You, turning my life over to You to do with me what You desire.. Thank You my Lord, for loving me and caring for me..."

Knowing this Father, and practicing this, does bring relief - release...Thank You sweet Jesus, our Savior and Lord... ... ...

Mirrors of Our Souls...   Jan 5

Ezekiel 36:26,27
"And I will give you a new heart—I will give you new and right desires—and put a new spirit within you. I will take out your stony hearts of sin and give you new hearts of love. And I will put my Spirit within you so that you will obey my laws and do whatever I command."

Why is it Lord, that we shudder when we allow ourselves to really peek into our souls? Isn't it strange how we don't mind looking into a mirror and seeing the outside of our bodies and faces. How differently we might view our souls' reflections...

What a terrible thing, Lord, if when passing a mirror our very souls were exposed for us to see! How terrifying that would be, dear Lord, at certain times in our lives. We would avoid at all cost the possibility of ever having to look into mirrors again. For there we might see the reflections of our souls...

Yet, Lord, look at all the beauty You created in this world reflected in Your beautiful lakes and ponds! Some are nestled at the foot of mountains capped with snow. Others are beside sunny meadows. Wouldn't it be wonderful if we could reflect such pure beauty...

Lord, we can You say? But how? How can we change the images we have of ourselves in our very souls after looking there honestly? It is possible?

Tell me, Lord, tell me how...

"Follow Me. Follow Me by getting to know Me... Read about Me. Dwell on Me... Meditate about Me... Pray with Me. Soon you will see how I will change you - change your life – change your reflection of yourself. Where you once saw something in yourself that you wanted to hide, I will take it all away! Just as a muddied pond can be restored to its purest state, I will restore your soul so you may clearly, brightly, and purely reflect Me."

Dear Lord Jesus, how wonderful it is to finally realize there is a way for our images, our reflections to be changed! Why is it now that You have told me Your messages I see a special glow on the faces of those who love You most...Was it there before? Or do I only see it since You spoke to me?

Heavenly Father, what a wonderful world this would be if all our faces could reflect Your Love for us! This world would be full of reflections of beauty and love... ... ...

Hope   Jan 6

Romans 15:13
So I pray for you Gentiles that God who gives you hope will keep you happy and full of peace as you believe in him. I pray that God will help you overflow with hope in him through the Holy Spirit's power within you.

Our hope is in the name of the Lord! Oh dear Lord, that is so true! Thank You for being our Hope! How bleak our lives would be without Your Hope, never to be able to feel that something better will happen in our lives...

Without Your Hope, it would be like living in solitary confinement with no possibility of ever being released: day after day, week after week, month after month, year after year...Just thinking about that Lord, fills me with a frightening sympathy for anyone who does live like that...

Sweet Jesus, the sad thing about it is they don't have to live without Your Hope! All they have to do is to accept You into their hearts as their Savior and Lord, to be sorry for their sins. Then they too, can share the hope only You can provide! Then the remaining days they have left on earth can be filled with joy also: the joy, which only comes from knowing You, and loving You in a deep and special way!

Isn't it wonderful dear Lord, we can never run out of Your Hope; there is always some left over for another time! The more we use, the more there is! It's just like love; it's like a fountain flowing from an eternal spring! Come to think of it Father, there are so many beautiful things, which come from You! You are the source of all true Hope, Joy, Love, Beauty, Wisdom and Faith! Oh sweet Lord, everything worth having in this whole world comes from You!

When we were children we found it so easy to have hope. We would hope for the seemingly impossible, never doubting that our "hope" would come true! So many have lost this childlike quality or even worse, sweet Jesus, never even had it as children. Please reveal to them that with You in their hearts, they will never be without Your Hope again! This is Your promise, isn't it Lord?

There is an expression we have all heard so many times, "Where there is life, there is hope!" Dear Lord, for those who don't yet understand that You are the source of life, that You are the giver and taker of life, have pity on them. Give them the desire to find this truth…Let them know that Your Hope is possible because of You, Jesus Christ, Savior of the world!

What Is LOVE?   Jan 7

1ST Corinthians13:4-7

Love is very patient and kind, never jealous or envious, never boastful or proud, never haughty or selfish or rude. Love does not demand its own way. It is not irritable or touchy. It does not hold grudges and will hardly even notice when others do it wrong. It is never glad about injustice, but rejoices whenever truth wins out. If you love someone you will be loyal to him no matter what the cost. You will always believe in him, always expect the best of him, and always stand your ground in defending him.

In this world there are so many people we love and many who love us. Yet when it comes down to a real commitment, do they really love us? Do we really love them?

Little resentments, little hurts (real or imagined) seem to climb in between us and our so-called loved ones. Do we really know what love is all about? Can we even come at all close to the real meaning of love?

Love means so many different things to so many different people...If only we could truly realize Your meaning of the word "Love" dear Jesus...

Your Love is the most perfect kind of love: unconditional Love toward Your children. You were the only perfect man born of human flesh. You were spotless in this world. You committed no crime, no not even the very least, against another human being. You were loving and kind to bird and beast; no living thing knew anything but love from You.

But when men could no longer stand Your kind of Love, they felt compelled to destroy You...You were the only One ever born of this world who should have been spared any of the world's agony...Yet you willingly laid down Your very life for us.

And so sweet Jesus, You showed the world what pure Love is. Like a spotless white lamb You unselfishly died for all of us. There were no recriminations, no shout of "But I'm not guilty!". There was only Your gentle acceptance of Your role as our Savior. That vicious, brutal murderous act by all mankind was received by You with the words, "Father, forgive them for they know not what they do."

Dear Savior of ours, greatest teacher of true Love, show us and help us to learn how to truly love, as You Love us... ... ...

Faith   Jan 8

Hebrews 11:1
What is faith? It is the confident assurance that something we want is going to happen. It is the certainty that what we hope for is waiting for us, even though we cannot see it up ahead.

Faith - are we born with faith? Some people seem to be blessed with this gift. It is a gift, a wonderful gift. It's knowing from the time of your first remembrance that you could feel there was a "Father" somewhere up in the sky looking down and taking care of you. It's feeling comforted just knowing He was up there behind those big, fluffy, white clouds.

As we grow older though, logic sets in, we begin to wonder if there really is Someone up there after all...Perhaps that was just a story, a beautiful one, but just a story we were told as we were growing up. Now that we are adults and can reason for ourselves, can it actually be true?

Faith is feeling complete confidence in something or someone. Now that has to mean something pretty strong, like the sun coming up in the morning and setting at the end of the day. We have faith it will be happening tomorrow and the next day and the day after. We have faith in that, because hasn't it been happening every day of our lives? Doesn't it get dark every night too? Well, that's something else to have faith in...

Come to think of it, there are really not too many things that I can have faith in. Let's see now, there are also the tides, and then there is Christmas I can have faith in. Well, we know very definitely that Christmas will be celebrated. We have faith in that!

Christmas...wait a minute, did I just hear a baby cry? A newborn baby? What does a baby's cry have to do with faith?

Lord, that was Your baby Son, Jesus, whom You sent down here to us? How did You ever have the courage to let Your innocent little baby Son be born here on earth? You had faith in us, Lord? Oh, not us, but You had faith in Your Son to come down here to live and die for us! You had faith in Him that He would become our Savior, and through His death on the cross, would become the most wonderful teacher of faith Himself!

The Son had faith enough in You, His Father, to lay His Life down for us, knowing He could trust You to keep Your promise to Him. Now He is back with You sharing the joys You promised Him. That's faith, dear Lord!

Father of perfect Faith, teach us to always have Faith in You... ... ...

Refreshment   Jan 9

Matthew 11:28-30
"Come to me and I will give you rest—all of you who worked so hard beneath a heavy yoke. Wear my yoke—for it fits perfectly—and let me teach

you; for I am gentle and humble, and you shall find rest for your souls; for I give you only light burdens."

"Come to Me all you who are burdened and I will refresh you..."

Dear Lord Jesus, what a comforting thought that is. How can anyone resist such an invitation? Every day of our lives we are made aware of the many burdens, which are being carried by Your children. For many it would be completely impossible for them to be able to go on without some help, some refreshment from You...

Lord, thank You so much for that refreshment, for that is what communication with You is...We could never be refreshed, never be comforted without You. We would go through life with more agony without You to ease our burdens.

We need to learn the truth of turning to You, by communicating with You, whether it be in conversation, meditation, reflection or prayer. Then in every decision we make we are refreshed by leaving these burdens at Your feet! It is like taking a huge sack off our shoulders after carrying it for days and days! What relief it is to be able to unload that burden! How much freer we feel going about our daily lives without this terrible weight on our shoulders...Life becomes enjoyable once more...

Can this apply to everything in our life, sweet Jesus? Everything? That's so hard to believe! It seems that we have just begun to be able to manage our affairs and be our own decision-maker and now You tell us we should turn everything over to You! It seems logical to turn over the problems and the burdens, Lord; they're a relief to be rid of! But to hand over all the fun of making up our own minds, that's something else, Jesus...Why do we have to turn over this part of our lives too?

Yes, Lord...We see it all now...There cannot be two captains of one ship...You cannot let us go in one direction and You in another; we would capsize. Especially when the waters become rough, it is more important than ever to have one person in command! Strange too, Lord, even when the waters become calm, it is more effective to have only one captain...

You have convinced us, Lord, to turn over the leadership of our lives to You. Please be the captain of our ship. Please direct our every stroke in life to where You know the waters will be the safest! Now we can really enjoy the voyage You have destined us for. We can relax knowing full well that You are in command! Thank You, dear Lord, we feel cooled and refreshed already, knowing You are there at the helm... ... ...

My Father's Work   Jan 10

John 5:17,19,20

But Jesus replied, "My Father constantly does good, and I'm following his example." Jesus replied, "The Son can do nothing by himself. He does only what he sees the Father doing and in the same way. For the Father loves the Son, and tells him everything he is doing; and the Son will do far more awesome miracles than this man's healing."

Jesus was constantly about His Father's work...What a beautiful thought! But how can we be about our Father's work? How can we learn from the way Jesus carried out the work of His Father?

We can't help but think it must have been easy for Jesus to go about His Father's work. He was Jesus and we are only mortals, but was it any easier for Jesus? Did people want to listen to Him any more than they want to listen to us? Wasn't there always someone in the crowd to say "Prove what you are saying!" How discouraging that must have been for Him ...

How many times when we have tried to do our Father's work did people get a distrusting look on their faces. How many times will we continue to try? Sometimes we wonder why God beckoned to us to become one of His fishermen. How quickly the doubts settle in...

Maybe I'm not really meant to be used as one of Christ's workers; maybe someone else should do it, because they could do it better than I...After all, as long as my soul is saved, isn't that enough? Why should I have to worry about my brother's soul? Shouldn't he watch out for his own soul?

But, why me Lord? Nobody wants to listen to me! I have no special talent; I have no special gifts...Oh, Lord, You will give me these gifts? You will help me to do Your work? You say that all I have to do is to ask You, and You will give them to me!

All right Father, I'm asking. I'm seeking. I'm knocking on the door of Your Heart for these gifts. And when You do see fit to send me the gifts I need to do "My Father's work," please send me a double portion of Your special Love! I need the kind You had for all of mankind, the kind which will make me truly care about my brother's soul...

In the meanwhile I'll watch to see where You are working and follow Jesus' example...I look forward to Your gifts that I too, may be about the work of Our Father... ... ...

Your Loving Touch   Jan 11

Matthew 14:35,36
The news of their arrival spread quickly throughout the city, and soon people were rushing around, telling everyone to bring in their sick to be healed. The sick begged him to let them touch even the tassel of his robe, and all who did were healed.

Dear Lord, in our many readings about You, we have found You used Your hands to touch and heal. What a joyful thought it is to know how many times You reached out to touch those in need. And Lord, there were times when others would touch You, or even Your garment, to receive Your healing grace.

Today, Jesus, as we meditate on these thoughts, we can see how even now our lives have been touched by You...It has been over 2,000 years since You walked these lands and still Your Loving Touch abounds! Thank You for all the wonderful things You have done in our lives and for touching us in such special ways to draw us closer to You! Lord, we want You to know that without You in our lives, we are meaningless; we are hopeless without Your special touch!

How can anyone not appreciate You, Jesus – You who came as a Man and walked here so many years ago? How can they not appreciate Your words, Your actions, Your Love which still touches so many lives! Lord Jesus, it seems inconceivable! Yet there are so many places we go, which seem to lack Your special touch in the lives of the people there...What a shame Lord, they have not found You! How empty their lives must be!

Please continue to touch our lives each and every day...Please remind us how important it is for us to touch the lives of those around us. When we touch someone else's life, perhaps with a word of comfort, a cheery smile or a special prayer, Your Love reaches through us to them…It is Your Loving touch which passes through us and brightens up another soul! It's like a beautiful golden chain, linking us all together through Your Love! Thank You, Father, for allowing us to be part of Your "touch"…Your Loving touch spans the centuries and reaches all over this earth!

Forgiveness   Jan 12

Ephesians 4:32
Instead, be kind to each other, tenderhearted, forgiving one another, just as God has forgiven you because you belong to Christ.

Dear Lord, I have a confession to make about forgiveness. When I looked up "forgiveness" I found it means: to give up resentment against, or the desire to punish; to stop being angry with; to overlook; to release…

Well, Lord, I do these things, at least some of them, so why do I feel disturbed after I have "forgiven" those who have offended me? Is it because I have left out something important?

Oh yes, that something is to forget… But Lord, what does forget have to do with "forgiveness"? You say forgetting is part of forgiving? You have told us we are to forgive as You forgave us. When You forgive us You remember our sins no more. That is how You want us to fully forgive others.

Why is it that once we finally decide to condescend and forgive someone their transgressions, we still like to hang onto them? Why after we have done the forgiving, can't we complete it by forgetting?

Teach us, oh Lord, to forgive and forget with humility and compassion! Show us how to finalize the whole experience of forgiveness by forgetting completely the whole incident we were trying to hang on to. How much sweeter will the forgiveness be for the person we are forgiving, if we will give that person a feeling of love and understanding as well as forgetting. This would give her or him a total picture of what You meant when You said, "and forgive us our trespasses as we forgive those who trespass against us."

If we would give forth humility, compassion, love and understanding, we would be taking the word "forgive" and reversing it…It would now read "givefor" or better yet, "give forth" of ourselves, in the act of forgiving and forgetting.

Now Father, will You please teach the people whose forgiveness I need, how to forgive me completely? How frightening it would be, Lord, if they were forgiving me like I used to forgive them… … …

"Take A Small Step At A Time"   Jan 13

Romans 8:13,14 (NIV)
For if you live according to the sinful nature, you will die; but if by the Spirit you put to death the misdeeds of the body, you will live, because those who are led by the Spirit of God are sons of God.

Here I am dear Lord; take me and do what You will with me…Yes Lord, here I am. I am imperfect, insecure in Your Love at times, but trying to grow to be a better me…It's hard Father. I want to take giant steps and I keep tripping myself up! I guess deep inside of me I know why…With smaller steps we can be steadier and more sure of ourselves in our walk toward You…Each time I take a flying leap ahead, You lovingly pull me back and say,

"Take it easy My child… Take a small step at a time…"

Thank You Jesus, for keeping me under Your wing…

Lord, there are so many of us who want to just leap ahead and grow so quickly once we find out the right direction! But going in the right direction is only part of our growth…There are so many paths leading in that direction. Sometimes we are inclined to try and take a shorter path, thinking we'll get closer to You more quickly!

Dear Jesus, there is only one sure path to You, isn't there? That's the path to Calvary, where You died for us and where we have to die too. We have to die to our old selves - to die completely and become a new person. Because You Love us so much, You gave up Your life for us…Just as You died on the Cross for us and rose again on Easter morn, alive and pure, so we have to die too. We have to become a new person with a goal of truth and purity…

That is the path we have to follow no matter how difficult it becomes, no matter how long it takes…Slow death is very painful, dear Lord, but we have something so beautiful to look forward to when we do die to our old selves! Each part of us that dies will be replaced by another portion of Your Love and Holy Spirit, until we become the beautiful temple You created us to be. We will then be able to reflect the Love and beauty of Your Holy Spirit. We will be truly a shining example of what You intended man to become! This is surely a cause worth dying for, dear Jesus. This path is worth all the falls, broken limbs, and smashed egos we have to undergo to finally become victorious in Your Holy Name: our Savior and Lord, Jesus Christ!

We will be the victors! So now dear Lord, we can pick ourselves up once again on this path where we find ourselves today. Hopefully we are rejuvenated, for another part of our journey toward You has been accomplished. Here's my hand, dear Jesus, I'm ready for that next small step... ... ...

How Many Ways Do We Love You, Lord?
Jan 14

Isaiah 9:6,7a
For unto us a Child is born; unto us a Son is given; and the government shall be upon his shoulder. These will be his royal titles: "Wonderful," "Counselor," "The Mighty God," "The Everlasting Father," "The Prince of Peace." His ever-expanding, peaceful government will never end.

Dear Lord, how many ways do I love You; let me try and count the ways! The ways we love You are reflected in Your titles. And no one in all this universe has as many titles as You! Yet for all the ones I can think of, there are more and more!

Creator of Heaven and Earth, King of kings, Prince of Peace, Lord of Hosts, Holy Innocence, Almighty Father, Author of Inspiration, Teacher of Pure Love, Divine Light, Good Shepherd of the Flocks, Miraculous Healer, Holy Purifier, Son of God, Provider for All Life, Holy Comforter, Lover of Children, Blessed Redeemer, Savior of the World, are but a few. Oh Lord, pages and pages could be filled with the different ways that say what You are to us...

Sweet Jesus, it seems the closer You draw me to You, the more I realize how many titles You have! Yet of all the ways to call You, Heavenly Father, there is one which seems to stay with me the most "Sweet Jesus"...When I think of You that way, dear Lord and Master,

15

all the tenderness You showed in Your life seems to surround me! I feel enveloped in Your Loving care!

Son of Man, You had the strength of a human man when You were on this earth. You were the picture of manliness. Yet the Bible tells us how tender and compassionate You were when the need was there. How very human You were!

John 1:1-3

Before anything else existed, there was Christ, with God. He has always been alive and is himself God. He created everything there is-nothing exists that he didn't make.

Creator of Heaven and Earth is a role so awesome, dear Lord, I cannot fully understand it! You are the Creator of all the Universe and yet You also called the little children unto You! You put Your arms around them and held them close! That's what I love so much about You, Sweet Jesus, Your pure Love for us, no matter what our roles in life may be. It is so comforting that You, Omnipotent God, can make each one of us feel special to You whoever we may be.

There is no one in this world who can Love us as You do, with all our failings, with all our good intentions that never seem to develop. It is only You, sweet Jesus, who is always there waiting for us to call You...

Today, it may be "Father!" Tomorrow, it may be "Please, Holy Comforter." While next week it may be "Miraculous Healer!" But always You make us feel You are there waiting for our call...Thank You, sweet and generous Jesus, for giving us so many ways to love You... ... ...

Heartache   Jan 15

Psalm 125:2

Just as the mountains surround and protect Jerusalem, so the Lord surrounds and protects his people.

In this valley of tears, there is much heartache. Now in my hour of need, I come to You, asking, seeking, knocking on Your Heart.

You have told us, many, many times, that all we have to do is to ask You. I am here now, dear Jesus, asking for the grace to be free of any anxiety which I have. This burden that You have allowed me to have is very heavy...In my moment of reality, my grief and fear engulf my heart and soul...Please dear Lord, remove this from my heart!

Let me know that as long as I have You, I am in Your Loving care; and whatever happens, Your Love will surround me and protect me from all else. You said, dear Lord, that need would be the bridge for bringing us closer to You. You know my great need; of all, You know...

I realize we are all precious to You, dear Jesus, but it seems You allow such difficult things to happen to us. We wonder why. Yet when we really think about it, we can see how You are taking us, a lump of uncut precious matter, and cutting us very deliberately, just like the most expert of all gem cutters. You are breaking off the unnecessary softness of life - honing, filing and refining us down to the priceless jewels You want us to be!

Each time You allow us to suffer these heartaches, You are adding brilliance to our souls. How can we reject such a beautiful plan? So now dear Lord and Master, knowing all of these things in my heart, how can I ask for anything but comfort?

Please, Holy Comforter, come into my heart and soul and relieve me of all anxiety. Help me to take each day as it comes, knowing full well that You have me in Your Blessed Hands...

You have the whole world in Your Hands, and yet You let me feel as if I am right there in the middle! Thank You, sweet Jesus, for Your comforting ways... ... ...

Note to the Reader

The above writing is a true experience a close friend had. Her doctor told her that she was riddled with cancer. She was prayed over. The Lord supernaturally healed her. The writing "Thanksgiving" following this tells of her heart's gratitude to God.

Thanksgiving   Jan 16

Psalm 30:11,12
Then he turned my sorrow into joy! He took away my clothes of mourning and gave me gay and festive garments to rejoice in so that I might sing glad praises to the Lord instead of lying in silence in the grave. O Lord my God, I will keep on thanking you forever!

Thank You, dear sweet Jesus! I came knocking at Your Heart and pleaded with You to answer my request! I asked, just as You have told me to do, time after time. I was seeking Your help...

Dear Lord! What a response You gave me! What generosity! I had only to call on You and You proved, once again in my life, that is all You want us to do! You want us to love You enough, to trust You enough, to come to You with our cares and troubles! We have only to place these burdens at Your feet and when we do this, You give us such a feeling of comfort!

But more than that, dear Heavenly Father, You take these problems and remove them from our lives! I can hardly believe how quickly You did it again! What Your Love can do in our lives! What joy You can bring into our hearts after carrying such heartbreaking grief! Truly there is no joy in all this world that can compare with Yours!

What can I say Lord? How can I show You my appreciation? No words seem adequate to tell You how much Your answer means to me...All that I can say is that I love You! It seems to be so tiny a thing to say in response to such a tremendous gift!

Know though, dear Jesus, that this tiny sentence "I love You" can start a whole chain of loving thoughts in my mind...The beautiful thing about love, is that it can be a growing thing!

I am hoping this little sentence "I love You" is going to grow and flourish in Your garden and that whenever You see it You will remember me and be blessed! Thank You again, sweet Comforter... ... ...

Messengers Of Jesus Christ   Jan 17

Titus 1:1-3

From: Paul, the slave of God and the messenger of Jesus Christ.

I have been sent to bring faith to those God has chosen and to teach them to know God's truth—the kind of truth that changes lives—so that they can have eternal life, which God promised them before the world began—and he cannot lie. And now in his own good time he has revealed this Good News and permits me to tell it to everyone. By command of God our Savior I have been trusted to do this work for him.

Dear Heavenly Father, Son of God, Holy Spirit, does this message from Paul come to us too? Do You want us to be Your messengers also? Now that You have awakened a spark in our hearts, do You want us to make the next move? We are weak, Father, we are not sure of ourselves. How can we, sometimes so inept to understand Your Scriptures, ever hope to be able to reveal the Good News to others? Many of us were not schooled in the understanding of Your Bible. Some of us have only become acquainted with it recently, although we may have flipped through the pages from time to time...

Sweet Lord, we don't have any confidence in ourselves when it comes to trying to understand Your Holy words. What if we make a wrong interpretation? Worse than that, Lord, what if we interpret it wrong to someone else? See Lord, what could happen? Then we have compounded the error. Lord what do You want from us?

"My children, read My Book; read My words. Read My Scriptures; study them. Trust Me; I will make My meanings clear to You. First you will have to make a friend of My Book. As you treasure your best friend, as you have taken much time for that friendship to blossom, so you must do the same with My Book. Look now to Matthew 22:29 and see what I said: 'But Jesus said, "Your error is caused by your ignorance of the Scriptures and of God's power!' Do you understand now? Do you understand that by My power I will reveal what you will have to know to help as My messenger?"

Dear Father, again You let us know that we do not trust You enough. We forget about Your Power to do whatever needs to be done! Nothing is impossible for You to do, even when it comes to helping us understand some of the deep thoughts and words which have perhaps, clouded the minds of great scholars! Thank You, Divine Teacher. We are ready to begin... ... ...

Holy Spirit   Jan 18

John 14: 16,17a (NIV)
"And I will ask the Father, and he will give you another Counselor to be with you forever – the Spirit of truth."

Holy Spirit, miracle of faith, fill our lives! Let us be Your vessels of love! Fill our hearts with so much love that we will have no room for anything else. Remove all our old selves. Pry out anything that is not pleasing to You. Scrape our hearts, scour our souls, and scourge us with such force that we will hardly recognize ourselves...Fill us with a dedication to our dear Father and His Holy Son, Jesus Christ...Let us be open to You, Spirit of Jesus Christ! Let us not be concerned about anything else, but filling ourselves with You...

Use Your fire to burn out anything that is coming between us. After we are cleansed again and again, dear Holy Spirit, use Your flame to start a glow in our hearts which will never die! Start a torch of such fierceness and stamina that it will never even flicker when a strong wind tries to put it out! Never let it be cooled by anything displeasing to You. Let us be Your flames going forth to brighten up the dark places in this world. Let us be links in the never-ending chain started at Pentecost so many years ago!

Oh Holy Spirit, never let the enthusiasm we have found in You leave us! Please, dear Spirit, now that we have found You, don't forsake us; don't abandon us!

Now that we are in the sunshine of life, never let the dark clouds hide us from You. We want to always bask in Your sight. You can see us; You are our guiding light! Thank You, dear and generous Holy One, thank You, thank You, thank You. We adore You for coming into our lives! We don't deserve what You do for us because of Your Love for us! You have such wonderful plans for us! Use us. Use us, sweet Holy Spirit...

We have done nothing to deserve You. We are finding out, in wanting You with all our hearts that You WILL fill them! You will overflow them with so much that we will be overwhelmed...Sweet Jesus, we are hungering and thirsting for You! We are anxious to do Your bidding...Tell us; show us. We can hardly wait to hear from You!

Dear Lord, the most important request we have to ask is that You promise never to leave us...Please show us when we need to be corrected. Give us a loving nudge and we will start afresh on our path toward getting closer to You...Thank You, dear Holy Spirit, thank You... ... ...

The Bible   Jan 19

Psalm 119:18
Open my eyes to see wonderful things in your Word.

The Book of Truth is the greatest mystery story ever written - the best biography of all times. Is it just a bunch of fairy tales or just another history book? All of these terms and more, have been said about the Bible...It's also been told that it is the most sold book of all ages and yet, perhaps, the most unread book for the numbers sold! Dear Jesus, what a paradox!

Why is it so many families feel the necessity to own a Bible, dear Father, and are content to display it as part of the home furnishings? Why does it lay there so long unread and lonely, my Lord?

When so many of us think of all the wasted years that Your Book laid there untouched and dusty, we feel so ashamed...Others have copies, which are worn and frayed from constant use! How blessed they are, dear Jesus, to have felt the call to get to know You Personally...But You can suddenly prick us as with a thorn, perhaps one from Your crown of thorns, and awaken us from the sleep of ignorance we have been in...As we awaken, we find we are hungry and thirsty for the nourishment contained in Your precious Bible...Thank You for arousing this desire in us, Holy Spirit, for it is the beginning of our growth!

Suddenly we find there is a longing, a desire so strong we can hardly wait to finish one chapter and get on to the next! There is so much to learn, so much to absorb! Thank goodness You allow us to become as sponges to soak in what You want each of us to place in our hearts...

Dear Jesus, please continue to let us thirst for this knowledge contained in Your Holy Bible. Even more than that, Lord, let us learn from Your words how to grow and follow Your plans for us.

Your Word is just as relevant today as it was when it was first given. Fill us with a hunger and thirst for You and Your Word, so that we may follow You, dear Lord and Savior... ... ...

The Pattern Of Our Lives   Jan 20

Exodus 39:3b
… it was a skillful and beautiful piece of workmanship when finished.

Creator of all life, bountiful Father, how amazing it is to let our thoughts reflect on the many millions of people who have been born since the birth of man…Of all these millions, it's utterly amazing to comprehend that no two lives were lived exactly the same! Even when they may have been born as a twin, triplet or of a multiple birth, each of their lives was still different in some respects.

Each one of us, consciously or subconsciously, weaves a pattern or design into our lives. Each decision we make about our lives affects the pattern of it. Sometimes it starts out quite beautifully; we know just the design we want. It will, we think, look so beautiful when we finish it!

Suddenly, the threads of our pattern become tangled; our lives become enmeshed in problems, which become so difficult we don't know what to do or where to turn! It seems the more we try to solve these problems the more complex they become…Finally, we are completely fouled up; the design we have been weaving is so tangled up with threads going every which way that we can hardly recognize it! Where did we go wrong? Which thread got tangled first? Which thread do we have to find to untangle the whole problem?

That's it, Lord; that's the solution! Find the key, or the special thread, which we need to straighten out our lives! Blessed are we, dear Father, when we are able to realize that not only are You the solution to our problems, but You are the real Weaver of our lives! You are the great Weaver at the Loom of Life working our sorrows, joys, tragedies, hopes and all of life's experiences into a beautiful pattern of Your design!

It's when we try to do the weaving ourselves that we get into trouble…When we turn our lives over to You, You are then able to make that beautiful design…

When our lives are over, You will show us these beautiful, individual designs woven into a special fabric which will be ours alone, especially woven by You, dear Jesus…

Just imagine how many marvelously individual patterns and designs there will be, dear Lord! Won't it be something for You to look and see these patterns laid out like a magnificent patchwork quilt! They will brighten up the whole world for all the Heavens to see!

Thank You, Creator of all Beauty, for all Your wondrous ways... ... ...

"I Did It My Way"   Jan 21

Matthew 16:24-25

Then Jesus said to the disciples, "If anyone wants to be a follower of mine, let him deny himself and take up his cross and follow me. For anyone who keeps his life for himself shall lose it; and anyone who loses his life for me shall find it again."

Lord, there is a song called "I Did it My Way". You have heard it thousands of times being sung and played down here on earth! We come to believe those words are important, Jesus..."I" did it "MY" way! We begin to wear these words like badges of special courage and merit! "I" did it "My" way!

We go through many years believing these words are the most important words in the whole world! What a fallacy, Lord! How stupid we are to want to be in complete control of our lives! How foolish we are to lock You outside of our lives!

It's true Lord, You have given us choices. We do have the choice to do with our lives what we want to...That's when we often become deceived. That is the danger right there!

Our egos become so great that now we begin to believe only we can be relied on. No one else fits into our little worlds, above all, not You Lord! You are way up there behind the sky, beyond our comprehension and we are down here...

On and on we go, singing that same tune. Time passes...To some come fame, fortune and power. Then that special day comes; the day of reckoning arrives...Could it be no one seems to be impressed with us anymore? Have we lost our standing so that no one wants to hear us sing our favorite song? Where do we go from here?

"Come, little one, do it My way."

Where did that voice come from? Who would be interested in me and in my problems?

"I am interested in you. You are one of My children. I care for you. I love you."

Thank You, Father, for reading my mind and looking into my heart! There are things I don't like about my life...I thought I was in charge of myself completely, that there was no need for anybody else. I found myself only using other people around me, never returning to them anything except what could benefit me!

Lord, thank You for bringing me back to the real value in life! Thank You for Loving me and caring enough to call me to You...Forgive me, Lord Jesus! From now on my song will be "I'll Do it Your Way"... ... ...

The Devil's Instruments   Jan 22

John 17:15

"I'm not asking you to take them out of the world, but to keep them safe from Satan's power."

Our God of power and might, take us under Your protective covering against the devil and his instruments of this world! Most of all, dear Protector, please never let us be used as the devil's instruments! Let us be knowledgeable to the wiles of this demon of the earth, and he is that—a demon! Let us remember that there is such an evil in this world...

There are many, many people who think the devil is something to joke about; to dress up for costume parties - to put on their children at Halloween time! Make us alert and conscious of the dangers, which can befall us if we are not made aware of how very powerful he is, and can be! Heavenly Father help us to be constantly on guard against him!

Dear, dear Jesus, we need Your watchful care more than ever, the closer we come to You! Satan is very jealous and would like to fool as many of Your loving children as he can; that's his pleasure!

Dear Father, in our very modern world, with every possible thing within our reach to satisfy any desire we have, we have become insensitive to the sweetness and purity of life...We have turned to anything new, different or exciting. We seek anything that could possibly bring us another satisfaction, another thrilling experience...

Satan provides more instruments of pleasure with each passing generation as never before in history! Guard us against this willingness to accommodate satan in his thirst and hunger for our souls! Oh Lord how he drools for our young men and women who were brought up to be the future of this world! They are the young, pure hope of their parents' eyes! Some are given all the education and material things they could ever possibly need! These young ones are the choicest, perhaps the ones least able to resist him, because they are not aware of him and his evil design for them!

Now the world seems to be honoring this monster...Lord, everywhere we go we can see or hear his name mentioned. Son of God, unite us as never before in the denunciation of this scourge. If we are not forearmed against him, we will be his unwitting pawn. We will become his very own instrument to be used by him, sometimes over and over again!

Here and now, by Your sweet name, Jesus Christ, we renounce satan for all time! Holy Spirit, strengthen us as never before against this evil and let us become victorious until the moment of our departure from this earth to our Heavenly Home!

Thank You, dear Protector and Savior, for Your Loving care... ... ...

"For Christ's Sake!"   Jan 23

Colossians 3:17 (NIV)
And whatever you do, whether in word or deed, do it all in the name of the Lord Jesus, giving thanks to God the Father through him.

Exodus 20:7
"You shall not use the name of Jehovah your God irreverently, nor use it to swear to a falsehood. You will not escape punishment if you do."

"Jesus!" "For Christ's sake!" Oh my dear Lord, how many times do we hear Your beautiful name taken in vain during our daily life! Of all the many thousands of words in the dictionary, why do men and women have to use Your blessed name as a curse or swear word?

When are they going to realize the only time to use Your name is to praise You? If only they would realize it, they would soon find out the uniqueness of Your name! They would learn that there is POWER in Your Name! They would find out that You would come into their lives and change them! Never again would they mutter Your beautiful name under their breath or shout it out in anger!

Dear Lord, please give us the courage to speak out in Your defense when we hear Your name being abused. Please let Your Love flow through us so we can explain how it offends You to hear Your name taken in vain...

Dear sweet Jesus, wouldn't it be something if You walked by just as they were calling out Your name in anger! You would look deep into their eyes without even saying a word! Just one look from You and they would fall on their knees in shame and sorrow. "It was just a bad habit, Lord; I didn't realize I was saying it!" they would tell You.

So dear Jesus, if there is anyone who doesn't understand how much this offends You, please open up his or her heart to this knowledge. Then they can turn Your beautiful name into a praise instead!

It's such a joy to praise You, sweet Jesus; it's such a joy to say Your name! It fills our hearts and souls with such love that we want to spread Your beautiful name everywhere we go!

Thank You Jesus, for coming into our lives! We will always praise Your Holy, Blessed name! Your name IS the hope of the whole world! Jesus Christ, You are the Savior of the whole world! JESUS, THERE IS POWER IN YOUR NAME!

Fishers Of Men   Jan 24

2nd Timothy 1:7

2nd Timothy 1:7
For the Holy Spirit, God's gift, does not want you to be afraid of people, but to be wise and strong, and to love them and enjoy being with them.

Dear Jesus, can You believe that loving You so much could ever cause a problem? Well, dear Lord, that's sometimes my problem, our problem! We become so filled with loving You we get completely carried away and just want so much to bring this same love for You to everyone we come in contact with!

Once we are filled with Your Love, we want to share it with others, especially our loved ones...Sometimes though, these same loved ones just don't seem to want what we think they should have!

Oh, dear Jesus, You are so understanding all the time...You are so gentle with all Your children...Please show us how to share Your Love with those around us, in that same gentle way! We are so eager to bring all our families and friends to You that sometimes we don't use the right words or the right attitudes in bringing Your word or Your Love to others...

Yet Lord, so many years ago, You filled Your apostles with the right words to bring thousands of souls to You! These were simple men with only one thought in their minds: to bring others to know You and love You...Whatever they did, please share this with us so we will not turn off the very ones whom we want most to bring You!

Please Jesus, let us be sensitive to know what to say and when to say it - what to do and when to do it...Holy Spirit, we ask You to fill our hearts and minds with only what You want us to do and say! Show us how to be prudent, yet bold enough to step out in faith at the perfect time...Teach us how to pray and to turn our loved ones over to You...Let us feel confident that You will be in charge of winning these precious souls - precious to us but even more precious to You...

Show us how to relax and let Your Holy Spirit take over! That seems to be effective when we stop and think about it...It's just like the old saying: "You can lead a horse to water, but you can't make him drink!". That seems so fitting an expression when we think of how hard we have tried to bring this special love we have for You to others...

The most important thing of all though, dear Jesus, is that You have filled our hearts so full of love! We thank You for all that love! We can never stop loving and thanking You for being so good to us! We praise Your Holy Name! We love You! We worship You as our God and Father! Now we will go forth with more confidence, because of You, to become real fishers of men... ... ...

"My Sheep Recognize My Voice"   Jan 25

John 10:27-30

"My sheep recognize my voice, and I know them, and they follow me. I give them eternal life and they shall never perish. No one shall snatch them away

27

from me, for my Father has given them to me, and he is more powerful than anyone else, so no one can kidnap them from me. I and the Father are one."

When we read these words, dear Jesus, Savior and Lord, they bring us great comfort...Yes, we are Yours...You are the Good Shepherd and You know Your sheep. You said You would never let anyone snatch us away from You. That is a powerful and heartwarming promise, Father!

It sounds so easy. It sounds like there is nothing for us to do, but just be protected by You, dear Lord! Is it that easy? Is it so sure that we will be saved from all harm? Can we be sure of this promise You made to us? Do we have to do anything ourselves to earn this protection, Jesus?

What is it, dear Shepherd? Yes, now we understand... Recognize You! Know You! Follow You, Lord! You really make everything so simple for us! Little children follow their father, toddling around behind him. They answer to his call and know he is their father. That's how simple it is! We need to be child-like in our acceptance of You! We are not to question what You have in mind for us, but to follow You with loving innocent hearts as children. Yes, Lord, it does sound simple.

But what about those of us who have been used to going our own way, who didn't have fathers who were good examples for us? We are used to making our own decisions and feel we are the only ones to decide which paths we will take? It's very hard to give up this independence which we've prided ourselves on! Couldn't YOU make some of the decisions but let us make the most of them ourselves? Why do we have to give up everything? We like the feeling of importance we get from setting our own course!

"Read My Scriptures again, My lambs..."

Yes, dear Father.

"My sheep recognize My voice, and I know them, and they follow Me. I give them eternal life and they shall never perish."

Never perish! Never is such a long, long, everlastingly long time! Therefore, whatever years we have left remaining in our lives do not seem too much to give, when we realize what You will give us in return, Lord...You are so generous to us, Jesus! We thank You for Your Loving protection!

We will follow You anywhere, Lord…Just lead us and we will stay securely in Your flock, Father… … …

Obedient Tongue   Jan 26

Matthew 12:35-37

"A good man's speech reveals the rich treasures within him. An evil-hearted man is filled with venom, and his speech reveals it. And I tell you this, that you must give account on Judgement Day for every idle word you speak. Your words now reflect your fate then: either you will be justified by them or you will be condemned."

Dear Lord, help us always to be obedient to You…There are so many times when we feel we want to do our own thing, to follow our own will…We find it difficult to follow Your way for us, dear Jesus. So often we enjoy hearing our own voices…You have given us a voice to speak our own thoughts and many times we get carried away with listening to ourselves speak on things, with such authority!

Heavenly Father, teach us to be obedient to You. Never let our tongues run away and try to impress those around us with our own thoughts. Teach us to be prudent and to be obedient to Your cautioning when we find ourselves speaking for too long a time or dwelling on something which is of importance only to ourselves!

We want to be pleasing to You, most of all. Teach us to use a quiet voice, a gentle manner and Your judgment, as to when and what to say when we speak…Let us realize that if we can contain ourselves until the proper time to speak, our words and voices will be more appreciated…Dear Jesus, we ask You this because we want to be obedient to Your every desire, and we want to be known as one of Your children.

Our tongues are one of the smallest parts of our bodies and yet they can be the most dangerous…It can shred reputations, send men to jail, destroy families. Oh, so many horrible situations can be caused by our tongues! Yet, dear Jesus, the most beautiful music can be heard from this same instrument. Babies can be lulled into a beautiful slumber; lovers can be awakened by a soft whisper. Mothers can hear their child's first words; precious vows can be made. Dear Lord, so many beautiful occasions can be made more meaningful just with our tongues.

Teach us, dear Lord, to know the value and danger of this wonderful part of our bodies...Let us realize that it is far easier to erase a word on paper than it is to retrieve an unkind word or even worse, an untruth about another human being...Let us also realize even though something true has happened to another person, many times it would be better to keep this truth hidden. It could do no good by passing it along. Sometimes it is better to let the truth be forgotten than airing it out in the sunshine of our neighborhoods...and our churches.

Yes, Lord, let us be obedient to Your desires in all these things. Let our voices be welcomed by our families and friends with love, and by all of those You put in our paths... ... ...

Change Me   Jan 27

Zechariah 13:8,9
"Two-thirds of all the nation of Israel will be cut off and die, but a third will be left in the land. I will bring the third that remain through the fire and make them pure, as gold and silver are refined and purified by fire. They will call upon my name and I will hear them; I will say, 'These are my people,' and they will say, 'The Lord is our God.'"

"Spirit of the Living God, fall afresh on me. Melt me. Mold me. Fill me. Use me." Ah Lord, that's the problem; that's the catch! I have to change; I have to be melted down...

Whenever I think of melting anything, there is always heat or fire connected with it in order to do the melting. You know, Lord, how much that will hurt! Can't Your Spirit fall on me without my having to be melted?

Changes are such difficult things to undergo in our lives...No matter what is to come from a change, whether this change is for good or not - changes are difficult...All right, Lord, I've made up my mind to change, so melt me...But, dear Heavenly Lord, please don't take too long to do it though or I might change my mind!

Jesus, can it be possible? You say that I am made of something precious and worthy of being melted down? Me, Lord? I am more precious to You than the most pure gold that was ever melted down? Oh Father, I never thought of it that way before! You want to melt me down and You want to remold me! Thank You, thank You, my God!

You want to remold me into a precious vessel and fill me with Your living water! Then You want to sprinkle this living water through me, Your precious vessel! Wow, Lord, that's a beautiful purpose You have in store for me!

Hurry, hurry, Lord, before You change Your mind! Melt me. Mold me. Fill me. Use me! I am Yours and You are mine! I will become Your vessel and You will pour forth from me!

Oh, Jesus, Fountain of all living water and all love, fall afresh on me – on all of us... ... ...

Forgiving Ourselves   Jan 28

Micah 7:19
Once again you will have compassion on us. You will tread our sins beneath your feet; you will throw them into the depths of the ocean!

Dear Jesus, teach us to be able to forgive ourselves. The burden of guilt, which we carry sometimes, is such a tremendous weight on our souls that we can hardly bear up under it! We seem to be able to forgive others... Why does it take us so long to understand the importance of forgiving ourselves, Lord?

Sometimes we carry this guilt for years and years until it buries itself so deeply in our souls that we can hardly recognize it! It takes away the joy that could be ours! It can take such a hold on us; it becomes like a cancer, slowly eating away at our spirits...

This guilt, dear Lord, can often be because of neglect or omission. Sometimes we were too selfish to give of ourselves to someone who needed something from us. Even worse is the guilt, which does not have to be ours...We have been blaming ourselves for circumstances over which we had no control!

Please Father, free us from this guilt which we carry. Show us how to love ourselves again! Show us how we can be free from these nightmares! Only You can do it! If only we could bring this guilt and place it at Your feet! Once we bring it out into the open and talk to

You about it, and admit that it exists, only then will You remove this agony from our souls.

How much easier it is for us to release our guilt, Lord. If only we would have the strength to very carefully examine our hearts, and then place these burdens at Your feet. One twist of Your foot can wipe them out forever, never to be remembered again! Teach us, Lord, no matter how great our guilt is, that You will release us from it!

Remind us of the two men who were being crucified on each side of You, dear Lord. One wanted to rid himself from guilt and start over again in Your Heavenly home. There, before the whole multitude watching and listening, he asked to start a new life with You. The other man did not want to humiliate himself and thereby lost his chance at Paradise!

Lord, remind us that when You forgive us, You also FORGET! You forget what has been causing us pain, and make us realize that You want us to forget also...All You want is a chance to cleanse us and wipe our slate clean!

Thank You, Holy Comforter, for accepting the burden that was just laid at Your feet...Your Loving forgiveness and kindness makes life worth living again... ... ...

Who Are You, Why Are You, Where Are You, Lord?
Jan 29

1ˢᵗ John 4:18,19,21
We need have no fear of someone who loves us perfectly; his perfect love for us eliminates all dread of what he might do to us. If we are afraid, it is for fear of what he might do to us, and shows that we are not fully convinced that he really loves us. So you see, our love for him comes as a result of his loving us first. And God himself has said that one must love not only God, but his brother too.

Who are You, Lord? *"I am your Creator."* Why are You, Lord? *"Because I love you."* Where are You, Lord? *"Everywhere!"*

Lord, all over Your world these questions are being asked constantly by those You have created; those You Love, even those who have not yet found You.

Manifest Yourself to them, please, Lord! You have shown Yourself to me so personally. It makes my heart saddened to realize there are millions in this world who have not come to You yet...They need Your Love and Your Joy! What joy fills my heart when I think of You! It literally spills over and songs of praise spring from my lips!

I can't be truly happy though, my Father. I know so many of my loved ones and others all around who are not experiencing this same beautiful, unending joy. They do not know the great "I Am" and Your precious Love for them.

Only You could have said so powerfully the words, "I AM". That little two-word phrase appears many times in Your Bible, Heavenly Father.

"I am the First and Last; there is no other God." Isaiah 44:6b

"I am the Light of the world." John 8:12:b

Yes, Divine Inspiration, You are the Light of the world! You are the First and the Last! There is no other God! We Praise You, God!

Because of who You are, it is possible for You to open the hearts of those who have not yet surrendered to Your Divine Love. May it spread over the whole world so it will be as if You poured honey down from Your Heavens until this whole earth was saturated with it! With so much love poured out on everybody those three questions would soon be forgotten. It would be evident then who You are, why You are, and where You are, Lord God!

What was that You said, Jesus? Love begets love? You want us to start loving others, not just saying it? We must put our words into actions like You did! You said "I AM" and You were! You said You were the Light and it was so. You shone so brightly by Your Loving actions long ago and the light from Your Love is still being generated down through the ages.

If each one of us would put our words of love into actions, this earth of ours would be saturated with Your Love. These loving actions would attract others to come to You. Then they would multiply until You could see the Love shining all the way to Your Celestial Home!

Symbol Of Love   Jan 30

John 15:12,13

"I demand that you love each other as much as I love you. And here is how to measure it—the greatest love is shown when a person lays down his life for his friends;..."

Dear sweet Jesus, You have told us that the greatest of all gifts is love. Yet when we normally think of the word "love" we think of a heart-shaped form. We have been brainwashed by our society to think in this fashion. In reality, though the symbol we should have in our minds is a cross! Usually when we do think of a cross we think of sadness or hatred instead of love...

Yes Lord, the cross, Your cross, represents love. The greatest form of love, which has ever existed, is a man laying down his life for another man. That would seem the most perfect action a man could do for another man. The most astounding part of Your Love, dear Jesus, was that it came from the only perfect man to grace this earth! You were the only perfect man to come forth, the one man who should have been received and treated with the greatest of all honors! For a perfect man to die for an imperfect man seems a contradiction, sweet Lord. Why could they not see Your perfection? Why did they need Your Body stretched out on a cross?

They didn't know that Your Heavenly Father had this plan in store for You...They didn't know that You, our Heavenly Father's only Son, could have pleaded with our Father for Mercy. You could have asked for another easier way to show God's Love for us...Yet, Perfect Lamb, You surrendered Your will in obedience to our Father and agreed to die for all of our terrible sins! What perfect Love! That's why the symbol of the cross should represent love instead of any other...Your death on the cross was the greatest act of Love ever shown since man was born...

Other humans have hurt many of us and our first thought is retaliation! Dear Lord, bring to our minds, when we find bitterness against another for doing us wrong, the picture of You on Your cross. You didn't lash out at Your enemies, because You accepted the will of Your Father.

Sweet Lord, whatever is done against us, no matter how much, let us know what our action should be. Show us how to respond to others at these times like You did, with a quiet acceptance. Fill our hearts with the thought that these things are temporary; for someday we will be sharing in Your Kingdom with You! Let us show others what

34

Christian love is all about. Let us think of You on Your cross, dying, for one reason only - because You so Loved us...

Thank You, dear perfect Lord, for this perfect form of LOVE... ... ...

Thank You, Dear Lord   Jan 31

Psalm 100:4

Go through his open gates with great thanksgiving; enter his courts with praise. Give thanks to him and bless his name.

Thank You dear Lord, for all the many wonderful things You have brought into our lives! We so often don't even appreciate them! We take so much for granted in our everyday lives. We should be grateful just opening our eyes in the morning and being able to look around our room. Some days we are blessed enough to see sunlight streaming in through our windows, to be able to hear the sound of birds chirping and the wind singing through the trees! These are things that we take for granted. There are so many people, sweet Jesus, who can't see with their eyes when they awaken in the morning. There are so many who can't hear nature's wonderful sounds! Thank You, thank You, Lord, for these things we have, which we don't give a second thought to...

How many of us hate to arise in the morning, dear Lord! We are night people and love to stay up late. We perhaps grumble when morning comes and we have to get up. We wish we could stay in bed forever! Lord, don't grant us that wish! Please don't! Thank You, thank You, Lord, for our being able to get up in the morning!

Some days, dear Jesus, we come in contact with people who just enjoy bad temper...It's such a temptation to want to reply to them in the same manner in which they have spoken to us...Please let us remember that the voice You gave us can sound so harsh when we are not careful...It also can sound beautifully pleasant, like a tinkling bell or warm molasses, when we want to make a good impression on someone. Remind us to take a moment to turn that unpleasant situation into a more pleasing one. Perhaps we can tell that person we understand they must have had a bad start and show them we care. We can wish them a better time for the rest of the day. Just a little pleasant word or two can turn an unpleasant start into a salvageable day for someone else, right Lord? Thank You, thank You, dear Lord, for giving us the ability to speak at all!

Wow, dear Heavenly Father, just thinking of these few things we take for granted: opening our eyes, looking around, getting out of bed, speaking a few kind words, makes us realize how very much more we should be thanking You. We could go on, and on, and on and on... ... ...

February

Jesus' Promises   Feb. 1

Luke 11:13

"And if even sinful persons like yourselves give children what they need, don't you realize that your heavenly Father will do at least as much, and give the Holy Spirit to those who ask for him?"

Dear generous Jesus, our Lord and Master, again You show us in Your Scriptures ways for us to gain and grow in Your Holy Spirit! You told Your apostles just before You ascended into Heaven on Your last day on earth that You would send Your Holy Spirit to them. The Scriptures show You did!

You also told sinful people like us that we could have the Holy Spirit too! All we have to do is to ask for Your Holy Spirit to come to us!

Paul, who was chosen by God to be Jesus Christ's missionary, tells us the following words in 1st Corinthians 2:10-16:

But we know about these things because God has sent His Spirit to tell us, and his Spirit searches out and shows us all of God's deepest secrets. No one can really know what anyone else is thinking, or what he is really like, except that person himself. And no one can know God's thoughts except God's own Spirit. And God has actually given us his Spirit (not the world's spirit) to tell us about the wonderful free gifts of grace and blessing that God has given us. In telling you about these gifts we have even used the very words given to us by the Holy Spirit, not words that we as men might choose. So we use the Holy Spirit's words to explain the Holy Spirit's facts. But the man who isn't a Christian can't understand and can't accept these thoughts from God, which the Holy Spirit teaches us. They sound foolish to him, because only those who have the Holy Spirit within them can understand what the Holy Spirit means. Others just can't take it in. But the spiritual man has insight into everything, and that bothers and baffles the man of the world, who can't understand him at all...How could he? For certainly he has never been one to know the Lord's thoughts, or to discuss them with him, or to move the hands of God by prayer. But, strange as it seems, we Christians actually do have within us a portion of the very thoughts and mind of Christ.

Dear Lord, Jesus Christ, thank You for allowing us the privilege of reading the Scriptures! Through them we have found so much can be ours just by our asking You...Imagine, dear Jesus; we can have You with us every moment by Your Holy Spirit being within us...Praise You, Almighty Lord God, and thank you for Your generosity to us... ... ...

Keep Your Eyes On Jesus   Feb. 2

Hebrews 12:2-4
Keep your eyes on Jesus, our leader and instructor. He was willing to die a shameful death on the cross because of the joy he knew would be his afterwards; and now he sits in the place of honor by the throne of God. If you want to keep from becoming fainthearted and weary, think about his patience as sinful men did such terrible things to him. After all, you have never yet struggled against sin and temptation until you sweat great drops of blood.

Have we quite forgotten the encouraging words God spoke to us, His children? In the next two verses He said,

"My son, don't be angry when the Lord punishes you. Don't be discouraged when he has to show you where you are wrong. For when he punishes you, it proves that he loves you. When he whips you it proves you are really his child."

Dear Lord Jesus, thank You for reminding us again that when we become fainthearted and weary, we should turn our thoughts to You, our leader and instructor. It's true, Lord, we think we have burdens and think we have a right to feel weary from them. We forget that in many cases we have made these very burdens ourselves...Help us to remember, sweet Savior, that You are perfect and yet You willingly died for our sins - not Your own sins because You are sinless...

Lord, please teach us to be strong against our temptations. Teach us to be wise and mindful of the need to throw off these temptations. It's true, Lord, no matter what our temptations are, we have never sweated great drops of blood as You did...You were tempted to forsake us, dear sweet Savior - so tempted that you sweated those painful drops bursting forth through Your very pores! Yet because of Your Love for us and Your Loving obedience to Your Heavenly

Father, You stood strong and unbending to the temptation of abandoning us! Thank You, our Lord and Savior for Your strength! Thank You, for what You are teaching us...

And Lord, for all the many, many times we have fallen because of our weakness, please forgive us. So many times, we know what is right, but our human side takes over and we find ourselves falling again. And Lord, thank You for letting us see when we have fallen...If You didn't let us see our sins plainly we could never grow in our attempt to walk closer to You! Thank You for disciplining us as a Loving Father...Thank You for these words of wisdom:

"My son, don't be angry when the Lord punishes you - it proves you are really his child."

Dream of Me   Feb. 3

Luke 10:39,40a,41,42

Her sister Mary sat on the floor, listening to Jesus as he talked. But Martha was the jittery type, and was worrying over the big dinner she was preparing... But the Lord said to her, "Martha, dear friend, you are so upset over all these details! There is really only one thing worth being concerned about. Mary has discovered it—and I won't take it away from her!"

Father, I am here - here at Your feet, thinking of You, wondering about You. I am so empty tonight. What do You want of me tonight? How can I do or say anything that would make any difference to You...

I know You are here beside me. Yet when I think of the depth of Your skies and the vastness of Your universe, I become filled with an awesome fright. Deep down inside of me I feel like a lost child must feel...

I wonder about You. I feel so insignificant. You are so incomprehensible! I just can't think of any words to describe You! You are bigger than life; bigger than death; bigger than this world, this universe! Yet how many times have You come to me and made me feel that I was the only important one to You and that my problems were of the utmost concern to You...

Does my existence really make any difference to You? Are You expecting more from me than I'm capable of giving You? Tell me, Father, tell me what You want from me...

"Sit there. Gaze up into My Heavens and dream of Me. Let your thoughts wander into the depths of your soul and float through all the barriers that reality ties you to. Free yourself and stay with Me in your thoughts. That's all I want from you today, to be with Me in the heart of you. Be still - no need for action, just your attention. I ask so little of you."

That is so true, Heavenly Father, so true...How patient You are, waiting and waiting until we decide when to come to You. How many long hours You wait for each one of us to come when it suits us best...We get caught up in this busy life and put You in the background until we can work You into our schedules. Oh, how many times we have done this when You ask so little of us...

Forgive us Lord, and please keep reminding us to come to You. To comprehend that You are even aware of our existence should make us super conscious of who You are and how lowly we actually are. Yet we make You play the waiting game. How thoughtless we mortals are...

Now let us slip back to our dreaming, surrender our earthly attachments, and put You back where You belong, Jesus. First in our thoughts, first in our hearts, first in our souls, that's where You belong. Knowing this, we can now sit at Your feet in our spirits, until You call us home... ... ...

Admitting Our Faults   Feb. 4

James 5:16 (KJV)
Confess *your* faults one to another, and pray one for another, that ye may be healed. The effectual fervent prayer of a righteous man availeth much.

Dear Father, here is another difficult task You want us to do: confess our sins by admitting our faults...Lord, it is hard even admitting to ourselves that these faults or sins exist. Now You want us to admit them to others! Surely dear Jesus, there must be some other way to be healed!

Oh, now we understand, dear Lord...We must be obedient as James explains above, to admit our faults to one another...For then we are able to see them out in the open to examine them. Then we will have taken a step toward being healed!

But, whom can we pray with about such personal things? Your Word mentions a "righteous" person...What about that word "righteous", Father? It can be troublesome because it may sound stuffy or stilted...Could we instead think more in terms of Christ-like? Yes Lord, we need someone who reflects patience, kindness and all the virtues You possess. We need someone who will respect our confidences and help us understand ourselves through You, sweet Lord...

There could be someone living nearby who is the one You'd have us to pray with...It could be a man, woman, priest, minister, teacher, neighbor or even a stranger. Perhaps that someone is already in our household and we don't realize it yet! Open our eyes, dear Lord, and let us recognize the Light of Your Love in them. Let this "righteous" person be revealed to us soon! May a warm and close bond be made, so that we can grow in our joint love for You...

Thank You Lord, for teaching us that all we need to do is pray in Your Love, with one another - with no hidden motives. Jesus, we are so grateful for these words from James...As we confess our faults and pray for one another Your Healing Touch IS released!

Help us dear Lord, to learn and obey this lesson which can draw us closer to You... ... ...

Death   Feb. 5

Hebrews 9:27,28a
And just as it is destined that men die only once, and after that comes judgment, so also Christ died only once as an offering for the sins of many people; and he will come again, but not to deal again with our sins.

Sweet Jesus, thank You for the hope You have sent us by Paul in the above verse. We are anxiously awaiting Your coming again! Paul was one of many of Your ambassadors who brought us this good news.

Yes, Heavenly Father, we are destined to die; each one of us must face this...Some of us await death with no fear at all, Lord, but some of us are frightened at the prospect of facing death and judgement...To some it can be such a lonely thought; while for others it can be a joyous thought!

Jesus, You faced such a cruel death with so many watching You die. You must have been lonely knowing so many there did not love You, but only wanted to watch You suffer and die out of sheer cruelty...

We are living at a time in history, Jesus, when most people die in a more humane way...Whatever death You have in store for us, please let us die in a state of peace with You...No matter what happens to our bodies, dear Jesus, please keep our spirits full of joy and our hearts eager to join You!

For those who fear death, which comes to all, once they accept You as their Savior and Lord, please send to them a strong feeling of security. Give them a feeling that as soon as their eyes close and they take their final breath, You will be there with Your Hand extended! You will be waiting to walk with them to their final home! Then, Lord Jesus, they would not have to fear this final step...Let them find the joy, which can be theirs before they leave this place, for it is only our temporary home.

Lord, we are so blessed that You have gone ahead and prepared such a place for us! It's because You love us that You have arranged blessings for us...You had no other purpose in mind, did You, Lord? And Lord, we're so relieved that our sins do not have to be dealt with again! You are so good to us!

When we think of the most beautiful things in this whole world, we then realize they cannot possibly compare to what You have planned for us! It becomes so exciting it's hard to contain ourselves! Yes Lord, we are eagerly and patiently waiting for You to call us Home... ... ...

Our "Work"   Feb. 6

2ⁿᵈ Timothy 2:15

Work hard so God can say to you, "Well done." Be a good workman, one who does not need to be ashamed when God examines your work. Know what his Word says and means.

Lord, reflecting on this, our work, we realize that there are many forms of work. Lord Jesus, though many of us are in different walks of life regarding our method of working, perhaps You have in mind for us something else...Perhaps You want us to examine deeply in our hearts, another kind of work.

Savior, in meditating here about this, several passages from 2nd Timothy have come to mind...Paul writes these words from Chapter 3:16-17:

The whole Bible was given to us by inspiration from God and is useful to teach us what is true and to make us realize what is wrong in our lives; it straightens us out and helps us do what is right. It is God's way of making us well prepared at every point, fully equipped to do good to everyone.

Jesus, do those last few words hold a key to the meaning of the whole passage? Those last few words "fully equipped to do good to everyone," is that the work You have in mind for us, our true work?

In Chapter 4 Paul continues writing,

And so I solemnly urge you before God and before Christ Jesus—who will someday judge the living and the dead when He appears to set up His Kingdom—to preach the Word of God urgently at all times, whenever you get the chance, in season and out, when it is convenient and when it is not. Correct and rebuke your people when they need it, encourage them to do right, and all the time be feeding them patiently with God's Word.

Father, is this our work, our real work? Paul continues in the same chapter, verse 5:

Stand steady, and don't be afraid of suffering for the Lord. Bring others to Christ. Leave nothing undone that you ought to do.

Yes, Lord, it is all very clear what You have in mind for us. We can be carpenters like You, fishermen like Peter, tax collectors like Matthew, etc. to earn our daily bread, but our real work is outlined above in your Scriptures. As we come to know what Your Word says and means, we are to live and work in obedience...

You want us to do this in the way Paul tells us in 2nd Timothy 2:25.

"Be humble when you are trying to teach those who are mixed up concerning the truth. For if you talk meekly and courteously to them they are more likely, with God's help, to turn away from their wrong ideas and believe what is true."

43

Yes, Lord, let us do the work You have chosen for us to do by obeying Your Word... ... ...

Brotherly Love   Feb. 7

Romans 12:9-13

Don't just pretend that you love others: really love them. Hate what is wrong. Stand on the side of the good. Love each other with brotherly affection and take delight in honoring each other. Never be lazy in your work but serve the Lord enthusiastically.

Be glad for all God is planning for you. Be patient in trouble, and prayerful always. When God's children are in need, you be the one to help them out. And get into the habit of inviting guests home for dinner or, if they need lodging, for the night.

Lord, there are some very powerful messages in those passages...You don't want any pretense on our part when it comes to love...You want us to really love...Just that thought alone is a mighty one! It reaches into our very souls for self-examination. This takes a lot of doing for some of us, dear Jesus...It's so easy to love others when things are going well for us and for the ones we are supposed to love. But reflecting deeply, we can see where there were times when we have not felt up to loving others as You want us to...

You also ask us to love each other with brotherly affection, Father. But remember what my brother did to me last year? You remember Lord, when we had that unpleasant problem and now we aren't speaking to each other...You ask us to take delight in honoring each other, but how can I honor my brother and really love him after that unpleasantness? He should be coming to me and asking me to forgive him, not honor him!

I don't understand about the "lazy" part coming right after the delight in honoring each other, Lord...You say, "Never be lazy in your work but serve the Lord enthusiastically"...Oh Lord, do You mean that I have to do the work about patching up the problems between my brother and myself? I have to do it enthusiastically too? Oh-h-h, that is part of really loving others, not just pretending to love them. And not only am I to love my brother, but I am to honor him! I see, my Father...

44

Now the next passage is more meaningful. This is in Your plan for me: to be patient in trouble and prayerful always…I am to be there when my brother or anyone else needs me…I should be there to help them. I am to share my food, my home or whatever I have with them. Yes Father, these are powerful messages coming from our powerful God! I ask You now, Father, to help me stand on the side of good and with Your help, to become a sincere, loving follower of You, Jesus Christ… … …

Do Not Deny Me   Feb. 8

Luke 22:59-62

About an hour later someone else flatly stated, "I know this fellow is one of Jesus' disciples, for both are from Galilee." But Peter said, "Man, I don't know what you are talking about." And as he said the words, a rooster crowed. At that moment Jesus turned and looked at Peter. Then Peter remembered what he had said—"Before the rooster crows tomorrow morning, you will deny me three times." And Peter walked out of the courtyard, crying bitterly.

"Do not deny Me, My child."

Oh, Father, how I have denied You…How many times have You called me and I turned away from You…Forgive me! Father, forgive me! Only You know how many times You have called me. Sometimes it was so strong and clear and yet I put You off, because it wasn't convenient to my desires or my plans. Sometimes it was a beckoning of Your finger, but I chose not to look Your way…Sometimes it was just the very slightest whisper, calling my name…Oh, Lord Jesus, how many times have I wounded You this way? How many times have You heard me tell the world how much I love You? Yet how many, many times have I turned my ear away from You? I feel so unworthy, being one of Your children, Father…

Lord, in my misery now, tears fill my eyes. As my heart aches for the pain I've caused You, I ask You to forgive me. Even more than that, Father, I ask You to remind me again and again, of these precious moments, which You have revealed to me. You have let me know how it grieves You because we have not spent more time together…

My excuses always sounded so good to me, but how trivial and silly they must have sounded to You, Father...This busy time in which we live becomes our excuse. The world has never been more active and busy. Time seems to fly by! One can hardly realize that weeks turn into months and before we know it, another year has passed.

Father of all, have You been happy with us this year? Have we grown at all from last year in Your eyes? Are we maturing as You are hoping we will, Father? Are the tears You bring to us an indication of growth and maturity? Oh, how we hope so, for it is only when You let us see ourselves in the Light of Your LOVE that we can recognize our failings and imperfections...Now we see how we have denied You by our neglect...

Peter cried bitterly when he recognized his failure to acknowledge You. Yet in Your great LOVE, You restored him so gently near the end of the book of John.

John 21:16

Jesus repeated the question: "Simon, son of John, do you *really* love me?" "Yes, Lord," Peter said, "you know I am your friend." "Then take care of my sheep," Jesus said.

It is Your Love, Father, Your Divine Love for us, which causes us to want to change. We honestly want to obey You and spend time with You, Heavenly Father...How wondrously You restore us! How gently You comfort us and forgive us! How sweetly You reassure us of Your Love...

Thank You, Father, for Your Forgiving LOVE, which was there for Peter and is still there for us...Let us no longer deny Your voice, but answer with Peter, "Yes Lord, you know that I love You." Then may we show our love by our obedience... ... ...

Gather Together   Feb. 9

James 5:13-15

Is anyone among you suffering? He should keep on praying about it. And those who have reason to be thankful should continually be singing praises to the Lord. Is anyone sick? He should call for the elders of the church and they should pray over him and pour a little oil upon him, calling on the Lord to heal him. And their prayer, if offered in faith, will heal him, for the Lord will make him well; and if his sickness was caused by some sin, the Lord will forgive him.

Dear Jesus, Holy Comforter, what greater source of comfort can we obtain from each other, than as we gather together to pray! Lord, help us share with one another the needs we have, to help lighten the burdens we all carry. Remove from us the shyness we might have, to confide to our loving brothers and sisters, when we need to call on You through them for help.

Father, help us to know the right time and persons to share with…Show us Lord, that we can feel confident in releasing our burdens in front of the ones chosen by You to listen and help us. Sweet Jesus, bring to us, sincere brothers and sisters who will share our prayers to You, for our needs. It may be for healing of our bodies, spirits, minds, or something else.

Teach us again, dear Father, about the need for prayer. Show us we have to be consistent in our prayers. But show us also, sweet Jesus, that just because You want us to be consistent, we don't have to be repetitious! Perhaps sometimes our prayers could take on another form – singing and /or praising! What more joy could You have, dear Father, than to listen to one of Your children lift up his or her voice in a song of prayer, praise or petition. You don't care if our voices are trained or untrained; they are all beautiful to You!

Thank You, Jesus, for sending the above words from James to us. He reminds us to be thankful to You for the good things which happen in our lives too. Sometimes we get in the habit of asking You for things, Lord, and we do not thank You for giving them to us. Then there are the things You provide us without our asking. We seem to forget You have provided them also!

So Heavenly Father, greatest provider of all, remind us to send up our praises to You! Let us be thankful to You and gather together in Your Name, especially when at times our lives seem full of suffering. Thank You for Your healing powers, Your comfort, and most of all, Your forgiving Love… … …

Power Of The Holy Spirit! Feb. 10

Acts 10:38
And you no doubt know that Jesus of Nazareth was anointed by God with the Holy Spirit and with power, and he went around doing good and healing all who were possessed by demons, for God was with him.

Dear Jesus, Your Holy Spirit remained a mysterious figure or phrase in some of our lives for so long! In fact, Your Holy Spirit seems to have remained almost anonymous down through the ages! Some of us were taught about God, Your Father and ours. We may have been taught about You, dear Jesus Christ, but somehow or other Your Holy Spirit seems to have been passed over by many...

For lack of a better explanation, dear Lord, it seems much like the atom. Until a matter of a few years ago, the atom had not been discovered to have the power that we now know it has! It was always there, but its full potential lay undiscovered and unused! Holy Spirit, that seems to have been what we've done with You! Although the Scriptures are filled with the words "Holy Spirit," Your full potential lay mostly undiscovered and unused...But once unleashed, much like the atom, what power You can promote! You can do anything at all; nothing is impossible for You, Holy Spirit!

Dear Lord, again in the Scriptures, Paul tells us these words in **Ephesians 1:13-14.**

And because of what Christ did, all you others too, who heard the Good News about how to be saved, and trusted Christ, were marked as belonging to Christ by the Holy Spirit, who long ago had been promised to all of us Christians. His presence within us is God's guarantee that He really will give us all that He promised; and the Spirit's seal upon us means that God has already purchased us and that He guarantees to bring us to himself! This is just one more reason for us to praise our glorious God.

Holy Spirit, as we ponder on the above words of Paul, we are thrilled to realize that You have branded us! You first of all fill us with this strange longing, this strange desire for wanting to know our Lord and Savior better...Then as we move forward slowly and You fill us more and more with Divine Love, we realize we have become "Jesus freaks" - fanatics for our Lord and Master!

Your Holy Spirit finally takes over our lives. You place Your Holy Seal on us to show we are some of those whom God has already purchased! And with that seal on us, Your power begins to make changes in us and draws us closer to our Father...Thank You, dear Father, Son and Holy Spirit for awakening our spirits to You... ... ...

Nourishment   Feb. 11

1st Corinthians 3:6-8

My work was to plant the seed in your hearts, and Apollos' work was to water it, but it was God, not we, who made the garden grow in your hearts. The person who does the planting or watering isn't very important, but God is important because he is the one who makes things grow. Apollos and I are working as a team, with the same aim, though each of us will be rewarded for his own hard work.

Heavenly Father, this is so true! Sometimes we place too much importance on the people in our lives regarding our relationship with You! Sometimes because of our feelings for a particular religious person we feel closer to You...Then when that person has to leave our lives, we may find ourselves drawing away from You! Show us that we must learn to nourish ourselves directly from You...

Paul tells us above in the Scriptures that it was his job to plant the seed to love You in the hearts of those around him. It was Apollos' job to water the seed of that love. As Paul plainly said, it was not important who the person was who planted the seed or who watered the seed. The important thing for us to remember is that only You make the seed grow! No matter how much watering a person does to make something grow, the seed of life grows only because of You, dear Lord Jesus! We must never forget this, must we, Lord.?

Each of us has different experiences in life which help us to grow into the person You want us to become. It is through these experiences that You teach us to love You and each other. It is Your Love, dear Lord - the seed of Your Love from which it all comes.

Show us that it doesn't make any difference who helps us along the way to our growing stronger in our searching for You. We search through the dark earth of life looking for the first ray of Your Love ...The daylight of Your all encompassing Perfect LOVE, sweet Jesus, awaits each one of us...It is a search Father, which each one of us must make primarily alone, just as the little seed planted in the earth must make its way alone to the surface for its very existence...

That's what Your Love is to us, dear Holy Spirit of Jesus Christ. It is our very existence for survival in this world. Father, show us how to nurture this seed with all the nutrients You alone know are needed...Thank You, dear Father...Thank You... ... ...

Loneliness Of Man   Feb. 12

1st John 4:9-12

God showed how much he loved us by sending his only Son into this wicked world to bring to us eternal life through his death. In this act we see what real love is: it is not our love for God, but his love for us when he sent his Son to satisfy God's anger against our sins. Dear friends, since God loved us as much as that, we surely ought to love each other too. For though we have never yet seen God, when we love each other God lives in us and his love within us grows ever stronger.

God, why do some men avoid another man? Why do people put down certain others around them? Why are some of Your children avoided and left lonely, Lord? There are so many people, grown men and women, who do not feel loved and accepted. They wander from place to place, seeking to be accepted to end their loneliness.

Perhaps they are some of the thousands upon thousands of babies brought into this world in an unloving atmosphere, through no fault of their own. They have grown up still seeking love. They may have seen love displayed in a beautiful tender movie, a simple love story or a loving family relationship. They may be seeking the same love and acceptance. Does love and acceptance happen only in the movies, on television or in books?

Can anyone be loved and wanted just for themselves? Oh Lord Jesus, how it hurts to see and hear about the suffering which some go through in these lonely situations...How can they find what they are looking for deep down in their being?

"I came. I walked these hills and valleys. I came to bring men peace; to bring men joy; to bring brotherhood. I came to give My Divine Love to all people. No one has to ever be alone again once they have found Me... I am everywhere. My Spirit lives on and on and on... Once you know Me there is never cause for loneliness again..."

Ah yes, Jesus, YOU are the answer! You are the only One who can cure all the ills of the human race, be it in the soul, the spirit or the body…You are all things to all men. You are a free gift; You are available to all who will accept You…You will accept and LOVE anyone who will come to You…You remove the loneliness from lives! You bring JOY! You bring PEACE! You bring humans together in loving concern, when You are in the center of them…

Because of You, at times mankind looks with compassion toward their sisters and brothers, no matter their race, nationality, or background. Because of You they can share their joys, their sorrows, their friendships, their deepest emotions…

Yes, Jesus, Savior of us all, You are the answer to our loneliness, and to so much more… … …

Thought Transgressions   Feb. 13

Mark 7:20
And then he added, "It is the thought-life that pollutes."

2nd Corinthians 10:5 (NIV)
We demolish arguments and every pretension that sets itself up against the knowledge of God, and we take captive every thought to make it obedient to Christ.

Dear Lord Jesus, what terrible burdens we sometimes carry in our minds…We try so hard to fight these thoughts that plague our minds with all sorts of temptations…Each of us is subject to his or her own sinfulness. What are mine may not be another's…But, Lord, no matter what these thoughts are about, we are filled with a heavy weight by trying to rid our minds of them. What is even worse, Lord Jesus, we sometimes give our minds over to these thoughts and let them go rampaging through our entire beings!

These "thought transgressions" can be like a pickaxe…They begin to pick away, little by little at our minds…If we let them, they will start to become larger and larger…The next thing, that happens is negative things start to come out of our mouths. From there, negative actions can take place, and suddenly, we are caught up in a very negative situation…

51

In the dictionary, transgression means "the breaking or violation of any law, civil or moral, expressed or implied; disobedience of any rule or command; a trespass; an offense." We have to make a decision regarding these transgressions of thought...We can let them take hold or we can get rid of them...The decision is up to each one of us, isn't it, Lord...Sometimes we want to hang onto negative thoughts. In some strange way, we let ourselves feed on them...Perhaps some injustice has been done. One can almost feel pleasure in rehashing the negative thoughts relating to that unfair action.

In growing up and maturing, we have to understand that life itself is not fair, not just...But if we dwell on this, it only turns us into a negative type of person...We must get on with life...We must learn to overcome the negative things, which happen to us...Is it easy? Not when we try to do it alone...

That's where You, Jesus Christ, come into the picture. As the Son of our Living God, You can make a difference. You do make a difference! Realizing that You, Jesus, can help us, we must start retraining our thought patterns. Whenever a negative thought or "thought transgression" comes into our minds, we must call upon You, Jesus, and ask You to fill our minds with positive thoughts. There is power in Your name! Jesus! We must say it over and over again until peace comes...Gradually these "thought transgressions" will no longer control us...We will have overcome them because of You.

Thank Your dear Lord...You always show us what we need to do, when we call to You from our hearts with our problems and cares...You can and do help us...You set us on the right path. You put a song of praise and thanks in our hearts and remind us that we must trust You...Thank You, Father God, for listening to us and for transforming our very thoughts...JESUS, JESUS, JESUS, there is POWER in Your Name!

Indescribable Jewel   Feb. 14

Matthew 13:44-46

"The Kingdom of Heaven is like a treasure a man discovered in a field. In his excitement, he sold everything he owned to get enough money to buy the field - and get the treasure, too! Again, the Kingdom of Heaven is like a pearl merchant on the lookout for choice pearls. He discovered a real bargain - a pearl of great value - and sold everything he owned to purchase it!"

Father, You are the One, the only One. Without You, we are nothing...Without You, we are lost! We are alone and wandering in this life without direction or hope. Finding You is the greatest treasure we could ever hope to possess...You are the Pearl of Great Value...Once this tremendous experience comes to us we can really start to live - to live life in the fullest sense!

When we come into the full realization of Your treasure, then we know we are to share this with others. In doing so, this treasure has the mysterious capacity to keep on replenishing itself!

That's the kind of a Father we have in You, Lord, there is no end to Your giving! The more we take from Your storehouse of treasure, the more You keep filling! This treasure completely saturates every area in our lives! No matter how much we give away, day after day, it continues to grow!

If only every man, woman and child in this world could find Your treasure, Jesus...Our hearts become heavy thinking about this free gift just waiting for them. If only they could have the opportunity to hear about You and get to know You...Lord, teach us to be willing to bring Your treasure to others, not to keep it to ourselves. Let us be sensitive to Your direction and obedient to share, as You lead.

Many will ask, 'What is this treasure you are speaking about?' Father God, Creator of all, how can we describe such an invisible, indescribable jewel? It is Your LOVE that fills eyes and spreads across a face in a beautiful smile...How do we describe LOVE? Your Christ-like kind of LOVE changes men's hearts and melts them into new creations. They are filled with Your kind of LOVE which becomes the most desirable treasure ever created...

Lord Jesus, please show every one who calls themselves Christians, that they are called to be an example of and to share this treasure of unconditional LOVE... ... ...

God Is Not A Denomination   Feb. 15

Galatians 3:26-28
For now we are all children of God through faith in Jesus Christ, and we who have been baptized into union with Christ are enveloped by him. We are no

longer Jews or Greeks or slaves or free men or even merely men or women, but we are all the same—we are Christians; we are one in Christ Jesus.

Heavenly Father, thank You for not being Catholic or Baptist or Methodist or Episcopalian or Lutheran or any other denomination! Please continue showing us that You are L O V E!

Many of us have been steeped in one faith all our lives, mostly because we were born into it with little or no choice of our own. Lord, please give us the maturity to realize You are for all of us and You show no partiality!

Lord, when are we going to come to the full realization that You get very offended when we try to exclude any one religion from our lives when they are truly God oriented? Please let us realize, Jesus, that You are for all of us!

We are all Your children and we thank You for being our Father! A good earthly father does not want his children to quarrel and go their separate ways. It is even more painful for You to see us divide ourselves into little groups and pull away from our brothers and sisters who are in Your family, Lord...

You created us in Your own likeness, Lord Jesus. You have been forgiving and forgiving of our selfishness and narrow-mindedness. How can we behave like that when we were created to be like You - Loving in the most pure sense...

Dear God, we are all equal in Your eyes; it doesn't make any difference what we call ourselves...Show us it is what's in our hearts that counts. Show us, it is our RELATIONSHIP with You, our God, the Father of our Lord Jesus Christ, which matters the most!

Love is what it's all about. How can we possibly expect You to love us when we are not loving toward our brothers and sisters of other denominations? It's just as if we live in one town and think the towns around us are not as worthy as we are. We think we alone should feel entitled to all of Your Love. Are they not entitled to the same sunshine, rainfall and blessings, which are sent to our town?

Dear Heavenly Father, You brought us into this world to be loved equally by You...You have more than enough Love to go around. It is to be shared by all of us no matter what we call ourselves...

Yes, dear Father, YOU LOVE us all... ... ...

Glue   Feb. 16

Psalm 51:17

It is a broken spirit you want – remorse and penitence. A broken and a contrite heart, O God, you will not ignore.

1st Peter 5:6,7

If you will humble yourselves under the mighty hand of God, in his good time he will lift you up. Let him have all your worries and cares, for he is always thinking about you and watching everything that concerns you.

Lord, I was just repairing something, as it had been broken for a long time...I looked at it occasionally and wished that it had not been broken, but it was...It didn't seem repairable, but I didn't want to throw it away...A dear friend had given it to me...Then Lord, You put the thought into my mind that it could be repaired...Using glue and patience I was able to put it together, without showing where it once was broken...All it took was a little glue.

Suddenly, dear Jesus, the thought came to me: You are like glue! Glue repairs and puts together things which are broken...That's what You do too, Lord, isn't it? You take the brokenness of Life... You repair the ones whose hearts need to be mended, situations corrected. You repair them. You "fix" whatever needs to be fixed...

When I needed to fix my broken item, I needed to get some glue...It had to be the right kind of glue which was specifically made for that problem...You are that kind, Lord!

You became our "fixer" when You died on the Cross for each one of us...When You did, You bought each one of us with that **ACT OF LOVE**...You became the answer for all our problems, our brokenness...You are the only One Who can repair us for the rest of our lives! When we come to You with our brokenness, we ask You to repair what is wrong with our lives, dear Jesus...

Yes we need to come...We are like my item, which lay there year after year broken. Occasionally I would think, "If only it could be put back together again." Yet I did nothing about it...I let it lay there...Then, Lord, You gave me the thought that something could be done! Get some glue! But I had to make the decision to do it, to do something about it...That's where we often get "stuck"... We are offered a solution, but our flesh often gets in the way..."Oh, that's not the answer; a little glue won't work..." Our negative attitude can take over and the solution is ignored...Brokenness remains...

But Lord, when we truly want to have the brokenness repaired, applying You as the glue, does make the difference between wholeness and brokenness...Oh, Father God, Repairer of our lives, please continue to guide us to where You know we should be. Please help us to do what should be done, to become the person You know we can become...

Thank You for Your mercy, Your tenderness, Your LOVE...Thank You, Lord, thank You... ... ...

Game of Life   Feb. 17

Psalm 119: 130,133 (NIV)
The entrance of your words gives light; it gives understanding to the simple. Direct my footsteps according to your word; let no sin rule over me.

Revelation 2:7b
"To everyone who is victorious, I will give fruit from the Tree of Life in the Paradise of God."

Life - what are you? Are You a mystery or a game? What is this existence that each one of us has to go through once we are born into this world...Why do each one of us have to struggle through so many situations without knowing the reasons or the answers? How many trials and errors do we have to make...How many are we allowed?

Jesus, dear Jesus, tell us; show us...So many of us are mixed up and don't know which way to turn.

"Yes, My child, life is like a game. It is the most important game you will ever play... As in every game there are rules. Once the rules are learned one can play and win. Those who want to abide by the rules, My Word, are sure to win. Those who want to skip over the rules are the losers. There is one great difference with this game from all other games. Everyone who plays this game can become a winner! There do not have to be any losers. The choice is yours."

Thank You, Jesus! Whenever You design a plan, it is made so that it is fair to one and all! You never choose favorites! You love us all, each one of us, as if we were Your only child! You want us all to win, don't You, Father...You are the One who is always there on the sidelines watching each play we make. You long for us to play by the rules. We thank You, Lord God, for Your wondrous ways!

There is another wonderful thing about the rules to Your game of Life, Father...There is no competition among Your children! You want us all to win, to come in first. Strangely enough, that's exactly how each one of us does come in at the end of the game - first! There are no second or third place winners; we are all first! Praise You, Jesus, for this wonderful privilege of being able to spend our eternity with You, dear Lord...

But, some will ask, where are the rules? Where is the book of rules to know this game so we may win? Of course, it's the Bible! Where else could we go to learn all about what You want us to know, Jesus.

Father, teach us to be patient so we can learn these rules in Your Word. They will guide us wisely in the difficult decisions and situations which will come into our lives. For only in following Your rules, Your way, can we be Eternal Winners... ... ...

Ladder To Heaven   Feb. 18

Genesis 28:12(RSV)
And he dreamed that there was a ladder set up on the earth, and the top of it reached to heaven; and behold, the angels of God were ascending and descending on it!

Thank You, dear Lord, for showing us how necessary it is to have a "ladder" to Heaven! It's true, Jesus - You are the Ladder!

It takes a long time, sweet Jesus, to realize that we do need a ladder...Sometimes it takes a lifetime! Most of all, we realize how terrible it was when we didn't even think a ladder was necessary...We were just going about our merry way enjoying all the things in life, taking for granted how wonderful our lives were...Life here on earth has been pretty wonderful for so many...Who needs a ladder? Who needs God? We're doing pretty well on our own! We can't be bothered with anything that might mess up the way our lives are going!

57

Shockingly something happens in our lives, which we didn't expect! It is something we didn't want to happen...What's going on here? We didn't expect that to happen! Take it away someone! Someone? Who's someone? Who will take it away?

All these years we've managed on our own! Why does it have to change now? We're mature people; we know what's best for ourselves! We'll work it out...

That's strange...We're trying to straighten out the problem but it keeps getting worse! We better get some help! Help? Who can help us? Who will help us?

Who is over there, shining in the sunlight? Jesus! HE can help us! Why didn't we see Him before? Well, things were going so great we didn't realize that we needed Him... ... ...

He then added, "I tell you the truth, you shall see heaven open, and the angels of God ascending and descending on the Son of Man." John 1:51(NIV)

Now I'm holding on to Jesus as my Ladder...Lord, I just had a terrible thought! What if that problem had never come into my life! I would never have discovered that You, Jesus, are THE Ladder! I would never have started coming closer to You...Thank You, dear Jesus, thank You for being our Ladder!

Red Lights   Feb. 19

John 12:36a
"Make use of the Light while there is still time; then you will become light bearers."

Dear sweet Jesus, we find ourselves rushing around day after day in our cars trying to accomplish more and more! We get so conditioned to rushing we resent the very important traffic system which was set up to safeguard us...

As we're speeding down the highways and arteries of our country we see the light changing from green to amber. We speed up to try and "make the light" so we won't have to stop for a red light!

Day in and day out we do this, little realizing how many times we are passing up a wonderful chance to stop. It is a chance to praise You; a chance to pray to You; a chance to thank You!

Instead of trying to "make a light," dear Father, teach us to slow down and take advantage of these precious moments in our busy lives! These little stops could be called "Prayer Stops" or "Praise Periods" in honor of You, for all You do in our lives, Lord! Just think, dear Jesus, how many extra prayers would be flooding Your gates and storming Heaven!

Perhaps there would be lives saved too, sweet Jesus; what a bonus that would be! Teach us, Lord, the need to seek every chance we can in our busy lives to find these precious moments to spend with You. They are the little joyful moments when we can perhaps raise our voices up in a burst of song and shout "Hallelujah, Praise God!"

Dear Jesus, please help us to take Your words from John to heart. They are so true. By taking advantage of the "light" while there is still time, we can strengthen our own prayer life so we will become "light bearers". People around us will see a change in our lives and wonder what has happened to us! You are the Light! Your Light will shine through us when we allow ourselves to make use of every moment to draw closer to You...

Every day, Lord, remind us of these words as we go driving about, trying to cram so much into so little time! Remind us of the chance to have a little "Prayer Stop" or "Praise Period" instead of just waiting for a red light to change... ... ...

See! He Is Arriving, Surrounded By Clouds!
Feb. 20

Acts 1:9-11

It was not long afterwards that he rose into the sky and disappeared into a cloud, leaving them staring after him. As they were straining their eyes for another glimpse, suddenly two white-robed men were standing there among them, and said, "Men of Galilee, why are you standing here staring at the sky? Jesus has gone away to heaven, and some day, just as he went, he will return!"

Praise God! We await Your return, Jesus! As Luke relates in the above Scriptures, You will return to earth in the same manner as You left! Awesome, Lord! Many say we are in the latter days, Jesus...We are filled with mixed emotions when we hear this...Only Your Father knows the exact day and hour...But one thing we know for certain, You will appear just as You departed...

Your Scriptures also tell us that in these latter days, there will be many "false prophets" proclaiming Your coming, Jesus...We must let the Holy Spirit guide us before reading or listening to one who appears to be a prophet.

Beginning in 2 John 1:7, it says very plainly what we have to do,

Watch out for the false leaders—and there are many of them around—who don't believe that Jesus Christ came to earth as a human being with a body like ours. Such people are against the truth and against Christ. Beware of being like them, and losing the prize that you and I have been working so hard to get. See to it that you win your full reward from the Lord. For if you wander beyond the teaching of Christ, you will leave God behind; while if you are loyal to Christ's teachings, you will have God too. Then you will have both the Father and the Son.

If anyone comes to teach you and he doesn't believe what Christ taught, don't even invite him into your home. Don't encourage him in any way. If you do you will be a partner with him in his wickedness.

Wow Lord, that's plainly said! You tell us very clearly in Your Scriptures what we are to believe and what we are to avoid!

Lastly, in Revelation 1:7a, You again show us what You want us to believe! John wrote it all down in a vision from God. It says:

"See He is arriving, surrounded by clouds; and every eye shall see him – yes, and those who pierced him."

Thank You Father, for Your Holy Bible that guides us and teaches us Your Truths... ... ...

Genius...   Feb. 21

1st Corinthians 1:26-29

Notice among yourselves, dear brothers, that few of you who follow Christ have big names or power or wealth. Instead, God has deliberately chosen to use ideas the world considers foolish and of little worth in order to shame those people considered by the world as wise and great. He has chosen a plan despised by the world, counted as nothing at all, and used it to bring down to nothing those the world considers great, so that no one anywhere can ever brag in the presence of God.

Lord, You are our Lord, our Savior - our all...Without You we are nothing. Sometimes we wonder about our own personal talents, Lord.

We look around and see so many examples of talent. We open up art books and see such gigantic talent! We travel and see magnificent examples of architecture and sculpture! Sometimes our minds perceive one person down through the ages as perhaps the greatest artistic genius of all...

Lord, for some of us Michelangelo comes to mind...What talent, what genius! How many examples of his work reflected things about You and all Your creations! As our minds drift off into wishful thinking, some of us perhaps wish that we could have had talent such as his! What dedication too, Lord, Michelangelo had; he devoted his entire life to his art!

Yet, a poem Michelangelo wrote when he was in his latter years, reflects these thoughts:

> "Well-neigh the voyage now is overpast,
> And my frail bark, through troubled seas and rude,
> Draws near that common haven where at last
> Of every action, be it evil or good,
> Must due account be rendered. Well I know
> How vain will then appear that favored art,
> Sole Idol long and Monarch of my heart,
> For all is vain that man desires below,
> And now remorseful thoughts the past upbraid,
> And fear of twofold death my soul alarms,
> That which must come, and that beyond the grave:
> Picture and Sculpture lose their feeble charms,
> And to that Love Divine I turn for aid,
> Who from the Cross extends His arms to save...
> *Michelangelo*

Lord, keep us ever mindful of our goal in life! Don't let us become blinded by our talents, whatever they are, no matter how great they are! Show us that it is only You who matter in our lives! Please show us we have to keep You in the very center of our hearts and souls...

This world of ours can become a deceiver for us at times, dear Lord, as You well know! Remind us constantly to keep close to You every day of our lives!

Flower Children   Feb. 22

Psalm 37:23,24

The steps of good men are directed by the Lord. He delights in each step they take. If they fall it isn't fatal, for the Lord holds them with his hand.

"Take My hand... Look neither to the right or left, for I have you securely in My care... Believe this so that I can take you where I want you to be..."

Oh Father! How we do believe You! How we do trust You! We will leave everything in Your Hands! You have brought us to a deeper understanding of how this can truly work in our lives!

You promised us so many times in Your Scriptures that if we trust in You, You will bring about the best for us! Now we are in a situation, which requires us to stand on these promises...

The world, Jesus dear, would tell us that we should be worried by the circumstances, which we are in! But as we know, dear Lord, Your ways are not of the world. We CAN stand unafraid knowing that You are there with us...No matter what may happen, what the timing may be, we know that You will continue to watch over us, for You are our loving, caring Father...

Oh, Lord, how we Praise You for claiming us as Your children! How we Praise You for loving us so much. You will be with us in all the many ins and outs, ups and downs of these days, which are unknown...We could imagine that it is like walking with a blindfold on. We take one cautious step at a time, but still being courageous enough to take that step...Steadily we go on, unsure of ourselves, but being sure of YOU. We know full well that You ARE there caring for us...

Yes Lord, we believe in You...We trust You...We know without doubt that You are the only One who can be relied upon! So we will go forward, trusting that You are with us and will bring us where You want us to be – just as You have said...

Wherever that place may be, whatever the circumstances may be, we know if You bring us there - then it is right...It is where we are to bloom, for You alone can make us flower... ... ...

"I Am The Way, The Truth And The Life"
Feb. 23

John 14:6,7a

Jesus told him, "I am the Way—yes, and the Truth and the Life. No one can get to the Father except by means of me. If you had known who I am, then you would have known who my Father is."

That's what is necessary for us to know...Jesus IS the Way! Jesus IS the Truth! Jesus IS the Life! And NO ONE, absolutely NO ONE can get to the Father God, except by means of Jesus!

Jesus - what a PRECIOUS name! What a POWERFUL name! What a BLESSED name! Jesus...Without our recognizing that name, that truth, our lives are meaningless... ... ...

But what is the way to You, Lord? Is it the same for each and every one of us? Is there some secret we have to find first? And the Truth, Heavenly Father, what is the Truth? So many Bibles have been written; some people have been confused by them. One says that only his Bible is the acceptable one. Another says only his Bible has the truth; still another says his is really the one to be believed...Lord, what are we to believe? Who are we to believe? Holy men argue this point.

Turn to the Scriptures You say? It is there for all to read in any Bible...Heavenly Teacher, Provider of all knowledge, thank You again for enlightening us. In 2nd Peter 1:20,21 and John 16:13a the answers are found.

For no prophecy recorded in Scripture was ever thought up by the prophet himself. It was the Holy Spirit within these godly men who gave them true messages from God.

"When the Holy Spirit, who is truth, comes, he shall guide you into all truth,..."

Yes Lord, You are the Truth. Throughout all Your Scriptures, You show us the Way too—the way to everlasting Life! Time after time You told us that we must love You enough to follow You - love You enough to deny ourselves. We must love our brothers as much as we love ourselves. Yes, Lord, to love divinely as You Love, that is the Way, that is the Truth, that is the attainment of Eternal Life!

But, Lord, there is always the problem of knowing the answer to a problem and following through with the answer. That is the difficult part. More than ever, now we need the power of Your name! We need the power of Your Holy Spirit! We need the Holy Spirit's Power to help us to follow through what we have found to be the Way, the Truth and the Life! Please help us each and every day, dear Jesus, for we want to follow You... ... ...

Turn To Me   Feb. 24

Luke 24:44-53

Then he said, "When I was with you before, don't you remember my telling you that everything written about me by Moses and the prophets and in the Psalms must all come true?" Then he opened their minds to understand at last these many Scriptures! And he said, "Yes, it was written long ago that the Messiah must suffer and die and rise again from the dead on the third day; and that this message of salvation should be taken from Jerusalem to all the nations: *There is forgiveness of sins for all who turn to me.* You have seen these prophecies come true.

And now I will send the Holy Spirit upon you, just as my Father promised. Don't begin telling others yet—stay here in the city until the Holy Spirit comes and fills you with power from heaven."

Then Jesus led them out along the road to Bethany, and lifting his hands to heaven, he blest them, and then began rising into the sky, and went on to heaven. And they worshiped him, and returned to Jerusalem filled with mighty joy, and were continually in the Temple, praising God.

Lord, there are so many heavy thoughts in these passages! First of all, You opened the minds of Your beloved followers. In an instant they were able to understand Your Holy Scriptures! Please Lord, be as generous to us; teach us to understand Your Holy Words. Please let only Your meaning come through to us when we make our attempts to understand this mighty legacy...Thank You, Jesus...

Now for the very important message in Luke 24:47b, "THERE IS FORGIVENESS OF SINS FOR ALL WHO TURN TO ME." No matter what sin we have ever committed - no matter how grave, wretched, or unforgivable we thought it would be, You promised us, IF we turn to You, You will completely forgive us!

You, Jesus, who are so perfect, know how imperfect we are! Praise You, Jesus! Thank You for Your Love and compassion for us! No one else in this whole world could be so forgiving and understanding of our offenses...These offenses are not only to society, but also more importantly to You, God. For You are so deserving of our undying dedication...

When You kept Your Father's promise to Your Apostles, You sent the Holy Spirit to be upon them and in them. They were filled with the power from Heaven! This same power You have promised us too, Lord Jesus! We can be filled with this same Heavenly Power by putting our faith and trust in You! Thank You, Jesus, thank You! The Holy Spirit is ours just for the asking!

These overwhelming things were not all You gave to Your loyal, loving followers on that day, Jesus. You filled their hearts with mighty joy! They were so joyful with love and praise for You that they were constantly praising God!

You ask so little from us and You promise to give us so much in return! All You ask is that we turn to You, Jesus...

Have YOU turned to Him?

Reaping The Harvest   Feb. 25

John 4:34-38

Then Jesus explained: "My nourishment comes from doing the will of God who sent me, and from finishing his work. Do you think the work of harvesting will not begin until the summer ends four months from now? Look around you! Vast fields of human souls are ripening all around us, and are ready now for reaping. The reapers will be paid good wages and will be gathering eternal souls into the granaries of heaven! What joys await the sower and the reaper, both together! For it is true that one sows and someone else reaps. I sent you to reap where you didn't sow; others did the work, and you received the harvest."

Lord, it doesn't make any difference how You use us, whether we be sowers or reapers, just show us the way...Dear Jesus, if each of us here on earth could be used to draw at least one lonely soul to You - just one! What a different world this would be...

65

Praise to You Lord, Savior of this world! Without You we would be forever in darkness and without hope...You are the Light of the world and the Joy of this world and the whole universe!

Your Scriptures are our nourishment, Jesus. Through them, we come to understand more fully what is meant by being a sower or a reaper. Perhaps it will only be one loving act on our part, some Christ-like action, which will attract one soul to You...Perhaps that one act on our part will be the seed, which will fall into a fallow spot in just one person. Perhaps too, this will lay dormant for many months or years before the seed begins to sprout. But grow it does until the time comes for the reaping! The sower might long have passed on to his or her Heavenly home where he or she rejoices with You, dear Lord Jesus. The work has long been finished and the reaper now prepares for the harvest. What joy is in the reaper's heart...

This once small seed is fully-grown and waiting to be harvested at the moment of its perfection! Yes, Father, Planter of all good, what joy there is in Heaven to be able to welcome another soul into Your company of angels and Your Heavenly Family!

Most of all, Jesus, our Savior, what joy there is for the one soul who has been saved! Oh, that every soul who was ever created by You could be saved! Oh, that every soul would bow down before You to honor and adore You! That is our desire, Jesus, Lord God! That You be adored, worshipped and praised for all eternity! You alone are our God! You alone are our Heavenly King...You alone are worthy... ... ...

We Believe You, Lord Jesus   Feb. 26

John 20:31
...but these are recorded so that you will believe that he is the Messiah, the Son of God, and that believing in him you will have life.

We believe You, Jesus! We believe You! We want to express our belief to You, by devotion to You in love and obedience. We support Your teachings, Your Holy Words, Your Scriptures!

When we love and obey You, then You reveal Yourself to us! We believe all the things, which You have taught us. These are what we want to live our lives by, dear Leader of truth...

There is so much to learn about You, Heavenly Father! Each wonderful passage of Your Bible tells us more and more about You. We hunger for the day when we will be face to face with You!

Meanwhile, we wanted You to know that besides loving You, adoring You, praising You, honoring You, we firmly BELIEVE in You...We believe so strongly that this consumes our whole lives and changes them. We praise You for this wonderful change!

Wherever we go now this belief in You shines through us and makes us reflect the power of You, Lord God! If only all people would turn to You, Lord Jesus...How can they not believe, Father God? It seems so strange to those of us who do believe in You...

So many know that the greatest celebration of the year is the day of Your Birth. So many, many know You died on Good Friday and rose again on Easter Sunday...They know all that and yet they do not all believe! Has anyone else ever resurrected after their death??? Has anyone else in the hundreds upon hundreds of years had their birthday, death and resurrection celebrated year after year after year? How much more proof do they need to believe that You are the only ONE: the only Son of God who came to earth for all mankind? Even the calendar we use today is based on Your birth, dear Lord Jesus!

Many say that You were a "good man". Some say You were a "good human being," perhaps a prophet, or a "good humanitarian". They will not believe that You came down from Heaven as the Son of God, who was born of human flesh and lived like us, but was without sin. They will not believe that You, perfect in all ways and sinless, died for us who are so sinful. Foolish, foolish men, how sad it is to see them seeking values of this world... You are patiently waiting for them to turn to You and believe in You...

Father, we do believe in You...Please help us to draw others to believe in You also... ... ...

Suffering   Feb. 27

Romans 8:17
And since we are his children, we will share his treasures—for all God gives to his Son Jesus is now ours too. But if we are to share his glory, we must also share his suffering.

Oh God, why do we have to suffer? What is suffering for, Lord? Why do some have to suffer while others seem to go through life unscathed and untouched? Truly Lord God, there are so many who have done nothing to deserve suffering, yet they have to suffer...

I don't understand it, Father God...Tell me what You want me to know about suffering...What is the mystery of suffering?

"Oh, My child, I did nothing to deserve suffering. I came into this world wanting to teach Love. Look at Me. See Me. See how I was led through the streets and under the archways with My hands tied. What was My crime? Why did I have to suffer??? For you - I suffered for you. You can suffer for Me. You can offer your suffering as a reminder of how I suffered for you, My child, and for all.

Remember it was My Father's Will that I come into this world and die for you, but I had a choice too, as you have. I asked My Father to remove the cup of suffering from Me. But I knew that unless I carried out His Will, you could not be saved. Do you understand now why there is suffering and that you must suffer too, to share with Me? I willingly suffered and died for you. When you are with Me you will understand fully as we spend eternity together... "

Yes, Father God, now we begin to understand, and can relate more clearly...Each time we suffer, let us picture in our minds what You went through for us as if we were Your only child, Lord. Then let us see You shining and glowing as Victor over all that You suffered, now resurrected and glorified! That is what it will be like for Your children who will accept what this life brings even though they may not have caused any of the circumstances.

Yes, Jesus, You were the Innocent Lamb led to slaughter without a murmur...Teach us to handle our sufferings as You did...Thank You for suffering for us... ... ...

The Gardens of Our Souls   Feb. 28

1ˢᵗ John 1:9

But if we confess our sins to him, he can be depended on to forgive us and to cleanse us from every wrong. [And it is perfectly proper for God to do this for us because Christ died to wash away our sins.]

Dear Lord, while struggling with some weeds today in my garden I tugged, pulled, twisted and used all my strength to get rid of those big, ugly weeds! I really worked at them, Lord! While I was wondering why it was so hard to remove the big, ugly ones and not so hard to remove others, You showed me the similarity between my garden and my soul...

You made me see, dear sweet Jesus, that when we neglect our gardens, for long periods of time, all kinds of weeds can come along and take over! It's just like that with our souls too, isn't it, Lord? When we neglect You for long periods of time and allow ourselves to be taken over with all kinds of sins and imperfections, the natural beauty of our souls becomes withered looking...

The longer we stay away from You, the worse our souls become. Then they are so choked and strangled by sin, we hardly know where to go or how to clean them up again! Finally when we do see the need to do so, we have to work doubly or triply hard to get ourselves back in spiritual relationship with You, dear Lord Jesus...

Just like the weeds, some sins are much harder to "pull out" than others...Try as we might, they hold on with the most tenacious grip! We find we do not have the strength to rid ourselves of them...What can we do about that kind, dear Lord?

Today when I struggled so hard, using all my body's strength to remove one weed, You made me see it was impossible to do on my own. You told me to use my common sense and get an instrument to help me. I tried with the first one, but with no success. No little garden hand tool was big enough to do the job! I had to use the most powerful tool I owned: a big shovel...

Lord, You showed me that it's the same way with sins. Those sins or habits we have allowed to really take hold of us and let stay a long time, cannot be removed in our own strength.

We finally realize we must go to You, dear Father. We need Your divine help! Only You can rout out these terrible sins and habits...We find ourselves powerless to do this job of removing the sins and habits we know have to be removed from our lives. You are the "big instrument" in our lives who can help us...

Ah-h-h, now we know, Lord Jesus, we must not neglect our gardens for one single day or else the seeds of the ugly weeds of sin which float all through our world will take root in our lives again!

When we allow You to keep us weeded, then You can look down into the gardens of our souls and be pleased to see how beautiful they are... ... ...

Going Home   Feb. 29

Titus 3:4-7
But when the time came for the kindness and love of God our Savior to appear, then he saved us—not because we were good enough to be saved, but because of his kindness and pity—by washing away our sins and giving us the new joy of the indwelling Holy Spirit whom he poured out upon us with wonderful fullness—and all because of what Jesus Christ our Savior did so that he could declare us good in God's eyes—all because of his great kindness; and now we can share in the wealth of the eternal life he gives us, and we are eagerly looking forward to receiving it.

Lord Jesus, You are our Lord! You are the mighty One! You are the Creator! You are all Powerful and Mighty! We praise You! We glorify You! We sing Your praises with joy in our hearts!

When we come to know You in a personal way, we become so excited our hearts almost burst with longing and desire to join You in Your Heavenly place, our future home!

Home - we'll be going home to our real home, our final home! Trying to realize this in our earthly minds sends us into such excitement we can hardly bear to wait! Father, You will be there! You, Creator of all, will be there, just waiting for us to come home to You...Wow, Lord Jesus, what glorious things await us, things that our tiny earthly minds cannot possibly understand or comprehend...Why should we ever fear death? Death is the gateway to our Heavenly home where only You and goodness prevail! We thank You, Lord God, for wanting us; for waiting patiently for us; for making us feel that we are special to You, Father...

Oh, Jesus, Friend of all mankind, Holy Spirit the Comforter of all those who yearn for Your compassion, how can we ever feel that we in any way deserve to spend our eternal lives with You...Please keep showing us that it is only Your Divine Love, Your Divine gift of Love, which makes it possible for us to be with You for all eternity...

Father God, Your Son's death on the cross was Your gift to us, our way to Heaven...We could never earn a place there. Never, never could we deserve to be there...It is only when we accept Your gift by faith that we are able to enter Your Heavenly gates as Your children...

Imagine! We are Your kids! You are our Father! Your joy is to father us, Love us, and cherish us! Our joy will be to please You - to do anything our hearts can think of which will in any way bring a smile to Your face or laughter in Your voice!

Oh, dear Lord Jesus, if we dwell any more on these thoughts our hearts will become too heavy to bear the thought that we still must wait until we hear You call us to our Heavenly home... ... ...

March

Radiate, Smile, Love!   Mar. 1

John 15:1,2,8

"I am the true Vine, and my Father is the Gardener. He lops off every branch that doesn't produce. And he prunes those branches that bear fruit for even larger crops."

"My true disciples produce bountiful harvests. This brings great glory to my Father."

Precious Lord, how can my life make a difference to anyone else's? In the overall realm of things, what does my life mean in the huge scope of LIFE? What purpose does my life serve? What purpose, Lord, what purpose…

"Just as a flower gives forth beauty, gives color, gives forth fragrance, you must do the same. The flower has a life span of its own, as do you. I bring forth those who see the flower. I send you where you are to flower…

Rest in Me as the flower rests in its place. As the flower drops to earth, so shall you, when as the flower is spent, you also are spent. I will gather you up and bring you to a place with Me. For now you are to radiate, to smile, to love… "

Oh, WOW, Lord! You have meaning for my life! You are aware and watching over me!!! You have a plan for my life! I have a purpose for my life! How wonderful to be as one of Your "flowers"! What difference does it make how long one lives! Just as some flowers last a long time and others a very brief time, as long as we radiate, smile and love for You Jesus - that's what matters!

Oh, Father, Master Gardener, Pruner of Life, may the glow of Your Son, Jesus, in us cheer the hearts of all who come across our paths. May we be delighted to "flower" for You…

Let all who pass by be touched by the fragrance of YOU…Let all be lifted by the presence of YOU reflected through us… … …

And Rest In The Law Of Love   Mar. 2

Mark 12:32,33

The teacher of religion replied, "Sir, you have spoken a true word in saying that there is only one God and no other. And I know it is far more important to love him with all my heart and understanding and strength, and to love others as myself, than to offer all kinds of sacrifices on the altar of the Temple."

"AND REST IN THE LAW OF LOVE"…Lord God, when You placed these words in my mind, at first I did not understand what they meant…We have become conditioned to tense up when we hear the word "law" as if it is something to fear…Then You followed this word law with the most confusing word in all this world: LOVE…LOVE — how many of us know the real meaning of this word? More songs have been written; more promises have been made; more hurts have occurred because we have at times misunderstood the true meaning of this little four-letter word…

Love can make the world go round as the song says - but has it? Has it changed anything enough to show the world that LOVE really can make a difference in the lives of mankind? Is it possible LOVE can make a difference?

Ah-h yes, Lord, it can make a difference…We see it happening around us when those who come to know You, discover that knowing You, teaches them Your pure kind of LOVE. It is Your LOVE, which passes all understanding, the LOVE You had for all men by giving up Your spotless life for us…That's LOVE in its purest state! This is the example You set before us…There was and is only one law, which can possibly change the world - the law of LOVE…

It starts by teaching us to love our Lord God, our Creator. Then loving our brothers as ourselves completes this law of LOVE. Jesus, You never said it would be easy and You said it was Your Command…Now, Lord, this is where we have problems. This is why there has been so much misunderstanding about this law of LOVE. We must love our brother and sister when they are most unlovable! It is easy to love when they are lovable…Teach us to constantly keep our thoughts on You, Lord…Only in this way can we come into the full understanding of this powerful word – LOVE…

Then, Lord, please teach us that we must REST…We must stop churning and spinning our wheels trying to do the work ourselves, our way. By loving YOU completely, You will in turn shine through us and Your LOVE in us will make it possible for us to LOVE our brothers and our sisters…Yes, Father, teach us to "REST IN THE LAW OF LOVE"… … …

Memories   Mar. 3

Colossians 3:13-14a
Be gentle and ready to forgive; never hold grudges. Remember, the Lord forgave you, so you must forgive others. Most of all, let love guide your life…

Lord, here we are where we hope no one else can see us, especially ourselves…Perhaps if we keep perfectly quiet for awhile no one will ever know or find out the truth about ourselves. We can go on as if nothing has happened, and perhaps the resentments, hurts and bitterness will not come back again…But on the other hand, why do we have to give up those feelings? Those things happened to us, didn't they? Remember the time that, and then, remember the time when…Oh, wait a minute; r-e-m-e-m-b-e-r the time - that r-e-a-l-l-y was the worst of all? Well, we have a right to feel mistreated so why do we have to give up these painful memories? Each time we think of them and relive them they give us a certain sense of satisfaction…

How we "enjoy" remembering each hurt, each put-down, each act of neglect…Each time we remember detail by detail, a surge of anger, resentment or bitterness flows through our bodies. Then we re-enact all those painful circumstances once again.

Oh, Lord, free us from this kind of reckless thinking! Oh God of Power and Might, help us rid ourselves of these destroying thoughts, emotions and feelings before they completely tear down our relationship with You!

Show us how dangerous these painful memories can be to us! Show us how they can keep us from loving those who have hurt us…Show us how we can start out afresh and renewed in our relationships with our families, friends, neighbors, co-workers - whichever relationships need healing, Father God…

It is only Your Divine Love, which can truly turn a hateful, unloving relationship into a relationship of love and beauty, my Lord...Only You can heal hearts and bring about the most loving experiences among Your children, Father...And it is so important for us to be willing...

Praise You, Lord! We praise You for Your Goodness...You lift us up out of our daily problems once we turn to You for help, once we take our eyes off ourselves, our hurts, our bitterness, our unhappiness...

Yes, Father of Love, You graciously show us what we have to do, in order to heal these past painful memories. We have to turn them over to You - each hurt, each insult, each insensitive act committed against us. Then the peace and joy of Your healing Love can fill and renew us. Oh, Lord of Love, we thank You for Your wondrous ways of teaching us how to live and to forgive in this world of ours - and Yours... ... ...

"Have It Your Way"   Mar. 4

Isaiah 42:5,6a (NIV)
This is what God the LORD says - he who created the heavens and stretched them out, who spread out the earth and all that comes out of it, who gives breath to its people, and life to those who walk on it: "I, the LORD, have called you in righteousness; I will take hold of your hand."

As I gaze out upon the world today I see
Beautiful greens, blue sky, a bird, a bee,
Sloping hills, pastures green, lambs grazing -
All of this and much, much more. It's amazing!
Lord God, You created it all. Nothing can exist
Unless You create it. So why do we persist,
In trying to get our own way, hoping it is Your way...
"Ah, child, let ME take over, let Me," You say.
So, Father, thinking things out as I gaze away
I can now say, "Have it Your way; have it Your way..."
GNL

A Parent's Prayer For A Child   Mar. 5

Romans 3:23,24

Yes, all have sinned; all fall short of God's glorious ideal; yet now God declares us "not guilty" of offending him if we trust in Jesus Christ, who in his kindness freely takes away our sins.

Dear Lord, once You gave me a child. You in your generosity gave me a gift of life. That little bundle of flesh and bones, so helpless and small, has grown up. Dear sweet Jesus, did I fail You when You allowed me the privilege of being a parent? That's such a tremendous responsibility! I really tried, Lord, to always do the right thing; to make the right decisions, but in my humanity I did make mistakes...

Hopefully, dear Father, these mistakes, which I made, will not be held against this child, whom I love so much...

If You have to make someone pay for these mistakes, dear Lord, please do not let it be my child, who had no choice being sent to me. I accept full responsibility for the growing up years...

You don't want to punish either of us for the mistakes I've made, or the ones this child will make? But, Lord, I thought You always punished when mistakes were made! Thank You, sweet Heavenly Father; what a relief it is to my soul to know You don't want to punish us!

What is the secret, dear Savior, for not having to be punished for our mistakes? Oh, Creator of all things, Your Son, Jesus Christ, took the punishment for all mankind! Believing this, that Your Son's death on the cross was and is our only salvation? **That's the secret!!!** But it's not supposed to be a secret, Lord? Why didn't I know this before? Was it because I was not listening to Your words?

Loving and forgiving Father, please accept my apology. How could I have ever doubted that Jesus Christ was and is Your Son who died for my mistakes? How could I have come so close to Your ways and not have known Your message...Did You say You want all the world to know?

All right, dear Father, You have been so generous to me in giving me this child, now in gratitude, I promise to tell whoever will listen. I will tell Your message, that Your Son came to save the world and that He lived and died for our salvation!

And, Lord, one more thing, thank You from the bottom of my heart for giving me my child, whom I love so much... ... ...

Through It All...   Mar. 6

Hebrews 13:5b
For God has said, "I will never, *never* fail you nor forsake you."

Through it all, Lord, You were faithful to me...No matter what befell my loved ones, or me You were always there with us, through it all...

Looking back, You carried me through such difficulties; my heart beats faster at the remembrance of them...There were days and nights when it seemed things couldn't be worse, and yet You brought me through each experience...

Now I can see, You have caused me to be a stronger person; You have caused my faith to be unflinching. I can see the years, the experiences unfolding before my eyes. I can now marvel at the way You allowed them to happen and yet kept me and my loved ones alive...

My faith in You, Lord Jesus, has covered not only me, but also my loved ones...Oh yes, Lord, You and I both know that they have not all made commitments to you, but I have faith that You will bring them into Your family through Your Grace...

There is a song entitled "I Never Promised You A Rose Garden." So many of Your children think that if they are "good," You will give them a beautiful "rose garden" type of life...But even in the rose garden there are briars and thorns, which can prick us and make us, bleed...

That is part of Life itself, Lord, isn't it? There is the beauty of the rose, but also the thorns that are a part of it. We would like to have the roses, but not the thorns or briars...We would like to be pampered, waited on, served by others...

You know, Lord, the results that would come from that kind of LIFE... Most of Your children would become spoiled, selfish and conditioned to look at themselves as worthy of such a life. And so, because You LOVE us so much, You seldom allow Your children to sail through LIFE without problems of one sort or another...

That is when we realize You are there with us through it all...That is when we learn to continue on, no matter how dark things may look. That is when we see through the darkness, the glimmer of a new day, a new ray of hope, with confidence that You are always with us...

Yes, Lord, looking back we can see that the ups and downs of LIFE have actually helped us grow...Thank You, dear Savior, dear Jesus, for being with us through it all... ... ...

In the Garden   Mar. 7

Matthew 26:36,38

Then Jesus brought them to a garden grove, Gethsemane, and told them to sit down and wait while he went on ahead to pray.

Then He told them, "My soul is crushed with horror and sadness to the point of death... stay here... stay awake with me."

Oh, sweet, sweet Jesus... Here You are in the garden... some of Your disciples are with You... You have come here to pray... You know what is to come...

Because You also have a Will, you have the freedom to make choices. Your Father, Almighty God, has asked You to suffer until death... You are here agonizing about this painful decision...

Should You deny Your Father's request? Should You decide to agree to His awesome question? Your heart, mind and Spirit are troubled... You must make this earth-changing decision.

The garden—peace and quiet linger all about You... You realize that your comrades have fallen asleep. You go to them and awaken them. Then You return to that place where You were pondering and praying...

Time passes, minute by minute. Stillness fills the air. As You continue to pray, You realize the disciples have fallen asleep. As You go forth to awaken them, You hear the sound of footsteps, many footsteps. Then a voice calls out "Hello, Master."

Judas has come... He kisses You on Your cheek. You have already made Your decision. Yes, you agree with Your Father God... You will become the living sacrifice for all mankind. You will become the sacred Lamb, the sacrificial Lamb, for every human being who will ever be born on this planet.

You, dear, dear Jesus, without anger, animosity or rage, go peacefully with Your abductors. Now You have left the garden... but forever will be the presence there of Your stay that night of all nights. Yes, dear Jesus, Your presence will always linger in the garden, that most special of all gardens...

Thank You, precious Jesus, for making this sacrifice for each and every one of us... Thank You, thank You, thank You... ... ...

You Are A "WOW" Lord!　　　Mar. 8

Psalm 145:5-7
I will meditate about your glory, splendor, majesty and miracles. Your awe-inspiring deeds shall be on every tongue; I will proclaim your greatness. Everyone will tell about how good you are, and sing about your righteousness.

Lord Jesus Christ, what more can we say after we say "I love You"? There are no earthly words to describe You! You are a "WOW" God! WONDER OF WONDERS, that's what You are, Lord Jesus! You are the WORKER OF WONDERS! We have seen so many of Your Wonders ourselves. We could let our minds drift off into all kinds of fantasy and yet You are beyond all of that!!! You are WITHOUT WORDS to describe You! That's why we have to stay so open when we think of You or talk about You...Yes, Lord Jesus, Father God, Holy Spirit, You are a "WOW" God!

Many of us did not see You as this kind of exciting God...You seemed to be only a fearful God, a stern God who kept a strict account of what we were or were not doing in our lives...We had You all wrong, God...

You didn't change from what You always were! You are the same yesterday, last year, last century, last thousands of years, since time began! It is we, who have changed! It is we who have finally come to know You as a loving and tender Lord. You are also caring and just...How long You have suffered under these misconceptions, Father God...You were waiting for us to come to You, to want a loving, close relationship with You. You desire us to become intimate friends. You want to be able to give us all the loving care a sweetheart gives his intended bride...You want us to be receptive to this loving relationship. It is only then it can grow into the depth of love You have made possible between God and mankind...

Your Divine Love is the only kind of love that is a lasting one...Your Divine Love is the only kind, which can forgive us time and time again when we hurt You...Often this is not an intentional hurt on our part, but still, how shallow our love can be at times...

Yes Lord, You are Father, Son and Holy Spirit...You truly are a "WOW" God! Who else can be spoken about as God, our Father, Creator of all; Jesus, His Son, Savior of all; and His Holy Spirit, power and strength for all...

Yet this believable mystery of the Trinity points again to a WONDER OF WONDERS, a WORKER OF WONDERS, and a God who is WITHOUT WORDS to describe...Thank You, Lord Almighty God. Thank You... ... ...

Consolation   Mar. 9

Psalm 23:4,6 (KJV)
Yea, though I walk through the valley of the shadow of death, I will fear no evil: for thou *art* with me; thy rod and thy staff they comfort me.

Surely goodness and mercy shall follow me all the days of my life: and I will dwell in the house of the LORD for ever.

Oh Father God, I need to be consoled...I am hurting...I feel so down...Everything around me seems to be falling away...My head is heavy with the burdens I feel surrounded by...My heart feels crushed...I feel so useless, so useless...

My life seems to be empty of joy, peace...The days are passing by, one by one, and seem to go on to an endless succession of gray days. Life is seemingly without hope, without anything to relieve me of these feelings...

Oh Father God, console me...I need so desperately to be consoled...Is this all there is to life? Endless days are to be waded through, and there is no change in sight...Oh Father God, show me what I need to know to help me through this valley I'm traveling through...

I truly want things to be different, to be more meaningful. I do want to wake up each day with hope in my heart and a light in my eyes. I desire a song in my voice and a praise upon my lips...Father, dear Father, show me the way...

"My dear one, come close to Me... Come closer... I have My arms around you though you cannot feel them... But they are there, believe Me.

Your every situation is watched over by Me... Nothing will be able to affect you without My permission... Believe it! All is well. These are the trials in life that will help you grow... Have patience; have patience... I truly love you and am watching over you. Take comfort as I console you with these words... Peace will return and joy will spill over... Take comfort, dear one; take comfort..."

Light Of The World   Mar. 10

John 12:35-36a

Jesus replied, "My light will shine out for you just a little while longer. Walk in it while you can, and go where you want to go before the darkness falls, for then it will be too late for you to find your way. Make use of the Light while there is still time; then you will become light bearers."

John 12:44-46

Jesus shouted to the crowds, "If you trust me, you are really trusting God. For when you see me, you are seeing the one who sent me. I have come as a Light to shine in this dark world, so that all who put their trust in me will no longer wander in the darkness."

You are the beacon for the whole world to see, Jesus. Your Light is the only pure light that man has been able to find as he stumbles through this, sometimes unbearable, life...Only You can make this life bearable, Jesus, only You...

Sometimes a shadow falls across us after we have found Your Light, Lord. We grope around in the darkness alone and afraid. Sometimes a burden or heartache enters our lives. We find ourselves under a dark cloud trying to set ourselves again on the path toward You. We struggle on and on thinking we can find the solution ourselves. Foolish, foolish mankind - for it is only when we put You back in the center of our lives, that we find again, Your Divine Light, which never dims...

It is only when we allow ourselves to fall away from Your Light into the dark pits of this world that we separate ourselves from You, Lord...You never hide Your Light! You never turn Your back on us! You go on shining and shining for the whole world to see, IF we will only take a step toward You, dear Savior...

Lord Jesus, Light of all this world, shine forth through us...Take all that is in us, which blocks out Your Light from shining through us and destroy it! Take out all the self, all the "I", all the ego, which prevents Your Divine Light from shining out of us...Empty us, Oh, Lord, empty us...

We need to give up all those things, which keep us from becoming empty vessels for You to use. Then Your Divine Light can penetrate our entire beings and we will be able to truly wear the name "Light bearers"...

So, Father of Light, keep on shining and shining! Please direct our steps only in the paths of Your Light. Keep us out of that darkness which leaves us in such despair! We really want to become light bearers, Your light bearers, Jesus... ... ...

I Want Your Love   Mar. 11

Hosea 6:6

I don't want your sacrifices—I want your love; I don't want your offerings—I want you to know me.

Lord God, what can You do or say more clearly than what You said in Hosea 6:6? You told us you want our love. You told us You want a personal relationship with us...

If we were to receive by special messenger tomorrow, an engraved invitation to a meeting with a renowned figure, our hearts would beat so rapidly with excitement we could hardly contain ourselves! We would probably run to our telephones and computers to tell our closest family members and friends the wonderful news! We would probably then sit in disbelief that the invitation had come at all! Imagine, to us! How special we would begin to feel about ourselves! How strange we are...We become awed by certain renowned figures of this world that we each hold in high regard. Yet they are only human like all the rest of us with failings, as well as, perhaps virtues.

Yet we respond as if Your invitation to a loving relationship is not very important! We seem not to be impressed by this message from You, Lord Jesus, Creator of all. Your invitation does not come in a fancy envelope or with engraved words. But, Lord, when You invite us and ask for our love, You are the One who wants to give more love to us, than You expect back from us!

If only more of Your children would worship You, Father - You ask so little from us...We are Your creations! Who else can fashion a human body and place into this miracle of life, a spirit, which will live for all eternity? Why can't we all see who You are, what You are and why You are? Why can't everybody love You? Why, Lord? You ask for so little...You ask for so little... ... ...

"Father, Son and Holy Spirit"   Mar. 12

Matthew 28:19

"Therefore go and make disciples in all the nations, baptizing them into the name of the Father and of the Son and of the Holy Spirit,..."

We praise You God, for You are Father, Son, and Spirit for all mankind...You loved us so much that You took the role of Father, Son and Holy Spirit, so human life could be reached by You...You, God, are our Father! You are our brother, Jesus Christ, and our Savior! You are the Holy Spirit, the Comforter, who inhabits this earth at this very moment! You are ever waiting for an opportunity to show Yourself to us...

We thank You God, our Abba Father...Yes, You are all to us and we praise You for Your encompassing Love for us...You Loved us so much that You sent Your only Son, Jesus Christ. He came down here to be born, to live among us, and to DIE for us...You then sent Your Holy Spirit to be present on this earth until the end of time...Because of Your Love, each of us has an opportunity to invite the Holy Spirit into our hearts...

Through Your Divine Love, Father, You offer us many gifts, which can be ours if we so desire. We have only to deepen our relationship with You, with Jesus Christ and Your Holy Spirit. When this happens You are only too happy to bestow these gifts, not on us,

83

but through us. You are the Giver. We are Your servants so that these gifts can flow through us for Your Glory, Father, for Your Glory!

What are some of these gifts? They are wisdom, knowledge, faith, healing, miracles, prophecy, discernment, tongues and interpretation of tongues. Each one of these gifts is precious, Father God...Remind us, always, that they are only to flow through us. We cannot be possessive of them for our own satisfaction or ego.

Heavenly Father, let us pour out praise for Your goodness to us! Yes, only You deserve our praise and adoration, our thanksgiving...As we deepen ourselves and humble ourselves, You will continue to show us Your Love. You will give us the fruit produced by Your Holy Spirit. These are: love, joy, peace, patience, kindness, goodness, faithfulness, gentleness and self-control. You want us to always demonstrate these. You never want us to lose them, but to let them grow and grow and grow within us!

Father God, You created the beautiful rose. Many people say that there is perfection in one rose. They believe it is the most beautiful flower ever created by You...Someone once said, "a rose is a rose is a rose". These words sound confusing to us at times...To some, it also sounds confusing to call You Father, Son and Holy Spirit...

Lord God, this is where one of Your gifts is to be used, the gift of faith. We need faith to believe that it is so, because You said it is so. Faith is needed to believe that Father, Son and Holy Spirit are ONE! God, Creator of All, God of Power and Might - we do believe. We do believe! We do believe... ... ...

"Listen To Me"   Mar. 13

Luke 10:39,42

Her sister Mary sat on the floor, listening to Jesus as he talked.

"There is really only one thing worth being concerned about. Mary has discovered it—and I won't take it away from her!"

"Listen to Me and you will hear the small, quiet voice that I speak to you... Hear Me... I want you to be so close to Me... Stay at my side... Can you not leave what you have and give Me your attention? I ask for so little, so little. Come and stay with Me... See in Me all your

needs, all your desires... I alone can answer what you need to know...
Come with Me..."

Oh dear Jesus, so often we forget that You have need of us...You yearn for our love, our trust, our belief in You...You are all Power, Knowledge, Creator, and Holder of so many titles. Yet, You desire to be loved by us, to be needed by us! How absolutely amazing this is!

In the stillness of this moment, we know it is true...We are as an only child to You, Father...You want an intimate relationship with us: to know our every thought, dream, and awareness of our very existence...

You want us to be so close that our very breath touches You...Every hair on our heads is counted by You...No one has ever loved us as You do...

How can we refuse this calling from You, this relationship You desire with us? How can we? Do we not know how much this means to You? Can we not be sensitive to Your deep desire for us to come to know you, in the most special way? Oh, dear Lord Jesus, surely we don't realize what it means to You or we would be so close that it would take a miracle to separate us...How little we know of You, how little...

This is what we realize as we come into the awareness of what You desire for us. We need to know You in a far deeper way than we ever have in the past, deeper than we dreamed or thought possible...Oh Father, dear Father, forgive us. Bring us into this tremendous relationship which is possible only through Your deep LOVE for us. You desire to be One with us...We wonder at the mystery of You being God, Son, and Holy Spirit – and yet One with us! Please bring us into this Oneness with You, dear Lord and Savior...

We are waiting... ... ... We are listening... ... ...

Obedience   Mar. 14

John 12:26(NIV)
"Whoever serves me must follow me; and where I am, my servant also will be. My Father will honor the one who serves me."

Oh, Lord Jesus, it is true - obedience is so precious to You! That's what You find so pleasing isn't it, Father? How many of us say with our lips that we want to do Your bidding, but when the moment of truth arrives, then it becomes another matter…

Please deepen our spirits, dear Jesus, to truly know ourselves and to place our strong wills gratefully at Your feet. That is where our wills belong, Master…

You became the servant by washing the feet of Your apostles, Lord. That is what You want from us too, to put ourselves in the position of becoming obedient servants. When we do this, we are in servitude to You…Once we dedicate ourselves to Your service, then You can depend on us to be truly obedient to Your plan for us.

Oh Father, this is a tremendous step for each of us to take! Emblazon on our hearts that we are Your servants. We must make it our true desire to serve You freely! Each time an opportunity comes for us to show You that we are Your servants, sharpen our awareness. You are our Lord…You are God…Let Your desires to use us be our desires also…

But, Father, protect us from becoming unfeeling in these precious situations. If it is a task which You have asked us to do, day after day, month after month, please refresh us with an ever-flowing sweet acceptance and joy to do Your work…

How it must grieve You to see Your people go about their work dull and unloving…Enkindle in all our hearts the complete joy and happiness we can have by doing Your work! Teach us Father, in a way, which brings us into the fulfillment of Your earthly plans for us…

Yes, Lord Jesus, teach us to be obedient to Your Will… … …

The Face of Jesus   Mar. 15

2nd Corinthians 4:6

For God, who said, "Let there be light in the darkness," has made us understand that it is the brightness of his glory that is seen in the face of Jesus Christ.

Jesus, what do You really look like? Would I recognize You if I were to see You today—would anybody?

Does it make any difference what You looked like? So many people would like You to look "a certain way," their way - does it really matter?

Hundred upon hundreds of artists have painted You. Many, many sculptors have depicted You in their minds' eye and in solid form. Have any of them come at all close to what You really looked like? Some have shown You with brown eyes; some with blue; others with an indefinable color. Your hair: it's been brown, light brown, medium brown, dark blond, curly, wavy, and almost straight. It has touched Your shoulders, almost touched Your shoulders, cascaded down Your shoulders...

Did You have a beard, a mustache or was Your face clean-shaven? What color was Your skin? Was it dark, medium or fair? All of these questions had to be answered in the minds of the artists and the sculptors for them to express how they imagined You...

Would we recognize You today if You came to earth again for a day or two? Are You here already in the soul of each of the humans who have dedicated themselves to You?

Is it You we see, when the pureness comes through a person at the precious moment they are attuned to Your Spirit? Those eyes which sometimes meet ours with such inner beauty and love, are they really Your eyes meeting ours to let us know that You are here?

Oh, Jesus, what difference does it make how You have been portrayed...It doesn't really matter...What matters is that You were here and that You came to bring us Light! That Light shines forth from our brothers' and sisters' faces as they reflect Your Divine Love! In their eyes, hopefully we see Your eyes, Jesus, our precious Lord and Savior... ... ...

Becoming A Servant   Mar. 16

"Why am I last? Why am I always the last in everything? Why am I never asked my opinion, my thoughts, and my desires? I want to be somebody. I want to be in the center of things; I want people to look up to me...Is there really a place for me in this world that is not last?"
Matthew 20:26b-28

87

"Anyone wanting to be a leader among you must be your servant. And if you want to be right at the top, you must serve like a slave. Your attitude must be like my own, for I, the Messiah, did not come to be served, but to serve, and to give my life as a ransom for many."

Those are powerful words, dear Lord Jesus…These words have the power to change our attitudes, our lives…These words spoken by You, Jesus Christ, tell us what choices we have when we live in this world. You alone, give us the choice of being happy if we really believe in You. You will give us Joy and Happiness when we choose to be last. We will then be able to accept whatever comes because of the fullness of Your Spirit in us…

You alone can actually show such love and joy shining in our faces that all who see us will know something special has happened to us! You alone, Jesus Christ, can be the One to draw others to You, through us.

Now we can look around. and see the faces of mankind…Now we can understand that the feelings we had about being last, about being depressed, need not be ours! Now we can see that the ones who have You, Jesus, as their Lord and Master, are Your truly happy and joyful followers!

Those who serve You through serving others are at peace with themselves for they have found Your true message, Jesus… … …

Anyone who says he is a Christian should live as Christ did…and as we obey this commandment, *to love one another*, the darkness in our lives disappears and the new light of life in Christ Jesus shines in. 1 John 2:6,8b

Why, Why, Why?   Mar. 17

John 13:34
"And so I am giving a new commandment to you now—love each other just as much as I love you."

Oh Lord, in Life there is such unfairness…Each of us is born into situations over which we have no control. Some of us are born into average families, ordinary circumstances. Others are born into such abject poverty. Some are born with "silver spoons in their mouths"…

Why am I not the one to suffer some of the saddest, poorest circumstances, which many, many people in this world experience? I did nothing to warrant some of the blessings I did receive—and still receive…

Sometimes the thought "Why?" fills our mind and we ponder and ponder…

"These are some of the mysteries of Life," You say Lord, in the inner voice, which speaks to us when we truly search for answers.

Sometime in the future we will understand all things, won't we, Lord? Meanwhile, though we see these inequities, our role is to LOVE, COMFORT, and SHARE. We are to practice what You, Lord Jesus Christ, came to teach…Help us to be obedient to extend Your LOVE in whatever way You lead us…

A loving word or glance, a smile from the heart, a gentle touch of a hand, or a warm embrace: these things help as we pass through Life…Giving of ourselves, our possessions, our money, sharing our homes, all that we have, can make a difference in the mystery of Life…Thank You again, Lord, for all Your Blessings… … …

Lord Of Life   Mar. 18

Romans 14:8,12

Living or dying we follow the Lord. Either way we are his.

Yes, each of us will give an account of himself to God.

Dear God, You are the Lord of LIFE, the Father of Time. You are the Great Giver and the Great Keeper…We cannot draw our next breath without You! Those who fill their lives with power and self-importance think they are the ones who control their lives. Those who plan their lives for years in advance think they are the ones to decide their future!

Suddenly the moment of truth arrives - the moment when God meets man face to face! In that moment man looks at his life as if it were a string of moments; then it is gone…

When will that moment be for each of us, Lord…Only You know…You said that we have only to get through one day at a time. We are not to worry or to look ahead. We have only to turn each day over to You and You will take care of us, our needs and desires…

Father, it sounds so simple, yet so complex. Some of us have been taught, from the time we were very young, that we must make it in this life by ourselves and under our own power. We were taught to become competitive. We were led to believe, by this world's standards, that we must become successful in the eyes of others...How badly we have been deceived! Your Word has told us just the opposite...You have told us to depend upon You, totally and completely. We have striven, competed, and stepped over others to prove to the world that we are somebody special, somebody to be recognized...Oh, Lord, how mixed up we can become...

For only You, Lord of LIFE, are the Great Giver and the Great Keeper. You are the only One whom Life must center upon. Then when that moment of all precious moments comes, we will be able to say with all our hearts and souls, "Father, dear Father, take me Home with You now"... ... ...

Guiding Light   Mar. 19

Isaiah 58:11
And the Lord will guide you continually, and satisfy you with all good things, and keep you healthy too; and you will be like a well-watered garden, like an ever-flowing spring.

Oh Father God, I need You. I need Your guidance. Direct me; lead me...I have turned my life over to You, but I see now that this is only part of what it's all about! I've been so used to doing things my way; making decisions my way; going in my own direction...I need You to be firm with me. I need You to keep me in check...Father, I need You so very much...

I want You to come into my life and take charge of it. I want You to be so much a part of my life that I am constantly aware of Your presence within me...Oh Father, help me. I need You so very much...

Sometimes I'm strong; sometimes I'm weak...Let me be strong for the things that You want for me, and weak in my desires for the pleasures of this world. Without You near me constantly, I feel uncertain of myself...

What would I do without You...Who would give me the courage to face each new day and each long night? There is no one else in this world whom I can think of to give me this courage - only You, Jesus...How very grateful I am that You are willing to be so much a part of my life. How very grateful I am that You are willing to be there constantly, whenever I call upon Your blessed name…Oh Jesus, guiding Light of my life, I will be eternally grateful to You for being my SAVIOR, for being all things to me…

Direct our lives so we will grow and multiply and be pleasing to You. Yes, Jesus, take each and every child of Yours and guide us through the difficult times, which each one of us faces while here on earth…

Lord, this encouraging verse above from Isaiah, shows us what will be done for us when we turn to You…Thank You, Lord, for Your sweet promise… … …

Security Blanket   Mar. 20

Matthew 18:3,4
…and said, "Unless you turn to God from your sins and become as little children, you will never get into the Kingdom of Heaven. Therefore anyone who humbles himself as this little child, is the greatest in the Kingdom of Heaven."

Oh God, oh God, how easy it is for us to put our hopes in some special person of this world…Sometimes it creeps up on us so gradually that often we don't even realize it…We want so much to be able to relate closely to some special person hoping to be guided by them to some special understanding or awareness. We are trying to find out what LIFE is all about. We are trying to fit into the best place for ourselves. Along the way, we see someone with that certain something, which draws us to them. It is so easy to let them become our "security blanket"…

Lord, let us see the danger in putting ourselves in these situations. Let us see that it is only You who can truly guide us and lead us to where YOU want us to be…

Men and women are so fragile; they are only capable of so much. When we put our trust in them, they can only let us down somewhere along the way, because of their humanness. Oh dear Jesus, keep reminding us to look only for YOU, to seek YOU out!

All through our lives people weave in and out; each one can offer us something. No one can offer us everything, except You, dear

God...Sometimes we don't realize the burden we place on some of these special people. Sometimes we don't realize that our love for them and our admiration can become such a weight that the person can become smothered by our need for them...Lord, let us understand they are only human; they have their weaknesses also.

Teach us, Father God, that each of us can be independent of any need to follow, sometimes blindly, another person whom we might consider "special." Teach us to understand that when we find something "truly special" in someone, that it is only You shining through them. It is nothing of those persons themselves.

The world says that we don't need a "Security Blanket." We are to stand on our own two feet...YOU say, "Become as a child..."

Dear precious Jesus, help us to become as children with YOU as our "Security Blanket"... ... ...

Spring Green   Mar. 21

Psalm 96:11,12
Let the heavens be glad, the earth rejoice; let the vastness of the roaring seas demonstrate his glory. Praise him for the growing fields, for they display his greatness. Let the trees of the forest rustle with praise.

Oh Lord God, Creator of all, as I gaze from this window, I see the beauty of Your creation - trees and vines abound! The lushness of it, bathed with Your Spring rains, causes me to exclaim Your praises!

Thank You for every leaf of greenery! Thank You Lord, for every twig waiting to burst forth with more! Oh Father, what a joy it is to behold this sight!!! Though the sky has been dull and cloudy day after day, Your rains have caused this view to abound with glorious shades of green!

Spring has burst upon us! Flowers are bringing up their sweet little faces to show the world the glory of Your beautiful colors! Truly these precious flowers are smiles from You to each of us who LOVE YOU...

Birds, Your beautiful little creatures, Your little friends, chirp and fill the air with their songs...Surely their little hearts are offering their praises unto You, dear God...You told us in the Bible of how precious these little creatures are to You...How that blesses my heart, Lord Jesus, and You love us more than them!

I have paused to listen to them, Lord...In the stillness between their songs, their praises, I lift up my spirit to You, Father God...My spirit is filled with love...My eyes have been filled with Your natural beauty...My ears have been filled with the sweetness of the songs chirped by these little birds...

How blessed are we who can appreciate the beauty of Your Creation! It is the handiwork of You, dear God! It expresses the intricate making of the tiniest flower with so much detail in it...Each leaf is a miracle from You...There are so many, many different shapes, sizes, designs, and colors of green. It must be one of Your favorite colors, Lord God!

Master, Creator, our hearts fill with the splendor of Spring! May we who live on this earth really try to maintain and help keep the beauty You have created for us...Let us realize the privilege of living on this earth which You created so long ago...Help us to understand that this earth is only on loan to us, while we are here...Father God, thank You for blessing us with the greatness of this awesome beauty... ... ...

Ocean Of Life   Mar. 22

Psalm 107:28-31
Then they cry to the Lord in their trouble, and he saves them. He calms the storm and stills the waves. What a blessing is that stillness, as he brings them safely into harbor! Oh, that these men would praise the Lord for his loving kindness and for all of his wonderful deeds!

Oh Lord, I feel like I'm a little boat in the ocean of Life...At times, most of the time, I feel like I'm moving toward the horizon and You are the horizon...

But sometimes Lord, the waves rise high around me. Though I seem to battle to make progress, I find myself slipping back...Oh, Lord - these are the times I find myself so unsure...

Should I just let myself be carried along and make no attempt at continuing, trusting that wherever I am You will take over? Or do You want me to keep struggling and pulling constantly?

Oh Lord, what is it You would have me do?

"Take time, make time, to pray... Drifting along needlessly can be a waste of time. Prepare yourself through prayer for the battles and storms that do arise. Victory is Mine and what is Mine is yours..."

Oh thank You, sweet Lord, sweet Shepherd! Though the waves can be very high and overwhelming, we know that You are with us through each onslaught. We must take ONE day at a time, and believe that whatever decision You help us make, will bring us closer...

Lord, please help us to have the desire to battle through these storms of Life...Each one of us has our own particular battles.

Lord Jesus, thank You for the Victory of Your Life! You are the perfect example and source of strength. Each of us who calls You Savior, Redeemer, Master and Lord can feel assured of Your Loving kindness...For surely You are faithful to hear and answer our prayers...You will bring us safely into harbor with You... ... ...

The Mystery of You...   Mar. 23

Job 36:26

"God is so great that we cannot begin to know him. No one can begin to understand eternity."

1st Corinthians 13:12

In the same way, we can see and understand only a little about God now, as if we were peering at his reflection in a poor mirror; but someday we are going to see him in his completeness, face to face. Now all that I know is hazy and blurred, but then I will see everything clearly, just as clearly as God sees into my heart right now.

Dear God, You are a mystery...We long for the intimacy of knowing You...Yet it is a mystery to think of meeting You! It is a mystery to us as to what You look like...What will it be like to know You fully, as You have always known us...

Oh God, when we dwell on these exciting thoughts, it absolutely boggles our minds! All the mysteries, which have ever crossed our minds, will be as clear as the clearest crystal...All the things we thought were not possible will be possible! You will make all things perfect for You are Perfection itself...

Yes, Lord, You are a mystery…What are YOU like? You must be larger than LIFE! Will You be able to spend intimate moments with each of us? Will Your voice be of a quality never heard before? Oh God, how exciting it will be getting to know You face to face!

Perhaps each of has special thoughts and dreams about You, Father. Perhaps each of us imagines in our minds what You will be like…But You will reveal Yourself to us when our time comes…

In this LIFE, Father, as You well know, everything comes to an end at some time or another. Nothing lives forever, nothing…That is why we cannot understand what Eternity is. The most wonderful part of being in Heaven with You, is never having to leave You, never ever!!!

Oh Lord, let us realize how few days we have here…Let us realize it is such a short time compared to Eternity…Let us continue to bring the "Good News" to our brothers and sisters. The message of Your Son, Jesus Christ, and His "LOVE" is the "Good News"!

None of us knows when we will take our last breath before we greet You, Lord… We do not know when we will see You face to face, to understand the mystery of You…

As I reflect on these thoughts, are You standing there with Your Hand beckoning to me?

Why Do We Believe?   Mar. 24

John 16:13
"When the Holy Spirit, who is truth, comes, he shall guide you into all truth, for he will not be presenting his own ideas, but will be passing on to you what he has heard. He will tell you about the future."

Lord God, who do we believe? Teach us please, to learn the difference between being taught something, which seems the truth and really finding and believing the Truth…

Who can teach us the truth? Can man? No…Man cannot. Only the Holy Spirit of the Living God can bring us to the Truth…

We can become so very deceived in what we accept as God's Truth…Man often confuses religion and church with God's true message…Many of us are born into a particular faith or denomination and carry on year after year accepting some things, which have little Truth.

Does any one religion or denomination have all of the Truth? Only the Holy Spirit can tell us that...Truth does not reveal itself by ability. Truth does not reveal itself by intellect. When we are talking about searching for God's Divine Truth, only His Holy Spirit can reveal this to us...

Men are imperfect and often err and churches are made up of men. We must be on our guard and not allow ourselves to fall into the trap of following tradition. This applies to our depending on our heritage as well. We must test the spirits as God's Word instructs us to do. In 1 John 4:1 we are told the following:

Dearly loved friends, don't always believe everything you hear just because someone says it is a message from God: test it first to see if it really is. For there are many false teachers around,...

Does this mean that we should desert our churches and go off seeking new ways and ideas? Only You, Father, can direct us or tell us where You want us to be. Only You, Holy Spirit, know the Truth and if we seek Your Truth sincerely, You will not deny us but lead us there Yourself...

We must learn to become sensitive to what our Father is calling each of us to. Then it will become very clear, as to what our Father wants us to become or where He wants us to go... ... ...

Rainbows—God's Eternal Promise!   Mar. 25

Genesis 9:13-17

"I have placed my rainbow in the clouds as a sign of my promise until the end of time, to you and to all the earth. When I send clouds over the earth, the rainbow will be seen in the clouds, and I will remember my promise to you and to every being, that never again will the floods come and destroy all life. For I will see the rainbow in the cloud and remember my eternal promise to every living being on the earth."

Oh, Father what a beautiful promise! To see a rainbow is to know that You are looking at it too! What a thrilling experience it is to see a rainbow—to see You working them into our lives to give us hope; to give us promise; to show Your LOVE for us!

And today Lord, what a fantastic rainbow You did create! It completely encircled the sun and was entirely up above where it was closest to You! You wanted us to see how You can do new things with a rainbow! You wanted us to be assured that You are remembering Your promise to us! You wanted us to know we need have no fear of anything that may lie ahead...You are our God; You are our Lord. You are our Master; You are our Guardian. You are our Savior...

We love the way You want to please us, God, to show how You Love us! You show us how You enjoy creating these beautiful masterpieces of color just for us! How loving a God we do have! How we thank You, Lord, for being so good to each of us...

And now Lord, whenever I see a rainbow, I am going to remember the promise, which You gave to every living being on the earth...Let this visible promise remind me to share all of Your wonderful promises!

My desire, Lord, is for every human being to see not only one rainbow in their lives, but many! Let them learn that it is You who make rainbows possible! Let them know about all the wonderful promises You have made to each one of us...Thank You, Heavenly Father, thank You... ... ...

Power In The Name Of Jesus!   Mar. 26

Proverbs 18:10 (NIV)
The name of the LORD is a strong tower; the righteous run to it and are safe.

Oh, what would I do Lord, if I found myself in a very, very vulnerable position? What would I do Lord, if I were to be physically attacked with no one there to come to my aid? Oh Lord, what could I do? What should I do?

"Call upon My name! There is power in My name! Call upon My power, which is so great it would dispel the attackers! My angels are also part of My power! They will guard and protect you, but you must call upon the name – JESUS..."

97

Oh, Jesus, Jesus, Jesus - there is truly power in Your name! Oh, what a relief it is to know! We can really know and believe with all our hearts, that You do have Power over ALL situations!

We can be helped by Your Power…We can use it, or we can ignore the very Power of You! It's as if we were sitting in a room and as the natural light disappears, we choose to continue to sit in the dimming light.. As the darkness settles in, we then complain we are in the dark!

All we had to do was to flick on the switch allowing the power of electricity to bathe the room in instant light! Oh, we really are dullards so often in our lives…

Oh, dear, dear Jesus, please keep reminding us daily of Your self…Remind us of Your Love for us, Your protection and guidance. Remind us also that it is we who must do our part. We must grow in our dependence and trust in You and in Your power…

JESUS, JESUS, JESUS! There is POWER IN YOUR NAME… … …

Goodbye World, Hello Jesus!   Mar. 27

1ST Corinthians15:55-57

O death, where then your victory? Where then your sting? For sin – the sting that causes death – will all be gone; and the law, which reveals our sins, will no longer be our judge. How we thank God for all of this! It is he who makes us victorious through Jesus Christ our Lord!

You are our all, Jesus: our food, our joy, our Life, our future! Yes, Jesus, our future is with You! What a glorious day it will be when we shall leave this place and say, "Goodbye, world, hello Jesus!" That's the future we are looking forward to!

Oh, Jesus, how our hearts ache for those who do not have this beautiful time to look forward to. They have lived their lives believing this life is all there is…They have cheated themselves out of the glory, which You have promised, when we believe in You! Yes, we all have a right to claim the promises You made!

So many are lying in hospitals, nursing homes, or their own homes. They are without hope, dreading each day as it comes. They drag through endless empty hours, day and night, fearing the unknown future with such foreboding spirits. Their eyes are empty and their faces drawn, Father...They believe that death is the end instead of the beginning of their true Life, their eternal Life...

Your sacrifice of dying on the cross freed us from the dreariness of an empty life here...You, Jesus, Son of God, went to prepare a future home for us in Heaven...In Your final Kingdom, there will be no pain, no hunger, no hurts, no humiliations, no sorrow, and no sadness...There will be Joy, Love, Peace, Beauty, and Gentleness. Everything good will be there, for God is goodness and His Presence will abound everywhere! There will be such sights that our human minds cannot picture or comprehend them! There will be such LOVE that it will be overwhelming! There will be no darkness for where God our Father, and Jesus His Son and Holy Spirit are, there can be nothing but pure LIGHT!

Oh, Father, let all know with assurance that there is more than just this earthly life! The emptiness they are experiencing now can disappear! Let them know who You are before they leave this place so they too can say, "GOODBYE WORLD, HELLO JESUS!"

Jesus Christ Is LOVE   Mar. 28

Matthew 22:37-39

Jesus replied, "'Love the Lord your God with all your heart, soul, and mind.' This is the first and greatest commandment. The second most important is similar:' Love your neighbor as much as you love yourself.'"

Oh, dear God, I'm troubled...So many of Your followers misunderstand Your message – L O V E! That's all we are to do, to LOVE with Your Divine Love, with Your understanding. Your one complete plan is for us to LOVE...

Why do we have all the splitting of hairs? Why do we have to get hung up on the complications of men's ways? These confuse the issue - the simple message You came on Earth to give us is to LOVE...

No place in Your Holy Bible says that we must be of one denomination, one special group. Instead we are to be of one Body: The Body of Christ! We must learn to put aside differences, but dwell on JESUS – JESUS CHRIST IS LOVE! JESUS CHRIST IS LORD!

JESUS CHRIST IS, WAS, AND WILL ALWAYS BE! That's all we have to keep in our thoughts, only that...

Lord Jesus, You were able to do in three years what it takes some of us a lifetime to learn. This is a paradox in a way, because You were man, yet You are God...We understand that it could take all our lives to come into the deepest understanding of what Your message teaches us. We are to first love You, Lord God, and then we are able to love those You put in our lives...

It is a simple message; yet it takes a lifetime of doing...Each day gives us a new set of circumstances, new challenges to confront us. Each day we must learn to put ourselves aside, to allow Your Divine LOVE to flow through us to others...

Some days this is so easy; some days this is fun! Some days it becomes very discouraging, Jesus, because there are those out there who misunderstand our love and good intentions. Father, when we are faced with days such as these please remind us that You, too, suffered rejection and rebuffs...You were ignored and talked down to...
Ah-h-h yes, Jesus, remind us...

Then please refresh us with Your Divine LOVE...You were so loving that You accepted these hurts without complaint. When we remember this, it gives us strength to continue to be loving also. You taught Your followers countless years ago all about Your kind of LOVE...Please continue to teach us today, how to LOVE!

"My Child..."   Mar. 29

John 10:27 (NIV)
"My sheep listen to my voice; I know them, and they follow me."

Romans 8:16a
For his Holy Spirit speaks to us deep in our hearts, ...

"My child, and you are My child, we have made such progress together... I have taken you through the years and watched over you... You have grown under My Care...

May I call on you to continue listening to Me as I suggest things for you to do? I have only those who are willing to help Me in this world. Listen to Me... Listen closely to Me and you will hear My directions to you.

If you hesitate to do My Will, I will have to call on another to complete the task at hand.

Yes, many are called, but few are chosen. Are you willing to be a chosen one?

Softly My Voice calls to My chosen ones... They are those who have learned to listen for the sound of My Voice gently in their ears... Yes, My child, if you chose to be one of the chosen, listen for the sound of My Voice..."

Expectations   Mar. 30

John 15:12
"I demand that you love each other as much as I love you."

My Father, the road becomes so difficult as we draw closer to You...You show us more and more what we must become, what we must do,.. It is what we must become which allows us to do...

Oh, my Heavenly God, whose Presence, in the form of the Holy Spirit, is truly here...The road is surely narrow and rough...

I want to be all that You want me to be, but—I find myself failing, failing, failing...I cry out to You in dismay, for I know deep within my heart, I have disappointed You...

Oh, Father, there is so much in this world to do...Yet, I am so insignificant—how much difference can I make to what needs to be done?

I try and that seems to fail...How much do You expect of me, Lord God?

Do I live up to Your expectations of me, in any way? Do You have expectations of me? You do? Oh, Father, please let me know what they are! Yet, can I really stand to hear what they can be...Quickly, Father, tell me what You expect?...

"To LOVE, LOVE, LOVE..."

Ah, that seems so simple, Father; that seems so simple. Surely dear Father, since You have reminded me again of Your expectations of me, to LOVE, You will pour Your LOVE, through me…

I am willing to be a vessel for Your LOVE … … …

Lord God, Use Me   Mar. 31

Isaiah 6:8

Then I heard the Lord asking, "Whom shall I send as a messenger to my people? Who will go?" And I said, "Lord, I'll go! *Send me*."

Hebrews 4:16

So let us come boldly to the very throne of God and stay there to receive his mercy and to find grace to help us in our times of need.

Oh God, how in our littleness, we slight You! We come to You at our convenience, then we have the nerve to say: "Lord God, use me!" Where You are, Lord God, angels, angels and more angels are surrounding You just waiting for an opportunity to serve You! While waiting they are singing PRAISES upon PRAISES glorifying You! Then our little voices filter through, after we have decided to give You a few moments of our time, and we say, "Lord, I'm ready now, so use me…"

You God, The Mighty One, the Creator of all the splendor of the Universe, You listen to us! You hear us and in Your almost unbelievable way, look down upon us with a Love for us which is overwhelming!

You let us know that though we come to You in our own, sometimes selfish ways, You are always ready, willing, and able to care for our needs. You let us know, as Your Word tells us constantly, that You are our Father. You are just waiting to hear from us, to establish a deep relationship with us. Our needs are important to You, large or small! Nothing is ever too insignificant to bring to You!

When we, in a moment of great generosity, ask You to use us, sometimes we wait with clenched fists fearing that You will put a burden on us. Show us, please, Lord God, that whenever You do use us, even though things don't always go the way we want them to, they are always under Your watchful and loving eye…Nothing can ever get too difficult for You to handle...We can be used by You since we have You as our Father to step in and help us over the rough spots...

Lord, it would be wonderful for us to see Your mighty splendor and magnificence as John did in Revelation! You are our Creator! You are the Almighty God of the Universe! You are beyond words to describe!!!

Then our finite minds might be able to understand our relationship with You, ALMIGHTY GOD, and our own dear FATHER...What a blessing it is to be used and loved by You... ... ...

April

The Key   April 1

Isaiah 33:6(NIV)
He will be the sure foundation for your times, a rich store of salvation and wisdom and knowledge; the fear of the LORD is the key to this treasure.

Yes, Lord, You are the Key to the treasure of our salvation, our entry into our Heavenly home...This world is full of keys, Lord God. How many do we have to try? Our goal should be finding the only one which unlocks all the mysteries You made, when You created this Universe...

You are the Key to all things, all of life's experiences...Some are fortunate and find You right away in their search for the Truth. Some try key after key finding disappointment after disappointment...Yet You are standing there with the Key in Your hand outstretched to each and every one of us...

Jesus, Son of God, please bring us to a closer understanding of what You are all about...Bring us to the depth of understanding which You alone can bring...Show us that it is never through our intellect that this can come about. It has to be from the depth of our spirit, calling Your Holy Spirit to come to us with Your Perfect Truth.

Once we have found the Key, Jesus, please don't let us keep this Key to ourselves...Let us go out and tell all those who are willing to listen and share this joyful discovery of Your treasures! Master and Savior, please help us to share this delight with Joy and Enthusiasm. Never let us become possessive of this great discovery!

How many search this earth for hidden treasures as they look for the keys to unlock them...As children we read stories of these hidden treasures and what excitement filled our hearts as we got involved in the mystery of these discoveries...Teach us now, Jesus, to become involved, deeply involved, with discovering the mystery of all Your treasures, which lay waiting for us! One Key, You Jesus, can unlock all the treasures we'll ever need for all eternity!

Oh, Lord of Lords, King of Kings, Son of God, continue being patient with us until You bring each of us into our eternal home! Continue to offer the Key to Your Heavenly Mansions to all who come to You...Thank You, dear Jesus, for being our Heavenly Key... ... ...

Prepared Hearts   April 2

Acts 16:13b, 14

...and we taught the Scriptures to some women who came. One of them was Lydia, a saleswoman from Thyatira, a merchant of purple cloth. She was already a worshiper of God and, as she listened to us, the Lord opened her heart and she accepted all that Paul was saying.

Oh Lord, prepare our hearts. Prepare the hearts and spirits of the people who need to hear what You want them to hear...Father of All, please prepare the path...Prepare the way, for You said that You ARE the Way...

Father, as we go along and feel the desire to become one of Your workers, give us the tools, the wisdom, the courage, the guidance we need to do Your Will. It is so easy to be misled by our own desires, our own thoughts...

Holy Spirit, enter into communion with our spirits...Then gently, but firmly, guide us to where we should go...Tell us what we should say, how we should pray...We are so helpless without You to lead us...

With You though, we can surely do the work that our Father desires us to do! We can become Your reflected Light! We can glow with assurance because of You!

And Brother Jesus, do not allow us to choose those whom we think need help...Guide us to exactly the one You want us to help...How easily we get confused in this area, Jesus...How much more smoothly things go when You are there guiding and leading...Sometimes when we decide whom to help we end up pushing, shoving and dragging them. We think they need fixing up - changes made in their lives...

We become judgmental sometimes, Lord Jesus, and feel as if our decisions are the best and the only ones to be considered...Spirit of the Living God fall afresh upon us! Allow us to look deeply inside ourselves and realize that YOU are the only Judge. We are merely Your servants, Your helpers...

When we do this, it is so exciting to see how beautifully Your Plan does work! Oh Father, dear Father, please continue to guide us…Let us be sensitive for the need to follow Your Plan…Guide us to the heart, which has already been prepared for our coming. Then let us be faithful to share the Good News! So many need to hear that You Jesus Christ are the Redeemer and Savior of this world… … …

Spending More Time With You   April 3

Matthew 6:6 (KJV)
"But thou, when thou prayest, enter into thy closet, and when thou hast shut thy door, pray to thy Father which is in secret; and thy Father which seeth in secret shall reward thee openly."

Oh Gracious Lord, Bountiful Father, Lord of Blessings, I feel overwhelmed when I realize how You have blessed me during my lifetime!

Yes, there has been blessing after blessing…Yet as You also know, there have been sufferings intermingled with the blessings…

Some of these sufferings have been "heartbreakers"…But it is only by spending more time with You that these sufferings can not only be tolerated, but experienced with Hope…

Spending more time with You - what does that really mean Lord? Do You want us to be ever on our knees before You? Do You want us to actually go into a closet?

"No, My child, there are many ways to spend more time with Me… You have only to put all thought of anything or anyone else out of your mind and concentrate on Me… You will find soon, that in doing this, we can experience a depth of friendship, which you could never imagine. Come, spend more time with Me. I can be in the woods, near the water's edge, or enjoying a balmy night… I can be any place you quiet yourself and bring Me into your thoughts so that an instant communication can commence… I, Your Lord God, treasure these moments with you… Come, spend more time with Me…"

Oh yes Lord, cause me to realize how wonderful these times can be! Cause me to realize how much they mean to You! Sometimes it's so hard to realize that You, God of the Universe, can actually enjoy time with me, with each of us! That is such an awesome thought, Lord...

May we come together more often in the future by our willingness to spend these times, these precious times, with You Father God...And Lord, thank You for loving us so very much, and desiring to spend time with each of us... ... ...

Our Loved One   April 4

Isaiah 57:2

For the godly who die shall rest in peace.

Dear Lord Jesus, our loved one died today...Yes Lord, we realize that death is part of LIFE...But, Lord, we don't understand...We don't understand why You took her away from us who loved her so deeply...

We didn't want her to leave us...We wanted her to stay awhile longer, a lot longer...Why Lord, couldn't You let her stay with us?

We prayed to You, Father. We pleaded with You, Lord Jesus...We were constantly knocking on the door of Your Heart...Time went by - days, nights, and weeks went by...

So many were praying to You to melt Your Heart and release her from her illness and restore her health...You have done it countless times before, Lord Jesus...

She was so special, yet a simple person...Everyone who knew her had only good to speak of her...So why Lord, couldn't You leave her here longer...We don't, we simply don't, understand...

Yes Lord, we understand our coming into this world and our leaving it is in Your Hands...You are in control...For reasons known only to You, You decided to call her home...It is part of the mystery of LIFE...

We are grateful Lord, that You removed her from the pain which she was suffering...We are grateful that she had a peaceful, graceful death...

We are grateful for the LOVE she gave while she was here. We are grateful for the loving memories that we each have stored in our hearts.

We are grateful because we are assured that she has found her place in Your Heavenly home. You prepared that home for her and for each of us who believe, truly believe, in You...So dear Lord Jesus, thank You for all the years that we did share with her...

In her own simple way she left a clean slate...She was a peacemaker, a good wife, mother, grandmother, friend, and neighbor - a person who loved her family and others...

Thank You, Lord, for giving her to us for the time we had her. May her new LIFE with You bring her eternal peace, joy and contentment...Thank You again, Jesus, for our loved one... ... ...

Remind Us   April 5

1st Corinthians 13:4-7,13

Love is very patient and kind, never jealous or envious, never boastful or proud, never haughty or selfish or rude. Love does not demand its own way. It is not irritable or touchy. It does not hold grudges and will hardly even notice when others do it wrong. It is never glad about injustice, but rejoices whenever truth wins out. If you love someone you will be loyal to him no matter what the cost. You will always believe in him, always expect the best of him, and always stand your ground in defending him.

There are three things that remain—faith, hope, and love—and the greatest of these is love.

Remind us, Lord Jesus please, over and over again; remind us to LOVE, LOVE, LOVE! You came to us because of LOVE...You created us to LOVE...

Yet it's so hard to remember, so hard to do, Lord...The world conditions us to fight for our rights, not to let the next person get the best of us...The world tells us to pull ourselves up by the bootstraps, if necessary to step on others to get where the world tells us we should be going.

Lord, when we come right down to it, it seems as if Your ways and the world's ways are so completely opposite! You tell us to become servants and handmaidens. You tell us to turn the other cheek...You even tell us to give our jacket as well as our shirt to our brother in need...The world tells us to get all we can, because if we don't, someone else will...You tell us to care about our brothers and sisters in the world before ourselves; the world tells us to watch out for number one, ourselves...

Oh, Lord of LIFE, please keep reminding us that it is You whom we want to please, not ourselves...Remind us that if we really love You, then we will love those who are different from us, those who are out of harmony with us, or we with them...Let us see them with Your eyes, Your LOVE...

Let us learn to love without conditions attached, with Your unconditional LOVE...Let us see that You LOVE us just the way we are, and we must love others just as they are...

It sounds so simple: to love...Sometimes we have to learn to receive love...Sometimes it is very difficult to receive LOVE, because we feel unworthy of being loved...Father, dear Father of LOVE, teach us ever so tenderly, how to receive love, if we are in need. It is as important to receive as to give love...

There is a great healing in the true act of Christ-like LOVE...Lord God, sending Your Son Jesus, to die for us, was the greatest example of this healing LOVE...

Jesus, as the greatest teacher of LOVE, please teach us to love as You intended.

Remind us, Father, to love... ... ...Remind us, Father, to love...
... ...

God Came As Man   April 6

Luke 1: 31,32
"Very soon now, you will become pregnant and have a baby boy, and you are to name him 'Jesus.' He shall be very great and shall be called the Son of God. And the Lord God shall give him the throne of his ancestor David."

Philippians 2:6,7
(Jesus Christ) who, though he was God, did not demand and cling to his rights as God, but laid aside his mighty power and glory, taking the disguise of a slave and becoming like men.

GOD CAME AS MAN...Can we comprehend this? Can we actually understand that God, Creator of all, came here to this little planet and lived among us? Man's smallness of mind limits him to disbelieve often times...Who was Jesus? Oh, He was a good person;

He had a good message. Perhaps He was even a prophet...Oh, dear God, the injustice of it all, the injustice of it all...

GOD CAME AS MAN...God took on our human form and lived among us. God lived among us! He took on all the human characteristics, which we labor under. He felt pain, humility, LOVE, joy, hunger, loneliness...Though He was God and man, He took on the humanness we have...God, in Jesus, was in all senses, flesh and blood like you and I...

How good our God was to do this! It was not beneath Jesus to take on what God had created. Even though He knew the weaknesses and imperfections that we have, He was willing to come... If we were perfect, there would have been no need, no reason for Jesus to come...

What is God's Master Plan? Does the president of a huge corporation report to the lowest man in the work force his plan? No - the man believes that the president knows what's best for the corporation. He has faith in the president to make his plan successful.

So, in a sense, it is with our God. He has a Plan: a mighty Plan! Because we do not understand it, we sometimes lose faith in Him. Part of His Plan was to send His Son Jesus to earth and take upon Himself the image of man. Jesus loved us enough to experience what it was like to be human...He loved us enough to suffer for us...

GOD CAME AS MAN...He came as a babe like you and I. He was completely dependent on others to care for Him as we were when babies...Then if we follow His Plan, as we grow, we become dependent on Him! That is His desire for us - to become dependent on Him! Through God becoming man, we can better understand Him and who He is... ... ...

My Purpose   April 7

Psalm 145:1,2,10,13

I will praise you, my God and King, and bless your name each day and forever. All living things shall thank you, Lord, and your people will bless you. For your kingdom never ends. You rule generation after generation. (Scriptures combined)

My purpose, Lord – what is my purpose? Why was I born? Do I have, really have a purpose? Was my birth an accident? Was it intended to happen?

How can my life be meaningful? How can I make a difference in this world? Has anything been gained by my being born? Has anyone been affected by my being here?

I gave birth to children; perhaps, that was the reason I was born...But, for my own life, Lord - what is the real purpose?

Lord, that's something only You can really know, I suppose...But to me, it seems as if there was no reason for my being born...

"If for nothing else, My child, My dear one, your purpose is to love Me – worship Me, adore Me, praise Me, glorify me... Rest with Me... Turn out all thoughts of the world and come to me in the silence of the day, the silence of the night... That is your purpose... Once you are free of this life, that you now know, you will be able to look back... In retrospect, you may discover another purpose, which I have for you... This you need not know at this time..."

Oh, Lord, thank You...My spirit feels lightened...I felt so burdened by life, so disheartened...I know now that I don't have to feel burdened about the reason I was born...I WAS BORN! You DID give me LIFE! That's enough to know! You desire me to LOVE YOU, WORSHIP, PRAISE, ADORE, and GLORIFY YOU! You want me to come to You, to rest with You...That's my purpose...Yes, Lord, that's my purpose...

Is this the purpose for each one of us?

Greater Works   April 8

John 14:12a

"In solemn truth I tell you, anyone believing in me shall do the same miracles I have done, and even greater ones,..."

Lord God, we can be all things to all men through You! Jesus said when He was here that we, the later generations, would do all He did and MORE!

It's so true! Man, through the miracle of his mind, has invented such marvelous methods of spreading the Good News! We have only to turn on the television to see and hear a disciple of Yours speaking words that are being heard by millions of people all around the world! We have only to put a tape in a machine and be able to listen, over and over again to the same words until they are embedded within us...There are so many more ways too — books, radio, newspapers, magazines, telephones, videos, CD's, and computers!

You are a FANTASTIC LORD! You have allowed Your Hope, Your Holy Spirit, to manifest Himself so profusely in these present days! What mighty things are being accomplished, Father!

You allow us to be used by You, empowered with Your Holy Spirit, to do Your work! WOW! It is nothing of ourselves, never of ourselves...Can an electric light shine without the power of electricity being turned on first? We can only be used as we allow ourselves to be, nothing more than that electric light bulb, empty and waiting until ready to be used...

Yes, Lord God, we must remain empty of ourselves if we are to be used by You. But with You, what fantastic things can be accomplished! When You choose to use us we CAN further Your Kingdom... ... ...WOW, LORD!

Planting Loveseeds   April 9

Matthew 25:29a
"For the man who uses well what he is given shall be given more, and he shall have abundance."

1ˢᵗ Corinthians 16:14
...and whatever you do, do it with kindness and love.

"Lord," we say sometimes, "what do I have that can be used? I am nobody special...I am just an average person. I have no special gifts or talents..."

Oh Father God, please help us to look deep into ourselves. Let us see that the greatest gift we can give, the greatest reason for our being born, is to L-O-V-E...

Impress on us, Father, that this is a precious gift, a mighty gift! If all of us for one generation would start teaching Your selfless kind of Love to the little ones, what wonders could be seen! If we could sow seeds of Love all around us as we walked through Life, what beauty would come forth!

Many of us remember the story of Johnny Appleseed. One man spent his life planting apple seeds from one place to another. He hoped You, dear God, would send the sun and showers to nurture those seeds into beautiful apple trees! One man cared and loved enough to bring countless people the fruit of his love: beautiful blossoms, apples, comforting shade on hot days, perfumed air...

Jesus let us look inside ourselves to see what we can do with what You have given us...Let us reach out to those around us and like Johnny Appleseed, bring our gift to strangers who cross our paths. Perhaps it will be nothing more than a heart-warming smile, but that smile coming from the heart, can cheer another whose spirit is low...

As we use what God has given us, and use it freely and generously, more will be forthcoming! For as the Scripture above in Matthew said, "For the man who uses well what he is given shall be given more, and he shall have abundance." We have Jesus' promise on that!

When You, Jesus, promise us something, we can rely on it! So as the apple trees came forth from the seeds lovingly sown by Johnny Appleseed, we will see our seeds of Love multiply. Hopefully they will multiply until the air is filled with its sweet fragrance - perhaps after we have long gone...

We are on this earth for such a short time, let us plant those seeds of Love this day and every day... ... ...

Lord Of LOVE   April 10

Luke 6:27,28

"Listen, all of you. Love your *enemies*. Do good to those who *hate* you. Pray for the happiness of those who *curse* you; implore God's blessing on those who *hurt* you."

Oh Lord Jesus, the mystery of this world is that Your Ways are the exact opposite of the world's ways! We have been led to believe that if someone hates us or mistreats us, we should return the same treatment to them...If we continue to respond in the same way as our oppressors treat us, we can become so hardened that it may then become a way of life for us...

Suddenly we hear YOUR words...They sound strange, almost ridiculous! How can it be done?

113

"Love your enemies. Do good to those who hate you. Pray for the happiness of those who curse you; implore God's blessing on those who hurt you."

To implore means to beg; to cry out to; to weep for! But God, how can that be possible? How can we beg You to bless those who are so mean and hurtful to us? Is this not being a hypocrite? Can it be possible for us to really manifest a true love for them? Where will it come from? We feel so empty inside...

Oh dear Lord, that is the answer...If we can empty out the hurts, and the unhappiness, then YOU can fill us with Your unconditional LOVE! As we allow Your LOVE to enter into us, then miraculous things can happen! We can then LOVE our enemies! We can then do good to those who hate us! We can pray sincerely for the happiness of those who curse us...We can then implore, or beg God's blessing on those who have hurt us...What a relief this can be!

Now we are free! We are free from the burden of negative feelings, Lord! Oh how wonderful it is to be able to feel and say that we are no longer bound, but free to love and care for even those who do not understand us...Thank You, dear Jesus, Lord of LOVE... ... ...

"Come Or Stay..." April 11

Ecclesiastes 12:14
For God will judge us for everything we do, including every hidden thing, good or bad.

"Do you love Me? If I were to call you to come to Me today, or to stay, what would your answer be?"

Oh Lord, would that my answer be, "I'll come, Lord, I'll come!"

But in reality, what would each of our answers be? Are we ready, this moment, to face our Creator? Are we ready to place our life before Him, pleased with what we've done with it?

Are there any improvements we would desire to make to change our lives? It is examination time - time to zero in on our lives and scrutinize them as if under a microscope...

114

The microscope enlarges, magnifies whatever it sees. Can we face this, understanding all that we did, spoke, or thought will be exposed for our Creator to see?

Then there are the times and situations that we are responsible for not doing, saying, or thinking, as we should...There were actions which we did not do when in our hearts, we knew we should have. There were words we should have spoken, but we kept silent. Then there were thoughts we suppressed, when they would have led us to act or speak...

"Do you love Me? Do you love Me? Do you love Me?"

What is our answer? Are we ready to go today, this moment? Do we want to stay here longer, perhaps change our actions, speech, or attitudes before leaving this place?

"If I were to call you to come to Me today, or to stay, what would your answer be?"

What would our answer be...What would our answer be...You, Lord, already know, for You know our hearts...And thank You, Jesus, for Your forgiveness for all the things we have done or neglected to do...

What would your answer be?

"Tell Others"   April 12

Romans 10:8-13

For salvation that comes from trusting Christ—which is what we preach—is already within easy reach of each of us; in fact, it is as near as our own hearts and mouths. For if you tell others with your own mouth that Jesus Christ is Your Lord, and believe in your own heart that God has raised him from the dead, you will be saved. For it is by believing in his heart that a man becomes right with God; and with his mouth he tells others of his faith, confirming his salvation. For the Scriptures tell us that no one who believes in Christ will ever be disappointed. Jew and Gentile are the same in this respect: they all have the same Lord who generously gives his riches to all those who ask him for them. Anyone who calls upon the name of the Lord will be saved.

WOW, Lord Jesus! Again Your Scripture tells us we have a free gift when we believe that You are our Lord! Our salvation, our Eternity is assured when we claim You as our Savior! Telling others that You are Lord will further confirm it! Oh Father, how generous You are to us! You ask so little of us, so little...

You make it so simple for us and yet we often complicate Your simplicity...When we find things easy, it seems we feel that it cannot be worth as much as when we gain something after a difficult struggle...

Lord, sweet Lord, have patience with us please...Teach us that though man complicates things, You are there ready to untangle things and make Your messages easier for us to understand.

Man turns to churches, religions, cults, etc. for truth...Father, we implore You to release Your Holy Spirit, the Spirit of Truth, in even a greater way to open our eyes! Let us see what You created us for. Let us see that we have only one purpose for our lives. Let us see that it is Your Divine Love which You want us to demonstrate...

As we spread Your name and claim You as our Savior, Jesus, You are readying our places with You...We will not be disappointed for our Eternity will be filled with the Glory of You - the MAJESTY OF YOU!!!

Thank You, dear Lord...Thank You from the depths of our beings... ... ...

The Living Water   April 13

John 4:7,10,14
Soon a Samaritan woman came to draw water, and Jesus asked her for a drink. He replied, "If you only knew what a wonderful gift God has for you, and who I am, you would ask me for some *living* water!" "But the water I give them," he said, "becomes a perpetual spring within them, watering them forever with eternal life." (Scriptures combined)

Dear Lord Jesus, it's raining outside. It thundered loudly a few minutes ago...Now the rain is slowing down and there's a quietness coming about...Some little droplets are still coming down...The earth is absorbing the rain; the flowers will really appreciate this wonderful drink of Your rainwater...

It's Your water, Lord, Your water...When You were tired and thirsty once, Lord, You stopped by a well to rest. You had no vessel to dip into the well. Soon a woman came to draw water, so You asked her for a drink.

What a blessing for her that she came at that particular time! Little did she know that it was to be the most important time of her life! She thought she came for ordinary water, well water...

Then Lord, You spoke to her and told her about the Living water! Your water is the Living water, which brings eternal life!

She became thirsty for Your Living water, Lord, and her life was changed, never to be the same again...

We can see what ordinary rainwater does for the plants, flowers, trees and all of God's nature around us! Why can't all men and women understand the necessity for each one to believe and accept Your Living water, Lord? For this Living water truly brings real LIFE to oneself...Your Living water never runs dry, never evaporates to nothingness. It is always available...

Thank You Lord, for Your Scriptures. There we can read, over and over again, Your teachings about Yourself. In John, You so plainly describe for each of us, the true understanding of what "The Living Water" means.

Thank You Jesus, for having patience with each of us as we turn to You for perfect understanding...Without You, Jesus and Your Holy Spirit, to teach, guide and speak to us, we would be lost forever...It is You alone Who can make an eternal difference in our lives. We are so very grateful for Your Living water... ... ...

The Mystery Of Time   April 14

Psalm 31:14,15a
But I was trusting you, O Lord. I said, "You alone are my God; my times are in your hands."

Oh Lord, there is so much to learn about LIFE! How long will it take? How much time do we have? Some of us have wasted so much time already...Lord, it takes time to learn - time...What is time in Your sense of the word, Lord? Does it have anything to do with obedience, Father?

Do You allow us to learn something, or do we allow ourselves to learn something? Then when we learn, do we learn for one time? Do we have to experience and re-experience this learning?

Are You allowing our LIFE experiences to continue along a certain path until we can really learn what You want us to learn? Do You allow us to repeat and repeat until our weaknesses are made into strengths, Lord God?

Oh, Lord...The mystery of time - is time measured in experiences, dear Jesus? Do You place certain people, circumstances, situations in our paths just to teach us what we lack the most? Do we need to be taught again and again? It seems so, Lord, it seems to be so!

Father, this is difficult at times in our lives! Please continue to place in our paths all the necessary circumstances and people to help us understand what we have to learn...That unlovable person who seems to be so hard to be around - let me see that person with Your eyes...Let me LOVE that person with Your LOVE for Your LOVE is pure and good...

Let me see that though I failed this set of circumstances, and came through the test so badly, You will help me. You will be patient with me, and wipe the slate clean so I can start over again...

Help me to understand, Father, that though I may have only one day left in this world to change my LIFE to what it should be, to please You, that it can be so...

Help me to understand, Father that learning about LIFE can come to me in a twinkling of an eye, because it will be in YOUR Eye...Thankfully all things are possible because of You...

Though the Clock of LIFE is ticking, ticking, ticking, only You, Father God, still the Clock of LIFE...

Thank You, Lord, God, for taking the time to be so patient with us, with me... ... ...

Doubting Thomas   April 15

John 20:29
Then Jesus told him, "You believe because you have seen me. But blessed are those who haven't seen me and believe anyway."

118

Dear Lord, how disappointed You must have been when one of Your very own disciples would not believe You had risen from the dead...

Thomas said, "I won't believe it unless I see the nail wounds in his hands—and put my finger into them—and place my hand into his side." (John 20:25b)

He wanted three examples of proof, dear Jesus, before he would believe!

We are so shocked by his lack of faith! We find it hard to believe one so close to You, could be so unbelieving! Yet, every day, we who love You do the very same thing. We doubt You...Oh we do it in different ways, Lord, but it amounts to the same thing...

We teach our little children to put their faith in You, Lord. Yet the next time a terrible problem enters our lives, we start to doubt that it can be solved! We know we Love You and You Love us, but we don't have enough faith in You. We doubt that You can handle the problem! Maybe You can take care of little problems, but not those great big ones which only come to certain suffering people like us!

Finally when we have tried every way we can think of to solve the problem, we turn it over to You! Maybe You, Lord, can solve it! Jesus, how patient You must be with us! You wait so patiently for us to finally turn to You...Lord, it's a wonder You even listen to us! With our doubting hearts we come to You as the last resort!

As You said to Thomas,

"Don't be faithless any longer. Believe!" (John 20:27b).

Then when You answer our problems, all we can say is what Thomas said to You:

"My Lord and my God!" (John 20:28a).

Yes dear Lord Jesus, You are our Lord and our God! Please keep proving to our dull hearts that You are our Lord and our God! We can be so painfully stubborn like Thomas at times...Please keep showing us as often as necessary how wrong we are when we don't believe everything You want us to!

So many people have unchangeable faith — the kind of faith that doesn't need to be proven to them. It is the kind, which only deepens as they become more trusting of You...Will you help us to have this kind of faith, dear Jesus?

Praise God!   April 16

1ˢᵗ Thessalonians 5:18
No matter what happens, always be thankful, for this is God's will for you who belong to Christ Jesus.

Psalm 146:1
Praise the Lord! Yes, really praise him!

Oh, Father God, when are we going to learn that we have to PRAISE YOU in ALL circumstances?

We have so long been used to thinking that we should only praise You when good things happen to us! Yes, we often remember to thank You and praise You when things have gone our way…But when adversities come, we question why they should even happen to us! Why us, Lord? What have we done to deserve this?

For a long time we have had the notion that if we live our lives by "goodness" then only good things should happen to us! When troubles come, we even have friends and relatives who look at us and think or say, "What have you done to deserve this?" We too, begin to wonder what have we done to "deserve" this real burden in our lives…

It's hard for us to understand that our Father God would allow this to happen to us…"If He really Loved me, then why should this happen? Have I really caused God to look down upon me without love? I really thought He Loved me…"

"No, My child, I have not stopped loving you… I do love you…You are very important to Me… I have allowed this thing to happen to you… It is with My approval. But if I allowed only good things to happen to you, you would become very spoiled. You would become very selfish and self-centered… The more good that I allowed in your life, the more you would continue to expect…

I also want you to love Me at times when the 'goodness' is removed from you… Will you still love Me then? Will you still praise Me and honor and adore Me? Will I still be the first in your life? Think upon these things, My child, think upon these things long and hard… I wish to strengthen you. I desire you to become so strong that

120

no matter what happens to you, you will continue to praise Me in all things, in all circumstances. Through them all, know that I love you beyond your very own comprehension..."

Oh Father, thank You for bringing this understanding to our hearts. We are not being punished when adversities happen. You are only giving us opportunities to grow...

Oh Praise You, Lord Jesus! Praise You! Praise You in the morning! Praise You in the noontime! Praise You when the sun goes down! Yes Lord, Praise You in all things! All honor and glory belong to You, Lord God! You alone are worthy to be praised! PRAISE GOD! PRAISE GOD! PRAISE GOD!

In The Stillness With You   April 17

Psalm 46:10(NIV)
"Be still, and know that I am God; I will be exalted among the nations, I will be exalted in the earth."

In the stillness of this moment I come to You, dear Lord Jesus...I come seeking Your word, Your direction, Your thoughts for me...There is only quiet, silence...Father, know that though I hear nothing, though nothing comes through to me, I still want to stay here in the stillness with You...

Perhaps that is all that You want of me, to be still with You...Perhaps that is one of the most special things I can give You. I give You my complete attention in this special silence, which seems so deep. I feel totally alone with You, dear Lord Jesus...

Father God, there is really so very little that we can give You...You really don't need us and then again, we know deep down in our hearts that You want us! When one loves another there is a longing to be close and in constant communication...One thing we should really be secure in is that YOU LOVE US! You proved that beyond a shadow of a doubt. Millions of people know that You died on the cross because of Your LOVE for us...

So when these precious, silent minutes flow by, we can feel secure in knowing that You are there sharing them with us...No words spoken, no song of praise sung, no words of prayer, no requests - just the nearness of You...

121

Lord, when do these precious moments come? Oh, whenever we are quiet, still, and listening for You. They come as quickly as the blink of an eye or flick of a finger...During these close moments, precious Love flows from You to us like the nourishment from a mother to her child...We become refreshed, renewed...

Oh, sweet Father of Love, how wonderful it is to be in the nearness of You! We know that You are always ready and waiting for these special moments. You treasure them perhaps more than we! Oh Loving Father, accept our thanks for Your many wondrous ways! Accept our love for being the Father to us, Your children. Dear Father, we await our next moments of tranquillity with You... ... ...

Be Of Good Cheer   April 18

John 16:33

"I have told you all this so that you will have peace of heart and mind. Here on earth you will have many trials and sorrows; but cheer up, for I have overcome the world."

Thank You, dear Jesus, for having John speak these words...They are words of comfort, yet words of difficulty...But they tell us that with You, because of You, we can be victorious! Just as the song goes "I Never Promised You A Rose Garden" You never told us that LIFE would be easy here on earth...

In our reflections about LIFE we can see that having easy lives does not help us grow...Generation after generation has tried to make LIFE easier for us. Inventions have been made to make our lives so much easier than our forefathers; it is breathtaking!

Improvements come along so quickly that some of the things we buy are improved upon before they are worn out or are only a few years old! Man continues to make our lives easier...We have more leisure time than ever before...

But when difficulties or troubles come into our lives, we wonder where things went wrong. What did we do to bring this about? We sometimes think it is some kind of punishment we have to suffer through...

We forget that, You Jesus, Almighty God's Son, told us that we would have many trials and sorrows. It is the way we accept these trials and sorrows, which makes a difference in our lives...We can accept them and know deep in our hearts that You are watching over us no matter how difficult these trials are. When we can rise above them and not let them drag us down, then we have taken a step forward in our journey of LIFE...

Dear Jesus, teacher of LOVE, teacher of LIFE, you DID overcome this world! We do believe this...

No matter what our lot in LIFE may be, no matter how unfair it may seem to us or to those around us, we know, as Thomas did when he saw Your wounds, that You are Jesus Christ, the Risen Savior...

Yes, Lord Jesus, we can be of good cheer, for we know You are our victorious Lord, for You overcame the world... ... ...

Extension   April 19

John 15:5,8

"Yes, I am the Vine; you are the branches. Whoever lives in me and I in him shall produce a large crop of fruit. For apart from me you can't do a thing."

"My true disciples produce bountiful harvests. This brings great glory to my Father."

Oh Lord, YOU are everything! I am nothing. Yet, I can be everything with You working through me, when I empty myself and let YOU flow through...I am Your extension! I can reflect You! At one point in my life I would have thought that to be a sacrilegious thought...Now, because of Your Holy Spirit's revelation to me, desiring me to know - it can be so!

How else, dear Father, could You work here on Earth? You have no eyes, ears, or hands with which to recognize and meet the needs of Your children. Lord, Your work cannot be accomplished unless we become Your extended hands, eyes, ears, and heart.

One needs hands to pick up a telephone and call someone in deep sorrow, trouble or anguish...Ears are necessary to listen to those around us who need to be heard. Eyes are needed to see the hurt in the eyes of another. Someone must see that others are in need of food, clothing, finances or help of some kind...

Yes, Jesus Christ, our Lord, our Savior, our Master, our Brother - You work through us, as Your extensions. Together we can bring about miracles in this world!

Always though, we must remember that it is You, and only You, who can accomplish what has to be done. If we should forget that it is You, we may be carried away with the thought that we are accomplishing these things. To You always goes the credit, the glory, the thanks, the praise, for allowing us to be part of Your Work...

Father, please keep a constant watch upon us so we will not forget. May we keep thankful words upon our lips for You from whom the POWER comes ...Let us remember an extension is not the whole; an extension is nothing without the source...YOU are the source, Jesus, YOU are the source...

You are always there and YOU can be made visible!!! Lord Jesus, dear Lord, this is an overwhelming thought! We have an opportunity to make You visible! When we allow ourselves to submerge, completely in You, Lord God, You can be seen through us...Only You can be seen!

You, who are His disciples, peek inside yourselves and see JESUS! Then, invite Him out for the whole world to see!

The One Most Unknown...   April 20

John 15:26
"But I will send you the Comforter – the Holy Spirit, the source of all truth. He will come to you from the Father and will tell you about me."

Holy Spirit of the Living God, Your Presence is here...You are the Spirit of God, our Father. You are the Spirit of Jesus, His Son! You are here with us now...You are always present. There is no place where You are not...

You have been the mysterious One, the One in the Trinity most unknown...Yet, You have been present with each one of us since our Father sent You to us. You are the One who empowers us with such power that if we truly understood it, we would hardly believe it!

Some of us have spoken Your Name thousands of times and yet not understood...The knowledge of You has gone unnoticed for much too long! You are longing to be sought after, to be recognized, to be needed, to be our Comforter – our Counselor...

Holy Spirit of the Living God, please take the misunderstanding and ignorance about You away...Please make Yourself clear to us so that we can come to know and feel Your Presence as the special Helpmate that You are...

Jesus said that He would send You to us; He called You the Comforter...So many of us need that comforting...So many of us long for that special feeling which can come only from You...

When we call upon You, we see very clearly Your workings...You bring things together as no other can! We see the way pieces fall into place to cause extraordinary happenings! We see teachings that You want us to learn become so plain and true...Oh Holy Spirit of the Living God, we do appreciate You! We seem to have taken a long time to find You, having gone round and round – in and out...But now we praise God our Father and Jesus, His Son, for allowing us to have You and draw closer to You...

Truly, You ARE here! We CAN come to You and know that You will make the difference in our lives! You WILL strengthen us for the struggles we all experience. Thank You, Holy Spirit, we treasure Your Presence... ... ...

Under My Own Power　　　April 21

Romans 5:8
But God showed his great love for us by sending Christ to die for us while we were still sinners.

Under my own power - that's how I've lived. That's how I want to live...I want to live under my own power. I don't need anybody...I can do it all, all by myself! Who needs anybody else!!!

"Dear one, you think that you don't need anyone... Dear one, I, your Creator, your God, choose to need you! Don't you realize that I created you, watched you as you were being knit in your mother's womb? I watched you take your first breath, watched you grow from infancy to childhood. I watched you grow from childhood to adolescent, from adolescent to adult. I want a relationship with you... Why do you think you were born?

I wait and wait for you to come to know Me, to want to have communication with Me... Do you not know how important you are to Me? You have tried living under your own power... You see where your life has taken you under your own power...

I would ask you to come under My wing, to come under My power. This power, My power, will have a different effect upon your life... You will not desire to have your own way again. Coming under My wing, you will see My power released in a way you could never accomplish unto yourself... Come unto Me, dear one, come unto Me... I love you dearly..."

You, God, You? You Love me? You L-O-V-E me? But God - why? How could You Love me? If You watched me growing up and saw all the things that I have done, how can You say that You really Love me? I've done things that I thought would turn You away from me...How can You really Love me after seeing what I've done?

"Dear one, I sent My Son, Jesus, down to earth two thousand years ago. He lived as a man, went about the business I sent Him to do for Me: to teach mankind what I wanted learned... He taught about LOVE... He lived only 33 years, because men put Him to death on a cross. He took upon Himself your sins – yes, your sins. All of mankind's sins, He willingly died for. Because of His and My LOVE for you, He died... If you were the only one on earth, He still would have died – just for you... That's how much I LOVE you... That's how much He LOVES you... Now can you understand My LOVE for you?

Read about Me, about Jesus, about the Comforter – whose real name is the Holy Spirit. In the Bible get to know all about Me. Then we can become so close that you will no longer want to be under your own power, go your own way. We wait for you to share Our friendship with you..."

Defend Us, Oh Lord!　　　April 22

John 10:27
"My sheep recognize my voice, and I know them, and they follow me."
1st John 2:27

But you have received the Holy Spirit and he lives within you, in your hearts, so that you don't need anyone to teach you what is right. For he teaches you all things, and he is the Truth, and no liar; and so, just as he has said, you must live in Christ, never to depart from him.

Defend us, oh Lord...Protect us from all those who would tear us down and try to pull us away from where You lead us...Keep us from listening to others who may lead us away from Your Plan, dear Father...

Where do we go? What do we do? What shall we say without You to guide us? We are nothing without You, Jesus...Father, You know the desires of our hearts; You know that it is to do Your Will, and not our own...Protect us from the many ways we can be led astray...Only You know what is best for us, Lord. Only You can keep us on the right path to where You want us to go...So many of our loving friends try to persuade us to do what they think is right for us, Lord...They mean so well, but we must listen only to Your Holy Spirit. We must listen in such a sensitive way that we can learn to discern what it is that You want us to do, to say, and to become...

Defend us from ourselves most of all, dear Lord Jesus...It is so easy to become deceived by satan into thinking that we are doing the correct thing. We need to listen intently to what You want from us, Lord. It is so easy to become self-righteous, so easy...

You know all the tricks of satan, Lord. You know how anxious he is to tear us down so that we can be looked upon with ridicule and contempt. You know how anxious he is to make us, as Christians, look as bad as he possibly can. Please protect us, dear Father, from falling into these situations. Some of us are just babes and so unwary of what is happening to us...

Teach us to become so willing to do Your Will and not our own, that we will become strong and dependable for You, Lord God! That should be the one true desire of our hearts, to be true to You!

Meanwhile, Lord, put Your protective arms around us and draw us close to You in the safety of Your bosom. There we will be cherished as no other can cherish us. There we can stay until we grow strong from Your strength and able to let Your Light shine through us...Thank You, Heavenly Father, thank You... ... ...

127

God Gives Wisdom   April 23

Proverbs 1:23

"Come here and listen to me! I'll pour out the spirit of wisdom upon you, and make you wise."

In 1st Corinthians 2:1-16 the Scriptures tell us:

Dear brothers, even when I first came to you I didn't use lofty words and brilliant ideas to tell you God's message. For I decided that I would speak only of Jesus Christ and his death on the cross. I came to you in weakness – timid and trembling. And my preaching was very plain, not with a lot of oratory and human wisdom, but the Holy Spirit's power was in my words, proving to those who heard them that the message was from God. I did this because I wanted your faith to stand firmly upon God, not on man's great ideas.

Yet when I am among mature Christians I do speak with words of great wisdom, but not the kind that comes from here on earth, and not the kind that appeals to the great men of this world, who are doomed to fall. Our words are wise because they are from God, telling of God's wise plan to bring us into the glories of heaven. This plan was hidden in former times, though it was made for our benefit before the world began. But the great men of the world have not understood it; if they had, they never would have crucified the Lord of Glory.

That is what is meant by the Scriptures which say that no mere man has ever seen, heard or even imagined what wonderful things God has ready for those who love the Lord. But we know about these things because God had sent his Spirit to tell us, and his Spirit searches out and shows us all of God's deepest secrets. No one can really know what anyone else is thinking, or what he is really like, except that person himself. And no one can know God's thoughts except God's own Spirit. And God has actually given us his Spirit (not the world's spirit) to tell us about the wonderful free gifts of grace and blessing that God has given us. In telling you about these gifts we have even used the very words given to us by the Holy Spirit, not words that we as men might choose.

So we use the Holy Spirit's words to explain the Holy Spirit's facts. But the man who isn't a Christian can't understand and can't accept these thoughts from God, which the Holy Spirit teaches us. They sound foolish to him, because only those who have the Holy Spirit within them can understand what the Holy Spirit means. Others just can't take it in. But the spiritual man has insight into everything, and that bothers and baffles the man of the world, who can't understand him at all. How could he? For certainly he has never been one to know the Lord's thoughts, or to discuss them with him, or to move the hands of God by prayer. But, strange as it seems, we Christians actually do have within us a portion of the very thoughts and mind of Christ.

WOW! Thank You, Holy Spirit, for revealing to Paul, the above mighty thoughts and insights! We are POWERLESS of ourselves, but full of POWER because of YOU! We are empowered through You! Do we realize that our prayers may actually move the Hands of God? What a privilege and gift the Lord gave us when He taught us to pray...It is a thought almost too great to digest! We actually have a portion of Your thoughts, Christ, within us! How can we measure up to this?

Jesus, You made it possible! You found us useable...You bring out something good in us, despite ourselves...Oh dear God, Creator of all, Father of Wisdom, may You continue to teach us, through Your Holy Spirit, what You want us to learn and to become...YOU alone give us wisdom! You have our everlasting gratitude, dear Savior... ... ...

Unbelief   April 24

Mark 11:24

"Listen to me! You can pray for *anything,* and *if you believe, you have it*; it's yours!"

Acts 16:31

They replied, "Believe on the Lord Jesus and you will be saved, and your entire household."

Oh, my dear Lord, I come to you, imploring You to release Yourself in my loved one! Lord, I love him so and want so much for You to manifest Yourself to him! He needs You! He cries out to You and wants to really believe...

Lord, what is it that is preventing him from being set free from this ache in his heart? Lord, please show him that he needs to open up his heart completely to You...

Lord, please let Your peace flow through him. Give him the great gift of believing in You, truly believing in You! He wants it so much and yet finds it so hard to believe in You...

He's Yours, Lord. Bring him into Your Presence and let him know what it is like to be in Your Body of Believers, Your

Family…He sees it in others and yet cannot feel it himself. Have pity on him, please dear Father…

I plead with You, Lord Jesus, to bring him close to You. If I have only one prayer answered, that's my heart's desire…

Oh Lord, take him by the hand; lead him to Your self…Embrace him…Please tell him he is Yours…Tell him that You love him dearly and that You will never let him go…

Thank You, Jesus, thank You, for I know with all my heart that You WILL answer him. You WILL bring him into a deep relationship with You…

Yes, My Lord Jesus, I believe this for all the "hims" and all the "hers"… … …

Note to the Reader: Years later, God brought a young minister to him and he gave his heart to the Lord, 19 days before he died. Praise unto You, Almighty God, for being faithful to our prayers for his salvation…

The Bottle and I   April 25

Galatians 2:20

I have been crucified with Christ: and I myself no longer live, but Christ lives in me. And the real life I now have within this body is a result of my trusting in the Son of God, who loved me and gave himself for me.

The bottle and I – look at it, standing there, full to the brim…I am that bottle…You are that bottle…As I look at it, I see myself…I see my whole being is like that container…I am full to the brim as the bottle is, but I am filled with self…There are so many words to describe "self" – pride, ego, arrogance, even "holier than thou"…These are just a few of the words. Some more are: hatred, selfishness, anger, greed, ambition, jealousy, fear, loneliness, power…Perhaps we contain a combination of these…If each of us really looks inside ourselves, we can see what we are filled with…

The bottle stands so rigid; it is so full…How can what is in the bottle come out? If it continues to stand rigid, without bending at all, it cannot empty itself…However, if the bottle were to tip over, ever so slightly, it would spill some of what is inside…Is that what I have to do? Do I have to bend to be emptied of self?

As the bottle tips over more and more, the contents spill out more and more...It tips itself until now it is completely empty...There is nothing left to indicate what once was there - only space...The empty bottle can now be used...

The bottle can be filled with water to sprinkle a beautiful rose bush...It can be filled with liquid fertilizer to nourish a fruit tree...It can be filled with milk for a hungry baby...The bottle can also be filled with juice to quench the thirst of a tired farmhand...The bottle could even be filled with wine to be part of the precious Bread and Wine of Communion...These are some of the ways the bottle could be used...

But how about me? How about you? As we become aware of this concept, we are faced with a decision...Does it mean anything to me? Am I going to do anything about it? CAN I do anything about it? WILL I do anything about it?

If I am emptied of self, what will fill the space in me? Ah-h-h, through the Power of the Holy Spirit, we can be filled with the Holy Spirit!!! We then can be used as the empty bottle can be used!

What can we become now? If that bottle, made only of the cheapest glass, can be used for so many purposes, what more wonderful purposes could we be used for?

Oh God, please give us Your strength to be willing to be involved, to be used for You...It is only possible because of YOU...Help us, dear Lord, to truly be emptied of self. Then as we are filled with Your Spirit, we can be used by You, to reach others...For it is only in emptying ourselves, that we can make room for Your Personality. In reality, then only YOU will be seen...Jesus, we only want YOU to be seen!

Here I am, Lord...How do You want to use me?

"Come Near To Me..."   April 26

James 4:8a (NIV)
Come near to God and he will come near to you.

"Come near to Me... Come nearer to Me... I have so much to share with you, to teach you... How can you think that I do not care for you? You do have a meaning for Me. Yes, you do...

Do you find it hard to believe this? But, it is true... It's true... Come and stay near to Me and I will bring you through what you need to understand and accept... Not a day passes but you are watched over by Me... Not a night that covers you goes unattended by Me... I care; I do care...

What if things are not as you would like them to be at this present time? Do you not know that I am the One who does make a difference? Do you not believe this? You must believe this...

Forever I have been... Forever I will be... Time cannot change what I, God, have ordained...All things will work out for your own salvation... Salvation is what I came to bring you... It is My gift to you... Take it, for it is given you with the sweetness of My life – a truly pure gift...

So, draw near to Me... There is much for you and I to share together... There is much joy, peace, and contentment ahead for you, as you stay close to Me... I truly will make a difference in your life, if you will come close to Me. Come near to Me... Come near... Come near... ... ..."

You Are the Flame   April 27

John 8:12b

"I am the Light of the world. So if you follow me, you won't be stumbling through the darkness, for living light will flood your path."

Praise God! Yes, Praise Your Holy Name! You alone are to be worshiped and glorified! You alone are to be adored...All you who abound this earth, Praise His Holy name!

May each one of us who call You "Father," Praise You! May we raise our arms in praise, in homage...To praise is sometimes to raise our arms to Heaven, to surrender ourselves to God, our Creator...

Yes God, for You are present through Your Holy Spirit—let us draw in Your nearness, Your very essence...For You are Perfection and it is that Perfection which draws us to You...

You are the Flame! The Light! We are the moths...We flutter near You, nearer and nearer, never caring how close we come...Yet knowing that as we draw closer to You, Your Flame, or Light, will burn us...It will burn out the impurities within us...We flutter closer and closer for we cannot resist You, once we have seen Your Light!

Oh, thank You, Light of the World, for always being there to light the way; to guide our paths; to steady our steps...You take us and change us so that we can be new creations because of You...

Father, in our weak moments, be at our side...Never leave us; never forsake or abandon us...We need You so very much, so very much...Yet it's amazing to realize that our need for You is a delight to You! You want us to need You...You want us to call upon You, to call Your precious name...

Father God, Savior Jesus, Precious Holy Spirit, thank You for being all things to us...Thank You for letting Your Living Light shine into our lives... ... ...

The Rose   April 28

Song of Songs 2:1(KJV)
I am the rose of Sharon, *and* the lily of the valleys.

Oh Lord, in the perfection of Your Creation, You created an exquisite flower — the beautiful rose.

Our attention is drawn to a beautiful rose – the color, the fragrance, the fullness of the petals...But each rose is borne on a stem with thorns also. In our eagerness we may grasp the rose and be pricked by the thorns...Then in our humanity, we can become angry and blame the rose...

Yet most of us know that roses grow on thorny bushes. If we want that beautiful rose, we must learn how to approach it so that it becomes a joy for us...In Life too, we seek to discover the joy among the many thorns. How do we learn this?

We must learn as the trials and tribulations of Life prick us. But how? The Scriptures teach us ways of attaining peace and joy, which can exist in a world of thorns and roses...In a way, that's what Life is all about...

You, Lord, are the most Perfect Rose of all...We need to realize that despite the thorns of Life, searching for You is more than worth the anguish, pain, and tears...When we realize that You are the very center of our existence, then we can better understand what Life is all about...

Real Life is becoming aware of You and searching to find You... It is perhaps, smelling Your fragrance before coming upon the PURE TRUTH of who YOU are...Real Life is grasping that sacred TRUTH and never letting that TRUTH leave us!

Oh Lord, may each one of us search and find You in the deepest way...May we reflect, as the beautiful rose does, the beauty of Your Love, even with the thorns of Life... ... ...

Master   April 29

Luke 16:13a

"For neither you nor anyone else can serve two masters."

Matthew 20:26-28

"But among you it is quite different. Anyone wanting to be a leader among you must be your servant. And if you want to be right at the top, you must serve like a slave. Your attitude must be like my own for I, the Messiah, did not come to be served, but to serve, and to give my life as a ransom for many."

Master, do we actually have a master? If so, who is it? What is it?

These questions can provoke a lot of other thoughts...Perhaps many of them are unsettling...We think of ourselves as free...We think that no one or no thing has charge over us...But is this really true?

As each of us thinks about this, we can come up with many, many different answers...

Those of us with strong personalities are not going to admit (even to ourselves) that there could possibly be a "Master" in our lives. The very thought of that is thrown out, as far as possible...

Those of us with more average personalities may allow that there could be a "Master" in our lives. Perhaps, if we have time we may even seek a deeper answer...

Then there are those who actually make a sincere search looking inside themselves, as if under a microscope...They look to see what or who could be a hidden master, or masters. Masters can be disguised in so many different ways: money, power, ego, fame, sex, drugs, alcohol, nicotine - - - these are negative masters.

Masters can also appear in another form, that we may seldom think about...Some of these could be our husbands, children, homes, jobs, material items...

It is the person who is born of the Spirit who finds the Truth and the true Master, Jesus Christ...He, Jesus, the Master, was also the servant. He said whoever wants to be first must be last and become a servant...

Are we able to do that, to serve our brothers and sisters here on earth while we're here for our Master, Jesus Christ?

That's what we all have to ask. That's what our Master, Perfect Master, wants to see in all of us...Let us stop to ponder... ... ...

Who or what is my Master — your Master...

Paradise   April 30

Ecclesiastes 3:11(NIV)
He has made everything beautiful in its time. He has also set eternity in the hearts of men; yet they cannot fathom what God has done from beginning to end.

Paradise - can it be found here on Earth? One would think so when one sees some of the magnificent beauty that there is in this world...

One can look at the lushness of the greenery, the profusion of beautifully colored flowers. One sees the crispness of the white clouds against the blues of the sky and the different shades of the ocean as the waves roll up upon the smooth sand of the beach. Everywhere the eye looks, there is more and more beauty...Paradise - at last it's found...

But, Paradise is more than natural beauty...Paradise has to include oneself...If one is to enjoy the perfection of Paradise, one has to have also found the paradise of the interior soul and spirit...

How many men and women have come upon the natural beauty of Paradise but have not been able to truly enjoy it... Their spirit and their mind were so caught up in other things they could not truly enjoy the Paradise they had been searching for...

How disappointed they were; they are...Yet some others can come upon the same place and find such peace and joy. They have found the Pearl of Great Value, Jesus Christ! Their joy and peace can hardly be contained!

We must first ask the Creator of Paradise into our hearts...Paradise then comes from within, and then meets with the beauty without...May we each find Jesus, who is the Pearl of Great Value, before we seek a Paradise here on earth... ... ...

May

A Little Pain　　　　　May 1

Philemon 1:7
I myself have gained much joy and comfort from Your love, my brother, because your kindness has so often refreshed the hearts of God's people.

I don't mind a little pain, Lord; I don't mind...Sometimes we get so used to everything going well, and then suddenly something happens - a fall, a car accident, or a sharp pain...In each case nothing serious happened: no broken bones, no need for an operation...

It was just a little pain, but why do we have to have any at all, Lord? It's so much easier to get through Life without any. Who needs it anyway?

We do Lord? Why? Oh, if we didn't experience pain sometime in our lives, we really couldn't appreciate the times without pain! Yes Lord that's it. It's part of learning to appreciate the "good days" in our lives...

Reflecting on the thought of pain brings us into the realization of those who suffer and have suffered, day after day, night after night...

It can leave us with a sense of guilt, Lord...Why do some have to suffer year in and year out? Often those who suffer did nothing to cause this pain...

Lord, what can we do when we come in contact with these situations? What can we do?

"LOVE them with My LOVE... Let them know that you care about them – a smile, a word of encouragement, a visit, a phone call, a card, or a letter... Let them feel, really feel, the LOVE that I shine through you to them... Radiate this LOVE of Mine... Radiate this LOVE of Mine to them..."

Lord, I'm so ashamed to even mention my little pains, at times in my life. But Lord, it I had not had pain, I couldn't have experienced these thoughts with You. I have come to a better understanding of how I must learn to help those who have to bear pain on a daily basis...

Help me, please Lord, to understand their needs, their situations. May Your LOVE shine through me to those who are experiencing pain... ... ...

Fear   May 2

Psalm 139:11,12

If I try to hide in the darkness, the night becomes light around me. For even darkness cannot hide from God; to you the night shines as bright as day. Darkness and light are both alike to you.

Fear - fear often is associated with darkness. We can be in very familiar places when there is brightness and light...But let the light suddenly go out, and FEAR with all its ugliness wants to pounce on us! This is true of physical darkness, but it is also true when our circumstances appear dark and frightening.

When the darkness comes upon us without our desire or consent, then we have all the more need to believe that God is there with us! The darkness gives us an opportunity to call on God immediately and claim His protective LOVE and care!

It is instant communication time! It is not a time to allow satan to put fear into our hearts and minds! It is a real opportunity to declare to God, to ourselves and whoever else is around, that we are convinced of His LOVING Presence!

With firm control on our will, we steer it to the very mind of Jesus Christ. With praises on our lips, we can overcome this fear, this darkness!

Then as the praises flow with our mind on God Himself, we are in His custody! Whatever happens after that is completely in His Hands as we have given Him our permission to take control...

Peace transcends and we are at rest in the situation...Thank You God, for Your peace. In Philippians 4:7 we are told,

...God's peace is far more wonderful than the human mind can understand. His peace will keep your thoughts and your hearts quiet and at rest as you trust in Christ Jesus... ... ...

Employed By Your Love   May 3

Luke 9:59-62

Another time, when he invited a man to come with him and to be his disciple, the man agreed—but wanted to wait until his father's death. Jesus replied, "Let those without eternal life concern themselves with things like that. Your duty is to come and preach the coming of the Kingdom of God to all the world." Another said, "Yes, Lord, I will come, but first let me ask permission of those at home." But Jesus told him, "Anyone who lets himself be distracted from the work I plan for him is not fit for the Kingdom of God."

Oh Lord Jesus, Master and Savior, the words spoken by You, according to Luke, are powerful, almost frightening...The insight of the Holy Spirit continues to make us aware of the deepest truths. We can see that it is only because of a great love for You that we can be called to Your service, to Your employment...

We can only be employed by You because of LOVE...We are drawn to You first, because of the great LOVE, God, our Father, has for us. Because of Your forgiving and unconditional LOVE, through Your sacrifice for us, we can truly offer ourselves as servants or employees of You, Jesus Christ...

So often though, in the decision to become workers we can say what the two men above said, "Yes, BUT..." Oh that little "BUT..." Dear Father help us to not be distracted from the work You call us to do...

We don't have to be ordained through a church to become employees! Each one of us, wherever we are, can be the hands, ears, eyes, heart of You, Jesus, in our world. The bonus is Eternal Life! The benefits are Peace and Joy that pass all understanding...

Thank You, precious Jesus, for blessing us so... ... ...

"Holy" And "Wholly"   May 4

2ⁿᵈ Corinthians 7:1b

...let us turn away from everything wrong, whether of body or spirit, and purify ourselves, living in the wholesome fear of God, giving ourselves to him alone.

Only when we become holy can we become wholly…What does "holy" mean? One dictionary defines it as "Belonging to God; set apart for God's service; pure in heart."

What does "wholly" mean? Again, one dictionary defines it as "to the whole amount; completely; entirely, totally."

Lord God Almighty, You created us with body, mind, and spirit…In our comprehension of this, we sometimes want to separate these three integral parts of our being. We might go through acts of piety, but allow in our mind thoughts that can be deeply distressing to You, our Creator…We may fill our minds with godly thoughts, but still find our bodies are not fully submitted to You…

Just as God, Jesus, and Holy Spirit are ONE, we must come to a similar agreement within our own humanity.

We cannot let any one part of us overrule…We must come to a decision in which all three are in unity with Your Spirit within us…

Now, if we are open to the mystery of the Holy Spirit, we are ready to give Him our total selves. When we do this, a beautiful harmony takes place! Not only are we totally one as a person, but we actually can become ONE with the Holy Spirit of our Living God!

As we seek to become holy, pure in heart, that becomes our one desire. Holiness can take control of ourselves! We then can become wholly set apart for Your service…Thank You, God, for this privilege…It truly is a privilege to be in Your Glorious service… … …

Habits   May 5

1st Peter I: 14

Obey God because you are his children; don't slip back into your old ways—doing evil because you knew no better.

1st Peter 3:11,12a

Turn away from evil and do good. Try to live in peace even if you must run after it to catch and hold it! For the Lord is watching his children, listening to their prayers; …

Lord, why is it the bad habits we have are so hard to break, and the good habits we have are so easily broken?

140

I have tried hard so many times to break habits, which I know need to be broken. I knew that for my well being I needed to break them...But, try as I might, they would hang on and on...Then the good habits I've tried to make part of my life would disappear, often before I realized they had gone...Later, I would realize the "good" habit I once had was now something in my past...

Lord, what can we do about this? Can anything be done? Do our sinful natures regarding negative things in our lives, have to win?

Each of us, deep down in our hearts, wants to break these negative habits. We must truly search ourselves in the light of truth...Each of us wants the positive habits to come forth in our lives. When it comes to the bottom line, when we look deep within ourselves – hopefully we know.

Again Lord, what can be done about this? Do we have to vacillate as if blowing in the wind? Do we bend this way and that way, never standing firm in a true commitment to break that negative habit once and for all?

Show us Lord...Tell us, Lord...

"Make a commitment, child, first. Then turn to Me and ask for My help. With your determination to continue on and your constant turning to Me for encouragement, you and I together can make a difference in your life. I am always there waiting for you to communicate with Me about this habit. Turn to Me constantly and then you will see, in days to come, that the habit, which once was so difficult has now become part of your past... I am your present. I am your future. Keep turning to Me in all situations; I will not disappoint you."

Oh Jesus, how wonderful it is to have You for our Friend. How wonderful it is to realize that You, Almighty God, God of Heaven and earth, are within "earshot" of our call to You...

Oh Jesus, thank You from the bottom of our hearts for never failing to listen, and for offering to be our strength... ... ...

"But I Didn't Do Anything!"   May 6

1st Corinthians 6:19,20

Haven't you yet learned that your body is the home of the Holy Spirit God gave you, and that he lives within you? Your own body does not belong to you. For God has bought you with a great price. So use every part of your body to give glory back to God, because he owns it.

They asked me what I did, Lord...And I said with such a rush of words: "But I didn't do anything!"

Then You came immediately into my thoughts and showed me that I did do something to cause that particular situation...

Oh, Lord, how often we want to think ourselves innocent in situations which have come about through no one else's fault but our own...This can be related to physical illness, abuses of our bodies, our minds, or our spirits...

As I looked back into situations I was surprised to see quite often, Lord, how some act of my own resulted in a detrimental situation to myself...Sometimes Lord, it came about because of such a small decision on my part...

If I were to put this thought, which became an action, into a familiar phrase, it would be "I took a chance!" Taking a chance - as I recall some past experiences Lord, I see so many instances where I "took a chance" and it backfired...I was the one who ended up with the problem...

Our bodies are Your temples, Lord. You said so in Your Scriptures. We should be doing our utmost to guard against anything negative...We must guard our own attitudes, words and actions...

Oh Lord Jesus, we know that we must step out in Faith! Please show us the difference between stepping out in Faith or "taking a chance"... ... ...We truly want to be in Your Will...Please help us gain the wisdom to know the difference, dear Lord... ... ...

"Seeds Of Love"   May 7

Ephesians 5:1,2
FOLLOW GOD'S example in everything you do just as a much loved child imitates his father. Be full of love for others, following the example of Christ who loved you and gave himself to God as a sacrifice to take away your sins. And God was pleased, for Christ's love for you was like sweet perfume to him.

Father, I have been gazing at a very soft and fluffy creation of Yours...It is the bloom of the pampas grass...When I cut it from the parent plant several days ago it was formed in a feathery stalk. I placed it in an arrangement and it looked so flowing and graceful...

Now, Lord, I am finding little fluffy puffs all over! As the seeds expanded, they have separated themselves from the stalk.

As I picked up these little individual seeds and surrounding delicate strands, almost like angora hair, they want to cling to my fingers! As I look closely at them and study them, the thought comes - if only LOVE would cling to those around us, as these little creations want to cling to my fingers...

If only we could be like the parent plant and send out hundreds upon hundreds of little "seeds of LOVE" to all those You put us in contact with! If only these little "seeds of LOVE" would cling, ever so tenaciously, to those people. If only these little "seeds of LOVE" would implant themselves in others, to spread the LOVE that is so needed in this world - if only...

Yes, Lord, the first step is to be willing...I see that very plainly now...We must pray to be more willing. We must pray that when You want us to become a "seed of LOVE" we would cling with Your LOVE to the one You have singled out...Then when You send us to another, and another, or bring another to us, we can LOVE with Your LOVE and Your strength...

May we remain faithful in our love for You as we bring LOVE to those sometimes so difficult to love...

Oh, Lord, let us become Your "seeds of LOVE"... ... ...

"Sweet Gift Of Life"　　　May 8

Acts 17:25 (NIV)
And he is not served by human hands, as if he needed anything, because he himself gives all men life and breath and everything else.

John 3:5
Jesus replied, "What I am telling you so earnestly is this: Unless one is born of water and the Spirit, he cannot enter the Kingdom of God."

"I didn't ask to be born!" "Why was I born?" Oh Lord, so many people in this world say these words and regret being born – even children...

They carry these thoughts with them. They see no Joy; they have no Joy… Some of them grow up feeling so inadequate – unsure of themselves. Never do they hear a pleasant word…Never do they receive a compliment… Negativity surrounds them. No one has ever affirmed them. They almost tiptoe through life hoping not to disturb… Some become nervous or "high strung"… Oh Lord, what a pity! One might ask" What's the answer – is there an answer?"

The answer is to first look at Life itself. What is Life? In John 14:6 Jesus says,

"I am the Way—yes, and the Truth and the Life…"

Until we know You, Lord Jesus, we cannot be truly grateful for our lives, whatever our circumstances. That's what we have to do! We have to believe that Life is a gift instead of a burden!…No matter how much our lives are mixed up, You God our Father will begin to respond to our appreciation of this gift of Life! It is only when we realize that Life is a sweet gift from God, that we are able look at things differently…

We now see ourselves in a different light. Gradually, as time goes by, we can look back and see how our gratitude to God has turned the tide of our lives…We have changed!

Now we can see that without this precious gift of Life, we could never have known about You, Jesus Christ, our Savior and Lord… Now we can be assured of a place in our Heavenly Home with our Father and Jesus! For without this sweet gift of Life, we would never experience the greatest gift of all, eternal Life with our Creator, God our Father…

Thank You, Jehovah God, thank You, thank You for this sweet gift of Life… … …

God's Pure Truth   May 9

John 8:12

Later, in one of his talks, Jesus said to the people, "I am the Light of the world. So if you follow me, you won't be stumbling through the darkness, for living light will flood your path."

He was the Light…He is the Light…He will always be the Light…

Jesus Christ is the Light of the World, Light of the entire Universe! It is He who shines Light for us here...

Oh, thank You God, Creator, for giving to us on this earth, faith to believe in You! Oh what a precious gift is faith!

And oh, what a responsibility it is to have faith...How we must guard our faith or we can be led into darkness...For awhile it can look like dusk; it can be gray - a mixture of light and dark...Oh, how very careful we must be! It is so very easy to slip into imitation light...

Imitation light? What can that be? Can it be??? Oh, yes, oh yes...There are those going about with "religion" stamped on themselves through their own efforts...They wear the symbol of Jesus Christ's death on the Cross, around their necks...Yet they do not have the True Light!

Oh, Light of the World, Jesus Christ, Son of God, You are Savior for each one who will truly believe in You...Have Mercy upon each of us who seek God's Pure Truth, and please lead us to it in the deepest sense... May we treasure this Truth until we meet You face to face... ... ...

But What Else Should I Do, Lord?   May 10

James 4:8a
And when you draw close to God, God will draw close to you.

But what else should I do Lord? I try to be a "good" person. I even go to church sometimes...I don't steal, rob or hurt anybody. I mind my own business; I stay out of trouble...Isn't that enough?

I know people who do dishonest things. I see how they live...They seem to have everything going for them...Everything seems to work out for them! How come Lord, how come? Yet for me, I have a hard time sometimes just paying the bills, trying to keep up with everything...I think I'm a "good" person; I really do. Remember the time I helped that person who needed help? You saw what I did Lord, remember? Now that person doesn't even seem to remember what I did to help. Sometimes I wonder if I should ever help anyone else. What do I get out of it anyway?

I always thought that if I tried to live a good life, good things should and would happen to me. Yet You see, Lord, that my lifestyle can't even compare with others. They go their own way without any thought except to get to the top of the heap...

"Yes, you have tried..."

But what else should I do, Lord?

"Meet Me in the morning; meet Me in the noontime; meet Me all the day through... Come to Me in the evening; come to Me in the night... I'm always there waiting for you... I want to be your best friend, your confidant... You have never taken Me to your bosom, your heart... I long for a closeness with you that you have never given Me...

Once this happens – joy, unspeakable joy, will fill you. You will never again wonder at those around you. Your life will be complete in every area, once you and I come into this relationship... What else should you do then? Tell others about Me; share what has happened to you since we have deepened our friendship... You will then become a fisherman for Me, calling in those who are lonely, worried, and unhappy...

Does this answer your question, 'But what else should I do, Lord?'"

Prayer   May 11

Ephesians 6:18
Pray all the time. Ask God for anything in line with the Holy Spirit's wishes. Plead with him, reminding him of your needs, and keep praying earnestly for all Christians everywhere.

Dear Jesus, Love of my heart, I thank You for Your instant availability...In just a flash, or half a heartbeat, You are instantly in communication with us as we turn to You in prayer...It astounds my mind to realize that You, Creator of this whole Universe, are ever available to communicate with each one of us, as we come to You...

Sometimes this need is for our loved ones, or ourselves. Sometimes it is for someone we don't even know, sometimes just a name in the newspaper...But whatever the reason, whoever the person or situation, You are ever present to listen to our prayers of intercession...

Oh Heavenly Father, what a wonderful sense of trust fills our hearts...What a wonderful sense of peace descends upon us...Oh thank You Jesus, for this truly precious gift You have given us...This gift of Yourself comes to us from the very heart of You. That is what prayer does! It reaches into Your very Being and You then take over the situation at hand...

We now can feel secure in knowing we have done the very best thing a person can do for another - pray for them...

It's such a wonderful feeling to realize that our very words, or even silent thoughts, go directly up to You! Our prayers do have power! That power is not from us, but the power of Yourself as You plan out what is best for each and every need...

Truly this is a gift, much misunderstood and often forgotten, or overlooked. This gift has the power to change situations, save lives, affect so many facets of Life...

Thank You again, dear Lord, for this precious gift...May our faithful prayers touch Your understanding Heart filled with Mercy... ... ...

Discouragement   May 12

Psalm 40:1-3

I waited patiently for God to help me; then he listened and heard my cry. He lifted me out of the pit of despair, out from the bog and the mire, and set my feet on a hard, firm path and steadied me as I walked along. He has given me a new song to sing, of praises to our God. Now many will hear of the glorious things he did for me, and stand in awe before the Lord, and put their trust in him.

Lord, I feel so discouraged. There is a bleakness about me which I cannot seem to shake...I look around me and nothing brings pleasure to my heart...

In this discouragement, I feel so lonely too, Lord, so lonely...

The weight of it all seems to be so heavy...I literally feel a burden on my back...My head and shoulders droop with this dismal feeling...Oh, Lord, pull me out of all this...

Time seems to be standing still, but yet the days are passing so quickly that they are all seemingly the same...Where once I could look and see something positive, I see only the same bleakness surrounding me constantly...There seems to be no ray of hope, no rainbow to brighten my days...

The loved ones in my life seem to be so distant from me...The love, which once brought joy to my heart from and through them, now seems to have dissipated - become lessened. The burdens they go through pull me down, because of my love for them. I feel so helpless to help them...

Oh, Lord, free me from this gloom! Pour into me Your Peace, new refreshment for life, and a new hope, Lord...Please pick me up and pull me to Your Bosom, to be nourished there until I become strong again...I need You! Lord, I need You... ... ...

Thank You for listening Lord, and giving me some encouragement as I rest with You now...I feel it slowly pouring into my mind, my spirit, and my body...I feel the burden lifting, being removed...

Oh, Lord, thank You for constantly being with me whenever I feel the need to throw myself upon Your mercy! Thank You, Lord, for being merciful, for being so caring...

Now I can look around and see the sunshine lighting the earth around me! A new glow fills the air, fills my heart! Thank You, Lord God...Thank You, Father... ... ...

Jesus, There Is Power In Your Name!   May 13

John 14:12-14

"In solemn truth I tell you, anyone believing in me shall do the same miracles I have done, and even greater ones, because I am going to be with the Father. You can ask him for *anything,* using my name, and I will do it, for this will bring praise to the Father because of what I, the Son, will do for you. Yes, ask *anything,* using my name, and I will do it!"

Jesus! Jesus! There is Power in Your name - Power, awesome Power! We have only to believe in You, believe in such a way that Your Almighty Power comes through us and makes all the difference in the world! Oh, if we would believe this, our very lives would be startlingly different! People would be able to look at us and know that we, as Christians, ARE different!

It depends on us as to how this mighty POWER can work in our lives and the lives around us...We are to be examples...One cult states that Christianity has failed, but YOUR POWER has NOT failed!!! Christians have failed Christianity many times down through history, as You know, Lord...But looking back, there are many shining examples of those who loved You above all else...

This mighty POWER that emanates from You is like the power in a huge factory. But unless someone turns on the switch and lets the power surge through the equipment, it is completely useless. It can do no good...

You, God, have allowed us to share in this POWER, through Your Holy Spirit! You have given us such a wonderful opportunity to use this POWER! But unless we call upon it and use it, it is not showing the mightiness of YOU, our Creator!

The inventor of the electric equipment in the power plant wants people to use his equipment to prove how great his creativity is...God, our Father, wants us to call upon HIS POWER also! He delights in our calling upon Him and the POWER, which comes through Him...

Miracles result from the POWER OF GOD! Miracles are happening all the time because of the POWER OF GOD! The more we believe in the POWER OF JESUS' NAME, the more miracles can and will happen! Our faith in You releases this POWER...

Jesus, You told the disciples that if they had only a tiny grain of Faith, small as a mustard seed, they could move a mountain! That Faith in You, Lord, generates POWER! Oh Jesus, please empower us to do what You want us to, for Your Honor and Glory!

JESUS, JESUS, JESUS, THERE IS POWER IN YOUR NAME!!!

Your Eyes - My Eyes   May 14

Ephesians 4:23,24
Now your attitudes and thoughts must all be constantly changing for the better. Yes, you must be a new and different person, holy and good. Clothe yourself with this new nature.

Let me see with Your eyes, Lord...My eyes only see what I want them to see...My eyes center on my life, my self...Oh yes Lord, I have surrendered to You; haven't I said the words? I said them more than once…Yet, Lord Jesus, as I see my life now, my eyes are clouded often with my own self-centeredness…

I want to be heard, listened to. I want to make sure that I am not overlooked…I'm a person, right Lord? Why should I have to put up with some of the treatment the world wants to shove at me! If I don't speak up for myself, who else is going to? Don't I have the right to get impatient with the way I am treated sometimes, Lord? I have to watch out for number one, don't I?

"Dear one, your eyes are clouded. They are filled with self, but that can be changed. As I work in you, My Spirit will take the scales away that cloud your vision – to see what I want you to see. Now you only see what you want to see…

My eyes have the ability to see right through to the heart of each situation… My eyes see the truth… This takes desire – deep on your part, to learn to do. Once you have decided, deep down in your spirit, to overlook much of what is happening around you, you will be able to zero in on the crux of each situation. Together with Me, you will be able to see things you never were aware of before…

Little by little, you will change. Your attitude will change. Your eyes will become clear to see each situation so that your thoughts, your words, your actions will now be much different than before…"

Oh, Father God, I do want to see with "Your eyes…" I want the scales to fall off these eyes. Then I can have the insight You want me to have. As I focus on what You'd have me to see, I can become a better vessel for You to flow through… … …

Incomplete   May 15

Ephesians 3:16-19 (NIV)
I pray that out of his glorious riches he may strengthen you with power through his Spirit in your inner being, so that Christ may dwell in your hearts through faith. And I pray that you, being rooted and established in love, may have power, together with all the saints, to grasp how wide and long and high and deep is the love of Christ, and to know this love that surpasses knowledge—that you may be filled to the measure of all the fullness of God.

Father, I am so thankful to have been found by You. I know deep in my heart, Jesus, that I cannot be, I do not want to be - without You…I feel that I would be incomplete without You…

What does incomplete really mean? In the dictionary I see it states: "lacking a part or parts; not whole; not full; not finished; imperfect…"

These words, these meanings, they really tell so much! Yes Lord, I am incomplete when You are not a part of me! Without You I am not complete! I feel empty when Your Holy Spirit does not fill me…I am not finished until You become my Finisher in eternity… I am imperfect without You…

WOW Lord, I had no idea when You called me out of bed to sit down and write about the word "incomplete" what You had in mind! It's true! All the words describing "incomplete" can so aptly be applied to each of our lives when we start to meditate on them…

We thank You Lord Jesus, for being the One Who Completes our lives! Yes Jesus, You bring wholeness to us! We can call upon You to fill us with Your Holy Spirit! With Your Holy Spirit within us, we can go out into the world and make a difference to those who come across our paths…

Perhaps it may not be an earthshaking situation for someone. Perhaps it might be a little thing to them, but it may have a far-reaching effect…

Use us to draw others to You so that they are not incomplete any more…You make us whole and full…Thank You Lord, for You are the great Finisher, who makes us complete… … …

Hebrews 12:2a(KJV)
Looking unto Jesus the author and finisher of *our* faith;…

Christianity   May 16

Matthew 16:15,16(NIV)
"But what about you?" he asked. "Who do you say I am?" Simon Peter answered, "You are the Christ, the Son of the living God."

Oh Lord, when I stop to think about Your being here on this earth, it seems so strange to me to realize that Your Ministry was carried out in so few years…

Why, Lord, so short a time? Even Your followers didn't seem to grasp Your Message very well...

Before You went to Calvary to die for Your followers and for each of us, Peter denied You three times!

There were so few to take Your Message to the world...Looking back through the centuries, I am amazed that such a small group could have multiplied into so many!

Lord, when I realize that there are many, many who call themselves Christians, but have no real understanding of what "Christian" means, I feel sad...I have met many people who after being asked if they are a Christian will reply, "No, I am a _____ or _____, etc." naming so many different Christian denominations!

When told that they had named a denomination, which is known as Christian, they seem surprised...That sadly says many may "belong" or were exposed to Christianity, but they never received the full Message that You came to share...The Message never reached their spirits...But thankfully, there are many, many "real" Christians in this day and age to bless and revere what You came to teach, dear Jesus...

You did not come in vain...Even though Your time on earth was short, it was more than sufficient! Thank You Jesus, for taking on the responsibility, which Your Father God, asked of You...You willingly came - You willingly shared the Message...You willingly went to the Cross, for us all...

The Christ...Jesus Christ...Christianity...Are we sharing the Message ourselves? Are we being "reflections" of You, Jesus Christ, to those who don't know You?

Jesus, You asked the question: "Who do you say I am?" Let us answer with Peter, that You are the Christ, the Son of the living God.

Are we telling others who You are???

Invisible Skin   May 17

Philippians 3:21
When he comes back he will take these dying bodies of ours and change them into glorious bodies like his own, using the same mighty power that he will use to conquer all else everywhere.

152

What is the color of your skin? What is the color of my skin? What happens to our skin when we die? What color will it be then? Will it make any difference then???

Sometimes Lord, people get into discussions about the color of skin...This happens lots of times - too many times, right Lord?

Skin is only the outer wrapping keeping all our parts together...Why so much consternation over the color?

In 1 Thessalonians 5:23 Paul refers to three parts of man: body, soul and spirit. You, Lord, have chosen to make skin to cover our bodies in various colors. You have chosen to decide who gets what color...So why can a human being, created by You, feel that he or she is someone special just because of their color? He or she had nothing, absolutely nothing to do with the decision!

Since we'll only have this "skin" a temporary time, say even three score and ten, it is nothing compared to our "real" life to be lived in Eternity with You, Lord God! That old skin, whatever the color, merely drops away, and the "real" life will then be lived!

For it is our spirit which lives on and on and on and on - FOREVER! Our earthly skin will have long been dried up into nothingness...

Brothers, sisters, you out there, think upon these things...Let the beauty of our spirits shine out beyond the color which God, our Creator, blessed us with. It is the inner Light that Jesus wants to have shine forth through each of us... ... ...

Job 19:25,26(NIV)

"I know that my Redeemer lives, and that in the end he will stand upon the earth. And after my skin has been destroyed, yet in my flesh I will see God;"

Hurt By And In The Body Of Christ   May 18

Luke 6:28, 36,37

"Pray for the happiness of those who *curse* you; implore God's blessing on those who *hurt* you."

"Try to show as much compassion as your Father does. Never criticize or condemn—or it will all come back on you. Go easy on others; then they will do the same for you."

In a precious little daily devotional I read, "If anything vex you, deal with that and get that righted with Me before you allow yourself to speak to, or meet anybody, or to undertake any new duty..."

Oh Lord, I've been hurt by someone in the Body of Christ...Lord, I feel as if I want to scream out "that's not true; it wasn't like that!"

Why Lord, in the Body of Christ, is there so much division? Why, Lord? You know, Lord Jesus, that my only desire is to be a loving vessel in this world...

In the Body of Christ, there are those who set themselves up as shepherds, leaders, whatever the title. Sometimes there is very little of the genuine unconditional LOVE, which You came to teach, in evidence...

You have witnessed all that has happened...You know the truth...The inner me really wants to shout out "Let me tell you what really happened"! But You want me to lay it all down at Your feet...It's hard, Lord...It's hard...

My mind wants to run back to all the details...My mind wants me to tell this one and that one! I want to write a letter or do something to "correct" the situation! And all this happened in the Body of Christ! Oh, Lord my God, how my spirit grieves...How You must grieve; how You must hurt, Lord - all in the name of "Christ."

But Lord, I see that You want me to lay it aside and get my eyes on You...I must keep You uppermost in my heart and mind...So I will, Lord, I will...Thank You for Your revelation today...I love You, Lord Jesus. I truly do...

And Lord Jesus, please shower down forgiveness, mercy and blessings on those who hurt others in the Body of Christ...Teach us that whatever happens to us we must practice forgiveness. We must forgive those who injure our reputations...Whatever the area in which we or others are hurt, it must be forgiven and forgotten...

It isn't easy, Lord, to ask You to forgive, to show mercy and then to have blessings shower down on those who do untold damage to us. But You have asked us to do this and this we must do. If we declare that we are followers of You, dear Lord Jesus, we must obey Your teachings...

Thank You Lord, for teaching us about Forgiveness, Mercy and Blessings...May we copy Your example... ... ...

Two Little Words   **May 19**

Psalm 139:23,24

Search me, O God, and know my heart; test my thoughts. Point out anything you find in me that makes you sad, and lead me along the path of everlasting life.

Lord, how two little words can make such a difference in a person's life! Those two little words "know thyself" popped into my mind and sat there until I let them unsettle me...I know myself, Lord...Haven't I been living with "me" all the years of my life? I know myself! I don't need to examine my life—it's not that bad...

"Is it that good, child, is it that good? I created you; I know your full potential... I know all about you. I've heard your excuses... I know who you blame for your failures... Why not come to Me and we'll have a long talk... You can be yourself with Me; there is no reason to make excuses to Me... I will help you to get to know yourself... It is only then that you can truly make a change in your life. Once you have looked at yourself with truthfulness, you will see where you need to change. I will help you. You can rely on Me. I will always be waiting for you to come whenever you are disheartened or troubled... Trust Me, My child, trust Me..."

But Lord Jesus, it will be so hard! How can I change - I feel so weak and helpless...

"Yes, child, I know how you feel... But you have to believe that with me helping you, you can change! You can be the person I created you to be. The fullness of your new life will then amaze you... Trust Me..."

Oh God, I needed to hear that! I need You! I can't make it without You! With You, I feel I can make the effort! I will take one step at a time, one day at a time, Lord, with Your help...

I know now You only expect the best that I can do...You consider my circumstances and surround me with Your unconditional Love. Lord, knowing that helps me take hold of my life...

Oh God, I thank You for Your unending loving-kindness and forgiveness...Your generosity of LOVE for me is awesome...No one has ever loved me like this before...Thank You God, thank You Jesus Christ, thank You Holy Spirit... ... ...

Lord, Help Their Unbelief   May 20

John 6:44

"For no one can come to me unless the Father who sent me draws him to me, and at the Last Day I will cause all such to rise again from the dead."

Oh God! My loved ones - they are standing fast against You...They won't recognize You Jesus, as God! They say You might be a Prophet; they say that You were a "good" person while here on earth...But they will not recognize that You are their Creator, their God!

This saddens me so much, dear Lord, so very much...They seem so stiff-necked...How can they react this way when You have done so much for them? You have loved them, suffered for them, died for them and went to Heaven to prepare a place for them...

They have blinders on their eyes. Yet they seem so aware of other things in life...Why, Lord, why?

Yet these, though they are "good" in the eyes of others, will not submit themselves to You...You are the Pearl of Great Value, the only One who has done so much for them...You are the only One who waits constantly with unconditional LOVE for them...

Why is it some will come to You and eagerly desire to know more about You, hungering for more and more? Others come reluctantly, but they do come. Then they rejoice for what they've found in knowing and loving You...

It's a mystery to me, Lord...It doesn't cost a penny; it's a free gift. Yet they hold back as if the price were beyond their reach! Oh Lord, I plead with You for my loved ones. Please help their unbelief...

Through Your Power Lord, do whatever it takes. Please Lord God, draw them into Your Family. No matter how long it takes, please Jesus, bring them to the Father for all eternity...

I love them so...My love is not sufficient to draw them in, Lord, but Yours is...Please Lord God, draw them in! It may be in my lifetime, and that would be such a glorious happening, but Lord, it is in Your time and in Your way...

As long as we will be reunited in our Heavenly Home, for all eternity, that is all that matters...Oh thank You, Father God, thank

You, dear Jesus and thank You Holy Spirit…In that mystery which I don't understand, You, God are Father, Son, and Holy Spirit…I thank you from the bottom of my heart… … …

What Can I Be For You?   May 21

Luke 17:10(NIV)

"So you also, when you have done everything you were told to do, should say, 'We are unworthy servants; we have only done our duty.'"

What can I be for You, Lord? What do You need me to be? I'm willing Lord, but I only want to be what You want me to be—nothing more—but nothing less…

I ask You, Lord, to use me as a tool, an instrument, an empty vessel. Help me, please Lord, to empty myself so that nothing of me remains to clog the workings which You have set in motion…

You say You want a willing vessel, a willing instrument? You want one that will not direct You or make suggestions, Lord? Um-m-m - - that's sometimes the hardest part…We often presume to know how You should handle the situation that You have allowed us to be involved in…

What patience You have with us, Lord Jesus, what patience! Thank You Savior, that You are so patient with us! Thank You, Lord…

You are the Creator of all! Mankind is still discovering as the years pass on, that You are willing and wanting to use us!!! We become awed by this thought as it sinks into the depths of our spirits…

You, God Almighty, are willing to use us? Oh God, forgive the self in each of us, the audacity, the pride, the ego…Remind us what a privilege and a blessing it is that You can use any of us who may be called to serve You, our Almighty God…

And Lord, please remind us of the humility that is needed - so necessary, to be the vessel or servant for You to use…

Sometimes the child in us wants to run out and call to all those willing to listen, that You, Lord, have called us to do something for You…Sometimes we can allow ourselves to puff up and become larger than life because You have placed a call, though perhaps only temporarily, on us…Oh, Lord, please, please, deflate us…

Let all unnecessary stumbling blocks fall by the wayside…What do You need me to be??? What can you be for the Lord???

Comfort…   May 22

John 16:7
"But the fact of the matter is that it is best for you that I go away, for if I don't, the Comforter won't come. If I do, he will – for I will send him to you."

2nd Corinthians 1:3,4a
What a wonderful God we have – he is the Father of our Lord Jesus Christ, the source of every mercy, and the one who so wonderfully comforts and strengthens us in our hardships and trials.

As I sit here, Lord, with deep concern for my loved one, I need to be comforted…I need Your comfort, dear Jesus…

My loved one is ill, Lord, very ill…You know all about that, Lord. I have spoken to You about my loved one constantly…I keep waiting for a Miracle, one of Your Miracles, dear God…

The days drag on, the nights are full of anxiety…My loved one continues to suffer…Oh Lord, have Mercy, have Mercy! We each need Your comfort…

Yes, my Jesus, we need Your comfort…We need to feel that You care. We need to feel that Your LOVE for us will result in a miracle - a miracle that will restore my loved one's health! Oh Father, I thank You for what You are going to do! I thank You in advance for the miracle! I give You all the GLORY for healing my beloved one…Thank You, thank You, thank You…

Lord, the Psalms came into my mind…When I read Psalm 106:1-2, the words jumped out and into my spirit! It says:

Hallelujah! Thank you, Lord! How good you are! Your love for us continues on forever. Who can ever list the glorious miracles of God? Who can even praise him half enough?

Yes, Lord, who can ever praise You enough for all the miracles You have wrought…We come before You now, asking for one more miracle, dear Jesus…You know what it is…Now we thank You again for it in advance… … …For You are the Lord, the God of Miracles!

When the word "Miracle" is spoken of, or written about, Your name is connected to it!

PRAISE YOU, ALMIGHTY GOD...PRAISE TO YOU, JESUS CHRIST...PRAISE TO YOU, HOLY SPIRIT!

Some of the Psalms are so very comforting, Lord. It is amazing that some of the words spoken then, written then, are the very ones, which are in some of our hearts, this day, or this night...

Comfort from You was needed then, and comfort from You is needed now...Thank You, dear Lord, for Your Bible and for Your comforting Holy Spirit... ... ...

The Language Of God   May 23

1st Samuel 3:9,10

So he said to Samuel, "Go and lie down again, and if he calls again, say, 'Yes, Lord, I'm listening.'" So Samuel went back to bed. And the Lord came and called as before, "Samuel! Samuel!" And Samuel replied, "Yes, I'm listening."

Oh, Father God, how I love You...Thank You for speaking to me...Many would think it strange that I should say such a thing, that You speak to me...But I truly do believe You do...You need to correct me, correct my thinking, correct my actions...And, Lord God, when You do, I am truly grateful...

Sometimes I can get off track and lose my way...Sometimes I can get involved in thinking about how I'm going to "handle" a situation. Before I know it, I'm heading in the opposite direction from where You want me to go...So again I thank You, Heavenly Father, for caring so much that You chasten me out of Love...When we show appreciation for the corrections, this shows us that we are growing and maturing in our walk with You.

Though we may someday be stranded on an island with only sparse food and water, we can be spiritually satisfied through this language of Yours: the language of God...We can communicate with each other, Jesus...We can become closer and closer no matter what our circumstances are...Yes Lord, You speak the language of God...And when we come into this relationship with You, blessings come down upon us

"Come now, little one, settle in with Me... I am lonely for you. Are you lonely for Me? Satisfy Your Longing for Me, for I am here waiting to hear from you... I have much to say to you... Settle yourself... I have much to say to you..."

Oh Father, I truly love You! I long to be with You face to face! Thank You for all the blessings You have allowed me to share in - I am grateful...They are so numerous I can't list them all, Father...

May I truly quiet myself to hear what You have to say to me, Lord God... ... ...

"Yes, I'm Listening, Lord."

You Can Shut Me Down, Lord   May 24

Job 33:4

For the Spirit of God has made me, and the breath of the Almighty gives me life.

Yes Lord, You can shut me down...Just like a piece of machinery that suddenly dies down, You can shut me down too, Lord, in an instant!

I cannot take my next breath without Your permission!!! Breathing has become such an integral part of my being I am hardly aware of it...Yet, in an instant that next breath of Life can be stopped at Your Will...

That's an awesome thought! Somehow we begin to feel that we are in complete control of our beings—our minds, our bodies and, the often forgotten part, our spirits...

You, Creator God, Lord of Lords, King of Kings, Savior, can and do make it possible for each of us to go on breathing. We often accept our life span as something due us...But it is a gift, this breathing, this gift of LIFE.

Often we have come to think of our life as a burden and not a gift...Some of us are given especially hard burdens to bear — some not of our making...

Sometimes, though, we are the ones who have taken this precious gift of LIFE and abused it—abused it terribly...

Thankfully, Lord God, You are the only One, who can make a difference in our lives. We can be changed by our allowing You to breathe back wholeness into us…So now, Lord God, please help us to realize the wonderment of this gift of LIFE and to appreciate it!

Help us to make a conscious decision to make the extra effort so our lives will be more meaningful for You, Lord God, for You…In doing so, we will have an opportunity to return to You, dividends on the gift which You gave to us — LIFE itself…

Thank You again, Lord God, for the breath of LIFE… … …

The Cry For Love   May 25

1ˢᵗ Corinthians 13:4-8a

Love is very patient and kind, never jealous or envious, never boastful or proud, never haughty or selfish or rude. Love does not demand it's own way. It is not irritable or touchy. It does not hold grudges and will hardly even notice when others do it wrong. It is never glad about injustice, but rejoices whenever truth wins out. If you love someone you will be loyal to him no matter what the cost. You will always believe in him, always expect the best of him, and always stand your ground in defending him. All the special gifts and powers from God will someday come to an end, but love goes on forever.

Lord Jesus, we cry; we cry for those who are unloved and those who are unloving…What a burden they are carrying, both the unloved and the unloving…

One might look at the unloving and say that the burden isn't as great as the ones who are unloved. This is not true…

The big difference between the two is that the unloving, perhaps are unable to love. The unloved ones are capable of loving, but are not receiving love…

Society and some educated people would like to further the problem by saying, "Once you are deprived of love, you yourself, cannot love. If one has had a steady diet of criticism, one will grow up criticizing. If one has been hated and abused, one will grow up to hate and abuse."

Oh Lord, how very mixed up we are as a people! There are people in this world who try so hard to fill us with thoughts which are the very opposite of You…For it is only in learning of You, learning from You, that we can make ourselves different from the ugly patterns of human nature…

161

It is only in loving You, learning to love ourselves, and learning to love others that we can break out of the sickness of this seemingly loveless society.

Oh Jesus, Perfect Teacher of LOVE, we ask that we may become extensions of Your LOVE. Teach us to love all those around us, despite perhaps, our loveless past...Only You, Jesus can transform us into the loving vessels YOU want us to become!

For it is in becoming love vessels ourselves that others can visibly see the transformation You have caused in our lives... Lord, it is easy to love the loveable; that is no challenge! Jesus let YOUR PERFECT LOVE flow through us to love the unloving! Oh let us love the unloved!

The whole world is in need of love...YOUR PERFECT LOVE – the world cries out for it! Let us sincerely ask for this wonderful gift of Yours - - - LOVE! May we generously share it with others... ... ...

Our Real Family   May 26

Mark: 3:32-35 (NIV)

A crowd was sitting around him, and they told him, "Your mother and brothers are outside looking for you."

"Who are my mother and my brothers?" he asked.

Then he looked at those seated in a circle around him and said, "Here are my mother and my brothers! Whoever does God's will is my brother and sister and mother."

Oh Jesus, what a shocking thing it is, to read this Scripture without the understanding of Your Holy Spirit! For those of us who were brought up to feel that our family was the most important part of our life, it's a whole new way of thinking...Yes, our families are very important, but You Jesus, are the most important of all...You are the One, the Only One, when it comes to a decision between You and family. You never said to stop loving our family, or stop praying for them...

Beginning in Matthew 10:35 You said,

"I have come to set a man against his father, and a daughter against her mother, and a daughter-in-law against her mother-in-law – a man's worst enemies will be right in his own home! If you love your father and mother

162

more than you love me, you are not worthy of being mine; or if you love your son or daughter more than me, you are not worthy of being mine."

Oh Jesus, again Your words are so shocking! You are trying to get us to understand that our focus, absolutely must be on YOU!

You give some of us families and loved ones…They are a wonderful gift! Yet, it's only for a season…You give us opportunities to learn how to communicate, what You came here to teach us, IF we'll let You…Yes, we make mistakes, so many mistakes…There is so-o-o-o much to learn…Yet time after time, You keep on giving us opportunities to learn how to love – to love You, to love ourselves, to love others…

As we learn to put You first, the way You want us to, then we understand the above Scriptures…Oh Jesus, Lord of Lords, King of Kings, Master, Teacher, thank You for allowing us to become Your brother, Your sister, Your mother…Thank You for dying for us and going to our Father's Kingdom to prepare a place for us! How we look forward to being there with You and with all our Eternal Family…

Thank You, dear Jesus! Thank You, my Lord… … …

For Me…For You…   May 27

1ˢᵗ John 3:16-18

We know what real love is from Christ's example in dying for us. And so we also ought to lay down our lives for our Christian brothers. But if someone who is supposed to be a Christian has money enough to live well, and sees a brother in need, and won't help him—how can God's love be within *him*? Little children, let us stop just *saying* we love people; let us *really* love them, and *show it* by our *actions*.

You Lord Jesus, did it for me…You were sent by Your Father, God Almighty, to come to earth for me!!!

You came willingly - for me! You came to be born, to teach, to be crucified, to die - for me…You were resurrected - for me…You went to Heaven to prepare a place - for me… … …

For me! For me! For me! It boggles my mind, Jesus, my Savior and my Lord…I have gratefully accepted what you have done for me…

I know that so often I have not shown my appreciation for what You did for me...This has happened more times than I care to admit...

And now that I am reflecting on all You have done for me, I have to face up to this thought: what have I done for YOU, Lord? What have I really done for YOU???

Matthew 25:35-40

"'For I was hungry and you fed me; I was thirsty and you gave me water; I was a stranger and you invited me into your homes; naked and you clothed me; sick and in prison, and you visited me.' "

"Then these righteous ones will reply, 'Sir, when did we ever see you hungry and feed you? Or thirsty and give you anything to drink? Or a stranger, and help you? Or naked, and clothed you? When did we ever see you sick or in prison, and visit you?'"

"And I, the King, will tell them, 'When you did it to these my brothers you were doing it to me!' "

Yes Lord, we will do it for You, for You dear Lord and Savior...

Please, Lord Jesus, keep reminding us of what you have already done for us! Then we will be reminded of what we can do for You - for You, Precious Savior, for You... ... ...

How Long Will It Be?   May 28

Song of Songs 2:10

"My beloved said to me, 'Rise up, my love, my fair one, and come away.'"

Songs of Songs 7:10

"I am my beloved's and I am the one he desires."

Dear Jesus, how long will it be before I see You face to face?

"I'm calling you... I'm calling you... Only I know the future, the moment, the split second that I will call you to be with Me... Forever and a day we will be united... You need not know the moment, the time. You need only to be ready... I have a plan prepared for you... There are many hills, mansions, and much space, which I have prepared for you...

Be content with what you have for you are a special one... Why think about tomorrow when today is yet at hand, My little one? Today

164

can be filled with wonder and beauty – My beauty. I have created it for such as you...

You must come away to be with Me more often. You cannot hear Me above the din of the crowd, for you are special to Me...

So, breathe deeply now, rest... Rest your mind, your body, your spirit... Stay with Me for awhile... I can give you rest. My rest is like no other can give... Rest, My child, rest... ... ..."

Thank You, Father, for it is so true...You are the only one who can breathe new life, refreshment, and rest into our busy lives. You are so gracious and loving to us when we decide to stop and listen. May we come more often to hear Your words, which speak to our inner beings...Thank You, Lord Jesus, thank You... ... ...

So What!   May 29

Ephesians 5:21
Honor Christ by submitting to each other.

It happened again, Lord. It happened again! That person did it again - talked "down" to me as if I were a child...

You know Lord, that I am an adult. So why is that person continually talking "down" to me as if I were an ignorant, immature person...

Time and again I find myself in the same position. Then when I speak up in my defense, a big quarrel ensues...

Why can't that person "see the light," Lord? Why?...Oh Lord - You say why can't I see the light? Why can't I see that this is part of my learning maturity, spiritual maturity? This is constantly happening to me because my "self" has to be humbled? Oh, Lord...

Please, Lord Jesus, help me to submit myself to those whom you have placed in my life so that I can truly see Your Light...

It's so easy to blame the other person...Thank You, Lord, for opening up my mind and my spirit to accept these "put-downs"...Let them be used to help me grow by my accepting them. May I truly see the necessity of these experiences...

So now, Lord, let me say to myself when they come along, "So what Lord, so what!" Let me see them from Your point of view. It will happen and will continue to happen until I learn it makes no difference in the whole scope of Life...Please help me to realize that it is You teaching me, Lord, through this person...So, "so what," Lord, when it happens...And thank You for loving me enough to correct me...

Isn't it amazing how much we can learn when You show us these lessons from Your point of view? And, Lord, it seems so much easier to be willing to relearn these things when You are our Teacher...

Just think, You the Master, Creator of the whole Universe, are willing, so completely willing, to teach each of us exactly what we need to learn...Thank You again, dear Jesus, for today's lesson... ... ...

How Many Times, Lord...   May 30

Galatians 5:25
If we are living now by the Holy Spirit's power, let us follow the Holy Spirit's leading in every part of our lives.

Oh, Lord, how many times in my life did I let You pass me by - I was completely unaware that You were there...Did You want me to do a special thing for someone? Did You just want me to stand or sit still while Your Presence was so very close to me?

Only now did it occur to me to ask You..."How many times did I let You pass me by?" It is a disturbing thought...It ruffles my inner spirit...Oh, Lord, forgive me, forgive me...

Open my eyes Lord, to the next opportunity...Let me become so sensitive to Your Presence that I will only need a quick moment to realize what needs to be done...There are many, many out in this world with whom we need to share a loving touch. Remind me of a time in my life when a special person acting upon Your signal, made a difference in my life, Lord...

Yes, it's true; we only pass through this life but once. There is no going back...

People will say that this world is cold...But it's not, is it, Lord? For You made this world to be what it is...It is a beautiful place! But we, Your creations, are the ones who soil and mar the beauty of this world. We are the destroyers...Forgive us, Lord. Please continue to give us another chance to learn what You, Jesus, came here to teach us — to LOVE one another...

Dear Jesus, please give us the hearts to be sensitive to You as You pass by, for whatever purpose...Oh Lord, have we been insensitive to You as YOU passed by???

Have WE passed You by this day, Lord???

God Cares   May 31

Psalm 139:5,6
You both precede and follow me, and place your hand of blessing on my head. This is too glorious, too wonderful to believe!

God, You care! You care about me! No matter what seems to be happening, or what is happening to me, You care!

Psalm 139:17,18
How precious it is, Lord, to realize that you are thinking about me constantly! I can't even count how many times a day your thoughts turn towards me. And when I waken in the morning, you are still thinking of me!

You truly do care about me...You, the God of all Creation, are more than mere man can understand or even know about...You care for me! Truly, like it says in Psalm 139, it is too glorious, too wonderful to believe! Because the Scriptures tell me so, I do believe...

As You know Lord, I just finished reading a book* filled with true experiences of how You entered in, to work out individual miracles! Oh Father God, it was so exciting to read page after page about these! In Your very loving and caring way, You at the precise time, made the difference in so many lives...

You care! God, You care! You care not just for me! You care for each one who would turn to You. Some turn to You out of Love, some out of desperation. Then they find that it's true - God Cares...

How many of us have friends or relatives who seem to love and care for us...In our time of need, we turned to them. Then we found those we thought would stand up for us, crumbled before us...We were let down and the disappointment was so severe...

---

* His Mysterious Ways" (Guideposts Magazine)

167

When we turn to our true Friend, our Lord God, we find that He will never fail us in the true sense of the word...Dear Heavenly Father, God of the Universe, please continue to care for each one of us...Please let us feel the comfort of Your caring... ... ...

June

Your Book of Life   June 1

2ⁿᵈ Timothy 3:16,17

The whole Bible was given to us by inspiration from God and is useful to teach us what is true and to make us realize what is wrong in our lives; it straightens us out and helps us do what is right. It is God's way of making us well prepared at every point, fully equipped to do good to everyone.

Thank you Lord God, for Your Book of Life, Your Book of Love, Your Book of Hope, Your Book of Faith - the Bible...

Yes Lord, Your Book of Comfort and Compassion is the Book from Your very Heart. Your Book is all that we need to help us get through this life here on earth...

How wonderful it is, Lord, to pick up the Bible! We find the very words to uplift us! Everything we need to know about is in it – this one solitary Book is complete in itself!

You begin by telling of the Creation of the Universe and all that is in it! Next the story of Your chosen people, Israel, is told. Then there are the Psalms; many are so comforting...Proverbs follows succinctly spelling out rules to live by. Finally in the Old Testament are the Books of Prophecy telling of the Messiah to come and so much more...

This one Book also tells us about Your Life, Lord Jesus...And yet, all that You experienced is not recorded in this special Book...But, the reality of Your Life is there: Your Birth, Your Ministry, Your Death for each of us, Your Resurrection...

Oh, Lord God, there is so very much in this one special Book. Thank You Holy Spirit for inspiring those who brought forth the Bible... Please protect and encourage those who are even now translating and printing Your Word for everyone throughout the world.

How grateful we, who love this precious Book, are this day...Through the years, believers, who are now with You Lord, must have been thankful for the blessing of the Bible...We, who believe in it and are still here, thank You, Lord. Those who have just discovered this Book of all books, thank You also, Lord! May it never be taken away from us! May we never forget what You want us to remember, Lord Jesus.

May we never forget... ... ...

Umbrella Of Your Love   June 2

Psalm 3:3 (NIV)
But you are a shield around me, O LORD, my Glorious One, who lifts up my head.

Stretched out over us, Lord God, is Your umbrella of LOVE! It protects us; it shields us from storms and happenings that, at times, we are not even aware of...

Even when we step out from under this umbrella of LOVE, Lord, You are still willing to follow us—to bridge the gap between us...In our stubbornness, we often insist on forging out and rushing into the storms of LIFE only to be caught up in a downpour of negative experiences...

Yet at times we continue to rush off in any direction that signals us...We refuse to stand under Your umbrella...We don't need someone to baby us; we don't mind the storms, we say...

Suddenly our vision is completely obliterated by the storm! We run - we don't know which way to turn...

"Stay here... Stay here in the shadow of My LOVE, My umbrella of LOVE... I am here to protect you, to care for you, to see that you get to your rightful place... Why do you neglect My care? Why do you not heed My guidance? My LOVE spills out for you..."

Oh Lord Jesus, it is so complicated, yet so simple...We insist on having our own way, getting so mixed up in Life. We go this way and that...Things snarl up until we are all tied up in our own little snares.

We make our lives so complex...Yet Your way, Jesus, is a simple one...We hold back from Your way, because we think it has to be one of "giving up" the very things that have complicated our lives!

Oh Lord, help us...Please continue to pour mercy on us while we decide to come back to Your umbrella of LOVE...We can be so difficult, like stubborn little children...The child knows that the parent loves it, but it fights and stamps its feet. It has a temper tantrum until it finally realizes the parent only wants what is best for it...When the awareness of the parent's love comes, then the child settles into that loving relationship...

Yes Lord, we act like stubborn children so frequently...Help us to mature under Your umbrella of LOVE...Never let us wander away from it, for it is truly a shelter for all of our lives...Thank You Jesus, for being so patient with us... ... ...

If You Had Asked Me   June 3

Matthew 26:52-54

"Put away your sword," Jesus told him. "Those using swords will get killed. Don't you realize that I could ask my Father for thousands of angels to protect us, and he would send them instantly? But if I did, how would the Scriptures be fulfilled that describe what is happening now?"

Lord Jesus, if You had asked me if You should die for me, I would have said "Oh Lord no! No, Lord Jesus, no-o-o..."

But You didn't ask me...You didn't ask anyone. Yet You died for me...You died for everyone...It's so hard for me to comprehend this, my dear Savior, so very hard...

You made a choice too, Lord. Because of Your Love for the Father, Almighty God, You were obedient when He asked You to die for each of us sinners.

That's so strange...You, the only Perfect Human were willing to die for me, so imperfect...Some of us cringe at the thought of being called sinners...But each one of us IS a sinner no matter how much we may despise the thought...

Oh, Lord Jesus, if You had asked me, I would have, hopefully, tried to come up with a different plan to save You from dying...Your followers wanted to hide You from those who wanted to put You to death. They did not understand, neither do I.

God, Almighty God, had His perfect plan! You, dear Savior, had to die in order to defy and defeat satan once and for all! This plan was designed to set men, women, and children free...Each one of us has to decide in our hearts that You are the Savior of this Universe! I believe with all my heart that You are...

Dear Jesus, obedient Son of God, thank You so very, very much for dying on the cross for each one of us. I long for the moment when I can meet You face to face to thank You personally...

Thank You, Jesus, that You followed Your Father's plan... ... ...

The Mystery Of The Universe   June 4

Genesis 1:1 (NIV)
In the beginning God created the heavens and the earth.

How strange Lord God, that man in his intellect thinks he has the answer to the formation of the Universe...

Some call it "the Big Bang"... It is just as if for no reason at all, the Universe came into being...The beginning of the Universe is a mystery. It is Your mystery, Lord God, for You created it...

You know the exact time, the very moment it all began...You were there...You will be at the end also, for there will be an end when You call that into being...

For all Life is in Your Hands, Lord God...You know all about everything...

Each of us born on this very, very small part of the Universe called earth, has only to go to a planetarium. As we look up into the schematic of the Universe we see how very inconsequential we here on earth actually are...

Yet You, Lord God, sent Your only Son to come to our Earth! Jesus was born here, to live, to die, and to rise again! Then He departed to go to You in Your Heavenly Home...

So earth takes a very special place as part of the Universe. But man, whose intellect is becoming more brilliant, still knows so very little in the overall Plan of Your Universe, Lord God...

Man has fallen far since he first was formed so very long ago...Yet in all his yearnings there is one very important, very basic rule which You, Lord God, want him to learn — to LOVE...He must love his neighbor and his brother, as he loves himself...To learn that, he must first learn to love himself...Then, he can love others around him...

Thank You God, for not keeping LOVE a mystery. Thank You for sending Your Son, Jesus, to teach us about this truly wonderful gift... ... ...

I Am My Brother's Keeper... June 5

Galatians 6:2,9a, 10

Share each other's troubles and problems, and so obey our Lord's command...

And let us not get tired of doing what is right, ...That's why whenever we can we should always be kind to everyone, and especially to our Christian brothers.

In Genesis 4:9, You, God Almighty, asked Cain where Abel, his brother was. "I don't know," he replied "Am I my brother's keeper?"

He inferred, Lord Jesus, that he was not—that this was not his responsibility...He made it sound as if he were unrelated to his brother - so why should he care about him...

In this day and age, Lord, more than ever, You want us to be our brother's keeper...There is so much hunger, illness and need for caring in this world...

Millions of new lives are being born each year and of these millions so many are being born into hunger, into uncaring situations...Who should help them, Lord? Who should help them...

If I feel in my heart that I am my brother's keeper, then I am obliged to help...But, one can feel sometimes, "I am only one person. What can I do to make a difference?"

One person CAN make a difference, right Lord? With the desire in one's heart, coupled with Your desire, Lord, one person can make a difference!

Even if that person does not have material things or finances, offering up prayers to You, Lord, from a sincere heart, can make a difference...You, Almighty God, can touch a heart to help others...

We can be our brother's keepers right in the midst of our own neighborhood...Perhaps there is not a need for financial or material help, but a need to comfort. We may need to speak some words of wisdom from You, Lord, to someone. Perhaps we can do errands for a person unable to help themselves...Perhaps there are children who need a special hug or encouragement…But, are we willing to become our brother's keeper?

We CAN be our brother's keepers in countless ways… We have only to desire to help, and You Lord Jesus, will show us where the needs are. You ask each of us, Lord, the same question You asked Cain. Hopefully our answer will be:

"Yes Lord, I am my brother's keeper."

Rain   June 6

Hosea 6:3
"Oh, that we might know the Lord! Let us press on to know him, and he will respond to us as surely as the coming of dawn or the rain of early spring."

Your lovely rain is raining down, Lord…It started with a drop here, a drop there…Then a few more came. Then a patter of raindrops coming down on the rooftop made a very pleasant sound…

This sound, the sound of rain, has been seldom heard these past months. The earth all about has been crying out for Your rain, as a soul cries out for help…

Pitter, patter. Pitter, patter. The rain is slowly coming to an end…Oh Lord, we need so much more! We need enough to wet the ground and let it seep down several inches into the earth!

Oh Jesus, we need more; it's hardly enough…Strange though, on the beautiful sunny days we don't want rain. We want the sunny days to go on, day after day, without the inconvenience of rain.

Then we become aware of the dryness; it's all about us…Suddenly we realize that we need rain! We need rain! We want rain! Forget about sunny days; we need rain!

Lord, You have brought to my mind, that spiritually, we are a lot like this…As things go along well in our lives, we act as if we don't need You. In fact, we treat You as if we've never even heard about You…No thought of You enters our minds…

We go about each day enjoying ourselves. Isn't Life great! Isn't it wonderful! Then we begin to feel that things aren't as great as we thought…Dryness of spirit begins…What's wrong? The dryness continues until we have to face it straight on…

One has to stop and take note of what has happened. When one honestly does this, and seriously evaluates the situation, a realization enters in. It becomes very clear that the spirit within has almost dried up...It needs to be revitalized...But how?

We must turn to Our Father, Jesus, and His Holy Spirit. We must take time to meditate, to communicate with our Creator. We need to dwell on what Jesus came to teach us, realizing what He did for each of us...When our spirits are dry and in need, He is the One who gives peace to our souls. We then receive His Living Waters like spiritual "rain".

Oh thank You Father, for Your spiritual "rain" and also for the rain that our earth needs. Please continue to provide both as You see we are in need...Thank You for always being there for us, thank You... ... ...

Three Crosses   June 7

Ephesians 4: 22-24(NIV)
You were taught, with regard to your former way of life, to put off your old self, which is being corrupted by its deceitful desires; to be made new in the attitude of your mind; and to put on the new self, created to be like God in true righteousness and holiness.

There were three crosses, Lord, standing there...You were in the center, the middle...That's where You want to be in each of our lives, in the center - in the middle...

But Lord, to so many of us that's not where You are...You are on the outskirts of our lives. For some You are not even in sight...To others You are in the vicinity, but not in the center of their lives...Why, Lord?

"It costs, for Me to be in the center, child... It costs... Self has to be put aside, put down... Self does not want that... Self wants to be in My place, the center... Only after one thrusts self out of that central place can one experience what I have for each of My children... Understand that..."

Yes Lord Jesus, so much has to go out of our lives in order for You to come in and take Your rightful place...So much junk has to be flung out, permanently...Each of us carries his or her own specialized

175

bag of junk. Each of us has to be willing for it to go before You can reign in the center of our hearts...

We have to clean up our house - our home, where we live...Our dwelling place is not in a structure, but inside our bodies. That's where we truly live...Once we have cleaned up and thrown out, we can invite You to take Your rightful and welcome place in our hearts, in our lives...

When we realize the price You paid for us, Lord, it is a bargain for each of us! You paid the price of our admittance into the Glory of Your Heavenly Home for all Eternity! Oh Lord, the price we pay is so insignificant...

The shadow of the three crosses should remind us of You on that day, Lord...There were two others with You, one on each side...One was willing, even at that late time, to change. The other refused to put You in the center of his life, even as short as it was...Those three crosses should speak to us here and now...Those three crosses tell us very plainly what we can expect in our decision to accept or reject You, Lord Jesus...Which cross represents the path we choose?

Yes, Lord, You are so right. It costs, but the price is worth it...Lord God, the price is so worth it... ... ...

Saving Souls   June 8

John 6:44a
"For no one can come to me unless the Father who sent me draws him to me,..."

Why is it Lord, that it's so very, very hard to get people to accept You for who You are? There are so many who know that You are first in my life, but feel that they want no part of accepting You...

We long to share You with all those whom we come in contact with...

Is it my fault, dear Lord, that they don't want to become interested in You? Or is the time not right for them yet? Dear Jesus, we so wish we could bring soul after soul to You. This would be pleasing to You, dear Lord...

What hurts the most, dear God, is when those closest to us seem so indifferent to You...How that truly hurts...But Lord, not by power, not by might, but by Your Holy Spirit, will they come into Your fold...

Lord, if each of Your children were able to bring one soul to You, there soon would be a shortage of unsaved souls! How glorious that would be for You, Jesus, how glorious!

So, my dear Savior, we will continue to hope and pray for this. Before You call us home may there be more who will have accepted You as their Lord and Savior...Hopefully, You will have allowed us to be used as Your witnesses...

Therefore, Lord Jesus, we will content ourselves with three things to do: to remain hopeful, to continue to LOVE them, and to pray. We believe that it will happen at Your appointed time...

Thank You, Heavenly Lord God, for being who You are! Truly we could not make it without You, Father God...

So please Lord, help us to help others find what You have given so freely: Salvation...Thank You, Lord Jesus, thank You...

Distortion   June 9

2nd Corinthians 4:2

We do not try to trick people into believing – we are not interested in fooling anyone. We never try to get anyone to believe that the Bible teaches what it doesn't. All such shameful methods we forego. We stand in the presence of God as we speak and so we tell the truth, as all who know us will agree.

Distortion - oh Lord, how much about You has been distorted...It still lingers down through the ages...You came here so simply, born in a lowly setting, born to a very humble mother...

You came to be the example of how we humans should live...You lived Your life with truth, compassion, service...People were Your focus...You cared about them as no other...

Yet today centuries later, You are still misunderstood...Your coming here, Your message, Your LIFE has become distorted by so many...Distortion has taken the beauty and the truth away from what You gave Your very own LIFE for...

There are so many who commit suicide, because they have given up on LIFE...They somehow or other, missed the realness of

You…They either never knew You, or heard a distorted version of You… Oh dear Jesus, what a waste!

How that must grieve You, dear Lord…How it grieves us who call You, Father, Lord, Savior, Master, and Friend…Yes dear Lord, You are all these when we come into the true knowledge of You…

How sad it is for those who try and go through this LIFE on their own; how very difficult it must be…If only the whole world would wake up to the reality of You, dear Lord…How much JOY, PEACE of mind and HAPPINESS would be generated with the acceptance of You into their lives…

Oh Father, please help us to bring the essence of You, the TRUTH of YOU, the knowledge of YOU, the unconditional LOVE of YOU to others while there is still time…

Remind us, Lord, that we are our brothers' keepers. Remind us that it is a free gift, which You are offering to those who don't know You…There is no service charge! There is no fee!

Help us Father, to stop the distortion about You! Help us be an example of Your LOVE…Everything that You taught Your followers, teach us…Yes, Lord, help us to end the distortion about You… … …

Teacher's Pet…   June 10

1st John 3:1a

See how very much our heavenly Father loves us, for he allows us to be called his children – think of it – and we really *are!*

How many of us, while in school as little children, wished we could be the teacher's pet…It was a special honor to be the favorite of the teacher…

Lord, if the teacher had only one favorite, one pet, that meant in a sense, that all the other children in the class were left out…

Sometimes, as You know, Lord Jesus, teachers continued to have favorites in the upper grades as well. Many, many students were left out, through no fault of their own…

Perhaps they did not have curly hair, blond hair, or big brown eyes with long lashes or blue eyes…Perhaps they were not clothed in the latest fashions…Because of things like this, they were overlooked, grade after grade...It can cause bitterness sometimes, Lord...It can affect the memories of schooldays...Favoritism can be so unfair...

But, now Lord Jesus, things can be different! No matter what our age is, we can be YOUR pet, because You are our Teacher! Yes! Each and every one of us can become Teacher's pet!!!

All the hurtful memories of the past, all the unfairness melts away! For You, Jesus, Master, Teacher, choose each of us to be Your very favorite - Your pet!!!

WOW! And because, Jesus, You are in the Center, none of us will be jealous of anyone else! No one! For we know, with all our hearts that YOU are Just...

For you who were favored as a student by certain teachers, you also can continue being Teacher's pet! Jesus Christ, our Teacher, our Master, our Savior is a fair Teacher and Loves each one of us unconditionally...

You, thankfully, Lord Jesus, have no favorites for we are all Your favorites—Your pets!

What a marvelous feeling this can be—favorite of our Master, our Teacher, our Jesus - Teacher's Pet... ... ...

Scents, Sense...   June 11

Proverbs 3:21
Have two goals: wisdom – that is, knowing and doing right – and common sense. Don't let them slip away,...

We smell peach blossoms, apple blossoms, lilacs, gardenias, magnolia blossoms, and lilies-of-the-valley. The sweetness of their perfume, their fragrances, their scents can fill the air...

These scents bring to mind a different sense: common sense...What does that really mean, common sense? Does everyone have common sense, Lord? Can we acquire common sense? Do we need common sense?

"In the Scriptures, sons and daughters, are passages referring to common sense, also wisdom. I urge My children to seek these..."

But Lord, what is common sense? The dictionary has an answer: "Common sense: sound, practical judgment that is independent of specialized knowledge, training or the like..." It sounds like learning

179

to think things out, not to jump into quick decisions without "putting our thinking caps on!"

Oh Lord, You know how easy it is for us to jump into situations without thinking, without using good, common sense... Help remind us, to slow down and really think things out before we make the decision, which needs to be made...

You, Lord, designed us with such a complex body. Please help us to use each part of it in the way You designed it to be used, most importantly our minds. And Lord, You know how much we depend on You to help us come to the right decision for each particular situation...

Thank You, Father, for all Your Blessings...Thank You for the Scriptures which teach us about common sense...Thank You for Yourself, most of all... ... ...

Not Our Kind Of Love, Lord, But Your LOVE...
June 12

Romans 5:8
But God showed his great love for us by sending Christ to die for us while we were still sinners.

1st John 4:16,17a
We know how much God loves us because we have felt his love and because we believe him when he tells us that he loves us dearly. God is love, and anyone who lives in love is living with God and God is living in him. And as we live with Christ, our love grows more perfect and complete; ...

Lord, we need to pray for more love... We want to be able to love more freely, without any strings attached! Help us to love with no conditions, like Your unconditional LOVE...

Can this be possible, Lord? Usually when we love, we consciously or unconsciously put conditions on our love for those around us...Can we, with all our faults, with all our humanness, ever be able to love the way You do?

Your kind of LOVE, Lord, is so pure, so giving, and so free...No matter what we do, You LOVE us...That's one of the hardest things to understand about You, Lord...And it is also one of the hardest to accept...How amazing that You can LOVE us no matter what...

Of course, we finally realize that though You LOVE us unconditionally, You do not Love our behavior at certain times in our lives. Nevertheless, that unconditional LOVE for each one of us continues to flow from You...

What a blessing this is to finally realize this LOVE, Lord Jesus – what a blessing! Others around us may not flow with that kind of love for us. But through You, Lord, we can generate Your unconditional LOVE for them. This is because of Your unconditional LOVE for us which flows to them through us! WOW!

What a gift this is, Almighty God – what a gift...It is a gift to me, to each one of us...How exciting this is when I realize that I am included in this LOVE of Yours, dear Jesus...It is also for each one of us to pass on to another who is in need of Your Special kind of LOVE...

Praise be to You, Lord God! Praise be to You, dear Jesus! Praise be to You, Holy Spirit! All Praise be to You, Father, Son and Holy Spirit! All Praise be to You for Your great LOVE... ... ...

Betrayed   June 13

Matthew 26:47-50

At that very moment while he was still speaking, Judas, one of the Twelve, arrived with a great crowd armed with swords and clubs, sent by the Jewish leaders. Judas had told them to arrest the man he greeted, for that would be the one they were after. So now Judas came straight to Jesus and said, "Hello, Master!" and embraced him in friendly fashion. Jesus said, "My friend, go ahead and do what you have come for." Then the others grabbed him.

Oh Lord God, I feel betrayed...What happened all seems like a dream...I thought I was standing on firm ground...Suddenly it was pulled away and I fell sinking into shock and disbelief...Father God, how could this happen? You know that I was trying very hard to carry out my responsibilities honestly and lovingly...I have tried to be a peacemaker...

Now amidst the shambles of the situation, as I review what happened, it seems like I was in a nightmare—that it really could not

181

be happening. But now in the light of a new day, I realize that it did happen...

You, Jesus, know the real meaning of betrayal...You were betrayed, yet You were Perfect - are Perfect...You know the depths of betrayal...What an utter feeling of rejection and deep sorrow it is...

So, my dear Savior, because of what You suffered I can accept the situation...This betrayal came from one whose loyalty I had depended on. Their truthfulness could have confirmed what needed to be confirmed, but they denied the truth...

You know Lord, all the circumstances...You saw what happened; You heard it all...Deep down in my heart, in my spirit, I long to cry out! I want to vindicate myself, but others have believed the betrayer...

Yes, Lord, I accept this situation because of You...What does it really matter in the eyes of some...You know my heart; You know the truth...I am so very grateful, dear Jesus, that I have You in my life...I am so very grateful that I can turn to You, night or day and be comforted by You...I am so grateful for this happening, which seems so large today. It will grow smaller as time elapses. Oh thank You, Lord God, for bringing these hurtful experiences of life into proper perspective...

Life will go on and the hurt will disappear...Thankfully You, Lord God, dear Savior Jesus, will remain the same...You are the past, the present, the future. You are the same yesterday, today and tomorrow. You are my future life...You have gone on, Jesus, to prepare a place for me where there are no tears, no betrayal, no rejection, and no untruth.

Only LOVE, JOY and PEACE will be there in that Heavenly home! You are waiting for each of us to follow in Your path...Thank You Lord Jesus, thank You... ... ...

My Captain   June 14

Proverbs 3:5,6 (KJV)
Trust in the LORD with all thine heart; and lean not unto thine own understanding. In all thy ways acknowledge him, and he shall direct thy paths.

Independence: that was an important part of my being...It's good to be independent, why not? It meant to me that I could stand on my own two feet; I could make decisions for myself...I wouldn't hurt anybody else by my being independent...

It also meant to me "I won't bother you; so you shouldn't bother me!" In a sense "live and let live"...

Yet, Lord Jesus, I felt I had a relationship with You...I felt that I could continue to make all the decisions in my life and it wouldn't matter to You...How wrong I was, dear Lord, how wrong I was...Because it was my life, I really thought I was in charge...

As life continued, I gradually began to see how I needed help. I needed guidance. I needed the wisdom, which only You could bless me with.

I needed a Captain of my ship, my life...I needed to have You Jesus, climb on board and take charge of my ship...

Thank You Lord, for being willing to take over this rudderless ship and bring it to the port that You know is best for me.

I realize there will be stormy days and nights while You are steering and keeping on course, but because You are the Captain, I trust You in all Your decisions. I have put You, Almighty God, in control of my ship, my life...May I never question Your course for me...

I may go up to the bridge each day to chat with You, to pray with You, to communicate with You...Remember, Lord, the beauty of those beautiful white clouds against the blue, blue sky? Remember the gorgeous sunset we shared together last evening; remember the breathtaking rainbow we saw last week?

Oh Lord, Captain of my life, no matter what happens, our ship will sail on until the end with You and I together...Thank You, my Captain...Thank You... ... ...

That Voice That Speaks To Our Hearts   June 15

John 10:27

"My sheep recognize my voice, and I know them, and they follow me."

Galatians 5:25

If we are living now by the Holy Spirit's power, let us follow the Holy Spirit's leading in every part of our lives.

Oh God, how very thankful we are to hear that voice. Your very own voice speaks to us, each in a different way...To me Your voice is not an audible one—but a silent one...Though this sounds very confusing to some, others, dear Savior, understand because You also speak to them in this same manner...

Sometimes Your voice comes when we least expect it...We are caught up in doing our little busy things...We are not in the mood, sometimes, to hear this very distinct "silent" voice speaking to us...

How can a "silent" voice be heard? That is a mystery not easily understood... But it has happened so often that now I realize one very important thing — we must listen intently...

The second most important thing is to obey...That's the hardest part of all when Your silent voice speaks, Lord...Often You are telling me to do something, which I did not want to address. I wanted to handle the situation in an entirely different way...Then You enter in, my dear Lord...You tell me that You are expecting me to listen, and to choose to obey You... ... ...

This then, has caused me to respond to situations in a totally different way. But each time I obey You, my Lord, I see that Your Plan is the only answer in each specific case! My own feelings in the matter have to dry up and blow away...

How grateful I am, dear Lord, that You care enough to get involved in the goings on in my LIFE...The pettiness of circumstances seems to want to take over and cause a mountain to rise up where there was only a molehill...Peace like a lovely blue sky, lightly dotted with fluffy white clouds may then refresh our being when we let Your "silent" voice guide us...

Oh yes, dear Lamp unto our feet, please continue to speak to our hearts, with Your, oh so special, silent voice...May we become more sensitive to being aware of it, as we continue to listen and obey...The wisdom and guidance You pass on to us makes a difference in the way we act. Actions speak louder than words...

May our actions, Lord, become so Christ-like that others would be attracted to You, through our obedience... ... ...

Good Morning, Dear Lord... June 16

Psalm 23:4 (NIV)
Even though I walk through the valley of the shadow of death, I will fear no evil, for you are with me; your rod and your staff, they comfort me.

Good morning, Lord! You created the morning! You created the sun - the blessed sun that shines upon our Earth and brightens our days! Yes Lord, Your sun is shining this morning! It casts beautiful shadows, forming designs before our eyes...It shines down and causes the plants, trees, and flowers to grow...They lift their leaves, their limbs and faces up to You, Lord...They also say to You, "Good morning, dear Lord!"

The shadows sway back and forth in the breeze...They, even on a beautiful morning, can look almost ominous...What? A dark shadow looms in my beautiful morning? Is there a dark shadow in my life? Oh no, Lord God, that can't happen to me! Life is too wonderful for me! I can't handle that hovering dark shadow in my life! It looks like it will consume me, consume my life!

Help Lord, help! What's happening here? Everything was going so great for me!

"Yes, child of Mine, I am here... I am always here with you... Sometimes in the sunny times of your life, you put Me in the back part of your life... Once in awhile you say, 'Good morning Lord, good morning'... But where am I in the whole of your life? I want to be your best friend; allow Me to become your best friend... Reading your spiritual food for the day is wonderful, but don't forget about Me during the remainder of the day and night...

Yes, child of Mine, I am here... Whatever happens, whatever shadow may darken your life, I am here with you to brighten your life as only I can... I am brighter than the sun! I obliterate all shadows and make all things new... I am here, child of Mine, I am here."

Oh dear Jesus, thank You for Your comforting words...No matter what comes into my life, I know that You will always be with me... ... ...

The Secret of A Happy Marriage   June 17

Mark 10:6-9

"...For from the very first he made man and woman to be joined together permanently in marriage; therefore a man is to leave his father and mother, and he and his wife are united so that they are no longer two, but one. And no man may separate what God has joined together."

Dear Heavenly Father, here we are in an age where there are so many married people feeling the strains of their marriage and wanting to sever their bonds. It's happening all around us, Lord. What is the secret of keeping a marriage whole?

Lord, it is not for us to question Your command. We see that very plainly from Your words above. But, dear Father, what is the key to keeping marriages intact? There must be one, because there is a key to everything in this life if we can only find it! Please tell us where we can find this key or how to get it! There is so much need for it!

Thank You, dear Father, for again revealing what You want us to know! Reading Colossians 1:26- 27, Paul tells us,

He (God) has kept this secret for centuries and generations past, but now at last it has pleased him to tell it to those who love him and live for him, and the riches and glory of his plan are for you Gentiles too. And this is the secret: *that Christ in your hearts is your only hope of glory.*

Father, some will wonder at this secret! They will ask, what's that got to do with keeping a marriage from falling to shreds. They will have to study the entire message and note well the key word to the secret. Yes Father, the key word is "love". So many times this little word love, keeps popping up in our lives and unfortunately it is most always misunderstood...Paul said You were pleased to tell those who love You the secret! We first have to learn how to love, the unselfish way You want us to love...

We must learn the real meaning of love, a complete giving of ourselves to others in the way You want us to. Then we will see another part to marriage that perhaps we've never seen before. But there, plainly, in Your secret message to us is the most important part of marriage.

We must take God's message: "THAT CHRIST IN YOUR HEARTS IS YOUR ONLY HOPE OF GLORY" and think of marriage in the exact same way. "CHRIST IN YOUR MARRIAGE

186

IS YOUR ONLY HOPE." Thank You again, dear Lord, for opening our eyes to what You want us to see: our hearts and our marriage are one and the same! How plainly You speak to us if we would just look for Your truths and answers, dear Father! Your Holy Bible is just filled with wisdom!

We've always thought of marriage as a two-part contract, Lord - one man and one woman. Now we know that marriage is a contract for three. You are the first, then one man and one woman...You are the only hope, dear God, of success in marriage! You are the fixative holding the bond together! Without You holding fast to any marriage, there is little hope for happiness and success...This is what You wanted us all to know! Thank You, God, for sharing it with us...

Most of all, dear Jesus, never let us forget that we can only unlock this secret message from You with the little key, labeled "LOVE"...

If there is any doubt left in our minds as to what You want us to know, Paul again tells us in Colossians 3:18-19,

You wives, submit yourselves to your husbands, for that is what the Lord has planned for you. And you husbands must be loving and kind to your wives and not bitter against them, nor harsh.

Again there is that word, so small, yet so powerful: LOVE...That is the key to the secret of keeping marriage the beautiful relationship it was meant to be by our Heavenly Creator...We praise You, dear Lord, for this beautiful bond... ... ...

"IF..."   June 18

Philippians 4:4-7

Always be full of joy in the Lord; I say it again, rejoice! Let everyone see that you are unselfish and considerate in all you do. Remember that the Lord is coming soon. Don't worry about anything; instead, pray about everything; tell God your needs and don't forget to thank him for his answers. If you do this you will experience God's peace, which is far more wonderful than the human mind can understand. His peace will keep your thoughts and your hearts quiet and at rest as you trust in Christ Jesus.

Oh Lord, there are so many "ifs" in life...How can I know which "if" to take? If I do this, that will happen...If I don't do that, this will happen...If... ... ...

That little two-letter word can make such a difference in our lives - such a difference…"If only I hadn't done that, said that…" "If only I had the courage to do it…" "If only I could be successful like my friend…" "If only I could lose weight…" If only - if only - if only…

Lord, in reading the above verses from Philippians over and over again, we can see that verses four, five and six tell us to do things…In other words it seems again, that we have decisions to make…Verse seven holds a promise! IF we do the above three things, rejoice, act in a Christian manner and don't worry about anything, we WILL receive God's PEACE…It is more wonderful than the human mind can understand! Wow! Now that's quite a promise Lord!

A promise from You is the highest form of hope we can ever have, dear Jesus…We thank You for that promise and all the other promises which are in Your special book, the Bible…

How many times we have been told from others, ever since we were children: "If you do this, this will happen." If you don't do that, that will happen." "If you be good…" Lots of promises were made to us, as we grew older…Lots of promises were broken, too many of them…

But, a promise from You, Lord God, based upon verses four, five and six, does come true! You Do give the Peace that is so wonderful!

Oh Lord God, thank You for all Your promises…And now, hopefully, that little word "if" makes us realize what blessings can come "if" we obey… … …

Faults   June 19

Colossians 3:13,14(NIV)
Bear with each other and forgive whatever grievances you may have against one another. Forgive as the Lord forgave you. And over all these virtues put on love, which binds them all together in perfect unity.

"It wasn't my fault, Lord, I didn't do anything…Why do I always get blamed when things go wrong…It really wasn't my fault…"

"Faults: oh, I guess I might have one or two, or maybe even a few…But they're hardly noticeable, right Lord? At least, I hardly even notice them…"

188

It's strange though, how we can sometimes notice the faults in those around us...If only he didn't DO that! If only she WOULD do what she's supposed to do! Oh, Lord, how their faults can grow so large that they can become a stumbling block in our relationships...

It happens at home, at the office, driving back and forth to work, with our relatives, with our friends. Their faults pop-out and flourish!

Thank goodness my faults aren't as annoying as theirs! My faults are only "little ones". After all, no one is perfect!

Perfect, perfection - which leads us directly to You, Lord. You are the only Perfect One...Yet in Your Perfection, You gathered together with the imperfect...You Loved the sinners though You didn't love their sins...You were always there when sinners needed help. You came forth so many, many times offering forgiveness to a sinner...

Oh, so that's the reason we too must overlook others' faults, which bother us...You, who were and are perfect, forgave and overlooked the faults in those who were around You...So we, who are so imperfect, must forgive and overlook the faults in those around us...

Faults: we all have them...It is in dealing with them that makes a difference to those around us...We can be stubborn and get upset over their faults or we can overlook them...As we say a silent prayer to You, Father, we ask You to give us strength, courage and LOVE to overlook these faults. We are reminded of what You once said as You hung on Your Cross: "Father, forgive them for they know not what they do..."

Let us do the same, sweet Jesus... ... ...

Why, Lord, Why?   June 20

Job 33:12b, 13
For God is greater than man. Why should you fight against him just because he does not give account to you of what he does?

Oh Lord, You heard us cry out "Why, Lord, why?". In the natural we could only see and feel the agonies, the hurts, the rejections...

"Why, why, why?" our minds cry out! The mind always wants to be in control of things—all things concerning itself...

Yet, we are made up of so much more...We even think that the next important aspect is our body...Yes, how well we know how our

189

bodies can cry out! It's begging us to satisfy itself with food, perhaps alcohol or drugs. The cravings, the lust for bodily desires demands our attention...

The spirit is often forgotten...The soul which includes the mind, the will and the emotion wants control; it wants its demands satisfied. The spirit is low on the list of what the human being is all about...

But You, Lord God, created each of us with a spirit, a body and a soul...When the soul leads in one direction, the body in another, the spirit is left unattended and chaos results...Peace, that inner peace which only You God, can provide, is gone...

As we grope along questioning "Why this; why that," it's necessary to stop...We must look within the depths of ourselves to seek You. You are the God of Creation...We must then lay everything before You...

You dear Jesus, are the burden-bearer. You constantly have us close to Your Heart. You only want what is best for us and only You, in all Your Wisdom, know what is best for each of us...

All the mysteries, the "whys" and all the questions will become known to us when we meet You face to face...So until then, we must content ourselves knowing that You have us and all our circumstances in Your Loving Hands... ... ...

Pearl of Great Value   June 21

Matthew 13:45,46

"Again, the Kingdom of Heaven is like a pearl merchant on the lookout for choice pearls. He discovered a real bargain – a pearl of great value – and sold everything he owned to purchase it!"

Jesus, dear Lord, You used illustrations many times when speaking to the crowds of people who followed You around. It was Your way of teaching those who would listen. Some believed and others let Your words fall upon closed ears...

One such parable is when You spoke only to Your disciples when they questioned You specifically...Your explanation regarding the Kingdom of Heaven is given in the Scripture above.

But what did it actually cost to purchase that great pearl, Lord? Was it money alone? Does it mean we can buy our way into Heaven? Surely not, dear Lord, surely not!

For there are so many without the funds to pay for a great pearl, in order to get into Heaven…There are many worthy people, in the world's eyes, with the funds to buy their way in…But there are many, many more who are not considered worthy, to buy their way into Heaven. So Lord Jesus, please explain this to us:

"The cost, dear ones, may be different for each one who aspires to live with Me for all Eternity… First, you must recognize that I have already paid a price for each one of you to enter in. When I agreed to die for you, that was the initial cost. But there is a cost you must pay, each of you. No one enters in without paying… You, each of you, must recognize My Father, Almighty God, as the only true God. You must recognize Me as My Father's Only Son… You must admit freely to being a sinner… Then you must be deeply pained by the sins you have committed – those of commission and those of omission. You must ask forgiveness for these…

The final portion is you must recognize that it was I, who died for you. I open the door to the Heavenly Home I have gone before you, to prepare.

Understanding all these and with heartful consent, you have offered your portion of the cost. It is a very small price to pay for all that I have prepared for you, My cherished ones…

Realizing these thoughts, you will desire to live a different way of LIFE, if you have not already… So, My loved ones, each of your costs may be different but in essence, the same…

Do you now understand the parable about the pearl of great value?"

Dust   June 22

Genesis 2:7 (NIV)
And the LORD God formed man from the dust of the ground and breathed into his nostrils the breath of life, and man became a living being.

A tiny particle floated by, caught in the sunlight...Dust: a particle of what I am made of and of what I will become some day...I remember as a child I asked what those tiny particles were floating through the air...Dust - Lord, I never even thought of what significance dust would ever mean to me at that tender age...

What a miracle, Lord God! What a gift! Out of the dust You formed us and gave us the gift of life!

Then when our lives are over, the Scriptures again shed light on our future...In Isaiah 26:19 it says:

Yet we have this assurance: those who belong to God shall live again. Their bodies shall rise again! Those who dwell in the dust shall awake and sing for joy! For God's light of life will fall like dew upon them!

PRAISE GOD! THANK YOU LORD! No matter how many particles of dust we become, the miracle of resurrection will give us new bodies, which will be perfect in every respect! No more pain, no more problems, as our former bodies had...We are now perfect for our Heavenly home!

Lord God, thank You again for the miracle of Life! Psalm 139:1-10 reads:

O Lord, you have examined my heart and know everything about me. You know when I sit or stand. When far away you know my every thought. You chart the path ahead of me, and tell me where to stop and rest. Every moment, you know where I am. You know what I am going to say before I even say it. You both precede and follow me, and place your hand of blessing on my head.

This is too glorious, too wonderful to believe! I can *never* be lost to Your Spirit! I can *never* get away from my God! If I go up to heaven, you are there; if I go down to the place of the dead, you are there. If I ride the morning winds to the farthest oceans, even there your hand will guide me, your strength will support me.

How wonderful Lord, it is to know that though we, who will become dust someday, are so precious to You...Yes, we are all precious to You...We mean something to You, Creator, Master, Almighty God!!

Thank You Lord, for Your complex plan for us...If we look at it with the proper perspective, an excitement takes place! It is exciting! We are part of a Master Plan created by our Heavenly Father!

Thank You, Almighty God, thank You!!!

192

An Unseen Friend   June 23

John 14:15-17,26

"If you love me, obey me; and I will ask the Father and he will give you another Comforter, and he will never leave you. He is the Holy Spirit, the Spirit who leads into all truth. The world at large cannot receive him, for it isn't looking for him and doesn't recognize him. But you do, for he lives with you now and some day shall be in you."

"But when the Father sends the Comforter instead of me - and by the Comforter I mean the Holy Spirit - he will teach you much, as well as remind you of everything I myself have told you."

Holy Spirit, You are our unseen friend...We cannot see You...You are invisible, but You ARE real!!!

You ARE real! Many people today are not aware of You...Many Christians do not realize the importance of You! The Power that You are and what You can do for them doesn't seem to interest them...

When You left this Earth, Jesus, You had already told Your apostles about Your Holy Spirit...You referred to Him as the Comforter. And what else is the Comforter? The Holy Spirit is a helper, an unseen friend...

But what good is a friend if we do not call upon this friendship, which has been offered to us? A friendship cannot fully grow unless both parties are in close relationship with each other.

Communication is so necessary in a relationship...You are there waiting to comfort; to help; to share...If we don't come to You, Holy Spirit, we are cheating ourselves and grieving You...In this life, we really cannot afford to lose such a wonderful friend as You, Holy Spirit...

Then too, why would we want to deprive ourselves of You, our unseen Friend? It really doesn't make any sense!

Cause us to meditate upon those last days of Yours, Lord Jesus...Cause us to read and study the Scriptures. Help us to recognize the importance of You and Your Holy Spirit in each of our lives.

So, as these thoughts minister to our inner spirit, may we make a determined effort to recognize how awesome is this Gift given to us by our Savior and Lord, Jesus Christ...

May we deepen our understanding of what is available to us and Who is available to us! The power of God! The power of Jesus Christ! The power of the Holy Spirit - our unseen Friend... ... ...

A Flying Leap! June 24

Romans 8:38,39
For I am convinced that nothing can ever separate us from his love. Death can't, and life can't. The angels won't, and all the powers of hell itself cannot keep God's love away. Our fears for today, our worries about tomorrow, or where we are – high above the sky, or in the deepest ocean - nothing will ever be able to separate us from the love of God demonstrated by our Lord Jesus Christ when he died for us.

Oh Lord, the first thing I want to do when I leave this earth and see You waiting to greet me, is to take a flying leap into Your arms! I want to run as fast as I can and then take a flying leap into Your everlasting arms!

Oh, what JOY, what comfort, what security, what rest I shall experience...I want to stay there for as long as it takes for me to realize that I am finally with my true LOVE...

Oh yes, I have loved here on earth and it has been real love, from one human to another...But the LOVE between You and one of Your believers is the most true LOVE ever...

Once I'm there with You in my heavenly home, I can never hurt or disappoint You again...I can never make You sad...Oh, how that thought gladdens my heart at this moment...And, thank You dear Jesus, for loving me! Remember when I was so unlovable? And I am still unlovable at times, yet You continue to Love me...

When I recall some of my actions, some of the words that have been hurtful, some of my thoughts, I want to hang my head...I hate and despise the times I made You sad, Lord...When I realize the depth of Your forgiveness, the unconditional LOVE You have for me, it causes me to feel so grateful. Yet, I truly can't understand it...

You constantly think the best of me no matter how I mess things up...You see the good in me even when I can't see anything at all worthwhile in myself...

So Lord Jesus, now You can better understand why I want to run, to run so fast and take that flying leap into Your arms! I want to nestle down and stay there for as long as it takes to feel the security only You can give...

And when You set me down I will know I am truly home! I will know that I will be with You for all eternity! Oh, Jesus, thank You for loving me so very much – so very much... ... ...

Failure   June 25

Isaiah 49:25

But the Lord says, "Even the captives of the most mighty and most terrible shall all be freed; for I will fight those who fight you, and I will save your children."

How can I feel so close to You, my dear Lord, and still feel like such a failure? I thought I had done the best I could, but now I see that my efforts have not been effective...Still I continue because my Hope is in You...Of myself I plainly see that my efforts have dismally failed...I can only thank You, dear Savior, for giving us this Blessed Hope in You...

We see our young people going this way and that...All our efforts seem to disappear when we look at our children and perhaps, grandchildren...They were such a blessing to us at one time in our lives...What went wrong? Why did we fail? Where did we make such seemingly disastrous mistakes? When did this all begin to fall apart?

We, as parents, try so hard to be what we feel are good examples...Then we see as they grow, some of them toss away all the good work we have done to set good examples...Our hearts are crushed, dear Savior...Years which we have spent, seem as if they were wasted...Peer pressure appears to overrule the good we tried to instill in them...

Years pass on and on...Some seem to mature. Some say, "I'm a 'good' person. I don't need Christianity." Prayers after prayers are sent up to You, dear Father, as You already know...

"Be patient, dear one, all is not lost. The battle continues on, but I AM the Victor... Time is nothing to Me... You must trust and continue to pray and to believe. Keep close to Me and one day you will see success in your eyes, and Mine as well..."

195

Oh Lord, what would we do without You...Thank You, Lord, for standing fast for us and our loved ones, no matter what their ages may be...Thank You, Heavenly Father God, for Your awesome LOVE for each of Your children. You don't want to lose a single one of us! Thank You, dear precious Savior, Jesus Christ... ... ...

"Go Away! It Is Too Late!"　　　June 26

Matthew 25:1-13

"The Kingdom of Heaven can be illustrated by the story of ten bridesmaids who took their lamps and went to meet the bridegroom. But only five of them were wise enough to fill their lamps with oil, while the other five were foolish and forgot.

So, when the bridegroom was delayed, they lay down to rest until midnight, when they were roused by the shout, 'The bridegroom is coming! Come out and welcome him!'

All the girls jumped up and trimmed their lamps. Then the five who hadn't any oil begged the others to share with them, for their lamps were going out.

But the others replied, 'We haven't enough. Go instead to the shops and buy some for yourselves.'

But while they were gone, the bridegroom came, and those who were ready went in with him to the marriage feast, and the door was locked.

Later, when the other five returned, they stood outside, calling, 'Sir, open the door for us!'

But he called back, 'Go away! It is too late!'

So stay awake and be prepared, for you do not know the date or moment of my return."

Dear Jesus, as I was in thought, a man who recently died, came into my mind...You know who he is...He was here one day and the next day he was gone from this world...So quickly was he taken...In my heart Lord, I felt that he was ready, though his death was so sudden.

Then the thought came, Jesus...There was enough oil in his lamp; it was full...How much oil do each of us have in our lamps? Will WE be ready when that moment comes for us to meet our Creator face to face?

Age has no bearing on death...It can come when we are young, when we are in the best of health, enjoying the world's pleasures. It can come when it is least expected. It can come as a thief in the night...

People pay thousands of dollars for insurance to protect their valuables, their lives...Yet in many instances, Lord, they never think of insuring their souls. Their souls need to be assured of salvation, when their last breath is taken...Then their everlasting souls will live on forever with You, Almighty God!

You, Jesus Christ of Nazareth, ARE our insurance policy, which guarantees us entry into our Heavenly Home! You paid the premium when You went upon the Cross and died for each one of us...

Those who accept You as their Lord, and Savior, have their policies all paid by You! They are assured of their place in Heaven with You for Eternity! Thank You, Jesus, for being willing to be "our insurance policy". YOU are the oil in our lamps... ... ...

Have you checked your lamp to make certain it is full?

That Next Breath   June 27

Job 34:14,15 (NIV)
If it were his intention and he withdrew his spirit and breath, all mankind would perish together and man would return to the dust.

Oh Lord, we take for granted that next breath, the breath that keeps our bodies functioning...We get so used to breathing we completely forget that, of our own accord, we cannot do it! We cannot count on our next breath...We do not have the ability to breathe without You giving us this blessing - the breath of Life...

Yes Lord, as my body just took a deep breath, I was again made aware of that fact. I cannot count upon my next breath...It is You, Lord Jesus, Who decides if the last breath I took will be my last, or if You will continue to let me live on to breathe more Life into my body...

Each of us, as we arise in the morning, do not even know whether or not this will be the last day of our lives. We can make plans for the day, next weekend, next month, next year. The truth is we cannot be sure of our next breath…Yet we often act as if we are completely in charge of our lives.

How many who got up yesterday morning, were not able to get up this morning, because yesterday was their last day on this earth. Many, many were healthy and strong, with the will to live; yet yesterday was their last day here on earth.

Oh, Lord, cause each of us to realize that the gift of Life is truly in Your Hands…Cause us to appreciate You for that gift and to give You thanks for watching over us! Thank You for caring for us as we breathe each breath of Life… May we show You our appreciation for this awesome gift…

And Lord, when the time comes for our last breath, please let us be ready to meet You. Let us be able to face You with Joy!

Yes, Lord, may we be ready, as our last breath leaves our bodies… … …

Sin   June 28

Romans 7:21-25

It seems to be a fact of life that when I want to do what is right, I inevitably do what is wrong. I love to do God's will so far as my new nature is concerned; but there is something else deep within me, in my lower nature, that is at war with my mind and wins the fight and makes me a slave to the sin that is still within me. In my mind I want to be God's willing servant but instead I find myself still enslaved to sin.

So you see how it is: my new life tells me to do right, but the old nature that is still inside me loves to sin. Oh, what a terrible predicament I'm in! Who will free me from my slavery to this deadly lower nature? Thank God! It has been done by Jesus Christ our Lord. He has set me free.

Lord Jesus, how weak we can become at certain stages in our lives…While living as committed Christians, we can feel that sin never really can take hold of us again…But satan continues to lurk very close to us…He's always hoping and looking for us to take that step into sin…He knows our humanity, our weakness, so well we sometimes forget…

It is at that moment he jumps back into our lives triumphant! We only see that what we are doing "isn't all that sinful." But sin is sin…

We have only to let a short time pass and oh, how our conscience begins to speak to us..."Why did you allow yourself to fall down like that? You knew the situation was dangerous and yet you went right along with it..."

Then reality settles in...Remorse fills our beings...Then we realize how very weak we really are...Temptation had not come our way for a long time; we thought we were invincible...How wrong we were...How wrong we are to ever believe that...

It is only by Your Grace, Lord, protecting us that we don't fall more often...Yet when we willingly depart from You and Your protective Grace, we are vulnerable to sin...

No one can make us sin! Sin is our willingness to depart from what we know in our spirit to be wrong. As committed Christians we know the difference between what is acceptable to Jesus and what is not...

Lord Jesus, please forgive this failure, this sin...Please cause us to be more alert to circumstances, which can pull us down into sin...Please make us aware of the danger of sin so we will consciously decide we want no part in it. The burden of sin is too heavy to carry - the feeling of failure too overwhelming...

The worst part of it is the feeling that we have grieved You, Lord Jesus...We have failed You...We have been used to feeling close to You and now that sin has entered our lives again, the feeling of separation from You is so hurtful to our spirits...

Lord Jesus, thank You for Your forgiveness. Thank You for wiping our slates clean again as we truly come to You with contrite hearts. Ah-h-h...Already we feel better, for old satan has lost again...We now make a fresh start in our walk with You, Lord Jesus...Thank You for Your unconditional Love...Thank You...Thank You...Thank You, dear Jesus... ... ...

Hope Eternal   June 29

Romans 15:13 (NIV)
May the God of hope fill you with all joy and peace as you trust in him, so that you may overflow with hope by the power of the Holy Spirit.

Lord, my heart goes out to those who have not found Hope in You...Oh Lord God, Almighty God, Creator, how horrifying this thought is to me. To be without the Hope that I have in You would be terrifying! That thought shatters me! Oh God, I am so very grateful We found each other! All my Hope is in You...

Without Hope in You, there is nothing at all but drudgery here in this place...

Without Hope in You Lord, why go on in this world of ours...Without Hope there is no expected Joy for today or tomorrow...Without Hope in You, Jesus, nothing on earth can have the pleasure, which only You can give...

Oh God, please don't let me come to the point where I would lose my Hope in You...You are my Hope, my only Hope in all this world...

Friends, family, associates are all meaningless compared to my Hope in You, Jesus...But Lord, I do not want to be selfish. I want this precious Hope, which I have in You, to be shared by others...Please bring me to those who are deeply in need of Your Hope.

Suffering is part of this world, but suffering without the Hope You provide is double tragedy...There are so many lonely people, Lord...There are those who are so desperate, that they take their own lives rather than go on in this world...They had no Hope that Life could be different, because they did not choose to make a friend of You, dear Jesus...

Oh God, please bring Hope to all those who are desperate in this place, this world of ours...For You alone can do this...You do bring Hope...May this Hope bless someone especially at this moment, dear Heavenly Father...May they find Peace, because of their Hope in You...Thank You, Precious Lord, thank You... ... ...

I'm Listening, Lord...   June 30

Isaiah 28:23(NIV)
Listen and hear my voice; pay attention and hear what I say.

Psalm 121:8(RSV)
The Lord will keep your going out and your coming in from this time forth and for evermore.

"Listen..."

Yes Lord, I'm listening...I want to hear You speak to my inner self...I want Your direction, Your thoughts, Your desires for me...I want all that YOU want for me...

I'm listening, Lord...I'm listening...Speak to me clearly so that there will be no misunderstanding...

I feel You want me to close my eyes and rest...You want me to clear my mind so that I can concentrate on You...Yes Lord, I'm listening...

I feel as if I am nestled close to You, oh so very close to You, Lord...I feel contentment throughout myself...

"You are here, My child, at My bidding... Rest with Me... Take joy at knowing we are resting together... Keep your mind at peace... Breathe deeply... Breathe deeply... Relax! Now I have your attention... Now I can speak to you... There is a journey that you will be taking... You are safe... You are in My care..."

Oh Lord God, I don't understand...But because I am in Your care, because I trust You above all, I am at rest...I am in Your hands...

As You know Lord, I have made no plans for a journey, but You, being God, know what my future holds...Whatever the path, whatever the direction, I know that all is well because of You...

I am content because of You, Lord...Only You can bring each of us, Your children, to this state no matter what the circumstances are in our lives...May I continue to be sensitive to Your speaking to me...Yes, Lord, I am listening... ... ...

July

Mercy, Lord, Mercy   July 1

Luke 23:40-43

But the other criminal protested. "Don't you even fear God when you are dying? We deserve to die for our evil deeds, but this man hasn't done one thing wrong." Then he said, "Jesus, remember me when you come into your Kingdom." And Jesus replied, "Today you will be with me in Paradise. This is a solemn promise."

Dear Lord Jesus, have Mercy...Lord, have Mercy...You who are so merciful, Lord, have mercy...I look at myself, Lord Jesus, and I know that I need Your Mercy...

Sometimes we glide along for ages and ages not taking the time to look deep inside ourselves...Then when we do look inside, we realize that only Your Mercy, Lord, can bless us...

Yes, Lord, Your Mercy is a blessing to us - one that we are undeserving of, but which is so gratefully received...We cannot buy Your Mercy; it is not for sale...It will never be for sale...Yet Your Mercy was bought for us by the price You paid, when You allowed Yourself to be led like a lamb to be slaughtered...

It was Your Mercy which blessed the "good" thief who hung on his cross next to Yours. He believed in You and Your Mercy for him. He was promised a share in Your Heavenly Home! Oh Jesus, thank You for that example of Mercy! It blesses us! It makes Your Mercy real to us - believable to us!

Because of the Mercy You have shown to us, help us to be merciful to those around us...Let us be examples for others to follow so they in turn may be merciful to others...Mercy doesn't cost a cent...We can bless others by showing them mercy...It is part of our great Teacher's example to us so that we in turn can teach others...

Yes Lord, may we understand the fullness of the word Mercy. It is something that we cannot expect...It is given to us freely...May we be generous in giving mercy to others as You have done repeatedly to us, Lord Jesus...

Thank You, again, dear Lord Jesus, for Your Everlasting Mercy... ... ...

Peace and Quiet   July 2

2nd Thessalonians 3:16
May the Lord of peace himself give you his peace no matter what happens. The Lord be with you all.

It's strange Lord, the phrase "Peace and Quiet"...While I was expressing that phrase, I realized through Your wisdom, that it seems backwards!

Peace does not come before quiet time, at least, not usually...We need to settle down when it's quiet...As the quietness seeps into our spirits, then peace seems to follow...You are the great Refresher, Lord Jesus!

We need these quiet times, Lord Jesus...We need them as often as we need food and sleep...We are made up of body, mind and spirit...Each part of us - our body, our mind, and our spirit needs that quiet time.

Our bodies need the rest. Our minds need to stop the mental stimulation, which so often needs quieting down...Our spirits need the refreshment that comes when we, every part of us, truly quiet down...

As each part of us works in tandem, peace enters in...Our bodies feel relaxed. Our minds are without stress, and our spirits then rejoice as peace prevails...We are then one with You, dear Lord...

Oh Jesus let us long for these quiet times! Let us realize that it is not being selfish—but a necessity! It is a necessity because we must then share some of this peace which we experience, with others...

It may take the form of a sincere compliment to someone who needs to hear something positive...It may come in the form of doing a favor, a good turn to another...We have gained something ourselves from our quiet time with You...It is in keeping with Your way of LIFE that we give back to others some of what we have received from You...

One might say: "Oh, let him (her) get their own quiet time and then they will have that peace also!" But You and I know, dear Savior, that all the world does not know You...Many don't know that

You have so much more to give, if only they were aware of the real You...

There have been so many factions since You've come and gone, dear Lord...So many have lost the true meanings of what You came to teach...The rules have changed, been added to, been manipulated, been bent...It's no wonder that so many have decided that they don't want or need You...

Others have misrepresented You in their presentation of You...Oh, Lord, now we realize that is why You call each of us separately to You...You have a real work for us to do. You have a mission for us to accomplish...It is to LOVE, to LOVE our brothers and sisters of this world. That is why we need to come to You for this quiet time—to replenish ourselves through our time spent with You...

Peace and Quiet...

Quiet and Peace...

You Are In Charge, Lord   July 3

Isaiah 55:8,9
This plan of mine is not what you would work out, neither are my thoughts the same as yours! For just as the heavens are higher than the earth, so are my ways higher than yours, and my thoughts than yours.

Whatever happens, Lord, You are in charge...No matter how bleak the world conditions can appear, You are in charge!

In Habakkuk 1:3-4 it says:

Must I forever see this sin and sadness all around me? Wherever I look there is oppression and bribery and men who love to argue and to fight. The law is not enforced and there is no justice given in the courts, for the wicked far outnumber the righteous, and bribes and trickery prevail.

One has only to read the daily paper, Lord, to see what happened in Habakkuk's day, now prevails in our lifetime. One has only to listen to the radio or watch the news on television to actually see the evilness that exists here and now in the twenty-first century...How sad it must make You, Lord God, to realize that most men's hearts and motives have not changed since seven centuries before You were even born! Yet Lord, we can see down through the years, so little progress in man...Although every now and then, we may hear of a "good deed" done, because of the goodness in one man's heart...

In all of history, You have seen and are still seeing, what exists in the hearts of Your creation: mankind...In all of these years, You are still in charge, Lord...Like Habakkuk, we do not, so often, understand...Your ways are not our ways...We have placed our complete TRUST in You, Lord God...We KNOW that whatever Your plan is, whenever it takes place, it is the only answer in Your Eyes...

Trust - that's what You want from us, Lord, isn't it? No matter what is happening in this world, in our community, in our own family circle, You Lord God, Creator of the whole Universe, are in charge! You are in control! We are in Your care, because of Your Love, Your unconditional LOVE for us! So, away worries! Away cares! Away frets! GOD IS IN CHARGE! Praise You, Lord God! All Praise and Glory to You Almighty God!

GOD IS IN CHARGE!!!

Vacation   July 4

Psalm 121:3,4
He will never let me stumble, slip or fall. For he is always watching, never sleeping.

Today, dear Lord, You heard someone asking me, "When does God take a vacation?" You heard me laugh and say that God never takes a vacation!

Thank You, dear Creator, for never, never taking a vacation from us! In a way, it was a frightening thought!! Who could ever take Your place?

There is No One - No One! There is no one who could ever take Your place! I never want anyone but You to be there for me, for us...You, Father, Son, and Holy Spirit are as One. I accept on Faith that You are the One and Only for me...

You have been there throughout my life...You have shown me time and time again Your faithfulness...You have never deserted me. You help me with my burdens by taking them upon Yourself.

You comfort me; You allow me to be Your friend! What an amazing act of confidence on Your part, Lord, to allow me to be called Your friend…We all have friends in this world at one time or another in our lives. Blessed is a person who has friends and especially if they are loyal ones. You, precious Lord, are the perfect example of loyalty…You are always there for us. You always love us with Your unconditional Love, with Your forgiveness…Thank You, dear, dear Jesus…

No, dear Father God, do NOT take a vacation, even a very, very short one! That sounds very selfish, but Lord it is because we need You so! The Universe would turn black without You; all life would be so miserable without You…We love You! We want to know, to be assured, that You are where You've always been! Your Bible assures us that this is so…

Someday, when this earth and Universe have come to an end, You can take a vacation if You desire!! Your Heaven will resound with greater Joy than it's ever experienced before, because Your Plan and Purpose have been fulfilled…We will all help to celebrate with You, if You do desire to take a vacation! But knowing You as we do, being so loving and caring, we feel that You would not want to leave us…

Thank You, dear Savior, for Loving us so much…Thank You for Your forgiveness and Your faithful availability…What a gift You are to all of us… … …

True To Himself…   July 5

Acts 11:23b
… he was filled with excitement and joy, and encouraged the believers to stay close to the Lord, whatever the cost.

Oh Lord, I was just meditating on a young man's dilemma…The thought came, "Please Lord, let him be true to himself…" Immediately You spoke to me and said:

"Let him be true to Me first, then he will be true to himself…"

Yes, Lord, to be absolutely true to ourselves, we first must come into contact with You. But that first contact is only the beginning. We must move, want to move on from there…In any relationship there must be a willingness to get to know one another. It is that way with You, Lord Jesus...

When we make a commitment to You, not just a passing acquaintance, we are all the richer. For a relationship with You has real "meat" in it...It has the substance for a lifetime...But we must be true to that relationship.

When we are, truth comes forth in our lives...There is no more hiding this thing and that, even from ourselves...It cannot be a shallow life...Truth must be uppermost in our hearts, in our spirits...

Lord Jesus, I pray for this young man...I pray that, though he has failed several times already, that he will make a determination for You...He must finally decide that You are the only answer to his problems, his needs, his life! Lord, touch him...Open him up to Your reality...If he will only let the realness of You come forth, he will become the person You want brought forth.

Oh, Jesus, there is a world full of those who need the realness of You in their lives...Men, women, children all need the realness of You. As we draw closer to the end days here on earth we have seen how the morals of the world are changing drastically...We need You more than ever, dear Jesus! We need You more than ever...

Only You can touch the hearts of mankind...May Your Holy Spirit's Power to open hearts multiply, so that there will be a great desire for revival, true revival! The world needs this, Lord, as You know...Each soul here needs Your Holy Spirit's Power desperately...

May this happen, dear Savior, and may it happen soon so each person in this world will be true to You and true to himself - or herself... ... ...

Puny, Puny Me...   July 6

Psalm 119:141
I am worthless and despised, but I don't despise your laws.

Psalm 42:7,8
All your waves and billows have gone over me, and floods of sorrow pour upon me like a thundering cataract. Yet day by day the Lord also pours out his steadfast love upon me, and through the night I sing his songs and pray to God who gives me life.

Oh Lord, I try to realize the vastness of You, the awesomeness of You, the majesty of You! As I try to relate to You, all I can think of at times, is puny, puny me...

How do I have the nerve to think that I can relate to You, the Creator of all the Universe? How can I think that You, being God, would have anything to do with me?

I aspire to communicate with You, Lord God...What nerve! Who do I think I am to try to have a "oneness" with You...

Yet, Lord God, there is something inside of me that tells me You want to communicate with me also!

Sometimes I feel as one of the psalmists...I want to continue to aspire and relate with You. But at times, I feel that the unworthiness of myself is more than You can tolerate...

Dear Lord, lift up my spirit; lift up my heart! Let me know that You do find something about me worth relating to...I am so lonely...Lord, my spirit cries out for Your companionship...No one can take the truth from my heart that You do care!

Oh-h-h, a glimmer of Your Perfection filters down upon me! It leaves me with such peace...No matter what my earthly worth may be, no matter how puny I am, You, Mighty God, do care for me!

How wonderful this thought is: my God Loves me just as I am! Though I want to be absolutely perfect for You, Lord, You know that I am not...But Lord, I am trying; I will continue to try...I want to please You, Lord God...

Just think, here I am relating to my Lord, and You Love it!

You Love me...

Do you realize how much HE LOVES YOU?

"Reach Out And Touch Someone"   July 7

John 15:12
"I demand that you love each other as much as I love you."

Romans 5:8
But God showed his great love for us by sending Christ to die for us while we were still sinners.

Lord Jesus, the above phrase "Reach out and touch someone" is a phrase that a lot of us have heard...It is a commercial message...The bottom line is to cause people to utilize a particular product...

It has a good meaning too...Perhaps we Christians should adopt this phrase also, right, Lord? So many of us don't reach out enough to show the world that being a Christian is more than going to church on the Lord's Day...

If we Christians don't step out, and not just once or twice, we are not fulfilling what You, Jesus, desire us to do...Reaching out and touching someone means that we reach out with Your LOVE: Your pure LOVE...

We cannot reach out and truly touch someone if the bottom line does not have Your Love in it, Lord God...It must not be a mechanical reaching...It must be from the heart...

We can do this by giving of ourselves as we do something for someone else with no strings attached. Sometimes we might think when we do a good turn, that person should return another to us...No, no - that is not the basis for reaching out...

The basis is what You, Lord Jesus, did for each one of us in Your great LOVE...You, Lord Jesus, carried a huge, heavy wooden cross for me...You carried it for all Your children...After You carried it, You were hung on it. You were still breathing, suffering the agony of nails thrust through Your hands and Your feet...

Some were there who had reached out to You and crushed a crown of thorns upon Your precious head...Then someone reached out to You as You hung there and ripped open Your side, spilling out the last Blood and liquids from Your Body...

Yes, Lord, there were those who reached out to You with their ugliness and hatred...Now we can understand better by Your sacrificial act why we must reach out and touch others with Your kind of unconditional LOVE...

Soften our hearts, Lord Jesus, so that we may carry on what You came here on earth to teach: LOVE, LOVE, LOVE... ... ...

Silent Ears   July 8

Matthew 13:15 (NIV)

"'For this people's heart has become callused; they hardly hear with their ears, and they have closed their eyes. Otherwise they might see with their

209

eyes, hear with their ears, understand with their hearts and turn, and I would heal them.'"

Oh, Lord, there are so many in Your world with silent ears. They have ears for hearing all that they want to hear, but when Your name is mentioned, suddenly their ears are closed. They hear nothing; they have silent ears…

There are so many, Lord Jesus…There are the young, so busy, so full of life…There are the career people, whose sole attention is to become successful in the eyes of the world…There are the elderly, who would not listen all during their years of living in this world. Now in loneliness they are sitting in their homes or nursing homes. There are those living on the streets…All these have ears that have been silent to hear anything about You, Lord Jesus…They all seemingly, have refused to listen… … …

What wasted lives are those especially, Lord, who sit and wait for death to come. Hope is not a word that comforts them; many say there is nothing after death…How sad, Lord Jesus, how very sad…

At least those who are young have, hopefully, a lifetime to make a decision for You…And those who are striving for success may suddenly realize that success is an empty attainment…

Oh, if only they would open up their ears and let Your Truth filter in! Oh, if only they would listen and really hear Your messages! For You offer so much, Lord, so very much - Eternity with You! There will be no tears, no heartaches, no pain. In Heaven JOY, LOVE and PEACE reign with You, Jesus, and our Heavenly God, Father of us all!

Yes, Jesus, we don't understand it all now, but we accept on FAITH that what You taught Your apostles is true. All You shared with them will come to pass some day…Oh, Lord, please help us to help others come to understand You fully, while they are still here…

Lord, our hearts ache as we see in our minds' eyes, those who are elderly and know You not…Our hearts ache for them…Have mercy, dear Lord, have mercy; cause them to hear again about You, and open up their silent ears…

Dear Lord, You know at this very moment those who are closest to death. No matter what their age may be, please give them one more chance to say "Yes" to You…Please, dear Lord, please… … …

"Do You Love Me?"   July 9

Romans 14:19 (RSV)
Let us then pursue what makes for peace and for mutual upbuilding.

1ˢᵗ Peter 4:8 (NIV)
Above all, love each other deeply, because love covers over a multitude of sins.

"Do you love Me? Do you really love Me?"

Oh Lord, You know I do! You know I do! I'd do anything for You!

Anything covers so much - anything? Does it mean I have to subject myself to those unpleasant experiences, people or situations that I find myself in? You know, Lord Jesus, some of the time it isn't my fault...Somehow or other I seem to get involved in situations which I did not cause...

"Then you must become a peacemaker for Me..."

But Lord, I don't have the credentials for taking on that kind of responsibility!

"I will speak through you. Be willing to be My peacemaker and I will provide you with the wisdom you will need... Only be willing..."

Thank You, Lord Jesus...I am willing to be Your peacemaker...I will not take any credit for any successes, but give You all the Glory, for You are our powerful God Almighty!

Yes Lord, LOVE can cover even the difficulties in Life...It carries a lot of responsibility. It is so easy to say the words sometimes—I LOVE YOU...But when we truly understand the real meaning of LOVE, we become more mature, more understanding. Real LOVE is a PURE LOVE...

Father God, help me to continue to grow in carrying out all that You want me to understand concerning LOVE...For You are the epitome of TRUE LOVE - PURE LOVE...You gave Your LIFE for each of us...You willingly died a cruel death because You LOVE each and everyone of us no matter what our circumstances are...

"Do you love Me? Do you understand now what I mean when I ask you that question, dear one?"

Yes, Lord Jesus, I realize that when I say I love You, though You are in Heaven, Your LOVE can be reflected through me...My love for You can bless others...LOVE, pure LOVE, is so desperately needed in our world...

"Go now, and truly love..."

A Price To Pay   July 10

1ˢᵗ John 4:10,11 (NIV)

This is love: not that we loved God, but that he loved us and sent his Son as an atoning sacrifice for our sins. Dear friends, since God so loved us, we also ought to love one another.

There's a price to pay when we love, right Lord? Because when we love we have to be open...To be open means that whatever the situation, circumstance or position the one we love is in - we are obliged to become involved...

So there is a price to pay when we say we love someone...Love covers so many people in our lives. We have been conditioned to think that a loved one might necessarily be a sweetheart or spouse...There are so many others who fit into the "Love" category...

Each one in our family needs our love...Parents, children, siblings, grandchildren, grandparents, all our relatives need our love...Our friends need our love...Our neighbors need our love...The world needs our love!!! But how can we love the whole world? We say, "I am only one person, what can only one person do to make a difference?"

One person can do a meaningful thing for another...That person does something meaningful for another. Then that good deed is passed along to another and so a beautiful chain of loving deeds continues on and on...So if more than one person starts a chain of love, there can be love chains crisscrossing all over the Universe!

Oh Lord, what a blessing that would be to all the world! What a blessing it would be to You as You look down and see the love passing from one to another...

Yes, Lord, there is a price to pay when we love...But when we do, along with the price come blessings! The blessings may not be immediate, but they will come...

You, Lord Jesus, paid a price to set us free…It was the ultimate example of LOVE…The price You paid was extreme, is extreme…Because we are imperfect none of us could ever pay a price like that, Lord, as You were Perfect, without fault or blemish…

So Lord, dear precious Savior, may we thank You again for the example of LOVE, PURE LOVE, You left for us?

Thank You, dear Lord, dear Savior, dear Jesus…Thank You for paying the price…May we who profess to be followers of You, Jesus, be willing to pay a price when You deem it necessary…May we be a willing vessel to be used by You, to continue the LOVE You came down to teach us about…May we be a blessing to You, dear Lord… … …

Blow Wind, Blow!   July 11

Acts 2:2a, 4a (RSV)
And suddenly a sound came from heaven like the rush of a mighty wind, …And they were all filled with the Holy Spirit…

Blow wind, blow! Holy Spirit blow over all the earth! Surround this earth with Your Breath of freshness! Blow away the insensitivity of mankind…Blow away hatred, selfishness, anger, lust for power, immorality, and prejudice…And then blow gently into the hearts of mankind all Your worthy characteristics, Holy Spirit…Hopefully, these thoughts are like prayers to You, Jesus, for today the world is filled with war and evil.

Men are designing instruments to kill. Then these weapons are used to kill and cripple all who are in the path of these instruments of death…Everywhere we look evil seems to be more and more evident. Dear Jesus, it must be so discouraging for You to look down and see the circumstances mankind has caused here…

Oh, that it would be possible for Your wind, Holy Spirit, to blow away all evil thoughts that allow men to destroy and kill…Oh, that it would be possible to blow away the immorality that now exists in this world…Oh, that Your wind could blow innocence back into mankind…

This is possible, Lord Jesus, but ONLY when You are the POWER behind the decision to end all these tools of evil…For You

213

alone are Pure Goodness...You represent ALL Goodness! You are sensitive to every living person and creature...When one gets to truly know You, then hatred, selfishness, and anger disappear. Lust for power, immorality, and prejudice are also blown away!

Then the real human being appears, the human being that You, Lord God, Creator of all mankind, created. Then true goodness can exist throughout this earth...

The Scriptures tell us in Titus 2:11,12(NIV):

For the grace of God that brings salvation has appeared to all men. It teaches us to say "No" to ungodliness and worldly passions, and to live self-controlled, upright and godly lives in this present age,

Though we, as Christians, are in the minority, please give us the courage, Your courage to make a difference in this world...And dear Jesus, please bless us...Let us know how touched You are to see Your children continuing on, despite the world's negative condition...

Thank You, Lord, for the patience You have with us...Thank You, Lord God, thank You... ... ...

Nothing Lasts But You Lord, And Your Believers
July 12

1ˢᵗ Thessalonians 4:16,17

For the Lord himself will come down from heaven with a mighty shout and with the soul-stirring cry of the archangel and the great trumpet-call of God. And the believers who are dead will be the first to rise to meet the Lord. Then we who are still alive and remain on the earth will be caught up with them in the clouds to meet the Lord in the air and remain with him forever.

There will come a time Lord, when I will be completely forgotten...No one will remember that I even existed...

I don't know the names of my ancestors, several generations ago...It's as if they never existed. Time will pass and the same will happen to me, eventually...Will it matter to anyone that I ever lived? Probably not...

But the exciting realization is that You Lord God, know I exist now and You will always be aware of my existence! I will never be forgotten by You! No matter how many more centuries come and go, I will be remembered by You! Oh thank You Lord God, for Your enduring LOVE for me, for each one of us who calls You Savior and Lord...

For nothing here on Earth lasts; eventually it will all be gone...Nothing lasts but You Lord...What comforting thoughts these are: You will always be what You are, Who You are, Why You are, Where You are...

Thank You Heavenly Father, for calling me into Your Family of Believers...How I long for my loved ones to call You their Savior, their Lord...Thank You for the Faith I have that You Will draw them in...It may be in my lifetime; it may not. But because You have taught Your children to have Faith, I stand on that belief...

Yes, some day there may not be one shred of evidence that I ever lived, but that is not important...As the Scriptures say, our bodies will dry up and blow away...But our spirits, Lord, will live on as You promised they would...

It is unimportant for any one of us to be remembered, but only that You are remembered...You created the Universe. You are! You were! You will always be!

Nothing lasts but You Lord - and Your believers... ... ...

"Do You Have A Writing For Me Today?"
July 13

Habakkuk 2:2a (RSV)
And the Lord answered me: "Write the vision; make it plain upon tablets,..."

Lord, do You have a writing for me today?

"Yes child, I have one for you whenever you come to Me and desire to write down our thoughts together..."

WOW, Lord God! Wonder of Wonders! For that is what "WOW" can stand for! Wonder of Wonders, that's what You are, Lord God! Wonder of Wonders that You, Creator of all, would be willing to give of Yourself to me—to share Yourself with all those who desire a very special relationship... ... ...

Well Lord, what will it be today? What would You expressly desire for me to put on paper, this paper - this blessed paper...

Does this paper feel blessed to have Your thoughts written upon it, Lord Jesus? In my childlike delight, I think so...It came from a living thing, a tree. That tree, once living somewhere in this world which You created, has now the blessing of being used for You, dear Jesus. For this is a letter of LOVE between You and I...

This paper, once a miniscule part of a living tree, has been chosen above all other paper to reflect words between You and I...It is an instrument to be used by You, Lord God. I, too am only an instrument used by You to express thoughts prompted by our sharing these moments together...

Tree, now long gone, thank you for being a vessel...Hopefully you produced other trees in your lifetime, which will continue sharing themselves for mankind...May each of us who read these words be willing ourselves, to be used. May we be willing to plant seeds for others and to continue being vessels for You, dear Father...

Just as this paper is being used, Lord, to express these thoughts, I thank You again for the paper used to print Your Word, the Bible...Tree, then paper, then words – these communicate from a living tree to living souls...

May You, Jehovah, God Almighty, touch countless numbers through the pages of Your Living Word, the Bible...Thank You, Lord, thank You, for touching us with these special thoughts... ... ...

Take One Day At A Time   July 14

Matthew 6:34

"So don't be anxious about tomorrow. God will take care of your tomorrow too. Live one day at a time."

Lord Jesus, You have said in Your Scriptures that we need only take one day at a time...I'm so comforted to realize that again! That's as much as I can take care of, dear Lord...Even that sometimes, seems like too much...

But, through it all, we still have You...You are always there, no matter what the circumstances, no matter what...That's so comforting, Lord, so needful...You have also told us in the Scriptures that You are the burden bearer...We need only to turn over our problems to You...

Again, dear Lord that is such a comforting thought...It does not necessarily mean that the problem, the difficulty will disappear. But just knowing that You are the great "I AM" causes us to calm down...We begin to thank and praise You for the wonderment of Yourself and for all the blessings You have given us in the past...

The Creator of this Universe cares for us in our needs! It seems preposterous! How can this be? How can the Almighty God, the Alpha and the Omega, care for a tiny life who is suffering here on earth? How can we matter to so great a God? How can He know about each of us in a personal way? It's a mystery to us...

Tomorrow may come, but today is here...Today is what's happening and that is all we need to take care of...How we need Your guidance, Your wisdom, and Your protection, dear Savior...How we need Your caring, Your forgiveness, and Your unconditional LOVE! With Your help dear Jesus, each of us, no matter what our circumstances are, can make it through this one day...

Was that the chirp of a bird? Yes, Lord! It is another reminder which You told us about in Your Scriptures in Matthew 10:29:

Not one sparrow (What do they cost? Two for a penny?) can fall to the ground without your Father knowing it.

You provide for these little creatures, so surely You care for us, Your children...

So, Lord Jesus, thank You for reminding each of us that we need only to take one day at a time...We must leave it in Your Hands while we give You our thanks for all the blessings You have showered us with in the past...

Oh, Heavenly Father, thank You for the faith to take one day at a time... ... ...

Because Of You...   July 15

Lamentations 3:23
Great is his faithfulness; his loving kindness begins afresh each day.

Lord, the words "what difference can a day make" came to me from out of the blue! Immediately You quickly changed the phrase around and added one little word! What a difference it made! It becomes "what a difference a day can make!"

217

Yes, dear Lord, because of You, what a difference a day can make...Yesterday there was depression, despondency...Today - new hope, a freshness of body, mind and spirit has come about, because of You! There is LIGHT in the tunnel where once there was only darkness...

Yes, precious Lord, You are the LIGHT of the World; You are the HOPE of the World...Without You, dullness and drabness exist...One day becomes like another...Depression, deep depression settles in like a shroud...

Oh God, why do so many refuse Your LIGHT? Why? Why do some elect to accept You, to hold You in the highest esteem, while others refuse to acknowledge You...

Because of You, miracles still happen every day, all over this earth! If they were to be written down, the little miracles, the big miracles, the huge miracles, they would fill countless libraries!

Strangely enough, there are many who disclaim the miracles You bring about! They say it was just a coincidence of happenings...But Lord Jesus, we who have seen Your miracles, no matter what the size, know that You continue to perform them!

There are some doctors who cannot understand why a particular person is dramatically healed, because they cannot account for the healing...They shake their heads...Why do some feel reluctant to say, "This is a miraculous healing from our Almighty God!" Why do they find it so hard to bow to You in thankfulness for intervening in some of their cases?

But, You and we know, dear merciful Healer, it was all because of You...

Thankfully, it is ALL because of You - the LIGHT of the World... ... ...

You're My Brother, Jesus...   July 16

Luke 8:21
he remarked, "My mother and my brothers are all those who hear the message of God and obey it."

Yes, You said it Yourself, Jesus! In Matthew 12:50, You said: "...Anyone who obeys my Father in heaven is my brother, sister and mother!"

Wow, Lord Jesus! That's such an exciting thought! You are so very many things to me already: Master, Teacher, Savior, Lord, Friend and Sacrificial Lamb who died for me...

I've read that verse many times before, but it has just penetrated my inner being, my spirit...You, Jesus Christ, are my brother! Brother denotes so many thoughts...You are the big brother who is always there when the sibling is in need...You are the big brother who is there to counsel—to comfort, to encourage, to guide, and to be an example...But, You are so much more!

We don't have to have an appointment to see You or speak to You, since You came down to our level... That thought puts our minds spinning! But Jesus Christ is in the role now not of an earthly brother but as a Heavenly brother who is perfection itself - amazing!

We all need a big brother, one to whom we can talk - with no holding back...We all need a brother to confide in—to talk to, to share all that's inside us which needs to come out...

Thank You, dear Jesus, for these comforting words

"anyone who obeys my Father in Heaven is my brother, sister and mother!"...

Many of us have had earthly brothers...Some of them failed to be all we wanted or needed them to be...Others were a blessing to their siblings...Each one of us now, no matter how young or old, can feel with earnestness, that we do have a big, powerful, all loving, caring brother whose name is Jesus...He is a brother who answered His Father's call to die for us!!! Imagine, He willingly died for us - for you, for me!

We have no concept of the depth of His LOVE for us! He died for each of us, no matter how much we have failed...No matter how much we have sinned, He is still willing to be our brother...Like the song says: "Oh how He loves us, oh how He loves us, oh how He loves you and me."

Thank You, dear brother Jesus... ... ...

"Who Do You Say That I Am?"   July 17

Matthew 16:15-17 (RSV)

He said to them, "But who do you say that I am?" Simon Peter replied, "You are the Christ, the Son of the living God." And Jesus answered him, "Blessed are you, Simon Bar-Jona! For flesh and blood has not revealed this to you, but my Father who is in heaven."

"Who do you say that I am?" You asked that question to Peter, dear Jesus...He answered: "You are the Christ, the Son of the living God." That was the correct answer...

But what about us? Who do we say that You are? Are You a prophet perhaps, a good person or one of the several sons of God? Are You a "higher being", the Light, the "man upstairs"?

Why is it so hard to believe that YOU are God? Why not believe it? What or who do we have better than You to believe in, dear Jesus...It seems that all human beings have had the desire to worship a god of some kind...Some of these gods have been visible; others have not...There is, inside of us, a part that seems to want to pray to someone...Man is still discovering ancient peoples who have buried with them idols which they worshiped as their gods.

When the Bible became known to mankind, we were able to read for ourselves what was written centuries ago. It was written about the coming of a Savior: You, Jesus Christ...The Old Testament reflects this. Then in the New Testament, it was written about Your Birth...It was written about Your Life, Your Death, Your Resurrection...It was written about the Miracles You brought about for so many.

Yet there were so many who would not, did not believe in who You were...You must have sighed deeply many times at their unbelief, dear Jesus...It must have been so very discouraging to realize how many saw the Miracles and still turned away from You...When You drew near Jerusalem, You wept because of the continuing disbelief of many people...

There is an old expression that seems to be so appropriate: "You can lead a horse to water, but you can't make it drink..." Yes, Lord Jesus, that reflects on the Living Water You wanted to share with each of us...You are the Living Water...

We can understand the mystery of the Living Water by reading the Bible. When we ask Your Holy Spirit to open our spirits to Your understanding, we then can understand...

Who do YOU say that I am?

"You are the Christ, the Son of the living God."

The Door   July 18

Revelation 3:20,21

"Look! I have been standing at the door and I am constantly knocking. If anyone hears me calling him and opens the door, I will come in and fellowship with him and he with me. I will let everyone who conquers sit beside me on my throne, just as I took my place with my Father on his throne when I had conquered."

The door is the heart of man...Each of us must make a decision...Each of us must decide whether to open the door of our heart, or to ignore the knocking and keep the door closed.

In this world there is much to shut out the sound of knocking at our door...Even repeated knockings can be unheard, because of what we choose to cover them up with...

Music, for example - music can soothe tired nerves. It can lull babies to sleep; it can bring us into a spiritual experience...It can blast our ears and drown out all else around...This is just one of the many examples...

So each of us must make a decision to cause our ears to be sensitive to the sound of Your special knocking, Lord Jesus...Or we can decide to block that sound out of our lives and overlook it...Once we get in the habit of overlooking your communications, it becomes easier and easier to ignore and forget them.

But You, Lord Jesus, continue to knock...You said it Yourself; so it is true...You are waiting for each of us to open the door of our heart...You, Almighty God, stand at our hearts' doors waiting to come in.

Sometimes we open the door for a peek at You, Lord...Then we close it again hoping You will go away...Sometimes we open the door halfway and even speak a few words to You, and then close the door. But when we open the door fully, and invite You in, then we can begin fellowshiping together!

You will invite whoever opens the door to You and welcomes You in, to spend Eternity with You! What an exciting promise! Then when our time comes to leave this earth, we are whisked off to Heaven to spend our real Life with You, Jesus! How can anyone possibly ignore this?

"Look! I have been standing at the door and I am constantly knocking."

Sh-h-h-h...Listen, do you hear a knock???

Only Three Years...   July 19

Matthew 22:37-39

Jesus replied, "'Love the Lord your God with all your heart, soul, and mind.' This is the first and greatest commandment. The second most important is similar: 'Love your neighbor as much as you love yourself.'"

Three years, Lord, that's all You were in Your Ministry here on Earth...Yes, You were 33 years old when You went to the Cross...Then You died for us, for me. You only started when You were 30 years old...

That seems so strange to me, dear Jesus...One would think You would have started earlier, say at 25 years of age. But for some unknown reason to many of us, You started at 30 years of age and ended only three years later...Was that fact a secret only Your Father knew? Did You know You would have only three years to undertake the huge responsibility of teaching so many what You came to teach us?

When this thought came to me, it caused me to wonder about the shortness of Your Ministry...So much had to be accomplished—so many with whom to share Your thoughts, Your messages, Your illustrations in such a brief span of time...

Yet, more than two thousand years later, here I am dwelling on You. I am reading the Scriptures about You and meditating about You. I am believing You. I am Loving You. I am Praising You...

So dear Lord, the short length of time did not deter You from getting Your messages solidified and passed down to all generations since You walked this earth...

What an accomplishment! The truth which You spoke about so touched the lives of 12 men that they gave up their lives to follow You...They were eager to learn from You, to follow Your example...And, Lord, You truly were an example to them just as You still are today...

We have only to read about You and Your LIFE, and then ask You to give us understanding. Then, hopefully, we will also follow You...We happily take on the name of "Christian" because of You, Jesus Christ.

Three years or twenty years, we can see now that it was not the length of time You taught...It was the message itself: to love You and then to love one another as we love ourselves...Teach us, even now, dear Jesus that we must also learn to love ourselves...That is so difficult for so many of us...But it is so necessary to do before we can truly carry out Your message:

"LOVE ONE ANOTHER"... ... ...

You Are The Vine...   July 20

John 15:1-5

"I am the true Vine, and my Father is the Gardener. He lops off every branch that doesn't produce. And he prunes those branches that bear fruit for even larger crops. He has already tended you by pruning you back for greater strength and usefulness by means of the commands I gave you. Take care to live in me, and let me live in you. For a branch can't produce fruit when severed from the vine. Nor can you be fruitful apart from me. Yes, I am the Vine; you are the branches. Whoever lives in me and I in him shall produce a large crop of fruit. For apart from me you can't do a thing."

Thankfully, Lord Jesus, You are the Vine and we are the branches...We, the branches, need the LIFE flow from the Vine, from You...If we are cut off from the Vine, slow death, spiritual death, takes place...

This world is so complex, so opposite from Your teachings, Lord Jesus. It teaches that if someone hurts us, we should hurt that person back...You teach us to turn the other cheek.

Throughout the New Testament, there are several examples similar to this...Therefore, we need desperately to be connected to the

Vine, to You, Lord Jesus...For You are our sustenance, our nourishment...We cannot grow spiritually without you, Lord Jesus...

No matter what happens, we must remain connected to You...We can plainly see in Nature what happens to branches that splinter...They are weak; they cannot produce good fruit...

The vine has a purpose. It is to support the branches...It is necessary for the branches to exist. Without the Vine, there could be no branches...Therefore, we must realize, and we thank You, dear Jesus, for this realization, that You are the Vine...You also are the Key, the Beginning, the Giver of LIFE, and the Cornerstone...

All good comes from You, Lord God...Anything good has to emanate from You...You are the source - You are All...You are the Almighty Creator, the one true God...

We are in debt to You, dear Jesus...You make it possible to leave this LIFE and go to our real Home, because of Your Divine decision to go to the Cross - for us...Yes, dear Lord, Heaven awaits those who truly believe in You...

We, who are Your branches, are so grateful that You are the Vine...Yes, Lord Jesus, You are the true Vine... ... ...

The Majesty Of Yourself!   July 21

Psalm 93:1,2,5

Jehovah is king! He is robed in majesty and strength. The world is his throne. O Lord, you have reigned from prehistoric times, from the everlasting past.

Your royal decrees cannot be changed. Holiness is forever the keynote of your reign.

Lord, as I was gazing out upon Your ocean and Your sky, I suddenly saw in my mind's eye, the awesomeness of You, appearing as if rising from the horizon!

You filled the sky with Yourself! The majesty of Yourself filled my soul with excitement!

Oh Lord God, You are larger than the oceans, larger than the skies, larger than the earth! The wonderment of You is incredible! OH, PRAISE YOU GOD FOR THE MAJESTY OF YOURSELF! ALL PRAISE, ALL GLORY goes to You alone, Lord God!

Sometimes we Christians lose sight of that majesty! Sadly in this world sometimes Your name is used in a derogatory manner. Those who don't know You do not realize the POWER that You hold!

Kings and Queens of this world are catered to, bowed to, curtsied to; their every wish is met...Yet You, KING OF KINGS, hear Your name shouted out in anger, even as a curse time after time...

Oh Heavenly Father, they do not understand who You really are! You are the great "I AM"! You are the Beginner and the Finisher of this earth! KING OF KINGS! Oh, Father God, how we, who recognize You, long to see and hear You receive Your proper recognition!

Oh what a marvelous, exciting day that will be when all earth will resound with PRAISES flooding the air with Honor and Adoration for You!

You are Creator of the whole Universe, as man knows it today...Yet You know all - including everything which still waits to be discovered, because You created it all! Men think they have answers, but You are the answer and hold all the answers!

You know the mystery of the Trinity where You are God, You are Son Jesus and You are Holy Spirit. This is beyond our understanding, just as man does not understand how the Universe was created...

Because it is written in the Scriptures, we accept this mystery and know that it and all mysteries will be revealed to us one day in the hereafter...Oh, Your Majesty, Your Highness, may we never lose sight of the majesty of Yourself... ... ...

"Be Still And Know I Am Your God."   July 22

Psalm 37:7a (NIV)
Be still before the Lord and wait patiently for him;...

Zechariah 2:13 (NIV)
"Be still before the Lord, all mankind, because he has roused himself from his holy dwelling."

Stillness, quietness - it sounds easy to be still, to be quiet...Yet as the minutes tick by, it becomes harder and harder to be quiet, to be still.

Our thoughts want to wander here and there. Our minds churn out this thought and that thought…

Oh, Lord God, You ARE GOD! You are real! There is a "YOU" a real YOU!

"Be still and know I am your God…"

Yes, Lord…

"Be still and know I am your God…"

Yes, Lord God…

"Be still and know I am your God…"

Yes, my Lord God…

"Be still and know I am your God…"

Oh yes, my Lord and my God…

"Be still… Be still… Be still…"

Psalm 46:10 (NIV)

"Be still, and know that I am God;

I will be exalted among the nations,

I will be exalted in the earth."

The Mystery Of Healing   July 23

Psalm 66:18-20

He would not have listened if I had not confessed my sins. But he listened! He heard my prayer! He paid attention to it! Blessed be God who didn't turn away when I was praying, and didn't refuse me his kindness and love.

James 5:14-16

Is anyone sick? He should call for the elders of the church and they should pray over him and pour a little oil upon him, calling on the Lord to heal him. And their prayer, if offered in faith, will heal him, for the Lord will make him well; and if his sickness was caused by some sin, the Lord will forgive him. Admit your faults to one another and pray for each other so that you may be healed. The earnest prayer of a righteous man has great power and wonderful results.

Yes, Lord, healing is a mystery…It is especially mysterious when You, in Your Power, decide to heal someone…I have witnessed Your mysterious healing Power, Lord! I have seen with my own eyes the results of Your healing!!! It is wondrous, amazing, awesome!

On the other hand, dear Lord Jesus, I have witnessed those who have asked for healing and it did not happen...There's the mystery again...Why is one healed and another not??

No one here has the answer, do they Lord? It is You and Your Father God who bring about this mystery...We down here on earth have the responsibility of believing in You, praying to You, and then we are to leave the answer with You...

It's hard though, Lord, very hard when after much asking, much prayer, the healing never takes place...But we cannot fault You with the answers to our prayers; we cannot...Healing is a mystery...

When healing does happen, what JOY there is; what a Miracle takes place! All Heaven rejoices with us! Yes, Lord, You did it again! How we appreciate Your graciousness! Oh dear, dear Jesus, thank You for all the healings You have accomplished already! May we also share in future healings!

And, most importantly, dear Father, we give all the Glory to You and Your Son, for You are the Almighty God, and Savior of our souls...

YOU are the Great HEALER! Yet, Lord, healing is a mystery... ... ...

Harvest Is Ripe   July 24

Matthew 9:37,38
"The harvest is so great, and the workers are so few," he told his disciples. "So pray to the one in charge of the harvesting, and ask him to recruit more workers for his harvest fields."

Almighty God, Father of all Creation, You have shown me a very small vision...It is that the harvest is ripe...But in that vision I saw no workers, only a path through the field...

Oh God, how that must grieve Your Spirit. The harvest is great, but the workers are few...Dear Jesus, please give each of us who call You Savior, the desire to go out...May we go into the vineyards, the fields, to bring the Good News to those who are so in need of You...

227

We have already been blessed by having a tender relationship with You. This makes us realize even more how much those who don't know You personally yet, need You...

LIFE here on earth can be much more than just existence...For there are so many here who are just existing! That pure JOY which only You can give is not a part of their lives...That PEACE that passes all understanding is totally foreign to them...

Oh Father God, help us to make a difference in the harvesting of souls! Give us the Wisdom, the guidance, all that we need to step out to reach the unsaved...If we need holy boldness please supply all that we need to accomplish what You desire us to do...

For dear Jesus, we want to be in Your Will...We do not want to take one step in front of You or drag one step behind You...Yes Lord, we want only to be in step with You as we go about the mission of gathering souls for You...

Each of us, who call ourselves "Christian," has a responsibility in our commitment to You...We must be concerned about our brothers and sisters who do not know You as Savior, Lord, Master, Teacher...

If we cannot go ourselves, please place upon our hearts some means of helping others to do so...There is a harvest of souls just waiting for the Good News to be brought to them...

Yes Lord, the Harvest is great and the workers are few, but Lord, here we are...

Are you willing for the Lord to use you and your resources for His Harvest?... ... ...

"I Will Not Forget You"   July 25

Isaiah 49.15,16a (NIV)

"Can a mother forget the baby at her breast and have no compassion on the child she has borne? Though she may forget, I will not forget you! See, I have engraved you on the palms of my hands;..."

Oh my Lord God, when I read these words, I became so excited! The thought came—You have two palms! You said my name is engraved not only on one hand, but upon both!

The verse from Psalm 139:6 just came into my spirit:
This is too glorious, too wonderful to believe!

Yes, Lord God, it is a glorious thought! My name is engraved upon both of Your palms! Did you know your name is engraved upon both of God the Father's palms?

How very often I use my hands...As I opened up my hand and looked at my palm there were the usual lines there...I tried to visualize my name there...

Thankfully, God, Your hands are large enough to hold our names upon Your palms...Thankfully, Lord God, Your palms hold the names of all of us who call You Father God! That's so stunning a thought! It reminds me of the song "He's Got The Whole World In His Hands..." Yes, God, You do...

Oh Father God, how very much we have to thank You for – especially for the gift of LIFE itself! Your unconditional LOVE for each of us, and Heaven when we leave this earth, are more of Your gifts...

Thank You, thank You, Heavenly Father! Without You our lives would be drab and gray, without the Light of Yourself, Your Hope...Our future would be so severe without You living with us...

Oh Father God, dear Son Jesus, Holy Spirit of the Living God, please accept our deepest gratitude...Please continue to guide us, teach us...

Please help us, dear God, to pass on the Good News to others who come across our path...Then they too can receive Your assurance,
"I WILL NOT FORGET YOU!"

What We Become   July 26

Matthew 6:19-21 (NIV)
"Do not store up for yourselves treasures on earth, where moth and rust destroy, and where thieves break in and steal. But store up for yourselves treasures in heaven, where moth and rust do not destroy, and where thieves do not break in and steal. For where your treasure is, there your heart will be also."

Father, You give us the Gift of LIFE when we are conceived in our mother's womb...After we are born we begin to grow - but in what direction? Some strive to become this, or that...

We often ask little children what they want to become when they grow up...A fireman, a nurse, a policeman, an executive, a doctor, a teacher, an astronaut or a farmer, they may answer. But these are just roles...These are things to do to occupy time, to earn money and to support ourselves and possibly, a family.

What is our goal in LIFE? Is it only to become this or that because of a job title? Is this all there is to LIFE? Could there be more to it than playing out a role? Should there be more?

Yes, there is more to LIFE than achieving a gold watch, a plaque, stocks and bonds, or medals of merit...These are like accessories to garments. But what about the real you? What will the real you become?

Man is not just a body to be doing...Besides a mind to think and reason with, man has a spirit, a heart. This is the ESSENCE of man...This is the part of us that is eternal...This eternal spirit of man is what the Holy Spirit awakens to God's Perfect Truth. As our spirits are quickened to the reality of our need to know God, He WILL reveal Himself! It may take time, but as we continue to seek God, He WILL be found!

Dear Heavenly Father, we are made aware of our need for Your Son, Jesus, to come into our hearts, to renew our spirits. We learn from Your Bible, Father, how to live LIFE according to Your Teachings. As we learn we realize we have a choice to make. We must decide whether to accept or reject Your Truth and Your LOVE, Almighty God...

Have we spent all our time and effort on just doing, existing day by day? Has our energy been spent on storing up treasures, which are not eternal?

While there is still LIFE in us we have a chance to make up for lost time...If we have neglected our eternal spirits, it is not too late...Are we satisfied? Are any changes to be made? What we are, what we become, is OUR choice...

Thank You, dear Jesus, for the opportunity to appraise and change our lives when necessary. Thank You for the courage to make the right choices – to become all You desire for us... ... ...

Just To Be Near You...   July 27

James 4:8a
And when you draw close to God, God will draw close to you...

Oh Lord Jesus, my desire is just to be near You...Oh, how I wish I could, at this very moment, be near You...In essence I know You are near me, through Your Comforter, Your Holy Spirit, but I desire the presence of You in reality!

I know how this must sound to those who don't quite understand...For some in this world think of You, Almighty God, with fear and trembling...They have been taught to fear You without the other side of the coin: to LOVE You...

When we love, deeply, truly love, we desire to be with our loved one...That is our ultimate thought, to be with our loved one...We try and think up new opportunities to be able to be with the one we love.

True love is the greatest gift which humans can give one another...When we discover You, Lord Jesus, our understanding of You can be fragmented...For You are the Almighty God, Creator of this whole Universe! How can we, so inadequate, so insignificant, understand anything about You? You are so mighty, so all powerful, so all knowing...

One falls in love from afar and then that love draws closer. Time and circumstances draw each to the other...As time progresses, the love becomes deeper. The presence of each other, once seemingly unattainable, now becomes an intimate reality...

And so it is with You, my Lord...We desire a relationship with You, yet we hesitate because we do not know how we will be received. We are somewhat unsure as to the outcome...Will we be received by You? What are our chances? Will You accept us? Will You accept us the way we are???

"Yes, dear one – I accept you. Not only do I accept you, but I, your Almighty God, desire a deep friendship with you... I have chosen you... You are to be My friend... You are to be My best friend... I have deep affection for you... I LOVE you... I truly LOVE you... ... ..."

YOU LOVE ME! You, Almighty God, LOVE each and everyone who comes to You! Each can be Your best friend! All who long to be near You, WILL be near You one day!!!

Oh Father God, dear Jesus, Holy Spirit, how we long for that time when we meet You face to face...How we desire just to be near You - just to be near You... ... ...

Only You...   July 28

Psalm 89:1,2
Forever and ever I will sing about the tender kindness of the Lord! Young and old shall hear about your blessings. Your love and kindness are forever; your truth is as enduring as the heavens.

Psalm 96:3,4a (NIV)
Declare his glory among the nations, his marvelous deeds among all peoples. For great is the Lord and most worthy of praise; ...

Yes, Lord God, only You can make a difference...Only You can cause circumstances to change, hearts to change...No one else can do what You alone can do...

People sometimes cross their fingers, or knock on wood...Somehow or other they think this will protect them...They hope something will or won't happen by their doing these things...Strange how we have our little ways of reacting to situations...

Only You, Lord God, can make a difference, a real difference! When we come into a relationship with You, and continue on in a deep friendship, we can see how You DO make a difference...Oh Merciful God, how we thank You for that! How deeply appreciative we are when You enter into our lives and show us the difference...

One has only to look around at others' lives to see the loneliness, the despair, the anger, the hurt, and the sorrow...It is so sad to see this, especially when we know that IF they would seek You, believe in You, their lives WOULD change!

Sometimes people come to us, who are followers of You, dear God, and want us to pray for them...Sometimes these prayers are answered and because the answers came through our prayers, they want to thank us...Oh, God, how careful we must be regarding these situations, right Lord? It's YOU, and only YOU, who cause prayers to be answered -ONLY YOU!

You alone are to be thanked, praised, adored, and glorified! You alone are worthy, Lord God - YOU ALONE! May we continue to appreciate You in the way that only God our Father and Jesus Christ should be appreciated...

This whole world would be a better place, a peaceful place, if everyone could come into the pure TRUTH that only You can provide...

Then JOY AND SONGS OF PRAISE would pour out throughout this earth to rise up as incense to bless You, Lord...

YOU ALONE ARE WORTHY, LORD GOD!
YOU ALONE ARE WORTHY, LORD GOD!
ONLY YOU, LORD GOD, ARE WORTHY!

When The Earth Began   July 29

Colossians 1:16,17

Christ himself is the Creator who made everything in heaven and earth, the things we can see and the things we can't; the spirit world with its kings and kingdoms, its rulers and authorities; all were made by Christ for his own use and glory. He was before all else began and it is his power that holds everything together.

You were there God – Father, Son, and Holy Spirit - when the earth began...You caused it to come into being! It is a living thing, Lord God...You caused it to bring forth life...

We have only to look around us and see living, growing things...Trees, plants, flowers and grass are there to see...Oceans are teeming with living things! There are animals of all kinds, and birds filling the sky!

Yet earth is just a very small part of the Universe as we understand it...You, Lord God, brought forth the Universe! Even today man has not "discovered" the completeness of the Universe! Man only knows a limited amount... Man is still "discovering" new areas of the Universe!

Father, it is so hard to understand about the Universe...You caused it to come into being...Yet what was there before it came into being? This question has no answer here on earth. There is no way it can be answered while we exist here, I realize, Lord God...Yet I am satisfied in my very soul that though there is no answer to this question now, I know You are who You say You are: Creator of ALL!

Thank You, Lord, for sending Your Son Jesus to Earth to teach us so many things...Faith is one of Your teachings. Faith is believing in something which must be taken for truth without any proof...

So Father God, I want You to know that I believe You were there when the earth began...Though I have nothing to prove this, though there are many who would and do chose to believe otherwise, I truly believe that You were there...

You were there, God – Father, Son and Holy Spirit when the earth began...Thank You Heavenly Father, thank You - for being there then and also now... ... ...

Can't, Can't, Can't   July 30

Philippians 4:19
And it is he who will supply all your needs from his riches in glory, because of what Christ Jesus has done for us.

Lord I can't make it without You - can't, can't, can't...And besides, Lord, I don't want to make it without You...

I simply can't imagine trying to get through life without You, Lord Jesus...You have become so much a part of my life. I cannot conceive of being without You...

The mystery to me, which I've said over and over, is that anyone could think they can get along without You! That amazes me...That mystifies me...How can they believe that?

Whom do they call upon when they are lonely - when they are hurt, upset or depressed...? Whom do they give thanks to when they are blessed?

Perhaps not having You, Jesus, in their lives is why so many people are lonely these days. There are more people in the world than ever before! There are many people living alone; so many people looking sad; so many people being discarded by families, society...Yet we are living in the most affluent of all times...

Yes Lord, it's a mystery to me why people aren't coming to You in droves...For You are the only One to satisfy the heart's longing for lasting friendship, true friendship. You are the One to heal a broken heart...You are the One to restore relationships that have been broken...You are the One to bring Peace into the minds of those who have longed for peace...

Oh Lord, remind each of us who calls You Lord, Savior, God Almighty, that our Christianity calls for us to spread Your Good News...Many come into our lives needing You; let us carry this news to them like a banner waving on high! Jesus Christ is the answer! You are the solution for all problems, ailments, whatever! You are the only One who can and does make a difference in one's life!

Oh Master, Creator of all, give us the courage to bring this message of LOVE, FORGIVENESS, HOPE for all to experience! Your unconditional LOVE, understanding, and compassion is just waiting for each one who will open their hearts to receive...Have mercy, Lord, have mercy...Thank You, Lord, for Your unending LOVE... ... ...

The 'Why?' Is Up To You, Lord...   July 31

Romans 5:8
But God showed his great love for us by sending Christ to die for us while we were still sinners.

Yes, Lord, the 'Why?' is up to You. The 'Why?' is Yours...Sometimes we sit and wonder, Lord, why this or that happened in our lives...We wonder why something didn't happen...We wonder about it...A deep sigh comes over us - another deep sigh...

What are our beliefs? Do we believe in fate? Is it something that happens to us without our having anything to do with it? Are we puppets on a string to be manipulated this way or that without giving our permission? Who is doing the manipulating, if we believe in fate?

For those of us who are aware of You, Lord God, who BELIEVE in You, we know You are the Giver of LIFE. You have given us the will to make choices, and decisions. Some of these have worked out very well...Others have been negative factors in our lives...

But we, until we leave this life, will have to continue to make decisions, to make choices...And when we find that we have made a mistake, You can show us how to live with that mistake...With You, Almighty God, all things are possible!

When we trust in You, Lord Jesus, the going becomes smoother in the rough places...You don't necessarily remove the rough places, but You do make a difference while we are experiencing them...

Life goes on - day in, day out...The sun rises; the sun sets...Our hearts continue to beat as we breathe in and out...We don't need an answer to the 'Whys' in our lives...We learn to take one day at a time, trusting in our Savior, our precious Lamb who was slaughtered for us...Then a peace that passes all understanding comes and settles over us and in our spirits...

There are so many 'Whys' in this LIFE...But the bottom line is that You, Jesus, chose to die for us...That is the biggest "WHY?" in our lives...Why did You die for us, Jesus? Why?

"I did it for you and you and you, and you... I did it for all mankind... And, I especially did it for you, because I LOVE you... "

August

Blessed Be Your Holy Name!   Aug. 1

Philippians 2:9-11

Yet it was because of this that God raised him up to the heights of heaven and gave him a name which is above every other name, that at the name of Jesus every knee shall bow in heaven and on earth and under the earth, and every tongue shall confess that Jesus Christ is Lord, to the glory of God the Father.

Yes Lord, blessed be Your Holy Name! Praise Your Holy Name! Praise the name of Jesus! Praise Your name above all names!

Yours is the name that is recognized in this world, Lord Jesus. Even when there are those who do not acknowledge You, Your name is known...Oh Lord, when is the day coming when You will be recognized and acclaimed by all?

When one loves someone, one desires for others to love that special someone also...This is the way we who love You, Lord Jesus, feel about You...We want others, all others, to love You!

We want them, to not only love You, but adore You, worship You, praise You! Praise Your Holy Name! For You are the only One worthy in all of the Universe to be raised up on high, dear Jesus...

Blessed be Your Holy Name! Oh, dear Jesus let us call upon Your Holy Name time after time...There is Power and Peace in Your name above all names!

Yes, Lord, there IS Power in Your name! Let us say it over and over and over again! Let us exalt Your name! Let it stand for all You did when You came down from on high to live here on earth...

Jesus, Jesus, Jesus...Let us breathe in Your name; let us breathe out Your name...Jesus, Jesus, Jesus...

Your coming made a difference in this world, Lord Jesus...Let us show You that we believe that...Let us show You that we believe in You, in Your Holy Name...May we be drawn into saying Your name often. May we say Your name with our first awakening in the morning...May we drowsily say Your name as we fall asleep each evening...

237

May we speak Your name with our last breath on this earth as we go to meet You...

Jesus...Jesus...Jesus... ... ...

A Special Kind Of Love, Lord   Aug. 2

John 21:15a

After breakfast Jesus said to Simon Peter, "Simon, son of John, do you love me more than these others?" "Yes," Peter replied, "You know I am your friend."

Romans 8:38

For I am convinced that nothing can ever separate us from his love. Death can't, and life can't. The angels won't, and all the powers of hell itself cannot keep God's love away. Our fears for today, our worries about tomorrow, or where we are – high above the sky, or in the deepest ocean – nothing will ever be able to separate us from the love of God demonstrated by our Lord Jesus Christ when he died for us.

It's quiet, Lord...I just had my eyes closed...I was thinking about You...I pictured myself sitting at Your feet, hugging Your legs as a child would hug the legs of one of its parents...Then I realized I wanted to get closer to You...I wanted to lay my head on Your shoulder - to curl up and just rest myself against You...I felt the strength of Yourself...I felt contentment...I didn't want to ever leave the security of that place...

I began to wonder about my love for You...It's a special kind of love, Lord...There's no one else in the whole Universe who deserves this kind of love...I love no one else like I love You, Lord...It's a special kind of love...

Yet this special kind of love is experienced by every man, woman, and child who has put You in proper perspective...You are also Number One in their lives! Yes, Lord Jesus, You alone deserve this special love that Your followers feel toward You...Your Apostles felt that kind of love for You, also...It is reserved for You alone, for You alone are worthy...

Yet the mystery continues regarding this special love...How can we love You like that? We have never met You face to face! We have only heard about You, read about You...We accept You by faith.

I only know that the deepest satisfaction in my life is You, Lord Jesus...I don't understand it, but I am deeply grateful...In the world that we know, love means finding another person to share our love with...But Lord Jesus, the special kind of love which we have for You brings forth contentment, peace, joy...Just knowing what we've read and heard about You has touched the innermost part of our beings...You satisfy body, mind, and spirit...

We hear songs about "True Love" but unless You are the focus of that love, it is only a temporary kind of love...The special kind of love, Lord, that we have for You is imperfect, but it is from our hearts...Your LOVE for us lasts and lasts for all Eternity!

Thank You, Lord Jesus, for this special kind of Love which we share with You... ... ...

Now Is The Time   Aug. 3

Joshua 24:15

"But if you are unwilling to obey the Lord, then decide today whom you will obey...But as for me and my family, we will serve the Lord."

Now is the time - for what? Now is the time to eat, sleep, arise, work, play, love, and forgive? Now is the time to live? Now is the time to die??? Now...The present is ever ongoing, but it is ever the present...

Now is the time to make a decision...Now is the time to make the most important decision of our lives...That decision is to decide once and for all the direction our lives will take...Which road? Evilness or goodness? There is no middle ground...

Jesus Christ stands for Goodness! Satan stands for evilness...It's one or the other...Some "good" people think that they don't need to make a decision...How wrong they are...

In the Bible Revelation, 3:15,16 says:

"I know you well—you are neither hot nor cold; I wish you were one or the other! But since you are merely lukewarm, I will spit you out of My mouth!"

Each of us who has been born and has come into the age of reason has to make a decision in this Life. No one can escape making one. Even if we don't make a conscious decision, we have actually made a decision because we didn't make one!

239

Reading the newspapers we can readily see how much time each person who recently died has had...Some had many years, others much less, and still others only a relatively short time. Only our Creator, God the Father, has the knowledge about each of us regarding our life span. Can any of us afford to take a chance of dying without making a decision to join God for all Eternity?

Many think there is no hell...Many think that this Life they have is all there is...Many people today are caught up in exercising their bodies, following the correct diet...Yet what are they doing for their souls?

The soul of each of us lives forever...It never dies. You, out there in Life, stop! Stop and evaluate where you are - where you are going...

Stop! Stop to take stock of your Life before it is too late...

Now is the time if you have not made a decision...

Now is the time... ... ...

Harmony   Aug. 4

1st Peter 1:7a

These trials are only to test your faith, to see whether or not it is strong and pure. It is being tested as fire tests gold and purifies it – and your faith is far more precious to God than mere gold;...

Lord God, life can be so difficult at times...Surroundings may not change, but little things and experiences creep in to rob us of the harmony we had been enjoying... Someone who seems so insensitive to our desire for harmony, true harmony—often shatters it...

Why, Lord? Why can't the harmony continue each day? Why can't LIFE become so smooth that we could just sail through each day, each night, with a beautiful breeze...Why can't a delightful wind catch our sails and propel us along?

Once we fall in Love with You, Jesus, we want to continue on in this Loving experience...Then the mystery begins...If we are desirous of being part of this truly Loving relationship with You, why do those around us sometimes fail to understand?

Why can't they see that it is truly our desire to live in a harmonious environment? Oh-h-h-h, Lord, I just don't understand this...

"Testing, My child, you are being tested... If you were allowed to sail through life without a blemish, what would cause you to become strong? You would become weak and selfish... Now you are in training. I am allowing you to suffer these injustices... They are not life shattering... I am watching over you... The timing is Mine... But be assured that all of these hurts are known to Me. Try and rise above them. Try for Me, remembering what I suffered for you... I truly LOVE you..."

Oh, dear, dear Lord Jesus -My Savior and Redeemer - thank You again for showing me, us that we must never get so discouraged with LIFE that we forget what You did...

Oh, thank You again, dear Father, for sending us Your LOVING Son...Thank You, thank You, dear Jesus for teaching us... ... ...

Cinderella, Too...   Aug. 5

Isaiah 9:6 (NIV)
...And he will be called...Prince of Peace.

Since childhood we have heard and read about the stories that begin with "Once upon a time..." They usually ended with "and they lived happily ever after..."

When we came to the end of the story the characters in the story went off into the distance on a white horse. We were left with the feeling that they were then in a perfect setting. As we closed the book or heard the ending, we were happy for the characters...

However, life as we know it does not happen like that...Yet happiness is possible for us, but in a different way.

Take, for example, the story about "Cinderella." We see her as a very good person. She has an unhappy situation around her because of her selfish stepmother and two stepsisters. She is constantly being called upon to serve them and do the endless and thankless chores relating to family life. Then the Ball she goes to changes her life! The beautiful glass slipper she lost at the Ball, while dancing with the prince, now is tried on everyone to see whom it fits. She is found one day by the prince and the slipper fits—they ride off on the white horse and "live happily ever after..."

Now what about the rest of us? Who is our "Prince" or "Princess" who can come into our lives and carry us off, to a life of everlasting happiness...Disappointment settles over us and we each have to face life with the deepest reality...Is there anyone who can make a difference in our lives? Is there any lasting happiness here on earth? Is there really that beautiful experience "Just for me"? YES...

Yes, His name is JESUS. He came to this earth to teach about LOVE. We all want LOVE - we all need LOVE...We can hide it, deny it, reach for it, crush it, steal it, strive for it, try to pay for it...But the real LOVE, the pure LOVE is from GOD...Because of His LOVE for US, He sent His only Son, JESUS, here to teach us about this pure LOVE...

He is as the "Prince" in the fable! He is constantly approaching each and every one of us. Strangely now the Prince has a pair of glass slippers and a pair of glass shoes in His Hands.

Jesus is waiting for each of us to accept Him. His glass slippers and glass shoes fit each of us! However, some of us may squeeze into the slippers or shoes and they become very painful. Until we can adjust to them it will be uncomfortable because our feet have to change their shape as the footwear is made of glass...

Yet we want them because they belongs to PRINCE JESUS! There is something there which sets Him apart from all else, as the Prince was set apart from all men in the fable.

As we follow PRINCE JESUS, we find He is the most special Prince of all! With the glass footwear on, as we follow Him and learn His ways, our feet begin to conform to them. It becomes less and less painful to wear them and follow Him...There is more joy than just looking at the slippers and shoes - they become a joy to wear!

Now we are able to be as in the fable—now we can go off with JESUS! His LOVE is with us wherever we go! His LOVE is Eternal! The book will never close - the story will never end...Thank You, JESUS, PRINCE of LOVE and PRINCE of PEACE... ... ...

"I Haven't Changed!"   Aug. 6

Ephesians 4:23-24

Now your attitudes and thoughts must all be constantly changing for the better. Yes, you must be a new and different person, holy and good. Clothe yourself with this new nature.

"I haven't changed!" The person spoke so emphatically with the accent on the word "I"...

When I heard those words, Lord, I immediately turned my thoughts to You...You have taught me that I have had to change; it's necessary to change...

Some of us have a stubborn spirit. We feel very comfortable with ourselves. Why should I have to change? Time goes by...We still stand on our convictions. Often we don't examine them to see if they need to be aired out in the sunshine of Life...

Change: it's an uncomfortable thought...Even good changes can cause difficulties...Changes can bring joy, happiness; changes can also cause pain, sorrow...

Lord Jesus let me look at MY life...Hearing the person say "I haven't changed!" has caused me to peek inside my life and see what other changes I HAVE to make...

It seems, Lord, that LIFE is a continual school. Each grade has its requirements. Each of us needs to change and grow into the person we want to become...

There are times, Lord, when You show us that it is not what we want to become, but what YOU want us to become...Then it's time to change – again that word change...

Outwardly we are changing every day, but it is unnoticeable most of the time...As the years go by and we look back at photos taken some time ago, we realize that our appearances have changed...

But what about our souls? Oh, Lord, what about our souls??? Have You seen a change, a growth, Lord? Or have we said, "I haven't changed!" How sad that must make You, Lord...We realize at times we can go our own stubborn ways...Oh, dear Jesus, cause us to rethink our situations and do what is necessary for the transforming of our souls...Then, dear Lord, may we be changed because of our love for You... ... ...

"Abide With Me..."   Aug. 7

John 15:4 (RSV)

"Abide in me, and I in you. As the branch cannot bear fruit by itself, unless it abides in the vine, neither can you, unless you abide in me."

Lord, Your voice spoke the above words to me, from what I call an "inner voice"...I wanted to know exactly what you meant when You said, "Abide with Me..."

So, Lord, as has happened in the past, I went to the dictionary to see exactly what "abide" means...

Abide: 1. to rest, or dwell;
              2. to tarry or stay for a short time;
              3. to continue permanently and
              4. to remain, to continue...

The synonyms for "abide" are inhabit, dwell, live, lodge and rest...

Oh Lord, I was blessed by reading those words! You want me to do all those things with You! You want me to be with You! I feel You want an intimacy with me - a "one-on- one" relationship...

The word "abide" takes in periods of time. It mentions, stay for a short time, but then it also says "tarry" which means to stay longer than intended. It means to wait, and then "abide"...It means to continue permanently, to remain!

Lord, this is an amazing word, "abide"! It means You want us to stay as long as we want to stay! You want us to stay permanently, but You leave an open door for us to leave...We can return to abide with You for whatever time we are willing to give You...

You, Creator of the whole Universe, allow us to come and go as we desire! When we want to spend time with You, we don't have to make an appointment. We can just enter in as Your guest...It's awesome, Lord God, it's awesome...

And Lord, there's never a bill given to us for the time we've had together...It's a free gift! Oh, Lord, thank You for those precious words, those astonishing words "Abide with Me..."

May we come often to abide with You, dear Lord Jesus...May we come often - until we forever stay!

Spiritual Jealousy   Aug. 8

Psalm 139:23,24
Search me, O God, and know my heart; test my thoughts. Point out anything you find in me that makes you sad and lead me along the path of everlasting life.

Oh Lord - deliver us from spiritual jealousy...In Your Body of Christ, this ugly behavior takes place at times...It is so shocking when this is revealed to those whose spiritual eyes are open...

There should always be unconditional LOVE for each other in the Body of Christ. But satan is a deceiver who is constantly looking for ways to shatter the Lord's peace. As a result spiritual jealousy raises its ugliness as he uses a member of the Family of God to wreck havoc...

Oh Jesus, help each of us who are truly committed to You, to abhor this trait...Let us decide never to be a party to it...

In Your Scriptures Paul talks about the Body of Christ in 1st Corinthians 12:12.
Our bodies have many parts, but the many parts make up only one body, when they are all put together. So it is with the "body" of Christ.

Even as a baby toe, let each of us be willing to be the least, in the Body of Christ...Then if You Lord, call us, let us be willing to be whatever YOU want us to be...It is YOUR decision as to what part You want us to undertake...

Sometimes a role is placed upon someone without their striving for it...Another person desires that role...Jealousy enters in and YOUR Plan has been attacked...

Oh Lord God! Please, please open all the eyes of Your followers who call themselves Christians...To be called a Christian means to be a follower of You, Christ...Awaken us to this call that You placed in our hearts. Alert us to the reality of what it truly means to be a follower of You, to be a Christian...

Oh, dear Holy Spirit, our Comforter, comfort us...Give us a desire to be even that little toe...If our friends or acquaintances are called to be raised up by YOU, let our hearts rejoice for YOUR Plan, dear Lord...

Yes, Master, remind us of Your humility, Your gentleness, Your unconditional LOVE... ... ...

Last Chance   Aug. 9

1ˢᵗ John 4:15

Anyone who believes and says that Jesus is the Son of God has God living in him, and he is living with God.

1ˢᵗ John 5:20

And we know that Christ, God's Son, has come to help us understand and find the true God. And now we are in God because we are in Jesus Christ his Son, who is the only true God; and he is eternal Life.

Dear Jesus, some of us enjoy taking chances..."I can take a chance on this; I can take a chance on that..." Suddenly the bottom falls out and the chance, which was taken, causes havoc in our lives.

Some of these chances can cause drastic changes in our lives. The feeling of deep despair can flood over us...We wonder why we insisted on taking a chance.

Taking chances in our daily lives can be risky. But taking a chance by not trusting You, Lord Jesus, as our Savior, brings eternal consequences...How many chances will we have? Will we get a last chance to believe in You?

"Every day is your last chance..."

Only You, Heavenly Father, know how long we have on this earth! Only You know when our last breath will be taken! Tomorrow may be too late...Today may be your last chance to come to Salvation...

When we leave this world and stand before You, Father, the Judge of all, some will be saying "Please God! Please give me one more chance!" But there will be NO more chances...For then, Father, Your Justice will fairly decide our eternal future...

"When you keep yourself close to Me, each and every day, there will not be any reason to fret about a last chance."

Oh, Lord God, that is the answer. When we come to Your Son, Jesus, and ask him to be our Lord and Savior, then we become close to You. Then we ARE in Your care! You watch over us...You work out the details in our lives when we abide in You and You in us...Thank You Father, for Your LOVING Care...Please keep us close to You, dear Lord... May we be willing to abide in You...

Thank You, Lord, that when we do make the decision to accept You as our Lord and Savior, we are secure in Your Unconditional LOVE for all Eternity... ... ...

Wisdom   Aug. 10

Proverbs 2:6 –8

For the Lord grants wisdom! His every word is a treasure of knowledge and understanding. He grants good sense to the godly – his saints. He is their shield, protecting them and guarding their pathway.

Yesterday, Lord, I was reading James 1:5,

If you want to know what God wants you to do, ask him, and he will gladly tell you, for he is always ready to give a bountiful supply of wisdom to all who ask him; he will not resent it.

Wisdom is being wise...Yes, Lord, we all need Wisdom. It's so great realizing as it says in James, we can just ask You and You will gladly tell us! You give us a bountiful supply!

There are so very many instances when we desperately need Wisdom, Lord Jesus...Oh, God, what generosity it is to receive the Wisdom of Yourself! What a gift it is from You!

But now I recall verses six, seven, and eight!

But when you ask him, be sure that you really expect him to tell you, for a doubtful mind will be as unsettled as a wave of the sea that is driven and tossed by the wind; and every decision you then make will be uncertain, as you turn first this way, and then that. If you don't ask him with faith, don't expect the Lord to give you any solid answer.

Yes, Lord, I see that there are conditions to asking You for Wisdom...We must expect an answer from You...You will not leave us dangling without an answer...It may take time and patience on our part before the answer comes, but it will come. That's where Faith enters in...Our Faith in You, Lord God, will not disappoint us...Our Faith in You demands an answer, sooner or later...

Looking back in our lives, we can see so many times when we were in need of Wisdom...Perhaps we thought it came only with age...But rereading verse five, there is no doubt that You, dear God, are glad to give each of us a bountiful supply. There are no requirements as to what age we are, what experiences we've had...

When we come to You, we must believe that You will answer us. That's where Faith and Wisdom work together! If we believe, then we will receive all that we need to answer those problems and situations, which come with Life...

Thank You for the Scriptures again, Lord...They continue teaching us what we need to know...Thank You, dear Lord, thank You... ... ...

You Are Our Only Hope, Lord   Aug. 11

1st Peter 1: 21

Because of this, your trust can be in God who raised Christ from the dead and gave him great glory. Now your faith and hope can rest in him alone.

You are our only Hope, Lord...In this whole world, who can we turn to but You? Who answers prayers, but You?

You ARE the Hope of the whole world! Without Hope, Life can be drudgery - a trial without any Hope of change...Yet there are so many in this world who scoff at belief in You...They have not experienced the Power of You in action, Lord!

Oh, the Power of You, Lord God! When we place our Hope in You, a mighty force takes place! It is beyond our understanding - but it happens!

Hope is an amazing experience...It requires Faith...When we place our Faith in You, Almighty God, You release a mightiness of Power! Then Your Love blends together with our Hope and Faith in a mysterious way...

Results happen! Changes are made! Lives are affected! Situations, conditions are no longer the same! The Power of You, Lord God in answer to our Hope, then our Faith, makes all the difference...

Yes, Lord God, You are our only Hope...Who else in this whole world can we go to? Presidents of Nations, Kings, Queens, Leaders in this world do not have the answers. It is quite evident that politicians do not have the answers...

What constant Hope can any of them give to us in our lives? No, Lord, they do not have the answer to our need for Hope in this world...

So, Lord God, let us cling to You! Let us wrap ourselves around You with all our might as if we are about to drown! For without our Hope in You, dear Jesus, we will drown in all the confusion...The negativity, the doubt, the indifference that is churning around us daily as we live in this world, would overtake us!

Please continue to show us how You do honor our Hope in You, our Faith in You, by Your LOVE for each and every one of us...

We need You, Lord...We want to share our Hope in You with others, Almighty God. Help us to share that You are our only Hope, Lord—our only Hope... ... ...

No Other Desire...   Aug. 12

Colossians 3:23,24b (NIV)

Whatever you do, work at it with all your heart, as working for the Lord, not for men,...

It is the Lord Christ you are serving.

Lord God, I want no other desire but to serve You...I want no other desire but that...I want to be Your Hands, Your Feet, Your Heart, Your LOVE...I desire to let Your LOVE, Your beautiful unconditional LOVE, come through me...Let Your LOVE touch those You know are in need of it... Help me, please Lord, to do so...

There are so many, many hurting people...As we pass them, often strangers to us, an opportunity presents itself...Then we find, though it appears nothing is amiss in their lives, that they are in need of You!

Once we share Your LOVE, they often open up to that need of You...Sometimes they don't know that they need a personal touch from You...Sometimes when asked if they are Christians, the reply is "No, I'm a _____, or _____, or _____," naming one denomination or another. These are always Christian denominations, but they have not yet discovered that "Christian" means believing in YOU, dear Jesus Christ...

Please Lord, take the scales off the eyes of those who are in need of Your precious Friendship, of Your personal LOVE...We all are so in need of it...Then, Lord, when You have been discovered in a more personal way, may they too have no other desire but to serve You...

Yes Lord, to serve You is the greatest call of all... We desire to serve You with JOY, with LOVE, with COMPASSION, with all that You bring forth through each of us who chooses to serve You...

We need not go "out into the Mission field" necessarily. But the Mission field can be our own homes, our offices, neighborhoods, factories, stores - wherever we are...

Oh Jesus, fill our hearts with excitement to serve You! It is exciting to see a face that seems to lack JOY suddenly burst forth with radiance, because of a touch from You...

Yes, Lord, let us have no other desire but to be Your servants...An elderly woman, on a dark, rainy night, once went out of her way to help another. In answer to "Why?" she said softly: "We are here to serve..." Let her example be to each of us a reminder that it is You we are really serving, dear Jesus; it is really You... ... ...

Pass You By...   Aug. 13

Matthew 25:44,45

"Then they will reply, 'Lord, when did we ever see you hungry or thirsty or a stranger or naked or sick or in prison, and not help you?'

"And I will answer, 'When you refused to help the least of these my brothers, you were refusing help to me.' "

I could never, dear Lord, pass You by and just say "Hello"...In my mind's eye, I could never do that...But, dear Jesus, do I pass You by when You are in disguise as someone needing a helping hand?

Do I pass You by, in the different circumstances that each day brings? How often does it happen, Lord, how often?

I am reminded of something that someone told me some years ago. The person was praying deeply and left word not to be disturbed...Sometime later, the person praying was told that there was someone at the door in need of help...But he refused to go to the door...

This praying person had kept asking to see You, Lord...It was his desire to see You...Shortly after the needy person left without any help, the Lord spoke to the praying person:

"You wanted to see Me. I came to your door, but you were too busy praying to see Me... You would have seen Me, if you had only come to your door..."

Oh, dear Lord, how many times have we passed You by...Our attention was somewhere else or the person in need didn't fit our requirements of a needy person...Oh forgive us, dear Jesus, for deserting You, time after time...

Oh, Heavenly Father, cause us to be sensitive to those who are in need...Remind us that whatever we do unto another, it is as if we are doing it for You personally!

Cause our hearts to beat with compassion for those less fortunate than we...Remind us of You, as we profess to be Your followers...

Please Jesus never let us pass You by again... ... ...

Fading Beauty   Aug. 14

2nd Corinthians 2:15
As far as God is concerned there is a sweet, wholesome fragrance in our lives. It is the fragrance of Christ within us, an aroma to both the saved and the unsaved all around us.

1st Peter 3:3,4
Don't be concerned about the outward beauty that depends on jewelry, or beautiful clothes, or hair arrangement. Be beautiful inside, in your hearts, with the lasting charm of a gentle and quiet spirit which is so precious to God.

Fading beauty is one of the things, which can be so hard to accept. Why is there so much accent on youth now, dear Jesus? Men are trying to hang onto their youth and women seem willing to try anything to prevent the fading of their beauty.

You bring to mind the expression "You can't judge a book by its cover." But what does that have to do with fading youth or fading beauty? Oh-h-h, inside a once new book, now with frayed cover, You place words of warmth, love, wisdom, and beauty! That book is loved very much by whomever reads it, because of what is inside...What a refreshing thought! As we learn more of your warmth, love and wisdom, we will be beautiful to whomever comes in contact with us,

251

just like a well-worn book! Thank You, dear Lord, for revealing this beautiful thought!

Speaking of beautiful thoughts, a picture of a rosebud just came into my mind: a rose perfectly shaped and of exquisite beauty! I can see it opening up very gradually, to its most perfect moment of color and fragrance! Lord, why can't we be as that perfect rose, forever kept at the moment of our youth? But - dear Lord, You're letting that beautiful rose look wilted! Why don't You stop it from wilting and fading?

Oh, now I see…You are picking off the petals one at a time and gently laying them away. They give off a very special fragrance, which will linger long after the rose has died…

That's what You are doing to us? You are taking away, petal by petal, things we had in our youth, which we no longer have. You are replacing them with different things - things which do not show on the outside! The fragrance of the living rose changed after it lost its beauty and a different fragrance now remains from the dried petals. You will do this to us also! As You take each petal away, You replace it with Your inner beauty and fragrance! This is all part of Your wonderful plan, because of Your great LOVE for us…

When we have faded away, the fragrance of our warmth, love and wisdom will remain after us. How blessed we are to know that it will continue to refresh those our lives have touched… … …

A New Heart!   Aug. 15

Ezekiel 36:26,27a
And I will give you a new heart – I will give you new and right desires – and put a new spirit within you. I will take out your stony hearts of sin and give you new hearts of love. And I will put my Spirit within you…

Oh God! You did it! You gave me a new heart! Oh my Lord, my God, another of Your Miracles has touched my LIFE! You are so wonderful, so awesome - so WOW! There are really no words to express how I feel!! "WOW" can mean "With Out Words" because words cannot tell You how appreciative we are, when we see Your mighty POWER! "WOW" can also mean "Worker of Wonders!" Dear Lord, that really describes You for You are the Worker of all

Wonders! You are the great "I AM!" What would we ever do without You!

My heart began to malfunction…All tests indicated something was amiss…A deeply committed Christian friend prayed "Oh God, give her a new heart!" The word "heart" appeared three times in the next few days as I read in my devotional books. I started to claim to all around "God is going to give me a new heart!"…

Ten days after the heart incident the doctor said there was nothing wrong with my heart! There was no explanation for what happened. My dear friend's prayer for me was answered! You God, made my heart anew! Oh God, You ARE the Worker of Wonders! There are NO words to adequately express my JOY, my thanks, and my restoration of health…You ARE a WOW God, truly You are!

You can do all things; You DO all things! Nothing is too insignificant for You to do…Oh God, Almighty God, if only all mankind would come to believe in You, to believe in the POWER of YOU!!!

We, who believe in You, are sad to realize so many do not come to You…If only they would, they would realize the difference You make…It is the difference between existing in this world, or experiencing the excitement of seeing how You change lives through situations and circumstances!

A new heart could mean several things…Hopefully, a new heart might mean that Your Holy Spirit, Lord, has entered into a heart that was cold to You…But this heart is now revived by Your wonderful LOVE…Hopefully all around this earth of Yours, hearts are being made anew…Broken hearts have been healed! Empty hearts have been filled with Your JOY, Your Peace, and Your LOVE…

Oh, Father God, Creator of all good, please continue to touch, heal, mend, and make new hearts, that have need of what only You can do for them… … …

If I Could Be   Aug. 16

2ⁿᵈ Corinthians 3:18

But we Christians have no veil over our faces; we can be mirrors that brightly reflect the glory of the Lord. And as the Spirit of the Lord works within us, we become more and more like him.

Holy Spirit, Jesus Christ, God our Father, Creator of all, if I could be, if I could be...What would please You, Heavenly Father? I close my eyes and see You sitting there, so Divine, so human. My love for You is so deep that if I could be something to please You, what would it be?

You created all the awesome, breathtaking beauty in this whole world. You who created birds, beasts and all living things, what would please You for me to become as I sit here and fantasize...?

Ah yes Lord, a butterfly - I would like to become a beautiful butterfly! I would like to be a butterfly so beautiful that You would want to gaze upon it! Only You could create a butterfly with such depth of color, design and shape that You would be pleased to have it about You...

And Lord, for me - what joy, what complete joy would I have! I would delight to ever so softly, land on Your shoulder, or arm, and linger there so close to You! Oh, my Lord Jesus! What an exciting thought! I would fly off again and float through the air surrounding Your presence, breathing the very essence of You, my Creator, my all - then I would return once again to You...

But, now back to reality - Lord, to a great extent that's what this life is all about, isn't it? Before a butterfly can become a butterfly it has to go through many stages of life, which are not beautiful. That's what has to be done in our lives. We have to go through many stages, which are sometimes not beautiful in order to grow into the beautiful person who You created us to be...Life is a continual growing process for each and every one from the moment of our birth. Some grow faster, some more slowly, but for each it is growth whether we want it or not...Sadly enough, some never get to the butterfly stage, and oh Jesus, how this must grieve Your heart...

When You gave us life You also gave us freedom to make choices. Father, what we become in our lives largely depends on the decisions we make with what You have given us. We can slowly go through each stage of life, and eventually become the beautiful person You know exists in each soul whom You created. We can become impatient with life and decide to take shortcuts and risk the fulfillment of Your desires for us...We can get stuck in our cocoons and never become the source of beauty You intended us to become to those nearby...That is the purpose of the butterfly, to bring beauty to those around them. It takes a long time for the inner beauty of the cocoon, the butterfly, to finally emerge...

Sometimes for us too, it takes a long time for our inner beauty to shine forth. It is the miracle of all miracles, though, when it does! It is Your Light, which shines through us, Jesus, and we become as beautiful as the butterfly emerging from its cocoon!

Let us use this inner beauty, which shines forth through us from You as a very special gift, Father...Let us bring to others around us the same reaction as if they actually did encounter a most beautiful butterfly. Let us bring to them a quiet moment of inner reflection of Your creative power and Divine LOVE, the most treasured gifts of all... ... ...

And So The Feud Ended   Aug. 17

Ephesians 2:13,14,16

But now you belong to Christ Jesus, and though you once were far away from God, now you have been brought very near to him because of what Jesus Christ has done for you with his blood. For Christ himself is our way of peace. He has made peace between us Jews and you Gentiles by making us all one family, breaking down the wall of contempt that used to separate us.

As parts of the same body, our anger against each other has disappeared, for both of us have been reconciled to God. And so the feud ended at last at the cross.

Dear Lord, why can't the words of Paul, Your apostle, be believed with more faith today? Why can't we live in peace with each other? You died for all of us, both Jews and Gentiles! You made no distinction when Your Heavenly Father told You His plan. You didn't say, "Father, I'll shed My Blood for one group, but not the others!" You laid down Your life for all of us, no matter what our race, color or religion. Thank You, Jesus, for being the only completely unbiased person ever to walk this planet!

At times we think we are so righteous. We feel we are true followers of Yours. Then a sudden negative thought pops up in the back of our minds. Oh, how quickly we try to cover it up with some excuse as to why we had acted in that unchristian way! The excuses come flying as we try to salve our consciences!

255

Paul said that we belong to You, Jesus! He said once we were very far away from God and because You shed Your Blood and died for us, we now have been brought very close to God! Paul also said that Your death was to end the resentment between Jews and Gentiles. How many of us have heard unpleasant things or remarks said about Your Jewish people, Lord...How many of us feel You disowned Your race in favor of the Gentiles? Lord, please help us to truly look deep into our hearts and see that no one race or color is any better than another! Please let us know it is what is in our hearts and souls, which counts with You. That should be one of the most important things to us!

Most of all please Jesus, teach us to love one another, truly love one another no matter what our differences are...When we learn this, Paul's beautiful words will have come true... ... ...

Through The Tears...   Aug. 18

Revelation 21:3,4

I heard a loud shout from the throne saying, "Look, the home of God is now among men, and he will live with them and they will be his people; yes, God himself will be among them. He will wipe away all tears from their eyes, and there shall be no more death, nor sorrow, nor crying, nor pain. All of that has gone forever."

Believing through the tears - it's hard, Lord Jesus, it's hard...Lord, help us, please, to get through the difficult times when suffering enters our lives - either for our loved ones, or ourselves.

We want to believe in You, to continue to believe in You, Lord God...Our very spirits are saddened...Our tears burst forth...Day after day, the suffering continues, the tears continue to flow...Our Faith is questioned...Why, Lord God, why? Has the suffering come because we did something wrong in our lives? Why, Lord, does suffering have to exist anyway...

There are many people in this world who cause others to suffer...Yet, in their own lives, everything seems to come up smelling like roses...The injustices continue in this life and it becomes very, very hard to understand, Lord Jesus... Babies, little children, teenagers, the elderly are not spared suffering—it's so unfair, Lord—it's so unfair...

"Yes, My dear one, it is unfair... Life, the life you live there on earth, is not fair... Justice does not prevail there... It is only here in Heaven that justice and fairness exist... One day you will see this... You will know that without any doubt... It is only then that suffering will cease to exist... It is only then that you will truly live..."

So, Lord, it seems that our tears will continue to flow...Our loved ones will continue to suffer...Heartache will still exist here...Pain will not be erased unless You, Lord God, cause it to be gone...

Meanwhile, dear Jesus, our Faith carries us on to another day, through that day, through that night...Our comfort comes from You...You told Your apostles that You would send the Holy Spirit to us and You referred to Him as The Comforter...Therefore, we place ourselves in Your Hands, Holy Spirit...Through the mystery of the Holy Trinity where You are Almighty God, Jesus Son of God and The Holy Spirit, the Comforter, we learn to understand...

May we each come into Your Grace to help ease the pain, the suffering, the tears... ... ...

This Strange And Wonderful Secret   Aug. 19

1st Corinthians 15:46-53

First, then, we have these human bodies and later on God gives us spiritual, heavenly bodies. Adam was made from the dust of the earth, but Christ came from heaven above. Every human being has a body just like Adam's, made of dust, but all who become Christ's will have the same kind of body as his—a body from heaven. Just as each of us now has a body like Adam's, so we shall some day have a body like Christ's.

I tell you this, my brothers: an earthly body made of flesh and blood cannot get into God's kingdom. These perishable bodies of ours are not the right kind to live forever. But I am telling you this strange and wonderful secret: we shall not all die, but we shall all be given new bodies! It will all happen in a moment, in the twinkling of an eye, when the last trumpet is blown. For there will be a trumpet blast from the sky and all the Christians who have died will suddenly become alive, with new bodies that will never, never die; and then we who are still alive shall suddenly have new bodies too. For our earthly bodies, the ones we have now that can die, must be transformed into heavenly bodies that cannot perish but will live forever.

Oh Lord, what a wonder thing to look forward to! These aching, tired bodies that we now have will be changed into new bodies! Just think Father, in the twinkling of an eye, it will be done, at the sound of the trumpet too! What a way to go, Lord!

For those who have already died, they'll be awakened by this trumpet sound, Jesus. In that same twinkling of an eye they'll be ready to start their new lives afresh! Just imagine no aches, no pains, no changing from youth to old age, no slowing down, and no inconveniences of any kind due to a malfunction of our bodies! Wow Heavenly Father, that really is an amazing thought!

Sitting here daydreaming about this strange and wonderful secret, which Paul reveals to us in Your Holy Scriptures, fills the imagination with all kinds of marvelous thoughts! Most important of all, Lord, as an added joy, there will be no sin! The battle will be over! We can release ourselves completely and let ourselves go, in our new heavenly spiritual bodies! Think of all the love, which will be there - Your kind of Divine LOVE, sweet Lord!

We'll be waiting as we listen for the trumpet... ... ...

Can All Paths Lead To You, Lord?   Aug. 20

Proverbs 3:6 (KJV)
In all thy ways acknowledge him, and he shall direct thy paths.

John 14:6
Jesus told him, "I am the Way – yes, and the Truth and the Life. No one can get to the Father except by means of me."

Whatever paths our lives have taken, we CAN still come to You...Yes, dear Lord Jesus, no matter which road we have been on, it CAN lead to You...You don't care what paths we have followed as long as we find You, JESUS CHRIST, at the end of it...YOU ARE THE ONLY SON OF OUR CREATOR GOD!

Today I was at the ocean, Jesus, Your ocean...Just sitting and looking at the vastness of it, brought such an awesome feeling...While I was deep in thought, I noticed a new stream of water coming from a distance away. It started out in one direction, broke into another, then another, and finally made its way down to the ocean...

These tiny droplets of water made up little streams, which found their way to Your ocean, Lord...It made me realize it doesn't make any difference what paths we have taken as long as we end up with YOU, OUR SAVIOUR, JESUS CHRIST!

There are so many roads in this world...If we think of Your oceans as being You, then all the little paths, lanes, roads, highways, and superhighways could be paths to You, Jesus. We can very readily see how many different routes we can take...

No matter what path a person has been on, they are never too far away to come to You, Lord Jesus...Some of us may have explored different paths, which led to a dead-end. We could have tried New Age, Buddha, Islam, or other false paths such as the many different cults...Many people consider their "good works" as an entrance into Heaven. "Good works" cannot be confused with God's Grace. The only entrance into Heaven is by way of accepting Jesus Christ. Thank You Father, that You can redirect us onto the TRUE path which leads to Salvation in Jesus Christ.

Your Word says that narrow is the way to Eternal Life and broad is the way to destruction...We discover that narrow way when we ask You, Lord Jesus, into our hearts to become our Savior and Lord...

It would be wonderful if we could all take a direct route to You...Ah-h-h dear Teacher, You let me visualize another lesson, a map...It's true Lord, most of the roads on the map wander here and there! But they eventually lead to their destination! Oh Lord, please keep drawing us to You even when we may wander at times away from Your Path...

May we learn to acknowledge You Lord, in all our ways, then You will be faithful to direct our paths. May our paths always lead to You, and You alone, dear Savior... ... ...

Praise, Honor and Glory Are Yours!   Aug. 21

Psalm 148:1-14

Praise the Lord, O heavens! Praise him from the skies! Praise him, all his angels, all the armies of heaven. Praise him, sun and moon, and all you twinkling stars. Praise him, skies above. Praise him, vapors high above the clouds.

Let everything he has made give praise to him. For he issued his command, and they came into being; he established them forever and forever. His orders will never be revoked.

And praise him down here on earth, you creatures of the ocean depths. Let fire and hail, snow, rain, wind and weather, all obey. Let the mountains and hills, the fruit trees and cedars, the wild animals and cattle, the snakes and birds, the kings and all the people, with their rulers and their judges, young men and maidens, old men and children—all praise the Lord together. For he alone is worthy. His glory is far greater than all of earth and heaven. He has made his people strong, honoring his godly ones—the people of Israel, the people closest to him.

Hallelujah! Yes, praise the Lord!

Yes, dear Heavenly Father, we praise You! We adore You! We bow down before You! We love You. We bless Your Holy Name! We honor You in every way possible, for You alone are worthy! We praise You especially for coming into our lives, for showing us how much You Love us! Thank You, thank You, thank You, most generous Father!

All we have to do is to read and reread the above Scriptures from the Old Testament and we become filled with the awesome reality of who You really are, Lord! You issued Your command and everything You made came into being! Wow, Lord, that's so powerful a thought when we deeply reflect on it! It is almost mind shattering! Who needs drugs or anything artificial to stimulate their minds, when You can do it for us just by what is in Your Holy Scriptures! Praise You Lord! They are true!

Praise, honor, and glory are Yours!
Praise, honor and glory are Yours,
Glorious God, King of Creation!
We Praise You, we bless You, we worship You in song.
Glorious God in adoration at Your feet we belong... ... ...

"I Am A Sinner..."   Aug. 22

Luke 18:26,27(NIV)
Those who heard this asked, "Who then can be saved?" Jesus replied, "What is impossible with men is possible with God."

260

"I am worldly; I am a sinner...I have a black heart, a heart of ice...I feel for no one...Nothing can penetrate my heart—it's dead to this world...I need none of your compassion—you're trying to pull at my heartstrings. It won't work...I have conditioned myself to my own beliefs...I have killed! I have enjoyed killing, took pleasure in killing...Don't think you can change me—I don't want to be changed...I will not change... I have a heart of ice...

I don't believe in your "God stuff." Where was He when I needed Him? You saw all that I suffered and no one came to save me, to protect me...So I had to learn how to make it in this mess of a world...I had to make it on my own, to prove to everyone that I could make it, that I didn't need ANYONE...

Look at my record. See what I did in this world. See all the crimes I committed, and there were many more! Do you think I am scared? Do you think I am afraid of anything? Well, you're wrong! I don't fear death—I'm not afraid..."

"Oh, My son, My precious one – you <u>are</u> precious to Me... I died a painful death on a cross for you... I would do it again today, if it would touch and soften your heart... For I LOVE you with all of My being... I, God Almighty, Creator of all the universe, LOVE you... Can you understand this? For it is necessary for you to understand this unconditional LOVE I have for you...

I do not approve of your bad behavior... I never have; I never will... But, My precious one, if you will be willing to turn to Me, your Creator, I will make a new creation out of you... You will be without blemish, pure as snow... Give yourself a chance to spend eternity with Me in Heaven... This is where I went to prepare a place, a home, an everlasting home for you... Give yourself another chance, My precious one..."

"Oh, God, how can I really know You? Too many years have gone by, too much evil has taken place in my life. How can someone like me change? It's impossible, God, it's impossible..."

"I am the possible God. All things are possible with Me... You have only to be willing... I will do the changing..."

"My God, my God, my God...Thank You, thank You!. Never in this whole world did I ever think this would happen to me. Thank You for forgiving me, God, thank you... ... ..."

* **Note to the Reader:** This writing is partially based on a true experience of a man on death row.

So Many Needs, Lord...   Aug. 23

Ephesians 6:18
Pray all the time. Ask God for anything in line with the Holy Spirit's wishes. Plead with him, reminding him of your needs, and keep praying earnestly for all Christians everywhere.

Oh Lord, there are so many needs to be prayed for, so many...It seems each day, Lord, You bring to our attention one or more persons who need prayer...Prayer is such a vital ministry...Prayer is so powerful; prayer is so necessary...Day after day, as we pray for the needs of these people, some even strangers to us, we see the answers come...

The answers are not always the ones we want, but when we pray effectively it is with no strings attached. We must never bargain with You, Lord...We must just bring the persons and their needs to You and leave them in Your Hands...As time goes by and some prayers are answered, we rejoice and give You the thanks, the glory...We are only the empty vessels through which the prayers for others pass to You...

Praying for others is an exciting experience sometimes! When the answer comes and it blesses the person in need, what deep joy there is in our hearts! Oh God, giver of all good, we thank You for answering the prayers of your faithful followers...

As we add still more names to "our prayer lists" we pray with expectation! We know that the way the prayer request is answered is completely in Your Hands, not ours...

At times, You seemingly do not give the right solution to our prayer requests. This is so very, very hard to understand dear Jesus...Why do You answer some prayers so beautifully and then at other times, the prayer seems to go unanswered? When one is praying for a loved one's recovery from a very serious illness You may seem not to hear...You allow the loved one to die – this is very, very difficult to accept.

It's hard because You send no note of apology, no message of explanation...In time, many are able to accept these very difficult

262

situations…But, sometimes their Faith is shattered… Some turn away from You. They have hardened their hearts against You. Dear Lord, please, somehow touch these hearts that are hurting so deeply…Comfort them and let them know that You allowed what You knew was the best answer to their prayers, though they do not understand…

Hopefully as time passes their Faith will be restored and they will put their trust in You again. For who else can they turn to, as You ARE our Almighty Creator…One day when they are joined with their loved one in Heaven, all the tears, the hurts, the loneliness will be forgotten. Then You will reign over them in GLORY as You reign over Heaven today…

So many prayers, so many needs, Lord - they are now in Your Hands. We look forward with great expectations to Your answers… … …

Shadows   Aug. 24

Psalm 36:9
For you are the Fountain of life; our light is from your Light.

Luke 1:78,79 (NIV)
"…because of the tender mercy of our God, by which the rising sun will come to us from heaven to shine on those living in darkness and in the shadow of death, to guide our feet into the path of peace."

Out of the corners of our eyes, shadows can play tricks on us…Something appears to be there, but really isn't…

You, thank goodness, dear Lord, are directly opposite to that thought…You are real; there are no shadows about You…You are a distinct personage…Yes, it's true that You cannot be seen now with the eyes of the world, but You can be seen through our hearts, our souls, our spirits…

You came, Jesus; You were seen and heard…You have been written about, spoken about…Even this day, Your name has been on the lips of thousands upon thousands scattered all over this earth!

How we PRAISE You, Father, for being WHO You are, WHY You are, WHAT You are…You, Creator of All, are EVERYWHERE! There are not enough words to properly describe You!

Shadows, grayness, darkness – these words can never be connected with You, Lord God! For You are the LIGHT! You shine wherever You are! Shadows scurry from You, for they cannot stand Your LIGHT shinning forth!

How dreary it must be for those who live among the shadows of Life...When we were born into this world, You dear Lord Jesus, gave each of us an opportunity to share in Your Life. As we come into Your Light, You begin to remove the shadows in our lives...

Sin causes darkness in our lives...Shadows lurk in the darkness...Shadows of all shapes and forms loom about us...Thankfully, dear Lord God, we HAVE a choice! We can choose LIGHT or darkness...We can choose the LIGHT of You, Heavenly Father, OR the darkness of sin...

Oh Father God, may the LIGHT of You, search out the shadows in the lives of those who need You so...May Your LIGHT shine so brightly that shadows can no longer exist...

May each of us search for any shadows in our own lives so that Your LIGHT and Your unconditional LOVE may sweep them away for all time...Thank You, Heavenly Father, thank You... ... ...

Isn't It Amazing...   Aug. 25

Proverbs 18:24b
...there is a friend who sticks closer than a brother.

Isn't it amazing, Lord, that You are my very best friend, and I've never seen You! Always Lord, I've seen You with my heart, but never with my natural eyes...

Isn't it amazing, Lord, that I've never even heard Your voice, with my natural ears, but I've heard Your "silent" voice for years within my spirit...Yes, Lord, it is amazing to me to realize how close we've become...After all, You created the Universe! I am here on earth among billions of people...Isn't it amazing, Lord!

You are the Great "I AM"! You are the Morning Star! You are the Beginner and the Finisher! You have so very many titles, dear Lord...But to me the first one that comes to mind is "Savior"...For without You sacrificing Yourself on the Cross for us all, none of us could ever look forward to a Heavenly Home with You for all Eternity!

The next best title to me is "Friend"...You are Friend, because I can come to You in any state...I know I can never hide anything from You...You see me just as I am...There are no pretenses between us...You know me like the palm of Your very own Hand!

Considering all of this, isn't it amazing that You LOVE me anyway! That's what comforts my heart so much...You see the best in me though I know I fail You often...Yet whenever I come to You, it's as if I am so special to You...

Thankfully God, each one born on this earth can have this amazing friendship with You also – IF they desire it...

Sometimes, human friendships break down through the years...Each of us here on earth can look back on friendships that we felt, at one time, would be life long...As we reflect back through time, we are amazed to realize that some of those friendships have vanished into nothingness...With You, thankfully dear Savior Jesus, that will NEVER happen – Your friendship remains throughout Eternity...

Oh, how we thank You, dear Jesus, for being so faithful to our friendship...Though we may have failed You, we are so very grateful that Your friendship toward us has never diminished...Isn't it amazing, Lord, isn't it amazing... ... ...

I Wonder, Lord...   Aug. 26

1st Corinthians 2:9
That is what is meant by the Scriptures which say that no mere man has ever seen, heard or even imagined what wonderful things God has ready for those who love the Lord.

I wonder, Lord, I wonder...What does that word "wonder" mean Lord? I shall look it up...

One of the meanings is "to want to know"...That's exactly my feelings, Lord; I really want to know...What do You look like? What does Your voice sound like? How tall are You? What color are Your eyes - Your hair? What does Your laugh sound like?

What is Heaven really like? What will we be doing there? Will we have responsibilities? Will we have different appearances? Will we be the age at which we die? Will we have individual homes? Will we be able to spend as much time with You, personally, as we would desire?

Yes, dear Lord Jesus, there is much to wonder about You...You came as an infant, a mere babe...Who would ever expect You to be GOD, our CREATOR too! It leaves me in awe to try and comprehend this stupefying thought... ... ...

Once here You led a very ordinary life...Hardly anyone visualized You to be anyone but an ordinary man, a carpenter...If only we could turn back the clock of Time and observe You in Your daily routine as a carpenter. Then we would continue to watch as You and Your mother Mary went to a wedding in Cana.

There it is told, You performed Your first Miracle, turning huge jars of water into wine...And excitingly, it is told, it was a premier wine! Of course, dear Jesus, we now know that when You did Your Miracles they were without comparison...

Yes, Lord Jesus, if only we could turn back Time and observe You...We would never have to wonder about how You looked then, what Your voice or Your laughter sounded like. We can only wonder about what You were like then, as we wonder about You now, as Lord of Lords and King of Kings!

The wonder of it all! We can meditate upon it but there are no answers here...We will have to patiently wait until the moment of reality comes for each of us...At our death, release from this LIFE and entrance into our Eternal LIFE will come because of You, Father...Then we will no longer wonder... ... ...

The Great Judge   Aug. 27

James 4:11,12

Don't criticize and speak evil about each other, dear brothers. If you do, you will be fighting against God's law of loving one another, declaring it is wrong. But your job is not to decide whether this law is right or wrong, but to obey it. Only he who made the law can rightly judge among us. He alone decides to save us or destroy. So what right do you have to judge or criticize others?

Oh Father God, I thank You that You are the great Judge, the Almighty Judge!

Sometimes we are tempted to criticize the actions or words of others...And in our humanness we wish certain types of justice would take place! Then You come into our thoughts and remind us that You are the Ultimate Judge...When reality settles in, we realize with gratitude, that we are not to judge...

Had we judged incorrectly, and the real truth come forth, how painful that would be to all parties concerned and to our own consciences...Thankfully Father God, that is Your responsibility and Yours alone...

For only You, Almighty God, know the heart of each individual...We can see only the outer appearance of another human being while You see body, mind and spirit...

What a lesson it is for each of us to learn.. Our judgement often results in cruelty to others...Cruelty seems to grow like a cancer in society...If every man, woman, and child would leave judging to You, what a difference this decision would make in our world here...Then there would be no prejudice...There would be harmony between nations...

Please Lord God, the next time we are tempted to judge others, remind us that You, Almighty God, are the only true Judge...You are the One who sees all and knows all. You are the only One to make the correct judgment...

And Lord God, when the time comes for each of us to be judged, we know we will receive the most perfect judgment...You are Righteous...You are also Merciful, dear Savior, so we will await our moment of Judgment with the knowledge that we will be dealt with in the most fair way...

You are always hopeful, until the last breath of life in our bodies, that we will make our peace with You...There are so many who don't realize how important this is...

Thankfully, dear Father God, You are willing to wait until that final breath before You Judge us...You are always waiting for any of Your Lost lambs to come into Your fold willingly...Your desire is to unite all Your children in Heaven for all Eternity...

Let us pass on this knowledge so that all will know of this wonderful opportunity to receive God's forgiveness and enter into Heaven... ... ...

I-ism   Aug. 28

Mark 8:34,35
Then he called his disciples and the crowds to come over and listen. "If any of you wants to be my follower," he told them, "you must put aside your own pleasures and shoulder your cross, and follow me closely. If you insist on saving your life, you will lose it. Only those who throw away their lives for my sake and for the sake of the Good News will ever know what it means to really live."

Oh Lord, how easily we can be lured into "I-ism"..."Because of me, this happened - because of me, he (or she) was healed, because of me, they were saved!" "Because of me - because of me..."

How full of self we are...Christians can play games with You too, Lord... They do not feel that YOU alone deserve to receive ALL the credit, ALL the Glory!

We are such fragile beings...We often feel that if we claim great things in the eyes of others, we become somewhat larger or more powerful...How foolish we can be at times!

Your Bible, Lord, tells us we must decrease; YOU must increase! Why is it so important? Dear Heavenly Father, You are the Master Creator! No matter how much knowledge we attain here, we can never fully understand the Greatness of You!

So our little petty selves must fall by the wayside...We must be willing to lay there, dead to self, waiting for the moment when You see fit to use us. The "I" in each of us has to become YOUR EYE...We must look for ways to become like You...We must serve others with YOUR EYES, Your LOVE, Your Heart, Your Compassion, Your Patience, Your Hands...

Dear Lord, until we can do this, we cannot really serve You, in the manner You desire us to...The "I" in us must die...Thankfully, Lord, You can be gentle with us when this occurs...But Lord, we know only too well that some of us need real healing from chronic self-centeredness...We literally need Your foot on our chests, before we realize that when You are finished with us, we will be happier and content...

So dear Lord, have Your way with us…We relinquish the "I" in us…Then You are given Your rightful due, rightful appreciation that belongs to You alone…

May we see with Your EYES from this time forth…And, dear Lord, our hearts are filled with gratitude for Your unconditional LOVE for each and every single one of us… … …

Before The Beginning   Aug. 29

Genesis: 1: 1-3 (NIV)
In the beginning God created the heavens and the earth. Now the earth was formless and empty, darkness was over the surface of the deep, and the Spirit of God was hovering over the waters. And God said, "Let there be light," and there was light.

We can only conclude by these words that You, Almighty God, were before the Earth began! You were before the beginning, Lord God!

Now the questions race through our minds! If You were before the beginning, who created You, Almighty God? Did You have a Creator? If not, how did You come into being?

You were not alone either, Father God, for in Genesis 1:26(NIV) it states,

Then God said "Let us make man in our image, in our likeness,…"

Us – You said us, Lord God…Who exactly was there with You when You brought this Earth into existence? In searching the Scriptures we find the answer in John 1: 1-3. There You tell us

Before anything else existed, there was Christ, with God. He has always been alive and is himself God. He created everything there is – nothing exists that he didn't make.

So, Jesus was with You, Father, in the beginning! And what about the Holy Spirit? Was He there too? In Gen. 1:2 it is written that the Spirit of God was hovering over the surface of the deep. This means that Father, Son and Holy Spirit were all there before the beginning!

But when was the beginning of Time, Lord? You, Creator of the Universe, know all about Time…How long ago did all this happen? Then again it really doesn't make any difference, but it is another one of our many questions…

Before the beginning – it is an awesome thought...Thankfully, Father God, it is not necessary to have answers to these questions! When we think about You, some of them do pass through our minds...But we can lay them to rest...When we meet You face to face some day, all these questions, these mysteries will be instantly made known to us...

There are no mysteries in Eternity...All knowledge will be ours through Your graciousness Father, for You, our LOVING Creator have ALL the answers... ... ...

Everlasting Arms   Aug. 30

Deuteronomy 33:27a
The eternal God is your Refuge, and underneath are the everlasting arms.

Moses spoke of Your Everlasting Arms to the Israelites before they crossed over to the Promised Land, didn't he, Lord? You told him to tell his people, Your people...What a wonderful thought - the Promised Land!

I just visualized a huge figure: You, God! I have wrapped myself around Your neck! You are my Refuge! And right beneath me are Your Everlasting Arms! Your Arms are stretched out supporting me, ready and willing to hold me forever...

Oh God, what a comforting thought...I can just "plop" into Your arms whenever I feel the need! I can stay there until I am completely rested and ready to face what I need to face...

Circumstances may not change, but just knowing I can depend on You completely, gives me such assurance! Oh Lord, I can close my eyes, breathe deeply and feel the comfort of Your Everlasting Arms...What satisfaction this gives me, what relaxation...

Jesus, Your Father, our Father, has blessed us with so much that we can hardly take it all into our minds...The Bible is filled with loving thoughts to help us through this life...

There is a "Promised Land" for each of us to go to when we leave this world. Once we truly grasp this, we can better understand what the Israelites felt when they entered their Promised Land!

There ARE real "Everlasting Arms" waiting for us! There IS a place, a "Promised Land" for us to go to! All the beauty that our God has created waits for us there...We look forward to sharing Your "Everlasting Arms". You are our Refuge for all Eternity...

Thank You, Father God, thank You...Thank You... ... ...

Today   Aug. 31

Hebrews 3:15

But *now* is the time. Never forget the warning, "*Today* if you hear God's voice speaking to you, do not harden your hearts against him, as the people of Israel did when they rebelled against him in the desert."

Today - what is it but only moments, minutes, hours in time...Yesterday was made up of only moments, minutes, hours in time...Tomorrow will also be made up of moments, minutes, and hours in time...

Yesterday is past now...There is nothing I can do about yesterday...Gratefully You have given me today, Lord - a fresh new day, a new start, a new beginning...Tomorrow may not be for me; it may not come for me...But, Lord, You have given me today...Is there something special You would have me do today? Is there any wrong that I could right today, Lord Jesus?

"Take time, My child... Think... Think slowly and longingly, desiring only to right something from your past... A letter perhaps – is there a letter that would bless and ease another's heart? Think, child, think... Ponder over this matter... Do not grieve your spirit over this, but dig deep into your past..."

Lord, if there is someone to whom I need to write, to correct something from my past, please bring it forth so that I can clear it up, so blessings may come forth...I don't want anything from my past to be a stumbling block—either to me or to someone else...Yes, Lord, if we are to right a wrong, today is the time to do it...Yesterday is gone, like a vapor that blew in the wind...Tomorrow may never come...Today is here and now...

Is there something between You and I, Lord, that I have to make amends for? Please, Lord, bring to my mind anything You have been hurt by my doing, or perhaps, my not doing...Sometimes we forget that not doing something can be more damaging at times, more hurtful, than our doing something wrong...

271

Today, Lord Jesus, You have given us today…It is another chance to bless someone. It is another chance to be blessed by Your forgiveness…It is another chance to thank You for all which You have blessed us with…Today's precious moments, precious minutes, precious hours - will they be our last? Will tomorrow come? No matter, we are in today…It is here in the now…Let us not tarry…Let us make today a special day, a special blessing…

Let today be a gift to You, Lord, by our praises, our thanksgiving…Perhaps today can be a gift of ourselves to someone who needs to hear from us…Today…Today…Today… … …

September

Broken Relationships   Sept. 1

Psalm 147:3
He heals the brokenhearted, binding up their wounds.

Jesus dear, You know how much I loved a certain item; someone special had given it to me...When it broke the first time, You gave me the writing "Glue".

When it broke again recently, after many years of use, I was so disappointed! I thought I could never replace it with another that would be as meaningful...

One day as You remember, Lord, I thought I'd found a replacement that would be almost as nice as the broken one. However, circumstances prevented me from purchasing it. Later I rushed back to purchase it, but it was gone...Disappointment came over me when suddenly my eyes fell on one I had not seen before! As I picked it up and studied it, I realized it was not only a replacement, but much more beautiful than the original which was broken!

As I was sitting here looking at the "new" one, I realized that You Lord, were showing me again, a lesson about LIFE...You showed me especially about broken relationships...Sometimes we find ourselves in a beautiful relationship; we feel that this person is the perfect one for us! Nothing could be better! No other person except this one could make our life complete...

Somehow the relationship begins to falter. Things just don't seem the same anymore. The LOVE, the JOY, the contentment has slipped away...Our hearts get broken...That "one" special person is no longer part of our world! Heartbreak is so painful...How does one repair a broken heart? Ordinary glue will not mend it as a broken item or toy a child loves so dearly...

Thankfully, dear Lord, as in the writing "Glue", You became the special glue for us! I quote:

"You, Jesus, are the only One who can repair us for the rest of our lives; etc."

Once mended by You, dear Lord, we are now bright, renewed! We can face LIFE again with new meaning! The broken relationship lies dead in the past...With a light heart we go on and leave the decisions to You, Lord...For You will answer our prayers as we send them up to You...

Now looking back, we realize the situation that we thought was once wonderful, has paled...There is no comparison to what You have now caused to be in our lives! Oh precious Father, how grateful we are to see the way You change circumstances, situations and relationships in our lives!

We see Your marvelous workings in our lives! Oh thank You, dear Jesus, for becoming the special glue for each of us... ... ...

Love And Marriage   Sept. 2

Ephesians 5:22,25
You wives must submit to your husbands' leadership in the same way you submit to the Lord.

And you husbands, show the same kind of love to your wives as Christ showed to the church when he died for her, ...

Dear Lord Jesus, this is a special day! Two dear hearts are celebrating their 50th wedding anniversary! Fifty years ago love meant marriage. But, we realize today, that love does not necessarily mean marriage...

Two young people met, were attracted to each other, fell in love and then made plans to marry...Love and marriage went together like bread and butter.

Love and marriage seemed like such a normal experience...Love and marriage seemed like it would bring instant "happiness"...It meant meeting the girl of your dreams or the man of your dreams and climbing up on a white horse to ride off into the horizon to live "happily ever after"...

"Happily ever after" - the dreams of youth and the freshness of love sweeps them off their feet...Reality picks them up...Happiness—it is such a fragile thing...One of the partners feels that if the other partner "really loved me" everything would be as they once dreamed!

274

Dreams and reality can be miles and miles apart!

Marriage is a blending of two personalities, hopefully, with one intent...Each one must love the other totally, and give 100% to the other...

When two can understand this commitment, beauty springs forth in the marriage. Contentment settles in...The marriage becomes much stronger, dear Lord, if and when You have been invited into the center of it...When this happens, the beauty and contentment can last throughout the marriage.

The problems, the burdens, the heartaches that befall, can be overcome because of You, dear Jesus, as You support them... Throughout the marriage, no matter what the pitfalls, You dear Savior, make the difference between success or failure...

May this special day, become a special blessing to these two dear hearts celebrating their 50th wedding anniversary...Thank You, Lord, for the example of what a marriage can become when YOUR LOVE is in the center... ... ...

A Man of Sorrows   Sept. 3

Isaiah 53:2,3

In God's eyes he was like a tender green shoot, sprouting from a root in dry and sterile ground. But in our eyes there was no attractiveness at all, nothing to make us want him. We despised him and rejected him – a man of sorrows, acquainted with bitterest grief. We turned our backs on him and looked the other way when he went by. He was despised and we didn't care.

Oh dear, dear Jesus, our sacrificial Lamb - You went to the slaughter for each of us...It grieves my spirit when I read the above words describing You...We, who truly love You, grieve...

You, dear Jesus, Perfection itself, were not only ignored, but despised...You were not only despised, but rejected...Any of us who has been rejected by another or others, can relate to this very painful experience. In a sense we can almost understand when we have been rejected...Your rejection, Perfect example of God's LOVE and goodness, shocks our very being...Just to meditate on the Scriptures above, brings a deep sigh from our hearts, from our inner spirit...How could this happen? We, who love You with our whole hearts can hardly understand this...

Some of us have been brought up to believe that goodness has its own reward...That is so misleading, Lord...There's a price to pay, we have found dear Master, when we choose to follow You...But no matter what the price, it is insignificant compared to the joys that accompany us as we come closer to You, dear Savior...

Yes, dear Jesus, You were a Man of Sorrows...Our hearts cry out for You and to You, when we realize the depths of sorrow You experienced...

Then we come into the realization of what followed Your death and resurrection! You now reign in Heaven with Almighty God, our Father! You have gone there to prepare a place for each of us who made the choice to follow You, the Man of Sorrows...

Oh dear, dear Jesus, how we thank You for being willing to do Your Father's Will...We can never, never thank You enough...Please look into our hearts and know how much we appreciate what You, the Man of Sorrows, did for each of us... ... ...

No Looking Back...   Sept. 4

Hebrews 8:12
"And I will be merciful to them in their wrongdoings, and I will remember their sins no more."

Once we have asked for forgiveness for our failures, our trespasses, with a sincere heart, You don't want us to look back, do You Lord?

"No My child, those times are in the past... But you must learn from your mistakes. They can teach you for the present and the future... To carry these failures, these transgressions, along with you would burden you so heavily that they would weigh you down when you should be sprinting ahead... Yes, now that you are free of them, you are able to perform with agility, the responsibilities I have assigned you..."

Oh Lord Jesus, the pain of the past was so heavy; my heart, my spirit felt so burdened...It's so refreshing to realize that though my past was filled with darkness at times, I can now feel a cleansing in my soul...

Oh, PRAISE TO YOU, FATHER GOD! Praise to You for allowing Your Son, Jesus, to come and bring us sinners - VICTORY! Jesus brought victory over the darkness of sin, victory so that we may spend our Eternity with You forever and ever...

You paid the price of this VICTORY, dear Lord Jesus, when You went to the Cross for us...And the amazing thing is that they did not drag You there screaming, "I AM INNOCENT!"...No, You allowed them to take You...You willingly laid down on that crude, wooden cross and let them nail You to that tree...

Oh, Lord, how You suffered for each of us...And as Your Blood, Your precious Blood, freely flowed, it was already cleansing us, these many hundreds of years later! What a magnificent act of Divine LOVE!

We are not worthy, will never be worthy of this unconditional LOVE and Forgiveness of Yours for us...We tell You now, if we've never told You before, how very, very grateful we are...

There really are no words for us to express our everlasting thanks to You, dear Jesus - there are no words appropriate...But You know our hearts and see in them what we fail to express in words. Thankfully, because of You, dear Jesus, we have no need to look back - only forward to our future with You... ... ...

I Wish...   Sept. 5

John 6:44a
"For no one can come to me unless the Father who sent me draws him to me, ..."

Lord Jesus, I wish, oh how I wish, that I could have lived while You were living on earth! How I wish that I lived in the town where You lived as You were growing up...

I know Your Word says that no one comes to You, Lord Jesus, unless the Father draws them. But I like to imagine when You were here on earth that Your simplicity would have attracted me, too. Maybe Your good humor and hearty laughter made you appeal to others.

On a day I wanted to be special, I would say to some others, "Let's go over to see what Jesus is doing!" Perhaps some would not want to go, but I would go so quickly to where You were...

As You worked among the pieces of wood, there would be the marvelous aroma from them...Each would have a different fragrance...As You shaped each piece, paring off the unnecessary, it was as if You were molding something precious...How blessed to think of the things You made with Your Own human hands...

It would have been difficult for me to see You leave Your carpentry work, when that time came...When You left You went to many places...Dear Jesus, I would have always been so happy to hear from others about You...

I would have had such a wonderful feeling about my friendship with You...There would always have been a feeling of happiness when I thought of You - the memories so pleasant, the friendship so dear.

As the years passed, a sadness would have filled my heart at what happened, when You, Jesus, revealed who You really were, the Son of the Living God! Because of this revelation they hunted You, caught You, humiliated You, beat You, crucified You...

Oh Lord Jesus, I wish, oh how I wish, that I could have lived while You were still alive...Perhaps I, like the few others who followed You, could have let You know how much we appreciated You, loved You...

When we love someone, really love someone, it often causes pain...Oh Lord Jesus, could I have stood by and watched what You suffered? Would I have loved You that much? Or would I have hidden myself so as not to be identified as Your Friend...

Do I still wish I could have lived while You were living on earth?

All The Skins...   Sept. 6

Romans 12:9,10

Don't just pretend that you love others: really love them. Hate what is wrong. Stand on the side of the good. Love each other with brotherly affection and take delight in honoring each other.

Dear Master, God of the Universe, I come to You in deep distress...Ugliness, violence has burst out again in Your land...

Some innocent people and some who were not, have been killed, violated, maimed...This is all under the cover of wanting "JUSTICE"! Oh dear, dear Lord, it's happening all over this world! When will it ever stop, dear Father God?

Some of us send up prayers to You about this terrible crime against humanity...But I see now that it will take many more prayers, on the part of us all, if we are to continue with some integrity...

There seems to be little respect for another's views or choices...The old saying "Live and Let Live" has lost its way. Then again Lord, perhaps that meaning had too little substance in it. It should have been "LIVE AND HELP LIVE"...

We ARE our brothers' keepers, whether we like it or not! For if we do not show this with deep sincerity, rebellion may take place...Rebellion plants its seeds in those who are lacking a fair share in LIFE...

What a blot on humanity these spiteful killings, lootings, and burnings are...The entire world is looking at this outrage...

You, for some unknown reason to us, created many colors of skin...There are red, yellow, brown, black, white and mixtures of all these. Why does the color of skin make such a difference? Why should it?

We, who love You sincerely, do not understand...Please, dear Lord Jesus, impress upon us - this cannot continue if we are to survive on this earth...We must learn to turn the other cheek! We must pray for those who do not understand Your message of unconditional LOVE...

Yes, my dearest Lord God, all the skins which You created are precious to You...Help us to respect those who are different from ourselves, whatever the color of our skin...

May we all become a blessing to You, soon, so as to blot out this terrible blight...Thank You, dear Father, for helping us to love and Forgive as You FORGAVE...May we continue to FORGIVE, and to love as You LOVE... ... ...

"Father, I Commit My Spirit To You" Sept. 7

Luke 23:46

Then Jesus shouted, "Father, I commit my spirit to you," and with those words he died.

Dear Jesus, You committed Your Spirit to Your Father, our Almighty Creator God with Your very last gasp...When these words came repeatedly to me, I wondered what You would have me understand about them...

My understanding now is that we, Your followers, who call ourselves Christians, should be commending our spirits to You daily. As You, dear Jesus, committed Your Spirit to Your Father centuries ago, I commit my spirit to You today...

Yes Lord, we offer up our spirits to You so that we can be in tune with You! We want our desire to be so in oneness with Your Holy Spirit, that we will obey You in a moment...We don't want to delay the working of Your Holy Spirit in our lives...We need to be of one accord so that when You need us, we will be ready, without question, to step out in Faith for You...

Dear Jesus, Your obedience to Your Father is deeply touching...When You were in the Garden the night before Your crucifixion, You saw what was going to happen to You...You were torn as to accept or reject that horrifying experience of the Cross...

But, obediently, You accepted this death, this painful death...You uttered, "Father, I commit my spirit to you." May we here now, over two thousand years later, truly desire to commit our spirits to You.

Father God, we need Your Power and strength to make this commitment. Once we are deeply committed to these words, "Father, I commit my spirit to you," our spirits will respond as You responded to Your Father, Almighty God...May we too respond in obedience to our Father's plans...

Lord, it is in giving up our own wishes, desires, and needs that this will be accomplished...In doing so we will be drawing closer to You, dear Jesus, dear Sacrificial Lamb, our dear, dear Savior... ... ...

For You Alone Are Worthy...   Sept. 8

Revelation 5:11,12

Then in my vision I heard the singing of millions of angels surrounding the throne and the Living Beings and the Elders: "The Lamb is worthy" (loudly they sang it!) "- the Lamb who was slain. He is worthy to receive the power, and the riches, and the wisdom, and the strength, and the honor, and the glory, and the blessing."

Dear Lord, so many people have been raised to be lauded, honored, and put upon a pedestal...Some have done it to themselves; some have been raised by others to be admired - to be glorified...

How sad this must make You, dear Jesus, when these very ones show You no honor, reverence or praise. The self seeks to be raised up by so many...What is it about human nature that it wants to be elevated above others?

Lord God, we understand that You alone are to be glorified, raised up and praised! We wonder how easily mankind can, sometimes, be duped into following people and placing them on pedestals...This is for You alone, Heavenly Father...You are the only One who is true Royalty...You alone are worthy of this homage, which is lavished upon many, many earthlings...

How I desire for the very stones of this earth to sound out Your Praises! Oh that the very waves of Your oceans would sing praises to You! How I long for the trees, as they sway in the breezes, to hum praises to You! Then all the earth would be sounding its praises to You, Almighty God! FOR YOU ALONE ARE WORTHY!

When that day comes and You return to earth then all these things will take place! How I will enjoy this praising for You, dear Jesus! How all the angels in Heaven will join in this harmony of sounds praising You!!! May the whole atmosphere resound with PRAISES unto You!!!

Dear Lord God, may all those who are alive, bow down before You! May every tongue confess that You and You alone are worthy! For You and You alone are the only true God! You are the Creator of the entire Universe!

Note to the Reader: A year and a half after the above was written by hand, I was typing it while I was on the Atlantic Ocean coast. Suddenly the waves began to roar, the trees swayed, and a great praising went up to the Heavens! It was a confirmation from our Dear Lord...

PRAISE UNTO YOU, ALMIGHTY GOD,
FOR YOU ALONE ARE WORTHY!!!

"Part Of Loving Me..."   Sept. 9

1ˢᵗ John 4:7

Dear friends, let us practice loving each other, for love comes from God and those who are loving and kind show that they are the children of God, and that they are getting to know him better.

"Part Of Loving Me is loving those that I LOVE..."

Oh-h-h, Lord God, that's perhaps the hardest thing about our relationship...You, in Your Goodness, LOVE every one, no matter their shortcomings or their behavior...Because I love You, Your expectations from me are to do the same...But because of my own shortcomings there are times I find it just too difficult to do! What am I to do? The feelings are real; I can't disguise them...What am I to do dear Jesus?

"Think child, about the times when you were unloveable... Your behavior was less than perfect... Yet in My LOVE for you, I overlooked your behavior and saw only you... I saw you as a child of Mine and believed in you... Can you not do the same for that brother or sister who is out of harmony with you? Part of loving Me is loving those I LOVE..."

Ah-h-h yes, Lord, when I reflect on some of the unChrist-like behavior that I have exhibited in my lifetime, I want to hide from the shame of it...Yes Lord, I truly want to forget that part of my life...

And Lord, thank You so very, very much for Your forgiveness to me...It is only in experiencing Your forgiveness that I can face You and the rest of the world...Your forgiveness has made a new creation of me...I can now face any situation or problem, which may enter my life. This is because of the strength and hope that I have received from You, dear Savior...

Refreshment has come...Peace of mind has come...Loving others has come, as You enable me to love them with no strings attached...I love others, because You LOVE me, Lord...Your LOVE is pure and enriching...

Lord, dear Lord, please enable each of us to understand all of the ramifications of loving others with Your kind of LOVE...Let us see the beauty in the different stages of another's life when we truly love them as You LOVE us...

Yes, Lord, one can see now that part of loving You is loving those whom You LOVE...Thank You, Lord for being the perfect example of unconditional LOVE... ... ...

Satisfy Our Souls   Sept. 10

Psalm 17:15b
And when I awake in heaven, I will be fully satisfied, for I will see you face to face.

My Lord, as I was gazing at a picture of Your face, I realized, once again, that no one living here on earth in our time has seen Your face...No one really knows what You looked like...

So many, many deeply love You. Yet we love someone whom we've never seen! That seems very strange when we think about it...Usually, dear Lord, when we love someone, we know very well what he or she looks like...On rather rare occasions we can even fall in love with someone unseen, because of hearing his or her voice...

To intimately love someone, whom we've never seen, would seem to be an unusual situation...But here we are Lord Jesus. Here we are, loving You...We speak to You from our hearts... It happens throughout all Your world! Communication between us is as frequent as we want it to be, isn't it Lord? All we have to do is be drawn to You and choose to have a relationship with you - and it happens!

Dear Father, You know what Your face looks like; we don't...As I gaze again at some artist's concept of You, I look at You intently...Love for You fills my soul...Yet I know that this is only a piece of paper - the frame is only earthenware...But, as I gaze deeply into Your eyes, I feel total contentment...It seems as if You are communicating Your LOVE towards me...The child in me delights in this, dear Lord, and so I continue to look at this picture with a sense of peacefulness...

We know, dear Savior, that whatever You look like will deeply satisfy our souls...That moment will come for each of us when we stand before You and look upon Your face. Then we will be filled! We will have the assurance forever that we will never be separated from You again!

We will be able to gaze upon Your radiant face forever! We will be ever thankful that we fell in LOVE with You, long ago while we were on earth...

Oh the JOY, the wonderful excitement of seeing Your face for all eternity fills us with delight! Thank You, dear Jesus, for giving us the opportunity to see You in reality one day... ... ...

A Walk   Sept. 11

John 15:13,14

"And here is how to measure it – the greatest love is shown when a person lays down his life for his friends; and you are my friends if you obey me."

Oh, Father how soon we forget...How soon we forget what You did for us by sending Your Son Jesus, to die for our sins...Yes, that was the ultimate plan...Your Son, Jesus, willingly died for me - for us, on that heavy wooden cross...

As LIFE continues for each of us, we get caught up in the struggle, the unfairness, the hurts. Anger seeps into our beings and we allow it to alter our minds, our spirits...Yes, LIFE is often unfair...We forget about Your death on the Cross...

Why Lord, why do we have to go through these painful episodes in our lives? Sometimes we look at those around us to see what is happening in their lives..."Look at that! I know that person who is having all the 'luck' is really a dishonest person. Yet look at the way things are going great for him (or her)!"

We, who call ourselves Christians, often see this in the lives around us...We wonder how it can happen..."Doesn't God LOVE us anymore? Doesn't He see how good we are?"

Now it's time to take a walk...Now it's time to close our eyes and visualize ourselves beginning our walk...There is a narrow path that veers to the right...As we progress, the path has a slight hill to it...We continue to move along the path and it starts turning ever so gently to the left. We notice now, the horizon facing us...

The air is still; the quiet enters our spirits...We stay on the path without realizing that it suddenly ends...At our feet a heavy post is imbedded in the earth...As our eyes see this post, we look up...

There looking down at us is the face of You, dear Savior...Your Face is stained...Your Body's limp...We gaze upon You and stand quietly before You...All the anger, resentments, sadness, emptiness, hatefulness seeps out of our hearts...Our memories of all the negative, suddenly drop there at the foot of Your Cross...Those who are carrying problems find their burdens lifted!

A voice speaks gently...Our ears open eagerly to hear...

"Father, forgive them, for they know not what they do..."

Oh Father God! Oh Jesus, precious Savior, thank You for the sacrifice You made for us - for me...Thank You for that walk to the foot of Your Cross...May the path leading to it become worn as we each come to You in grateful appreciation and adoration for what You willingly and LOVINGLY did... ... ...

"Yes, Now Go And Do The Same"   Sept. 12

Luke 10:25-37

One day an expert on Moses' laws came to test Jesus' orthodoxy by asking him this question: "Teacher, what does a man need to do to live forever in heaven?" Jesus replied, "What does Moses' law say about it?"

"It says," he replied, "that you must love the Lord your God with all your heart, and with all your soul, and with all your strength, and with all your mind. And you must love your neighbor just as much as you love yourself."

"Right!" Jesus told him. "*Do* this and *you* shall live!" The man wanted to justify (his lack of love for some kinds of people), so he asked, "Which neighbors?"

Jesus replied with an illustration: "A Jew going on a trip from Jerusalem to Jericho was attacked by bandits. They stripped him of his clothes and money and beat him up and left him lying half dead beside the road."

"By chance a Jewish priest came along; and when he saw the man lying there, he crossed to the other side of the road and passed him by. A Jewish Temple-assistant walked over and looked at him lying there, but then went on."

"But a despised Samaritan came along, and when he saw him, he felt deep pity. Kneeling beside him the Samaritan soothed his wounds with medicine and bandaged them. Then he put the man on his donkey and walked along beside him till they came to an inn, where he nursed him through the night. The next day he handed the innkeeper two twenty-dollar bills and told him to take care of the man. 'If his bill runs higher than that,' he said, 'I'll pay the difference the next time I am here.'"

"Now which of these three would you say was a neighbor to the bandits' victim?" The man replied, "The one who showed him some pity." Then Jesus said, "Yes, now go and do the same."

"Yes, now go and do the same..." You spoke these words to an expert on Moses' laws one day, Lord...He had been questioning Your orthodoxy...

People are still doing that today, Lord - questioning You or about You...So many still find it difficult to believe in You completely. Some who know You very well (they think) want to "split hairs" with You...

Some feel to "follow" You would mean having to change their lifestyles. They would have to give up all the "doings" and "havings"...They think then, there would be dreariness in spending their lives devoted to You...

Oh Lord, that's so far from the reality of understanding what it means to "now go and do the same"! There is such peace of mind when we give our lives over to You! It truly does pass all understanding!

Yet Lord, it does not mean followers of You suddenly find themselves living in a rose garden with flower strewn paths laid out before them...Each life is according to Your Will, when one turns over their life to You, Lord...But, in turning over our lives to You, Lord Jesus, we do not become puppets...A willing, loving servant serves its master without question...The servant-master relationship is enjoyed because of the deep love and respect between them. True followers of You desire to have You in that leadership role...

You, Lord God, allow US to question You! You want us to have an open communication with You! Just as the illustration mentioned above in Luke, You allowed Yourself to be questioned by the Jewish man. We don't know how he felt when You finished telling him about the good Samaritan and the Jewish traveler who was in need, when You told him "Yes, now go and do the same..."

But we today, over two thousand years later, must respond to that statement: "Yes, now go and do the same..." What is our answer? Shall we cross the street ourselves? Shall we look the other way?

Oh Lord God, we must search our hearts...May we be guided by the Good Samaritan and help our brothers, our sisters, no matter what differences there are between us...You created us all in the image and likeness of Yourself... ... ...

Lord Jesus, Thank You...   Sept. 13

Colossians 3:17
And whatever you do or say, let it be as a representative of the Lord Jesus, and come with him into the presence of God the Father to give him your thanks.

Thank You, Lord Jesus, for being You, for what would I do without You? Thank You, Lord Jesus, for LOVING my loved ones and me. I offer up my day to You, no matter how simple it may be...Lord Jesus, help me to be what You want me to be...Help me please not to disappoint You or to make You sad... Lord Jesus, I want to be a reflection of You. Cause me to see my failings so that I will correct them...

"Help me please, to LOVE with Your LOVE and to forgive as You forgive...Lord Jesus, thank You for LOVING me; I do love You...Yes, Lord Jesus, I do love You..."

These words were given to me many years ago and I pray them often. They remind me to look inside myself to see if I am reflecting Your Love and Your forgiveness to others. You use these words at times to correct my intended words and actions as I hear in my spirit -

"You cannot do what you are about to say or do..."

Your words, dear Lord, help me to check myself...They have LIFE to them and cause me to look again at the situation with Your Eyes, not my own...

My eyes upon the situation can at times blot out what You, my Savior, would want me to see. Sometimes the irritations of others cause me to want to correct them. Then, You point out to me, very plainly, because I call myself a Christian, a follower of You, that I cannot speak or act without Your permission...

Oh, dear Jesus, please let the words above penetrate so deeply into our spirits that nothing or no one can cause us to speak or act in an unchristian manner...We thank You again, dear Lord Jesus, for helping each of us to grow into the person You created us to be... ... ...

Imperfect   Sept. 14

Philippians 1:6 (NAS)
For I am confident of this very thing, that He who began a good work in you will perfect it until the day of Christ Jesus.

Good morning, dear Lord...As I look at a new picture frame that I recently purchased, I see a crack in it! Lord, how did this happen? It is imperfect now...

Imperfect - the word tumbles around in my mind...Yes, I will look up the meaning of imperfect...Oh Lord, this is a surprise! I have never considered that imperfect can also mean: "unfinished, not complete, lacking of something, not perfect..."

As I let these meanings filter into my mind, I feel grateful...I am grateful, Lord, because at times when I felt separated from You, I felt so imperfect...This feeling is a very disturbing one...It feels as if we can never arrive at perfection: to be perfect in Your sight...

Now dear Lord, knowing You have not finished or completed us, touches our hearts! We feel blessed! The lack within us will disappear...One day when we face You, You will see how we have grown in Your Eyes!

Oh Almighty Father God, though we know we'll never be perfect here, we long to go as far as we can toward perfection! We want to please You...In the Scriptures it states that we must aim for perfection...

Yes Lord, we are not finished yet...We are not complete yet...You, our dearest friend, are guiding us. At times You are urging us, comforting and consoling us. You whisper to us letting us know You forgive us and love us...We'll try our very best to continue on until our last breath...

Our last breath - oh dear Savior, let our last breath utter Your blessed name! Let our last breath give forth Praise and Thanksgiving to You...

Thank You, Lord Jesus, for having patience with us...Thank You, dear Father God, for sending Your dear Son Jesus to this earth of ours...Without You, dear Jesus, to teach us through the Scriptures, we would always remain imperfect. Without Your Holy Spirit working in us, we would remain unfinished, not complete, lacking of something...And, that something, dear Jesus, would be the perfection of You... ... ...

Solely Dependent Upon You   Sept. 15

Psalm 145:17-19

The Lord is fair in everything he does, and full of kindness. He is close to all who call on him sincerely. He fulfills the desires of those who reverence and trust him; he hears their cries for help and rescues them.

My dear Lord Jesus, may we always be solely dependent upon You...May we be completely independent of the world and solely dependent upon You...

As time passes, dear Lord, may we depend on You more and more each day and each night...May we, through Your generosity, not have to depend on others for our needs...

That is a very large request, we realize, to ask to be independent of others...But dear Master, because You are the authority in our lives, some of us yearn to be dependent on You alone...

As we wake each day and communicate with You, we realize more and more, how necessary it is that we depend solely upon You...Who else in this whole Universe can bring forth what You accomplish each and every day! We hear of Miracles happening here and there, but how many more are happening all over the world and we are not even aware of them!

God, You are the source of all goodness! Goodness – Your name God is in that very word! Virtue, kindness, generosity, and benevolence all reflect "goodness". That "goodness" comes only from You! Yes, Father God, You are the source of all LOVE; every "good" comes from You…How grateful are we who need no one but You to help us through our days and our nights…

How many millions scattered over this earth are dependent on drugs, sex, alcohol or tobacco to get themselves through each hour of the day and night…If only they would come to the realization that You, and only You, can meet the need for our dependency…

Dear Jesus, it is with grateful hearts that we come to thank You for not making us feel like a burden to You, because of our dependency on You…

Instead, You welcome us and delight in our dependence upon You!

Nails – Nails   Sept. 16

1st Timothy 2:9,10

And the women should be the same way, quiet and sensible in manner and clothing. Christian women should be noticed for being kind and good, not for the way they fix their hair or because of their jewels or fancy clothes.

Lord dear, I was sitting here looking at my fingernails. Suddenly You brought the thought of the other meaning of nails.

Nails were driven into Your Body…Nails hung You to that infamous Cross, which once was a tree…How often do we think of those nails, and the way they were used to help crucify You…

You, dear God, when creating us, gave us fingernails and toenails. They have definite purposes…Yet today, we see nails that are added to one's own. We see all colors painted on them…We see gold or jewels attached to these nails. Thousands upon thousands of dollars are spent on nails, perhaps millions…Today the care of nails is a huge business…

Oh Lord, there are millions of children starving all over the world. There are people made homeless through the failure of businesses. There are illnesses that need funds for research for cures and so many critical needs. If only a portion of these monies spent on nails could be used to help these desperate situations…

How much time is spent admiring the nails on our hands, changing colors, etc. How little time is spent on admiring You, praising You and adoring You...How often do we give thanks to You for all the blessings You have bestowed on us...

How often do we give You thanks for opening our eyes each morning...How often do we give You thanks for the ability to rise from our beds each new day...How often do we thank You for the gift of hearing, the ability to speak...

Oh Lord, there are so very many reasons to thank You...With so many people doing without, how often do we thank You for what we have, and pray for those in need?

Let us pause and enumerate all the blessings we've received in our lives...Yes Lord, we remember the blessings even in the difficulties and how you carried us through them...

We are tempted to be overly concerned with the temporary things of this life...But only Your Eternal Kingdom is of permanent importance...May we realize that those nails, which nailed You to that Cross, are part of our entrance into Your Kingdom! Thank You, dear Lord and Savior... ... ...

Grieving   Sept. 17

Ezekiel 17:23 (NIV)
On the mountain heights of Israel I will plant it; it will produce branches and bear fruit and become a splendid cedar. Birds of every kind will nest in it; they will find shelter in the shade of its branches.

Dear Lord God, I never expected to experience grieving for things that were not human or animal life...But I find my spirit in a state of grieving for what You had given LIFE to, many years ago...

I am reminded of the poem by Joyce Kilmer: "I think that I shall never see a poem lovely as a tree..."

You alone, God, can make a tree...You breathe LIFE into tiny seeds. They sprout and grow, and grow, and grow...Then one day a beautiful tree stands tall in the sunlight...It offers nests to birds, food for animals, shade for humans and households...When one is blessed by being surrounded by many of these magnificent gifts from You, Lord, great peace and tranquility exists...

LIFE seems so peaceful...When one observes each of these beautiful trees, one sees the different characteristics of each tree. One has great height, but its branches only spread out a few feet from the trunk. Another has great height and huge branches spreading out for many feet. Another has the ability to bear fruit, another nuts...Still others, each unto themselves, have different types of leaves, different shades of green...Truly living among these wonderful trees was a tremendous blessing from You, Lord God...

And now they are gone...In just two hours a mighty storm came through and with horrendous gusts of wind, blew these majestic trees into a maze of broken hulks...Where once beauty and tranquility existed, now devastation abounds...

Sky appears where once beautiful trees canopied the view...Yes, Lord God, mighty God, I am grieving...It is so difficult to lose these dear friends, for friends they had become to me...

Material things can be replaced in a relatively short time compared to the life of a huge tree. Twenty-five, fifty years or more were in the process of developing these trees to their maximum beauty...

Yes, new LIFE will come back as a gift from You, Lord, but other eyes will see the beauty someday, years away from now...For now, dear Father, I can only thank You for allowing me the privilege of living among all those beautiful trees while they were here...I will treasure these memories all the days of my LIFE...

From my heart I thank You again, dear Creator God... ... ...

In The Stillness Of The Night   Sept. 18

Psalm 63:6,7

I lie awake at night thinking of you – of how much you have helped me – and how I rejoice through the night beneath the protecting shadow of your wings.

"In the stillness of the night, I come to you seeking love, seeking affectionate thoughts of Me... I enjoy being with you... Can you understand this, believe this? Who do I have? Do I have any who will be willing to be My friend, willing to wake in the night to be with Me in spirit, to spend time with Me? Surely you can understand this, dear one..."

Yes, my Lord, I become lonely for You, too…As I awaken with praises on my lips for You, that comforts me…Yes, my Lord, I seek Your company as You seek mine…

Again I think it's so hard to believe that You, dear sweet Jesus, seek to spend time with me…Though I know deep in my heart that You LOVE me, it is still a wondrous thought to realize this…

You know how tired I was as I lay down to sleep this night…Yet You awakened me…Realization came to me that You wanted my attention. You clearly wanted me to awaken, rise up and spend this time with You…

We in this world can understand loneliness, Father God…Can it be possible that You would crave attention, affection, from one so insignificant? It is a wondrously complex thought…

It is still; the quiet seems so extremely deep…I am here Lord, listening…As we communicate, my heart is filled with gratitude. Happy is my heart, Lord, to spend this time with You…

Though I cannot see You, I feel so strongly Your presence here with me…Though I cannot actually hear Your spoken voice, I hear it in my heart…

Oh Lord, dear Lord, how my spirit longs to be with You…How I long to be with You for all time, all eternity…Thank You, my dear Savior, for calling to me, in the stillness of the night… … …

When Everything Is Said and Done…   Sept. 19

2nd Corinthians 5:10

For we must all stand before Christ to be judged and have our lives laid bare – before him. Each of us will receive whatever he deserves for the good or bad things he has done in his earthly body.

When everything is said and done, my Lord, it's YOU, YOU, YOU…Only You will have made the difference in all our lives:

No matter what achievements we have accomplished,
No matter what power we have had, Lord,
No matter what station in life we have held,
No matter how much money we have had.
It all comes down to YOU, YOU, YOU…

Each of us comes into Life alone. Each one of us will face You alone when this earthly body of ours drops away and our spirits arrive to stand before You...

Oh, Almighty Father, Creator of the entire Universe, we will stand before You in awe! All things in our lives will be out in the open – every word, action, motive, and thought will be out in the open before You, for all to see...

Words will not avail us...Truth, perfect truth will be the factor. Excuses of no worth, will fall faintly from those of us standing before You...No one ever born on this earth will be spared this experience. We can get no substitute to stand in for us – it will be a one-on-one command performance. It will be for one time only...We have only this once to face the judgement of either Heaven or Hell!

Is there really a Heaven? In Philippians 3:14 Paul says

...I strain to reach the end of the race and receive the prize for which God is calling us up to heaven because of what Christ Jesus did for us.

Is there really a Hell? Jesus makes this clear in Matthew 10:28.

"Don't be afraid of those who can kill only your bodies – but can't touch your souls! Fear only God who can destroy both soul and body in hell."

Do we have a choice between Heaven and Hell? Again the answer is in the Bible. In Matthew 7:21(NIV) Jesus says,

"Not everyone who says to me, 'Lord, Lord,' will enter the kingdom of heaven, but only he who does the will of my Father who is in heaven."

The will of the Father is explained by Jesus in John 6:40(NIV) which says,

"For my Father's will is that everyone who looks to the Son and believes in him shall have eternal life, and I will raise him up at the last day."

Yes Father, when everything is said and done, it is only You who will make a difference here and now in our lives when we choose You. But, the greatest difference will be in where we'll spend Eternity...

When one thinks of Eternity, one can only think of "forever and ever"...Our finite minds cannot really comprehend Eternity...There is nothing that we can relate it to...But once we believe in Eternity, it would be very foolish to risk the chance of spending Eternity in Hell. For Heaven is offered to us by our Savior, Jesus Christ, who died for us.

It is this faith in You, Lord, which causes us to believe that Heaven is real...Yes, dear Father, dear Son, dear Holy Spirit, when everything is said and done, it is YOU, YOU, YOU... ... ...

What Is Heaven Like, Lord?　　　Sept. 20

John 14:1-3

"Let not your heart be troubled. You are trusting God, now trust in me. There are many homes up there where my Father lives, and I am going to prepare them for your coming. When everything is ready, then I will come and get you, so that you can always be with me where I am. If this weren't so, I would tell you plainly."

Dear Lord Jesus, what is Heaven like? Suddenly as I wondered about this, I imagined a little bird flying toward me and landing on my hand...As I looked at this precious little creature, it began to sing! It showed no fear, but seemed to enjoy singing to me...What excitement flooded my spirit! Then a beautifully colored butterfly landed on my shoulder, slowly spreading its wings back and forth!!! Now I truly felt that I must be experiencing a little bit of Heaven right here on earth!

Yes Lord, I know it really did not happen to me but in my heart I feel that it did...Heaven could be - roses without thorns and flowers that do not cause hay fever, which bloom constantly without wilting and dying...

Heaven could be - little animals playing together without fear of one another...Pets there would not need grooming, feeding, or walking...The air would be filled with the music of our little feathered friends...Glorious colors would be displayed everywhere our eyes turned to...

These are only a very few of the things which may await us in Heaven! There will be no hunger; our bodies will never be overweight or under weight...Our skin will never become wrinkled, as we will remain forever young...

There will be no shortage of housing, as a home has been prepared by You, our Lord and Master, Jesus Christ, for each of us...There will be no stack of unpaid bills for You again, dear Jesus, paid the price for each of us already...

Heaven is a place of mystery...Heaven is a place already prepared for us to go to, as soon as our last breath leaves our bodies...

Oh Heavenly Father God, Father of all the Universe, enable us to help those in doubt of Your real Heaven...Help us please, to bring Your TRUTHS TO THOSE IN DOUBT...My spirit has been convinced by Your Holy Spirit, that Heaven IS real...Heaven is our eternal LIFE waiting for us, because of what Your Son Jesus did for us...Yes, precious Jesus, Your willingness to die for my sins and the sins of the whole world is, and was the greatest act of LOVE for all man kind... Thank You, dear Lord Jesus, thank You... ... ...

So Much To Think About   Sept. 21

Philippians 4:4-7

Always be full of joy in the Lord; I say it again, rejoice! Let everyone see that you are unselfish and considerate in all you do. Remember that the Lord is coming soon. Don't worry about anything; instead, pray about everything; tell God your needs and don't forget to thank him for his answers. If you do this you will experience God's peace, which is far more wonderful than the human mind can understand. His peace will keep your thoughts and your hearts quiet and at rest as you trust in Christ Jesus.

There is so much to think about, Lord, but then when we really get to the heart of everything, there's only YOU...Yes, Lord, there's so much to think about, day and night...

When we go to bed at night, it is often the time we spend thinking about things. We lay our heads down and almost immediately our minds start to churn...What about this? What about that? This is only the beginning...Time goes by; now our thinking has turned into anxiety, fretfulness and now the worst - worry...

Oh dear Lord Jesus, only You know how much energy and time is wasted on these emotions... It accomplishes absolutely nothing... Nothing positive comes out of worry...

Yes Lord, we need to spend some time thinking about decisions, etc. which we must make in LIFE...But, we must be careful not to allow ourselves to be caught up in the trap of worrying...

Not one of us gets through LIFE without having to think through decisions regarding problems and concerns...Praise to You, dear

Lord, for You have told us in Your Scriptures that we must TRUST You, instead of worrying about our situations...

Trusting You, dear Jesus, takes a great burden off us! When we leave our problems with You, after thinking about them, we can then relax and fall into a peaceful rest...While we are sleeping YOU are concerning Yourself with our needs...And Lord, there is no point in giving You our burdens before we go to sleep, and then picking them up again when we wake!

It is only by complete trust in You, Lord, that we can lead a joyful LIFE...The peace that passes all understanding can be ours!

Thank you Lord Jesus, that we can trust in YOUR care and rest in You... ... ...

You Must Be Brooding, Lord...   Sept. 22

Genesis 1:11,12, 25
And he said, "Let the earth burst forth with every sort of grass and seed–bearing plant, and fruit trees with seeds inside the fruit, so that these seeds will produce the kinds of plants and fruits they came from." And so it was, and God was pleased.

God made all sorts of wild animals and cattle and reptiles. And God was pleased with what he had done.

My Lord, You must be brooding over this earth. We have polluted and destroyed so much of it...Yes Lord, all of us living here must take part in the responsibility for damaging Your earth...

There was a time, Lord, when we little realized the damage that was being done...Suddenly we became aware of what was happening to the land and the sea.

Babbling brooks babble no more...Refuge blocks the flow of water to a tiny trickle...Some have already dried up. Where men made decisions to change the flow of water for financial gain, they now realize the folly of such decisions.

Oceans once teaming with all kinds of marine life are now in stages of depletion...Where once fisherman had full nets daily, they are reduced to looking elsewhere to make a living...

Oh Lord, how this must dishearten You...Men have poured putrid things into Your waterways, Your oceans...Where once clean, clear waters charmed this earth, now grayish, putrid, cloudy waters exist...

Dear Lord, you gave us this marvelous earth...It contained all and more than man needed to live...Along the way greed settled in...Now animals are being slaughtered for money. Parts of their bodies are taken and the remainder is left to rot away...Birds were and are killed for their beautiful plumage...

And Father, Your beautiful trees are being plucked out of Your magnificent forests leaving the land raw and useless at times...Where will all this pillage end? How long can this earth survive if we all don't help it? Each of us can help in some way. We must...

Still, You graciously give us sunshine and precious rain to help replenish the earth...Thank You, dear Lord, for all Your goodness to us. May we all become aware of this earth being a gift from You, as Life itself is Your gift...Hopefully, Lord, it is not too late... ... ...

Three for a Seesaw   Sept. 23

Ephesians 5:21,24,25
Honor Christ by submitting to each other.

So you wives must willingly obey your husbands in everything, just as the church obeys Christ. And you husbands, show the same kind of love to your wives as Christ showed to the church when he died for her,...

Love is like a seesaw, isn't it, Lord...This is especially true in marriage when it is so important for both partners to cooperate. Sweet Jesus, when we picture seesaws in our minds, we see only two people in connection with them...

We know from our experiences as little children that the first thing we have to do after getting on one end of the seesaw is to hold it steady, until the other partner gets on. If we are the second one to get on, the other person has to hold it steady until we have gotten on. Now the two sides are equal. Now the problem begins...Which one is going to give the first push to give the other partner the first "up"? Only one of the partners can go up first in order to start the seesaw's motion.

Lord, it's just like that in a marriage isn't it? One of the partners has to be the first to put the seesaw motion into action. Once one does, it gives a boost to the other partner and that partner is up high where it is usually so clear and bright! That's one of the main purposes of a seesaw, to give each one using it the opportunity to rise high where things are cool and refreshing...

That's the purpose of marriage too, Lord. When two people decide they want to be together in marriage, they agree to work together just as the two people who work a seesaw. One person's "up" is only achieved by the other person being willing to be down. That's where the Love starts to work. That's when Love puts the seesaw, or marriage, into real action!

Dear Jesus, we have the seesaw clearly pictured in our minds, moving up and down, up and down working so beautifully. Now we are aware of something else very important which is necessary for this action to take place. To use a seesaw, one sturdy board unites the two partners. In a marriage, a wedding ceremony unites the two partners. However, no matter how sturdy the board is or how equally distributed the weight of the partners, the seesaw cannot even begin to function until the most important part is there. It is the sturdy, supporting bar which runs directly in the center of the two partners. If the board is not centered properly, the seesaw cannot work right. One partner will get a shorter part of the board and one a longer part. It cannot work unless this important supporting bar is there...

Lord, in marriage, You are the supporting bar. You have to be in the center of the marriage for it to function properly. You are LOVE, perfect LOVE...Without You in the center of it, the marriage can't work as perfectly as it can with You in the exact center!

Dear Lord, thank You for this concept of Your LOVE...Thank You for teaching us that Love cannot be taken only. Love has to be given and taken, given and taken as on a seesaw! In order for us to love purely as You would have us love, we must learn to be constantly willing to give love. The more we give the more will return, then the desire in us will grow so strong we will want to again return the love we have just received!

Lord, it's a beautiful thing – Your LOVE! Thank You for showing us that it takes three for a marriage. When You are kept in the center, marriages will reap the joyful rewards... ... ...

Your Need For Me, Lord…   Sept. 24

Jeremiah 31:3 (NIV)
The Lord appeared to us in the past, saying: "I have loved you with an everlasting love; I have drawn you with loving-kindness."

Oh Lord, I find it so hard to realize that You, Almighty God, have a need for me…I find it so hard to understand that You want me to come to You in the silence of deep friendship as only two close friends can share…What is there about me that You in Your greatness would want to be near? Dear Lord, I simply can't understand it…

"You see, My child, I desire the hearts of My creations… I created you; you are My creation… Don't you see that? As a mother longs to have her child come to her knee, of its own accord, so I, My child, desire you to come to Me…

So come, dear one, come and sit beside Me… For I am with you, though you do not see Me… I find joy in the times you stop your busyness and give your entire thoughts to Me… Our friendship grows deeper each time we spend together…"

Yes, Lord, I am beginning to understand…I have just seen a rainbow and it reminded me of the promise You made to us in the Bible… (Genesis 9: 8-17)

It is no coincidence that the above words from You and Your rainbow came at the same time! A rainbow is the only visible promise mentioned in Your Bible, Lord…It is only one promise of the many, many You made to us! You also said You would never abandon us…With LOVE like that, dear Lord, it makes it easier to understand now, why You care so much for each of us.

Your unconditional LOVE is so overwhelming to us! You never said we have to get ourselves cleaned up sparkling white before You would come to us…You just want us the way we are, in our present condition. Then as we continue to draw toward You, You bring us into understanding how precious we are to You!

As our desire for You grows, we see the need to come to You…Desire, on our part, changes to need…Then we can reach that relationship where Your need for us, is more understandable, dear Jesus...

May our friendship reach such a depth, that we will constantly look for opportunities to spend quiet times alone with You... ... ...

Not Of This World...   Sept. 25

Isaiah 40:31

But they that wait upon the Lord shall renew their strength. They shall mount up with wings like eagles; they shall run and not be weary; they shall walk and not faint.

Lord, I was reading a lovely devotional message referring to the Scripture above from Isaiah. The thought came to me that we too, have wings, but they are not of this world...

It is Your wings that can sweep us up out of the dullness, sadness, loneliness and hurts of this earth...You lower Your invisible wings to us...We can choose to climb up on them or stay where we are...

Oh Lord God, I long to soar through the Heavenlies with You! I want to feel the release from this earth and experience the cool breezes hugging us...Only You, Lord God, can lift us up...We must relinquish our petty selves and desires...Then we can climb above our littleness, forget ourselves, and become new creatures...We can become reborn!

You, Lord Jesus, are the pathway to this freedom from earth's problems! You hold all the answers to our needs, as well as, our opportunities to grow spiritually! When we wait patiently upon You, Lord, no matter what the problems are, then we know that all Your Promises are going to be kept...

Knowing that, dear Savior, frees us to mount up with anticipation and envision Your beautiful wings. Your wings can carry us far away from the sordidness of our lives...We are still in the same circumstances and conditions, but now we are able to view them from Your perspective...

Yes Lord, Your invisible wings are not of this world, but it is a Joy to close our eyes and see them in our imagination! They are so beautiful, like gossamer and colored with the most delicate hues! We can visualize our stepping up upon them and stretching out on them as we feel the security of Yourself. No matter how high Your wings take us, we feel content as babes...Thank You, sweet Lord, for these beautiful thoughts...

May each of us desire to rise above our problems, as we look to You, Lord Jesus...As we view our circumstances from Your perspective, in Your Strength we can run and not grow weary, walk and not faint... ... ...

Sacrifice   Sept. 26

Hebrews 10:12 (RSV)
But when Christ had offered for all time a single sacrifice for sins, he sat down at the right hand of God, ...

Lord Jesus, dear Lord Jesus, You stood there as our Sacrificial Lamb...You spoke nary a word...What more could You say? You had said it all...Most didn't pay You enough respect to even try to understand Your mission here...Dear, dear Sacrificial Lamb, it is awesome to try to understand how someone as perfect as You, could have had so much animosity directed at them...

We often hear that if we are "good" only good things should happen to us...We only need to reflect a very short time, dear Jesus, to realize that is not so...Sometimes the harder we try to be "nice", the less we are understood. Suspicion arises..."What's in it for you?" is asked of us when we try to demonstrate generosity towards others...

The "goodness" in us is suspect...The Goodness, the Perfection of You, Son of the Almighty, was suspect...They, Your enemies, couldn't stand Your Goodness...It is so hard to understand this...

Those of us who love You, cry out in our spirits as we recall the treatment You received...To many of us, it is such a foreign thought to realize that others would want to see You crucified...

Sweet, sweet Perfect Lord, our hearts are still shaken at what You suffered for us...It is an overwhelming burden at times, dear Jesus...Yet we know that it had to be, for it was Your Heavenly Father's Plan...In order for us to enter into the Heavenly Home You desire to share with us, You had to die...

Thankfully, through the Scriptures, we are taught about God's Plan of Salvation for us! Because of Your willingness to obey this

Plan, we can be forgiven and come to know You as Savior and Lord...

What words could ever be adequate enough to thank You, dear Lamb of God? There are none! It is impossible to thank You with mere words...But, sweet Savior, please look very deeply within our hearts, then You can see the gratitude, the appreciation – though it is tremendously inadequate... ... ...

Mountaintop Joy!   Sept. 27

Psalm 90:1,2 (NIV)
LORD, YOU have been our dwelling place throughout all generations. Before the mountains were born or you brought forth the earth and the world, from everlasting to everlasting you are God.

Lord! You truly are without a beginning or an end! And as I gaze out at Your glorious mountains, so high they reach beyond the beautiful clouds, I am filled with an awesome joy!

Only You could have planned such a glorious sight! Everywhere one's eyes travel, Your glorious mountains are there!! Oh Father God, thank You for this stupendous sight! Thank You for creating these majestic mountains, some capped with snow, others lightly dusted...

Thank You, dear Father, for allowing Your children, at times, to have such joy! We cannot understand why You allow us to partake of this glory, this mountaintop joy, but our hearts are ever so grateful and appreciative...

Church bells are ringing out their joy at the glory of these majestic mountains! If they can sound such joy, how can we humans not ring out with our praises to You also?

Yet with all these glorious mountains to behold, we must realize that they are here only temporarily...Yes, these magnificent mountains will pass away, as we will, some day...

Thankfully, Father, Your Son - our Savior Jesus Christ, came here to teach us what You want us to know...He came; He taught. He LOVED; He died – all for us...He came to prepare the way to our real existence, our permanent home, in Heaven!

There we'll know true happiness! There we'll have mountaintop joy forever and ever! We'll not have to go to a special part of Heaven,

303

as we do here on earth to see beautiful mountains or oceans. Much more awaits us! There we will find our REAL dwelling place!!

And as Psalm 90:1 says,

LORD, YOU have been our dwelling place throughout all generations.

Oh thank You, Father God! We look forward to that moment of all moments when You welcome us home, with You for all Eternity... ... ...

Giving Of One's Self...   Sept. 28

1ˢᵗ John 4:7
Dear friends, let us practice loving each other, for love comes from God and those who are loving and kind show that they are the children of God, and that they are getting to know him better.

It's hard! Oh Lord, it's hard...Giving of one's self is one of the hardest things for us to do in our lives...In our minds we often say to ourselves, "I'll do this" or "I'll do that" for someone...Or "I'll be this" or "I'll be that" towards another...

Then Lord, when a specific time comes, we find that our own will drives us to do exactly what WE want regardless of anyone else...

To give material things, to give money, to give food, is so much easier than to give of ourselves...Our human nature often is spoiled and selfish...Though we have grown into adults, there are times when the spoiled child in us rears up and demands its own selfish way...

Oh dear Lord, help us to see our own selfishness when we take the time to examine our consciences. We sometimes look at others and recall their shortcomings. We know all their faults, don't we, Lord? But, dear Savior, we desperately need to see all of these shortcomings with YOUR eyes...It's so very easy to see the faults of others...

Please, Lord, help each of us to review our own nature...No matter how "good" we think we are, let us see with Your eyes where we need to correct ourselves...If we are to expect Mercy from You, we must remove the log in our own eyes, before we look at the imperfections in those around us...

To be able to do this, we need to give up our own way many, many times. Giving of one's self requires a deep desire to do so...It means coming to You, dear Savior, many times a day for strength and encouragement. You are our example of unselfish, unconditional LOVE…

When we take the time to recall how unselfish You were, dear Jesus, we can try again to surrender our selfishness…In a sense giving of one's self is a gift to another…You gave the supreme gift, dear Jesus, when You gave Your very own life…

Please, dear One, help us to be "givers" also… … …

A Grit Of Sand   Sept. 29

2nd Corinthians 4:7,17

But this precious treasure – this light and power that now shine within us – is held in a perishable container, that is, in our weak bodies. Everyone can see that the glorious power within must be from God and is not our own.

These troubles and sufferings of ours are, after all, quite small and won't last very long. Yet this short time of distress will result in God's richest blessing upon us forever and ever!

"A grit of sand, a particle of sand – out of this comes forth a beautiful pearl! I am the Pearl of Great Value! I came into this world to be that grit of sand, to be an irritant to you, to cause you to become a priceless pearl to Me, your Creator… Can you see this? Can you understand that I can irritate you, so you will stop your worldliness and take time to find Me? I am the One who can bring you the peace, which passes all understanding. Allow Me to do the work in you, so that you too may become a jewel, precious to Me…"

Oh Jesus, to become a pearl, a jewel for You is worth any price which we must pay…For once we become that, it is for all time! Your LIFE, Your DEATH, was and is the most meaningful happening in this whole world. By this LIFE of Yours, by Your DEATH, we are given the privilege of joining You permanently in Your Heavenly home!

Irritate us Lord…Allow whatever it takes to save our souls, Father God! Whatever the cost, dear Master, dear Savior, it is worth the price! Irritate us so that we can see YOU as that Pearl of Great Value! We shouldn't want to become so complacent with LIFE that we allow it to end without any value to You…We need to see that our LIFE needs to have some grit in it...We need some irritants, which will cause us to come to terms with what You came to teach us here...

Shake us out of our trudging along, or the "floating through LIFE" attitude...Instill in us the realness of You, dear Lord God...No matter who we are, we have the potential of doing great things, in and through You! Any one of us can be a breathtaking pearl in the lives of others! Because of You in us, we can become pearls for You...

Thank You, Lord Jesus, for Loving us enough to irritate us into changing...May we bless others and encourage others to understand the meaning of Your being the Pearl of Great Value... ... ...

Well, Lord, Another Day   Sept. 30

Psalm 118:24
This is the day the Lord has made. We will rejoice and be glad in it.

Well, Lord, another day - You have given us, another day...Thank You Lord, thank You...Days seem to run together in the sameness of our lifestyles...

Is today going to be much different than yesterday, Lord? Circumstances seem very much the same as yesterday...What difference can a day make? Each has the same 24 hours...Can this day be much different?

"Yes it can, because of Me, Your Lord, your Savior... I may call you to do an extraordinary act today... I may save your life today... So many things that I know about can affect you this day... All you need to know is that I am always with you, so concern yourself not with today..."

Thank You for Your comforting words, dear Father God...We so often find ourselves in the sameness of Life...We forget that there are millions of others who would eagerly change places with us...

We forget that there are millions who wander the streets searching for scraps of food...There are those who look for a safe place to lay their heads down, who search for something to keep themselves warm...These things are occurring in all the countries of this world...

Oh, Lord, forgive us when we act as if we are 'bored' with the sameness of yesterday and the days before...It only takes a short time of serious thinking to bring us back to the blessings You have given us...

And we can bless someone else today. We can be sensitive to Your guidance...Perhaps a long overdue telephone call can be made to cheer up a lonely, hurting person...Perhaps a card or letter would bless another...Perhaps we could visit an ill person in the hospital or one who is homebound...A financial donation may bless several people when sent to a deserving place...

Yes, Lord, another day has come—may this day bless someone who would have been forgotten about except for a reminder from You...Today is another day of loving protection from You - another day of opportunity to stop and count our blessings...Today is another day to thank You for being You, for saving our souls for all Eternity...Thank You, dear Savior... ... ...

October

Little Creature   Oct. 1

Psalm 32:7,8

You are my hiding place from every storm of life; You even keep me from getting into trouble! You surround me with songs of victory. I will instruct you (says the Lord) and guide you along the best pathway for your life; I will advise you and watch your progress.

Dear precious Jesus, I saw one of Your strange little creatures this morning…It was carrying quite a large house on its back…As I gazed at it the thought came that it was blessed to be able to carry its home, its hiding place, wherever it went…

My mind went on to make comparisons and suddenly I realized what the comparison should be for us humans…We should be carrying You with us everywhere we go, everywhere…Just as that little creature carried its home, its hiding place everywhere, we who are created in Your image, should keep You ever present with us…

Lord, it's a simple thought…But why do we make it so complicated? Why do we, who are traveling through LIFE as the little creature, so often refuse to take You along with us?

Like the little creature having the convenience of its home right on its back, why don't we realize what a blessing it would be to know that Your presence is with us? And, as the little creature hides itself inside its house, we then could hide ourselves within You…There we would always be protected and looked after by You…

How difficult we make our lives sometimes as we face LIFE…Yes Lord, You never said it would be easy. Yet You promised that if we gave You our burdens, ALL of our burdens, You would give us the peace that would pass all understanding…

What a wonderful promise! When we believe in You and trust in You, our lives do take on a peacefulness! Joy enters in too! Oh Lord God, Creator of this whole beautiful Earth, how we Praise You! How we thank You for Your generosity…

May we, like the little precious creature You gave LIFE to, carry You with us every step of each day… … …

Grateful Heart   Oct. 2

Psalm 9:1,2 (NIV)
I will praise you, O Lord, with all my heart; I will tell of all your wonders. I will be glad and rejoice in you; I will sing praise to your name, O Most High.

Dear Jesus, the sweet little birds, Your little birds, are chirping here and there under Your beautiful huge trees. They are PRAISING You, thanking You for all that You provide for them!

That is why I am here also, dear Lord...I am here on this very beautiful morning, here to PRAISE and thank You for all the many blessings you have provided for me...

The cool breezes caress my face, the sun shimmers on the waters and filters through Your magnificent trees! Surely Lord, this is a little piece of Heaven on earth!

Hopefully, Lord, there are millions of others thanking You for their little piece of Heaven on earth...Sometimes we take the beautiful natural surroundings for granted...Yet Lord, it doesn't take long to gaze around us, and appreciate Your generosity to us...

Our lives can get so complicated. It is at these very times that we NEED to look around and give You thanks. Sometimes we think something "big" has to happen to us or for us before we should say "Thank You, Lord! Thank You, God!"

All we have to do is to look around...If one truly feels that there is nothing absolutely nothing, to be thankful for, then it's time to look at one's self...

If one is able to walk, see, hear, and talk, then gratitude should be felt...Oh how we take these basic gifts for granted! Help us Father God, to have grateful hearts...

Oh merciful Father, how much we have to thank You for...Most of all we are grateful, dear Jesus, that You died for us...As the breeze continues to refresh me, as the birds continue to PRAISE You, I join them in their praises as we glorify You...We thank You and worship You...We adore You, for YOU alone are worthy... ... ...

The Mystery Of My Love... Oct. 3

1st Corinthians 14:1a

Let love be your greatest aim; ...

"Yes, child, there is a mystery about My LOVE... There is a mystery surrounding My LOVE... You wonder how I can LOVE those who are unlovable in your eyes? But in My eyes, I see them in a light of LOVE, My LOVE... My LOVE is purifying... My LOVE is a pure and perfect LOVE... There is no other LOVE like Mine...

Blessed are you who have come into the knowledge of this... Blessed are you who have felt this LOVE... Blessed are they who will open themselves up to My LOVE, for My LOVE is unique. My LOVE builds up. It never tears down... My LOVE has graciousness woven into it, compassion, all that a soul can ever need...

Call upon this LOVE of Mine... It is available to one and all... Yet because it is My LOVE, it is a mystery to many..."

Merciful Father, Teacher of true LOVE, help each of us upon this planet to understand the necessity of LOVE... Your kind of LOVE is critically needed in all our lives... There are so many hundreds of thousands, even millions, who are in need of Your LOVE... For Your kind of LOVE is like a soothing balm upon a soul... Your LOVE heals the hurts, misunderstandings, difficulties, and sorrows that come into our lives...

When we refuse to love or to receive love, we are the losers... We drown inside ourselves... In time our spirits, our inner selves, begin to shrivel up and we become dry and empty... Others turn away from us, because we can offer them nothing... We actually become good for nothing... Hopefully we begin to realize how empty we are as we see in others' faces, a glow of joy, peace, contentment... Then perhaps we will open ourselves up to Your LOVE – to receive and to give...

Oh dear Master teacher of LOVE, please show all those in need of Your mysterious LOVE, how to obtain it... You know, dear Lord, how desperately Your kind of LOVE is needed in this world!

If Your LOVE were put into operation today, families would become whole again! Wars would cease, as would the need for weapons. PEACE, LAUGHTER, and JOY would reign in our world...

Oh, Father of LOVE, help us to love… … …

You Are My Friend, God…   Oct. 4

Matthew 28:20b

"…and be sure of this – that I am with you always, even to the end of the world."

John15:14

"and you are my friends if you obey me,"

Yes God, You are our Friend! What an awesome thought that is! You, Almighty God, Creator of all Creation are our Friend! It boggles our minds!

Wherever each of us is at this moment, You are watching over us! We cannot be out of Your sight! Throughout the day, throughout the night, You are steadfast in Your LOVE for us…You care for us!

Through our ups and downs of Life, You are there. We can turn to You at any moment we choose to, and feel absolutely confident that You ARE there! We never have to make an appointment; we never have to wait until it is convenient for You to hear us…

How awesome it is! The older we are, the more we realize what Your friendship means…

Perhaps, You dear Father, have blessed us with true friends throughout our lives…If so they are to be treasured, dear Lord. Yet there are times that we cannot make contact with them…They are out of reach for some reason or another. But You, Almighty God are always available to us in the blink of an eye! May we all treasure this friendship with You, Father God…

Thankfully, we can continue on our paths through Life confident in Your care for us…As times go by, our friendship becomes stronger…Our friendship has been tested many times, but in Your Faithfulness, dear, dear Father God You have never abandoned us…

There are so many words to describe our gratitude for the friendship we have with You, dear Lord…But sometimes it seems as if we repeat the same words over and over again in trying to tell You how much we love You…Gratefully You know our hearts and can read them…As each beat of our hearts occurs, they too are saying

"Thank You, Lord...I love You, Lord...Thank You, Lord...I love You, Lord... ... ..."

Innocence   Oct. 5

Psalm 139:16
You saw me before I was born and scheduled each day of my life before I began to breathe. Every day was recorded in your Book!

2nd Corinthians 1:3,4a (NIV)
Praise be to the God and Father of our Lord Jesus Christ, the Father of compassion and the God of all comfort, who comforts us in all our troubles, ...

Lord, I always feel so sad when I hear or read about the death of a little child...It saddens my heart so much, that I almost feel the grief of the family...

And Father, I know how many prayers must be said when these precious little ones are ill or going through some catastrophe...Hopefully prayers are sent up to You for each one – countless prayers...

Blessedly You, in the mystery of Yourself, answer these prayers many times with positive answers! But Lord, today again, I heard of another little one who did not recover...

You took this child away from its family...Why, Lord why? This child was so young and full of innocence, a treasure to its family...

I sat here wondering, "Why? Why? Why?" Suddenly I realized You know all things, especially the future...You foresee the things to come...

You foresee the whole life of a baby even before its first breath...You look down the path of each of their lives. Could it be that You see where one of these little precious ones will go astray and lose their way?

That precious little life, so innocent, could be entrapped in such a way, that the pain to itself and all who loved them would be too much to bear...Perhaps this is why You lovingly take this wee one Home to Heaven...

May the loved ones of these dear little children understand that perhaps You took them Home to Heaven, because You LOVED them

312

so much...You wanted to spare them and their families from more pain and heartache...

Heavenly Father may You touch these grieving family members with Your Comfort...May they receive special blessings of Your LOVE and PEACE, dear, dear Jesus... ... ...

In The Storm   Oct. 6

Hebrews 13:5b
For God has said, "I will never, *never* fail you nor forsake you."

I was thinking about this past week, Lord, when the very worst of hurricanes had blown through. Then I realized that many parts of our lives are filled with storms of all kinds...

Some are actual, like the recent one, but oh, how many of us have storms of other kinds, which leave one's heart broken and askew...

Houses can eventually be rebuilt; material things can be restored...Finances can return...But hearts can take much, much longer to mend, sweet Jesus, as You know...

Yet each of us must remember as we go through these storms, You are always there...Yes Lord, for You alone can be depended upon...Sometimes we wonder why You allow us to suffer through these storms...

Why Lord, why me? Haven't I tried to live a "good" life? Haven't I tried to be a "good" person? Then why do I have to suffer these debilitating storms? You know how much I suffered recently...My life will never be the same...

"Yes child, your life will never be the same... You are in a new phase of life... You do not see it as better yet, but one day, looking back, you will see that there was a purpose to this loss, this suffering."

Lord Jesus, I do not see that this destruction in my LIFE could have a purpose...But because You tell me, as I look back, I will see the reason why one day - I trust You...

Suddenly I see a boat out on stormy waters. I picture Your disciples experiencing deep fears as You sleep, apparently unaware of the horrendous storm raging about...When they awaken You, You say to them:

"O you men of little faith! Why are you so frightened?" (Matthew 8:26b)

Next You stood up in the boat and rebuked the wind and waves. Then the storm suddenly subsided and all was calm!

That's what we need to do in the difficult storms of LIFE. We must TRUST You to calm us. Let us sense that no matter what happens YOU ARE THERE WITH US, and You promise never to leave us!

Thank You, dear Father, thank You... ... ...

I'm Destitute, Lord...   Oct. 7

Ephesians 2:8,9
Because of his kindness you have been saved through trusting Christ. And even trusting is not of yourselves; it too is a gift from God. Salvation is not a reward for the good we have done, so none of us can take any credit for it.

Without You Lord, I'm completely destitute...Anything that I have accumulated in this world means absolutely nothing without You...I put no worth in anything without You...

Matthew 16:26
"What profit is there if you gain the whole world - and lose eternal life? What can be compared with the value of eternal life?"

Yes Lord, everything is lost without You...

A rich man gathers and gathers more riches...Yet how much does he need to live? Ambition is one thing; greed is another...How many rich men do we hear about, scrambling here and there to build up their own personal empire...Then one day it comes crashing down.

History has shown us that wealth without a loving generous heart to accompany it reveals the fallacy of accumulating worldly riches.

In Your Scriptures, Matthew 13:45,46 says,

"Again, the Kingdom of Heaven is like a pearl merchant on the lookout for choice pearls. He discovered a real bargain – a pearl of great value – and sold everything he owned to purchase it!"

You are the pearl of great value to us, Lord...You are the greatest jewel in the entire Universe...Yet dear Lord, we all can have You, as our priceless jewel...In the mystery of Yourself You are available to all, and Precious Savior, You are a free gift beyond price!

What an awesome thought! The greatest gift in all this world, this Universe, is FREE!!! Oh, Almighty and Faithful God, Father of us all, remind us to call upon You! Yes, we can call upon You for everything! You are the constant source who meets all of our needs...There is no limit to Your LOVE for each and every one of us!

You have an overabundance of LOVE, FORGIVENESS, COMPASSION, MERCY, and TENDERNESS for each of us...In You, our Heavenly Father, we find all of our true riches...

Dear Lord, please draw us close to You so we may realize with all our hearts, that without You we are lost and destitute... ... ...

A Glimmer   Oct. 8

John 16:13
"When the Holy Spirit, who is truth, comes, he shall guide you into all truth, for he will not be presenting his own ideas, but will be passing on to you what he has heard. He will tell you about the future."

Dear Savior, how patient You are with us! As we travel through life we think we have the answers which satisfy ourselves...We think we have learned ALL that is necessary!

Oh, how self-satisfied we can become! But it's only a glimmer we have learned - only the merest glimmer! There is so much more!

As we continue along, truly seeking Your Truth, we see You are refining our thinking. Once we were satisfied with ourselves...After prayerfully listening to Your silent Voice, we realize that we are only on the fringe of it all...We are only on the edge of all TRUTH!

We must allow ourselves to be examined by You, Lord, and then look at ourselves with new understanding...We find surprises sometimes, when we do this! Are we stubborn - do we resist change? Are we willing to make changes in our lives?

Ah-h-h yes, this is when we must seek answers deep within...Where we once felt so confident, so content with ourselves, we can now see there is need for us to change...

Oh dear Jesus, dear Savior, thank You for Loving us through all our stages of growth! Don't ever stop! Please don't ever stop Loving

315

us, forgiving us, having mercy on us! We NEED to have our glimmer of Truth enlarged! We need to comprehend as much as You want us to know and understand...

Let us not waste the time You have blessed us with. Please keep calling us, nudging us to get our attention...May we be diligent to seek Your Truth, Holy Spirit, to allow You to continue enlightening us...For Life passes by so quickly...Time is so very fragile...

Minutes tick by, one by one, hours slip by...Days run into weeks, months, years...Oh dear Lord let Your Light shine through all the clutter of our lives so that we can separate the importance of You from the clamor of the world...

Yes, a glimmer now but oh, what waits for each of us as we continue to search for Your Perfect TRUTH! Thank You, Lord, thank You!

The Name of The Game   Oct. 9

Proverbs 3:18

Wisdom is a tree of life to those who eat her fruit; happy is the man who keeps on eating it.

Yes Lord Jesus, the name of the game is "put one over on you!"...So many, many in this world are trying to put things over on us, to fool us. They want to part us from our money, our security, to even deceive us in our beliefs! It's happening more and more as time passes...

People are becoming more clever about how to cheat others. They not only end up with our purses, etc., but then to add to this humiliation, we are thought of as being fools or stupid...But how do we learn to discern the truth? How do we acquire the wisdom and good judgement we need?

Proverbs 1:4-9

"I want to make the simple-minded wise!" he (King Solomon) said. "I want to warn young men about some problems they will face. I want those already wise to become the wiser and become leaders by exploring the depths of meaning in these nuggets of truth." How does a man become wise? The first step is to trust and reverence the Lord!

Only fools refuse to be taught. Listen to your father and mother. What you learn from them will stand you in good stead; it will gain you many honors.

Proverbs 2:6

For the Lord grants wisdom! His every word is a treasure of knowledge and understanding.

Proverbs 3:4,5

If you want favor with both God and man, and a reputation for good judgment and common sense, then trust the Lord completely; don't ever trust yourself.

Proverbs 4:5,6

"*Learn to be wise,*" he said, "*and develop good judgment and common sense! I cannot overemphasize this point.*" Cling to wisdom – she will protect you. Love her – she will guard you.

Father, if all your children would be faithful to the above Scriptures, there would be much less heartache and disappointment. You have set out the guidelines for us...We must learn to trust You in ALL decisions. When we do this day after day, year after year, we will be so full of wisdom AND common sense, that we will become safe from those who attempt to deceive us...

The great deceiver has many henchmen to do his bidding, to deceive us...It is our responsibility to seek Your wisdom so that we WILL overcome...

Yes dear Lord God, let us turn to You; let us absorb Your wisdom and common sense...Let us be generous and share these gifts with those who are in need...Let us not overpower others with these gifts, but gently share them.

With Your ever-loving thoughts renewing us, dear Lord, we will learn all that You would have us to...Thank You Father God for the blessings of Your wisdom... ... ...

Your Timing   Oct. 10

Ecclesiastes 3:1(NIV)

There is a time for everything, and a season for every activity under heaven:

Your timing is Perfect, Lord; our timing is "whenever"...Yes, Lord God, You are always right on time, no matter what we may think...

317

Our expectations from You can be quite selfish…"When are You going to do something about this problem, Lord?" we complain. We sometimes become impatient with You, Lord…

We can be so self-centered…"Why haven't You taken care of this yet, Lord? You know I've been waiting for an answer…Why is it taking so long?"

To You Lord, time is meaningless…Clocks and calendars mean nothing to You, Father…Man has set clocks, calendars - time itself, as being so important…

In the scope of Life, when all comes to a close, time seems to mean so very little…We are all on a journey here on earth…Each of us has a different life span…Some may live 100 years, while others have very few…Yet time itself is meaningless…You, Lord God, know exactly how much time each of us will have…

Sometimes we can squander Life…We can become so blasé about it…"I'm going to do…I'm going to do…Next year or in 5 years or in the future I'm going to… … …" Oh Lord, we think these plans, these dreams, will take place…

What we need to understand is that it's Your timing which counts, Father God! We must build a close relationship with You, Lord. Then we will understand that we must leave ALL things in Your Hands…Your timing is Perfect in our lives! We know, that YOU know, what and when is best for each of us…

Looking back over the past, causes us to realize that Your timing was exactly perfect, even when we didn't realize it…

Please Father, continue with Your timing, Your Perfect timing…Thank You Lord, for loving and caring for each of us… … …

"I've Called You…"   Oct. 11

John 10:2,3

"For a shepherd comes through the gate. The gatekeeper opens the gate for him, and the sheep hear his voice and come to him; and he calls his own sheep by name and leads them out."

"I've called you… You have not been as attentive as I'd like you to be… There was a time when you were so eager to hear My call…"

Yes Lord, You are so right...I know deep down in my spirit that You have called me unto Yourself...I cannot really explain or even understand why it seems that I drag my feet in coming to You, to spend time with You...

Yet in my heart I feel close to You – close but not like the closeness we've experienced in the past...It's me, Lord dear. Dear Lord, it's me. I allow so many, many things to come between us! They are such insignificant things, too.

I know that we can always excuse ourselves by saying that it must be satan...Well Lord, whether it's satan or not, I must overcome whatever it is that causes me to be separated from You...

For the bottom line is that we must accept responsibility for our actions, and for what we fail to do...It's so easy to find excuses for our failures...Dear Lord Jesus, forgive me...Forgive me...

When I stop to realize what a gift Your friendship is, what a privilege it is, I am so disappointed in myself for straying away from You. We are so easily drawn away from You by the cares and pleasures of this world. But anything which draws us apart is negative and hurts our relationship...

I don't want to grieve You, dear Jesus...I am reminded of Psalm 139:23, 24, which says,

Search me, O God and know my heart; test my thoughts. Point out anything you find in me that makes you sad, and lead me along the path of everlasting life.

Yes, Lord God, lead me...I need to have Your guidance, Your wisdom...Help me please, to separate myself from my surroundings so that I will spend more time with You...As You see fit to call me unto Yourself, day or night, may I come eagerly...

Let me not turn a deaf ear to Your sweet call... ... ...

Members Of God's Very Own Family   Oct. 12

Ephesians 2:18-22

Now all of us, whether Jews or Gentiles, may come to God the Father with the Holy Spirit's help because of what Christ has done for us. Now you are no long strangers to God and foreigners to heaven, but you are members of God's very own family, citizens of God's country, and you belong in God's household with every other Christian.

319

What a foundation you stand on now: the apostles and the prophets; and the cornerstone of the building is Jesus Christ himself! We who believe are carefully joined together with Christ as parts of a beautiful, constantly growing temple for God. And you also are joined with him and with each other by the Spirit, and are part of this dwelling place of God.

Thank You God, our Father. Thank You Jesus, Son of God. Thank You Holy Spirit...Thank You for constantly revealing Your truths in Your Holy Scriptures! It is very plain to see what You want for us when we allow You to show us Your truths, Your desires for us...

What a fantastic Plan You have for us, to become members of Your very own family! You want us to become citizens of Your country, to be brothers, sisters, comrades, friends, confidants! How wonderful it is to know that is Your desire for us!

You provide Your Divine Love through each of us, so that we can reflect Your peace, Your compassion, Your caring, loving ways...

When we come to the point of taking on Your ways, Father, hopefully we will draw others to You... You know that we all have our imperfections...Still, You promised us that we can become new and start afresh again...Holy Spirit, help us to really become brothers and sisters through Your LOVE... ... ...

Forgive Them Father   Oct. 13

Luke 23:34a (KJV)
Then said Jesus, Father, forgive them; for they know not what they do.

John 14:26
"But when the Father sends the Comforter instead of me—and by the Comforter I mean the Holy Spirit—he will teach you much, as well as remind you of everything I myself have told you."

"Father forgive them, for they know not what they do..." They know not what they do..."They" - who are they?

Why, that's me! I'm one of "they" I'm one of them! I'm one of the sinners of this world...Even though I've accepted You, Christ Jesus, as my Lord, my Redeemer, my Savior, I am still part of "they"...

Oh Father, Heavenly Father, help me to realize what I must become, in order to fully understand You and Your ways...

320

Some of man's concepts of You are not You at all! Oh Lord Jesus Christ, I ask You to reveal Yourself in Your fullness through Your Holy Spirit, to each who desires to know You in the deepest way…

For so long we have heard about You…We have read about You, sung songs about You, thought about You, praised You…But man's concept of You has been distorted so very often…

Show us how to be part of You, not "they"…For we long to be in total union with You, Jesus, Son of the Living God…

We long to be in oneness with You… … …

Ask   Oct. 14

1st John 5:14,15

And we are sure of this, that he will listen to us whenever we ask him for anything in line with his will. And if we really know he is listening when we talk to him and make our request, then we can be sure that he will answer us.

Heavenly Father, Your Scriptures are filled with so many wonderful promises! One thought stands out so clearly, Lord…You repeatedly tell us that You will give us anything we **ask** for! That word **ask** appears so many times!

In Matthew 18:19 You said:

"I also tell you this - if two of you agree down here on earth concerning anything you **ask** for, my Father in heaven will do it for you."

Again in Matthew 21:22, You said:

"You can get anything – *anything* you **ask** for in prayer – if you believe."

In Mark 11:24,25, You said:

"Listen to me! You can pray for *anything*, and *if you believe, you have it*; it's yours! But when you are praying, first forgive anyone you are holding a grudge against, so that your Father in heaven will forgive you your sins too."

In Luke 11:9,10, You said:

"And so it is with prayer – keep on **asking** and you will keep on getting; keep on looking and you will keep on finding; knock and the door will be opened. Everyone who **asks**, receives; all who seek, find; and the door is opened to everyone who knocks."

In John 14:12-14, You spoke again:

"In solemn truth I tell you, anyone believing in me shall do the same miracles I have done, and even greater ones, because I am going to be with the Father. You can **ask** him for *anything*, using my name, and I will do it, for this will bring praise to the Father because of what I, the Son, will do for you. Yes, **ask** *anything*, using my name, and I will do it!"

In John 16:24, You continue to tell us this important message:

"You haven't tried this before, (but begin now). **Ask**, using my name, and you will receive, and your cup of joy will overflow."

Dear Father, these passages are only a few of Your wonderful promises to us! You ask us to believe in You and to pray to You. You tell us to forgive others as we would like You to forgive us. You said to use Your Holy Name when we ask You to keep these promises to us…That seems more than fair, Lord!

We praise Your Holy Name, Jesus! We honor You as our Father, our Lord and Savior! We are completely dependent on You…Thank You for all the times You have answered us when we have **asked**…Thank You for the invitation to keep knocking on Your door… … …

On Our Lips…   Oct. 15

Acts 4:10b,12

"…it was done in the name and power of Jesus from Nazareth, the Messiah, the man you crucified – but God raised back to life again. It is by his authority that this man stands here healed!"

"There is salvation in no one else! Under all heaven there is no other name for men to call upon to save them."

Precious Jesus let Your name be on our lips as we pass from this world to be with You for all Eternity…Let us speak Your name over and over again as we make the transition from earth to Heaven! JESUS, JESUS, JESUS, JESUS, JESUS…Let Your name become embedded in our spirits so that whether we are coherent or unconscious, we will still breathe Your precious name… … …

Of all the names spoken on this earth, Yours Jesus, is the most precious, the most powerful, the most awesome! For You are not only the Son of God, our Creator – YOU ARE GOD!

This Life that we have been given as a gift from you, Lord God, is filled with mysteries...One of the biggest mysteries is how You, as God, were able to send Yourself to earth...You came in the form of Your only begotten Son, Jesus Christ, as a babe...This is too complex for the human mind to comprehend...

None the less, from the simplest of us to the most learned, all we have to do is to BELIEVE in YOU...When we have the most basic Faith in You, the gap between Heaven and earth is bridged...

Thankfully, dear Jesus, You willingly came here to be our example. You taught us how to go about living this Life that each of us has received. Thankfully we were given a mind of our very own. We can choose! We can make decisions! No matter how many years we are given here, it is a small price to pay to decide to follow Your teachings, dear Savior.

Many don't understand that in making a decision to follow You, it does not mean that we become robots, without a thought of our own. Many don't understand that there is joy, peace, and a sense of fulfillment, when we say, "Yes, Jesus Christ, my Savior...I want to be a follower of You."

So, dear precious Jesus, please enkindle within our hearts, thoughts of You, words about You, praises unto You...And may we leave this world with Your precious name on our lips... ... ...

JESUS, JESUS, JESUS... ... ...

...A Glow All About You...   Oct. 16

Hebrews 1:3a
God's Son shines out with God's glory, and all that God's Son is and does marks him as God.

Revelation 1:16b (NIV)
... His face was like the sun shining in all its brilliance.

Oh Jesus, I can hardly wait until I see You! I long to see You face to face, to see Your smile...Your face will be glowing! Your eyes will glow; Your smile will glow! There will be a glow all about You!

How can we, here on earth, not want to see You and be with You? We want to be around You! We want to see Your smile, to hear Your laughter! For You created laughter, joy, happiness, and so much more!

Our spirits crave to hear that laughter! Our hearts want to be warmed by it...There are those among us who also need Your comforting arms wrapped around them. We all need that. We need YOU, dear Lord Jesus...We need everything about You!

It's so easy to get discouraged here at times, Lord. The world seems to be more and more cruel. Then we realize that it's not the world, but some of the people in it who have become more insensitive to their fellowman...

Someone must make a more determined effort to help those among us who need a helping hand. Someone must comfort those in need, give a kind word, a sensitive smile or a warm hug...

Whose arms, hands, hearts, purses, can You use to do this Lord? Mine? But how can I make a difference? Can some of us truly make a difference? Oh Lord, You say that all we need is to have a willing heart... Thank You dear Lord, for Your encouragement...

What is this special feeling which has enveloped me now that You have spoken to my heart? Ah-h-h, a warm glow has begun to fill me! Some of Your glow has radiated from You into my spirit, into my heart!

May You continue to enlighten us as our days and years pass by, until we can look upon Your glowing face in our new Heavenly Home... ... ...

Old-Fashioned Revival Oct. 17

Isaiah 57:15(NIV)
For this is what the high and lofty One (God) says – he who lives forever, whose name is holy: "I live in a high and holy place, but also with him who is contrite and lowly in spirit, to revive the spirit of the lowly and to revive the heart of the contrite."

Revival or renewal means to stir up a new fire from the sleeping embers within our spirit. Please churn up the old spirit and refresh us with new life and the excitement of a fresh anointing! Yes, dear Holy Spirit, we need this desperately! Our souls are sorely in need of revival!

Come, oh Holy Spirit, come! As we look into ourselves, no matter how carefully we search, there is more room for You, Holy Spirit, to recharge us as You indwell us!

Many of Your children seem more aware and are more desirous of "something more". They feel a lack within themselves and they have already begun the search!

Oh yes Lord, let us search in such a deep way that we will become completely filled with Your Holy Spirit! What a powerful gift You left for us, dear Jesus! Let us avail ourselves of ALL You offer us...

What JOY there is! What freedom there is! What release is ours from the cares of the world! What comfort – what peace You offer to us...

Yes dear Lord, we must first remember to examine our hearts. We must confess our sins. We must confess the things we have done wrong...We must also confess the "good" things we should have done. As we empty ourselves, there is more room for Your Holy Spirit to fill us...

Now, we are ready for Revival - real old-fashioned REVIVAL! The flame is beginning to grow and hopefully it will burst forth in a glorious, life-changing, life-giving experience! Oh, Glory, Glory, Glory - REVIVAL is ready to visit Your people, Your Church again, dear Lord!

May this flame pass one to another, to another, and to another until we are all renewed! Thank You Holy Spirit, thank You!

You Are...   Oct. 18

1st Timothy 2:3-6

This is good and pleases God our Savior, for he longs for all to be saved and to understand this truth: *That God is on one side and all the people on the other side, and Christ Jesus, himself man, is between them to bring them together, by giving his life for all mankind.*

You are Savior! You are Master! You are Teacher! You are the only Son of God, our Creator! You are, dear Savior, all things to all mankind...Oh Father God, we are astounded when it sinks down into our spirits, the realization that You are ALL to us!

We humans are desperately in need of You! You are Comforter, Provider, Friend, and Healer...There is nothing lacking in You...Whatever our needs are, You are more than willing to meet them...

Meditating on what You are, Lord dear, and who You are, the title SAVIOR, stands out! Even if You were all things to all of us, except Savior, there would still be many wonderful examples from Your Life while here on earth!

BUT, dear Savior, Jesus Christ of Nazareth, without You there would be no HEAVENLY HOME for us!!! Death would come and we would be no more...We would dry up and only become a memory...You, precious Lord, as SAVIOR of the entire creation, have made the difference!

You were willing to leave Your Heavenly Home with Your Father and come to earth as an innocent Babe. You took upon Yourself humanity...You became one of us...You felt peacefulness, joy, happiness, sadness, and pain...You tried to teach what we all needed to understand, so we could learn how to live here. Some accepted You; many did not and still do not today...

You were willing to suffer humiliation, agony, and crucifixion for all of us...As You did, You asked Your Father in Heaven, to forgive those who were putting You to death...How much more could be expected of You? You gave Your ALL for us!!! And You are still more than willing to meet our needs at this very moment...

Dear Savior, dearest Jesus, please open our hearts more fully...For we are Your children when we declare openly that You are our Father...

YOU ARE standing at the door of each heart, patiently waiting for an invitation to enter in...While each of us has a heartbeat, let us not shut You out. Your desire is for each of us to be saved by You, our precious SAVIOR... ... ...

Little Moments   Oct. 19

Luke 10:39 (NIV)
She had a sister called Mary, who sat at the Lord's feet listening to what he said.

Dear Lord, I love You...I love You with all my heart, all my being. I desire to love You with all that I possibly can...Yet Lord, You know how much that is – is it really all that I can? Am I holding back and not aware of it?

Desiring to do something and doing it, is sometimes quite different...Words can flow from our mouths so easily and quickly – "I love You, Lord." Hopefully, Father, the words expressed are deeply sincere...

How can we love You more, Lord?

"Spend more time with Me... Find a quiet place... Settle in... Soon you will turn your thought and hearts to Me... I don't want to be a stranger to you. I want to be a friend to you, a very, very close friend to you. Let Me fill the empty space that longs for Me to enter in and fill the void... Let Me in... Let Me in..."

Yes Lord that is what we need to do...We need to seek special moments with You - moments which will increase into minutes, and at times hours with You...Then our friendship will grow so much that when we are not able to spend time with You, a deep sense of loneliness will take place...

Let us truly desire to meet together often – in the little moments that we can squeeze in many times in 24 hours. When we begin to do this, it is amazing how many little "rest periods" we can manage!

Each time we do this, we will feel more at home with You, Lord...We will feel refreshed in these special times. You dear Father, have shown us that You long for our company...That is amazing, almost unbelievable!

Thank You, Lord, for always being there, waiting for us, always wanting the best for us, always loving us. What would we do without You, Lord?

...The Rest Is In Your Hands Oct. 20

Ephesians 6:18
Pray all the time. Ask God for anything in line with the Holy Spirit's wishes. Plead with him, reminding him of your needs, and keep praying earnestly for all Christians everywhere.

Dear Lord Jesus, I can just talk to You; the rest is in Your Hands...I come with my prayer requests to You, day after day, night after night. Years are flowing by and when I look back and realize how many years, months, weeks and days have passed, I am amazed...

But, my dear Savior my coming to You is one thing; the rest is in Your Hands. I have no power of my own to change lives, to heal, to perform miracles. Thankfully, my precious Lord, You are the Mighty One; You have the Power that makes the difference in people's lives.

I ask. I pray. I implore. I beg for Mercy. It is You who decide. Thankfully, dear Jesus, You do not give this power to us! We would not know how to handle such God-given Power! It is a blessing that You are the holder of the Power!

So, I will continue to come, to seek answers to so many, many needs. The list grows longer as the years go by...Looking back into my prayer booklets, I see so many names, circumstances, and situations with "PTL!" (Praise The Lord!) after them! You have answered countless prayers, sweet Lord...

I have never understood why You have answered some and have not answered others. Yet I have prayed with the same confidence in You, dear Jesus, to answer them all positively.

Oh, I don't need to understand dear Lord? I just have to be willing to come to You, seeking? Oh thank You, precious Savior, for whispering this to me! You know, dear Lord, that I find much comfort coming to You. I know from the depth of my being that You are always listening to me.

Someday when we are face to face, Lord, I feel You will reveal some of these mysteries to me. So, I will continue to come...When I come to You, YOU know I come with a sincere heart.

I come on behalf of those You have placed in my life and whom I have a burden for. You know, dear Heavenly Father, that my first desire for each of those I pray for is SALVATION! All the other prayers are important, Lord, but Salvation is essential! Without Salvation we are lost!

Please, dear Savior, please save all those for whom I pray. I will be faithful to pray for them, but the rest is in Your Hands - Your Loving Hands... ... ...

Hands   Oct. 21

Psalm 63:4(NIV)
I will praise you as long as I live, and in your name I will lift up my hands.

Dear Jesus, in all the baby pictures which have been painted of You, You have your little arms stretched out towards us...Are You beckoning to us? Are You asking us to come closer to You? Are we afraid to come closer to You? Some of us would be...Others would want to pick You up and embrace You!

Each of us comes into this world with arms open to all around us. As children we learn to communicate by using our arms and hands. Then as we grow older our arms and hands seem to stay down by our sides or folded across our chests.

We often act as if the world is against us and we have to take a stand against everyone! We look at strangers with suspicion...The freedom, which we had with our arms and hands when we were babies, has become buried inside ourselves.

Now we are adults...We are in charge of our decisions. We don't need anyone else to influence our lives. Suddenly as we walk down a dark street one night a robber stands in front of us. "HANDS UP! THIS IS A STICK-UP!" We throw our hands up into the air! We are no longer in control of our lives...Isn't it strange how quickly we threw up our hands! We were obeying someone with a negative influence on us...

As this scene passes, one can stop and think about what has happened...We threw our hands up because of a negative situation...When would we raise our hands in a positive situation? Oh, some people raise their hands up when they go to Church...Why would they do that? Nobody is threatening them...Why then, would they do that?

"To honor Me, your Creator - by raising up your arms and hands to Me, you are saluting Me. You are giving Me the praises and honor I alone deserve."

Oh dear God, forgive me for my lack of understanding - my lack of appreciation for You, my Creator...Now I realize that when I free myself from the rigidity of my body, I feel a release of my spirit, which has been buried deep within me...

Thank You for what You have done for me by giving me the gift of Life itself...Thank You for alerting me to my self-centeredness...Thank You for revealing Yourself to us...Thank You, God, thank You for opening our hearts, our hands, and our arms up to You... ... ...

Perilously Close...   Oct. 22

1ˢᵗ Peter 5:8-11

Be careful – watch out for attacks from Satan, your great enemy. He prowls around like a hungry, roaring lion, looking for some victim to tear apart. Stand firm when he attacks. Trust the Lord; and remember that other Christians all around the world are going through these sufferings too.

After you have suffered a little while, our God, who is full of kindness through Christ, will give you his eternal glory. He personally will come and pick you up, and set you firmly in place, and make you stronger than ever. To him be all power over all things, forever and ever. Amen.

Yes Lord, we stand perilously close to losing our friendship with You...Your traitor satan, is ever after us seeking, sneaking, skulking around each of us, Your children.

He's after those, especially, who are close to You, Lord. To him, they are the choicest ones to snare in his traps. But, Lord God, when all those who love You, really put You first, all satan can expect is DEFEAT!

It is only when we are "on the fence" about You that we stand perilously close to losing our way. Satan knows each of our weaknesses. He is there constantly waiting for any of us, Your children, to weaken - to fall...

Dear Jesus, hopefully we can realize in time that we are in danger...Dear God, our Father, we need only to shout out to You from our spirits that we desperately need You! You are always willing to throw a lifeline to us!

Lifeline reminds some of us of communication...Perhaps when we find ourselves in these dangerous situations, it is because we have neglected spending time communicating with You. We have allowed ourselves to get caught up in our own little worlds. We become the center; we place ourselves on little thrones...We enjoy being in the center, having our little worlds revolve around us...

That's the danger, isn't it, Lord Jesus? We need to get off the thrones we have put ourselves on…We need to put You, dear Savior, in Your rightful place and that is on the throne within our hearts…

No one belongs there except You, dear Lord Jesus…You alone died for us, for me. You alone and no one else deserves to be the very center of our lives.

Thank You, Father God, for sending Your only Son, Jesus, to become our Savior, our life-line to You… … …

Search Me, O God…   Oct. 23

Psalm 130: 3, 4
Lord, if you keep in mind our sins then who could ever get an answer to his prayers? But you forgive! What an awesome thing this is!

Proverbs 17:3
Silver and gold are purified by fire, but God purifies hearts.

Yes, "Search me, O God, and know my heart…" As You know, dear Lord, these words taken from Psalm 139 are words to help us examine our hearts…It is easy to read the words from this beautiful Psalm, but we need to bury them deep within.

Father, mercifully, You are our true God…We have learned through the Scriptures that You are the God of LOVE and the God of FORGIVENESS…Gratefully, Father God, we can come to You expecting forgiveness, after we have opened ourselves up to You…However, this is not an easy thing to do. But in Your Loving care for us, You help us to go through this necessary step…

Thankfully there is no need for trepidation, anxiety or fear in coming before You, dear Father…Your unconditional LOVE spreads over us like the wings of a huge dove, where we can feel comforted…

Dear Father God, each of us is a sinner…No one, except Your Son, Jesus Christ, was or is without sin. Sometimes we want to deny that we are sinners. It is part of our nature to deny any wrongdoing in our lives.

It may take years for us to realize that there are sins of omission. What are sins of omission? In Luke 10:30-37 Jesus shows us what omission is:

Jesus replied with an illustration: "A Jew going on a trip from Jerusalem to Jericho was attacked by bandits. They stripped him of his clothes and money and beat him up and left him lying half-dead beside the road.

By chance a Jewish priest came along; and when he saw the man lying there, he crossed to the other side of the road and passed him by. A Jewish Temple-assistant walked over and looked at him lying there, but then went on.

But a despised Samaritan came along, and when he saw him, he felt deep pity. Kneeling beside him the Samaritan soothed his wounds with medicine and bandaged them. Then he put the man on his donkey and walked along beside him till they came to an inn, where he nursed him through the night. The next day he handed the innkeeper two twenty-dollar bills and told him to take care of the man. 'If his bill runs higher than that,' he said, 'I'll pay the difference the next time I am here.'

Now which of these three would you say was a neighbor to the bandits' victim?"

The man replied, "The one who showed him some pity."

Then Jesus said, "Yes, now go and do the same."

The Jewish priest and the Jewish Temple-assistant both were guilty of the sin of omission. They failed to do what they knew was right. They refused help to the bandits' victim.

Yes, Lord of Mercy, help us to search ourselves, search our hearts to a new depth of spiritual maturity...May our hearts be truly sincere in this search and may we feel cleansed and refreshed after doing so...Please make us ready to become Your obedient followers, dear Heavenly Father... ... ...

The Lost Sheep   Oct. 24

Luke 15:3-7

So Jesus used this illustration: "If you had a hundred sheep and one of them strayed away and was lost in the wilderness, wouldn't you leave the ninety-nine others to go and search for the lost one until you found it? And then you would joyfully carry it home on your shoulders. When you arrived you would call together your friends and neighbors to rejoice with you because your lost sheep was found."

"Well, in the same way heaven will be happier over one lost sinner who returns to God than over ninety-nine others who haven't strayed away!"

Oh Lord, I've been praying for one of Your little lost sheep. This sheep is tangled tightly in circumstances, as if caught among fierce briers...

You told us dear Lord, in Your Scriptures about the owner of 100 sheep and how one became lost. You told how the shepherd left the flock of 99 and searched until the 100th sheep was found...How loving that was, dear Jesus...

Now dear Savior, here it is today, many hundreds of years later. This little lost sheep is fully-grown. Because of that, one would think this one could manage life with maturity...This is not so, Lord...My spirit is deeply grieved...What happened, Lord, for this sheep to become so completely trapped by decisions and actions?

As I sit here with You Lord, wondering what I can do - I feel so helpless...What difference can I make in this life? Why would this lost one listen to me? Lord, please help me to reach out - please Lord, please...

"Tell this little lost sheep about Me. Tell of some of the times when I have helped you in your difficulties in life. Let it be known that I am Creator, Savior, and I am waiting for My lost ones to come to Me. Tell how great My Love is. Tell how I died for all the lost sheep. Tell about Me..."

Oh, Lord God, Creator of all the Universe, thank You for Your Loving kindness...How gracious You are! How wonderfully caring You are for Your children, no matter how young or old they are...

I Praise You, Heavenly Father! I wish I could give You all the Glory, all the Adoration, all the Praise that this earth contains, for You alone are worthy of our worship... ... ...

Heart's Desire   Oct. 25

Luke 12:15 (NIV)
Then he said to them, "Watch out! Be on your guard against all kinds of greed; a man's life does not consist in the abundance of his possessions."

Oh precious Lord, YOU are my heart's desire! There is nothing in this world that can give me the LOVE, the JOY, the PEACE of mind that YOU do give...

Yet Lord, there is so much to attract Your children away from You...The world keeps offering all these "things" to attract our attention...It's a "give-me, give-me" attitude from adults down to the smallest child.

So many are striving to acquire these "make me happy" items...When they do acquire them, the good feelings from the latest attraction soon disappear. Time passes and it's not long before another attraction comes along to be added to their supply of "goodies". The "give me, give me" desires crop up again and again...

Great amounts of money pour out for these attractions...Some go into financial failure due to acquiring these gratifications. If only they would look to You, dear precious Savior.. You are the "Pearl Of Great Value!" You have no price attached to You! You are a free gift to all who seek You!

We hear of many who acquire millions of dollars. Their lives appear to be an open book. Their names become known far and wide...Often we then hear that all the wealth acquired has not brought them contentment, but just the opposite. Their eyes appear empty - there seems to be no joy...

Oh Father, God of all Creation, we pray that many more souls will seek You...We pray that the peace that passes all understanding will be theirs because of You in their lives...

We are here in this world a relatively short period of time! When this brief span of life is compared to Eternity, one finds it hard to understand why all mankind does not rush into Your Everlasting, Loving Arms...

Dear Heavenly Father, please touch our hearts. Help us to desire to bring souls to You. Cause us to be sensitive to those around us so that they will desire You to be their first LOVE...

Thank You again, dear Savior, for LOVING us unconditionally... What a blessing that is to keep in our hearts... ... ...

At The Foot Of The Cross   Oct. 26

John 19: 17,18
So they had him at last, and he was taken out of the city, carrying his cross to the place known as "The Skull," in Hebrew, "Golgotha." There they

crucified him and two others with him, one on either side, with Jesus between them.

2nd Corinthians 5:19a,21

For God was in Christ, restoring the world to himself, no longer counting men's sins against them but blotting them out.

For God took the sinless Christ and poured into him our sins. Then, in exchange, he poured God's goodness into us!

Lord, to the foot of Your Cross I go...In my mind's eye, I see myself walking up a slight rise winding to the right...The horizon appears clearly...Then I turn slightly to the left continuing up the rise...While I am walking, my eyes are on the ground...Suddenly there I am at the foot of Your Cross...

My eyes slowly move up the Cross, Your Feet, then Your Body comes into my view – then Your Face...Your Eyes are open looking down into my upturned face...What compassion I see in Your Eyes, Lord...

Oh dear Savior, my dear, dear Savior - the sadness of my heart spills out to You...The sorrow for my sins floods my being...All the hurts of my life disappear – only deep compassion fills my soul...

Yes, we must all go to the foot of Your Cross, dear Jesus...Each of us has to face You...As we decide to take the first step to the foot of Your Cross, dear Savior, we will find that it becomes easier and easier...The more we go there, the closer we will come to You in spirit...We NEED to come to the foot of Your Cross, dear Savior...Without a deep understanding of what You, Jesus Christ of Nazareth, did for each of us, we cannot become Your true followers...

Please, dear God, help each of us to recognize what You did in Your Plan of Salvation. You sent Your only Son, Jesus, to earth to share Your Truth, which has been passed down from generation to generation. We don't fully comprehend the complexity of this Plan, which required the painful death of Your Son. But Your Scriptures tell us that atonement, a sacrifice, was necessary for our sins to be forgiven. You, Jesus, Perfect Son of our Father God, were the Sacrifice for us...

By Your Sacrifice of dying on Your Cross, dear Jesus, You generously opened the Gates of Heaven for each of us. This we must receive by Faith in You.

Christianity has to focus on Your Death on the Cross, and Your Resurrection, dear Savior...Without focusing on these truths we do not share in the fullness of Your Plan of Salvation, dear Father God...

Thank You, dear Jesus, for being willing to die on that Cross for all mankind... ... ...

"Enlighten"   Oct. 27

John 12:36

"Make use of the Light while there is still time; then you will become light bearers."

Ephesians 5:8(NIV)

For you were once darkness, but now you are light in the Lord. Live as children of light...

Lord dear, how strange it is when a certain word in our vocabulary suddenly strikes us in a very different way!

The word "enlighten" suddenly hit me. I had never connected it with You, Lord Jesus! Yes, You are the Light of the world, and oh, how grateful my heart is for that!

Sometimes we think being enlightened mainly means by the world's standards. We must gain more knowledge in this area, or that area...But then again, let's not forget that area...

I became more curious...You see me now consulting the dictionary! It has much to say about this word...It starts out with "to give light". Oh yes! That connects with You! You give Light! It continues: "to give clearer views." That reminds me of how You spoke in parables in the Bible to give clearer views to Your Apostles and followers.

Then it states: "to instruct, to enable to see or comprehend." That's what You spent most of Your life doing for those who would come to hear You speak. The definition continues: "to free from ignorance, prejudice or superstition." Again dear Savior, these were some of Your main teachings!

It continues on: "give clarification, to inform; to light up." Again this word reflects back to You, dear Master. You brought "Light" into a sinful, darkened world...

In Your teachings You asked that we become "Light bearers". That is the hard part, dear Lord Jesus, for You are asking us to imitate You...That seems impossible, dear Lord, due to our weakness and imperfections. But You also told us that we will be empowered through You, to be able to accomplish more than we ever thought possible! We CAN become victorious!

Because of our learning about You from the Scriptures, we can live a victorious life! We have become "enlightened" by You – our lives can be altered! We can also help enlighten others...

Thank You, sweet precious Lord, for being all things to us! You have made a way for each of us to follow Your Light and become "Light bearers"... ... ...

Vaccination   Oct. 28

2nd Corinthians 1:21,22

It is this God who has made you and me into faithful Christians and commissioned us apostles to preach the Good News. He has put his brand upon us – his mark of ownership – and given us his Holy Spirit in our hearts as guarantee that we belong to him, and as the first installment of all that he is going to give us.

Lord, You were there many years ago when I was vaccinated. That mark left on me indicated that I was immune to several serious illnesses. The scar, after many, many years, is still quite visible...It will still be there after all life has left my body...

In thinking of that, it suddenly occurred to me that I wish I could be vaccinated against SIN! I wish that with one injection I could be totally free of offending You, my Savior, for all my days...

Your mark would be on me for all to see. It would be there for me to look at every now and then. I would rejoice again for bearing Your mark of freedom from sin...

But, that is not so...Each of us has to follow Your Spirit moment by moment. This will show You we are sincere in our decision to follow You...We cannot let ourselves be blown in the wind, bending to sin one moment, and then feeling righteous the next...

The difficulties and temptations of life are always there...But You have told us that we are to depend on You for our strength in those times. You said You are the Burden Bearer, so we should give you all our burdens...

Oh that sounds so wonderful! Can it really be so, Lord Jesus?

"Yes, I am the Burden Bearer. Leave your burdens with Me... I will refresh you. There is no need of carrying them yourselves, My children... All is well."

Thank You, thank You, Lord! We don't have to fear any more feeling guilty or bearing the burden of past sins. We have given our hearts to You and You have placed Your mark on us...We are Your children, Your family...

Since we are Your children, we should rejoice more! We need to express the JOY, which only You can give! Oh, precious Savior, thank You for loving us, forgiving us, seeing the best in each of us...What comfort that is! What comfort that is...Thank You, dear Lord Jesus... ... ...

My Soul-Saving Savior   Oct. 29

1ˢᵗ John 4:14,15
And furthermore, we have seen with our own eyes and now tell all the world that God sent his Son to be their Savior. Anyone who believes and says that Jesus is the Son of God has God living in him, and he is living with God.

Yes, my dear Lord Jesus, YOU are my soul-saving Savior! When I realize what these precious words mean, I am filled with awe! I am filled with thanksgiving! I am filled with gratitude; I am filled with love...

No one on this earth, this planet of ours, could ever touch my spirit, my life, as You have...I simply can't imagine what it would be like not to have found YOU.

You are my LIFE, my JOY, my EVERYTHING! "Nothing can compare with You" as one of the little precious hymns says. I never could make it through one day, one hour, minute or second without the realization that YOU are my ALL!

You have saved my soul! Yes, dear Lord, I thankfully know there is a hell and You have saved me from that horrible pit of fire. Now because of You, Jesus, I have eternal Life in Heaven to look forward to.

Oh dear Jesus, my soul-saving Savior, thank You for coming into this world full of sin...Thank You for making a difference in my life...I shudder to realize what a blight would have been in my life were it not for You, dear Savior.

Gazing out my window and seeing the majesty of Your world allows me to marvel at its beauty! What You formed for us eons ago still causes us to become breathless at its awesome beauty!

At this time of year, magnificent color abounds all around us! Trees, shrubs take upon themselves hues of yellow, orange, red and blend together with the many shades of green...It is a joy to see! Oh the wonder of Your graciousness to us! Thank You, Almighty God, for the glory of this earth!

Thank You for sending us Your Son, Jesus, to be the Savior of this world...

May countless hearts be drawn to You and call You Lord and Savior! May our hearts fill with the desire to bring the unsaved into the joy of knowing You, and desiring to follow Your truths. Thank You again, our soul-saving Savior, from the depths of our beings... ... ...

"Turn the Other Cheek"   Oct. 30

Romans 12:21
Don't let evil get the upper hand but conquer evil by doing good.

It's so hard, dear Lord, to turn the other cheek...Once we have felt the slap, the putdown, the insult, and the blow to our ego, we want to retreat to some safe place...

We want to feel sorry for ourselves. We perhaps, want to express anger...We may want to get "even"...The thought of turning the other cheek and giving that person another chance of doing that again to us, repels us...Why should we be foolish enough to do that? Why, Lord, why?

In Matthew 5:39-40 we read,

"But I say: Don't resist violence! If you are slapped on one cheek, turn the other too. If you are ordered to court, and your shirt is taken from you, give your coat too."

Lord Jesus, these thoughts are very strange; it is difficult to understand them. Then in reading verses 43 through 48 You say:

"There is a saying 'Love your *friends* and hate your enemies! But I say: Love your *enemies*! Pray for those who *persecute* you! In that way you will be acting as true sons of your Father in heaven. For he gives his sunlight to both the evil and the good, and sends rain on the just and on the unjust too. If you love only those who love you, what good is that? Even scoundrels do that much. If you are friendly only to your friends, how are you different from anyone else? Even the heathen do that. But you are to be perfect, even as your Father in heaven is perfect."

We who have chosen to follow You, dear Savior, must turn to the Scriptures daily. We must remind ourselves of how You related with those who were not in harmony with You. If You tell us to turn the other cheek, Lord, we ask You for grace to give us the courage to do so...

Yes Lord, it's easy for us to say, "I'm a Christian"...Following in Your footsteps often takes us into situations which we, in the natural, could not tolerate...But because we have You as a loving role model to try and emulate, we can turn the other cheek...

Thank You for giving us the courage to be what You want us to be, to do what You want us to do... ... ...

That Special Word   Oct. 31

Isaiah 30:15a (NIV)

This is what the Sovereign LORD, the Holy One of Israel, says: "In repentance and rest is your salvation, in quietness and trust is your strength, ..."

Luke 24:46,47(NIV)

He told them, "This is what is written: The Christ will suffer and rise from the dead on the third day, and repentance and forgiveness of sins will be preached in his name to all nations, beginning at Jerusalem."

Lord, there are many words, which begin with the letter "R". Some of them are rainbows, radiance, recreation, rest, rain and so many more.

One word beginning with "R" is quite often overlooked, right Lord? It's a word that makes us feel uncomfortable. We would prefer to ignore it most of the time. You of all, dear Lord, know how important this word is: REPENTANCE...

The dictionary states: "repentance, the act of repenting or the state of being penitent; sorrow or regret for what has been done or left undone by oneself; especially sorrow and contrition for sin; such sorrow for the past as leads to amendment of one's ways; penitence; contrition."

As You well know, Lord God, today's society seems to be quite selfish. When we are selfish we don't want to see anything, but what will benefit ourselves. This must make you feel so sad, Lord...You are so generous to us... Being selfish, one does not want to ever hear the word "Repent" or "Repentance." It means we have to change our ways and we don't want to do that..."Why should I have to change? I'm very comfortable in my life style!"

Repentance is necessary...Necessary?? Because if we don't repent, don't have sorrow for our sins, offenses and shortcomings, we can't receive the gift to live in Heaven with Jesus! ...Oh, Lord... ...
...

The decision is up to us...It's a "Yes" or a "No"...Mercifully we have a truly Loving Lord... You, Lord, Love us UNCONDITION-ALLY! We must make the decision to accept or reject the gift of Forgiveness and Salvation offered to us...

If we decide to approach You, we need not feel anxiety or fearfulness...You are waiting patiently for us to come. When we do, we can feel, very much assured, that as we sincerely repent to You, since You know our hearts, we can then be at peace...

Then what contentment we can experience! Only You, Lord, can give us this inner peace...Thank You again, dear Savior, for going to Calvary for us... ... ...

November

Study To Be Quiet...   Nov. 1

Psalm 5:3 (AMP)
In the morning you hear my voice, O Lord; in the morning I prepare (a prayer, a sacrifice) for You, and watch *and* wait (for You to speak to my heart).

Yes, dear Father God, we must quiet ourselves to be able to hear Your voice...Your voice is a soft voice, yet no matter how soft, if we attune our ears and our hearts, we WILL hear it...

It seems, Father, that some of us find it difficult to know how to be quiet...It is only in learning to be quiet that we can hear Your still small voice...

Some of us may hear one particular phrase or sentence over and over again. That's because some of us may have a stubborn attitude; we need to learn the same lesson over and over again.

When we teach ourselves to find You, and as we quiet ourselves, we are blessed! A refreshment overtakes us and a sense of peace prevails! It is in the quiet time that we may be blessed by hearing You...Yet, in this very busy world of ours, trying to find quiet time seems almost impossible...

Dear Lord, please help each of us find our special place and time to listen for You...Sometimes You do not speak...But in this precious time, we can quiet our spirits, minds, and bodies...That alone is healing, which some of us need so very much...

When we do hear Your voice and we understand You clearly, how very touched we are...We realize that You, our Creator, have spent time with us!

Oh Father God, thank You for desiring to spend time with US! How absolutely kind You are to Your children! Thankfully we are all children in Your eyes no matter our age...Just as parents speak differently to each of their children, You speak to each of us in a more personal way...

May we continue to come to You whenever we are in our little quiet place, day or night. The hour is of no concern, nor the place. You only desire that we come to spend time with You. Thank You, O

342

Gracious Father, for Your unconditional LOVE for each and every one of us... ... ...

Willing Vessel   Nov. 2

Mark 8:34,35

Then he called his disciples and the crowds to come over and listen. "If any of you wants to be my follower," he told them, "you must put aside your own pleasures and shoulder your cross, and follow me closely. If you insist on saving your life, you will lose it. Only those who throw away their lives for my sake and for the sake of the Good News will ever know what it means to really live."

Holy Spirit, please empty me; empty me of all that is not of You...Shape me into what You have created me for...Please fill me Holy Spirit...Then You will be able to use me, once I have been emptied of self...Please reshape me and fill me...

I desire to be a willing vessel for You, my God, my Savior, my Comforter...You, Precious Jesus, said that if we put aside our own pleasures and pick up our cross, we could become Your followers...We are the ones who are now Your Eyes, Your Hands, Your Heart, Your Love...Without us, who call ourselves Christians, who will reflect Your Light in this world?

You desire a willing heart so that whatever You call us to do, it will be done in obedience and with Your LOVE...Sometimes we hear a call from You, but it comes at an inconvenient time. "Oh, not now, Lord, you know how busy I am. I'm so pressured already, maybe I can fit it in later..."

"My Child, when I call You, it is because You are the one best to answer My Call. Would I have called you if this were not so? Did you not tell Me more than once, that you wanted to be My Helper?"

Yes, dear Lord, we recall those times when we were fervent in our meditations with You...We declared that we would be a willing vessel for You, our God, our Savior, our All...

Oh how soon we forget our impassioned desires to please and serve You, Heavenly Father...Now we remind ourselves of these moments from our past when we have declared our love and desire to serve You...

Please, Lord, we now wish to rededicate ourselves to You...We want to be called by You as a willing vessel for You to use...As we meditate on these thoughts, we realize what a privilege it is to be called by our Creator!

Are we ready to hear from You, willing to serve?

What Would We Do?   Nov. 3

John 17:3 (NIV)
"Now this is eternal life: that they may know you, the only true God, and Jesus Christ, whom you have sent."

What would we do without You, Lord? What would we do???

We'd be like birds that could not fly! We'd be like flowers that could not bloom...We'd be like fish that could not swim...

We would be incomplete without You...The world would be without color for us...The birds would have no song for us...The air would be stagnant without the breeze to caress us, if You were not who You are to us...

Shadows would overcome us without You...Joy would have no meaning without You, Lord Jesus...Peace of mind would be impossible without You, dear one, dear heart...

LOVE, the great gift of LOVE, would not exist for some of us if it were not for You, dear Jesus...For You took us out of despair long ago and brought us into Your Light, Your LOVE...Without Your LOVE, we would not be able to truly live...We are just existing, if we are not really living the LIFE that only You can bring forth...

Existence is not living...Existence has LIFE in it, but not the LIFE that You alone can give one, dear Lord...One should not only exist in this LIFE; one should reach out and take what You came to this earth to give! One should reach out to get to know You in the deepest possible way...One should be willing, desirous of spending time to discover all about You, dear Savior...

LIFE is a gift! LIFE and LOVE are two of the greatest gifts of all the earth...Without LIFE one never has the opportunity to get to know You, Lord Jesus...LIFE is just the very beginning of the most wonderful journey...It is a journey that leads to a permanent LIFE when one finishes the journey here…This happens when we have made the discovery of You, dear Lord…

Discovering You, learning all about You, brings one's mere existence into true living…While on this journey we learn about LOVE…Living, learning, and LOVING are all parts of our lessons here…

Yes, Lord, what would I do without You? I shudder at that thought. For now knowing You, as much as I do, I can only thank You. From the depths of my being I thank You, first for the gift of LIFE, and then for Your unconditional LOVE… … …

"He Heard My Prayer!"   Nov. 4

Psalm 66:17-20

For I cried to him for help, with praises ready on my tongue. He would not have listened if I had not confessed my sins. But he listened! He heard my prayer! He paid attention to it! Blessed be God who didn't turn away when I was praying, and didn't refuse me his kindness and love.

Oh, Lord God Almighty, how many times I have come before You, asking You to listen to my prayers. I can't count the number!

How wonderful it is to be able to whisper in Your ear the needs of those You draw me to. The awesomeness of trying to understand this mystery is beyond me! The thought that You, Creator of all the Heavenlies, listen to one of Your children simply cannot be understood with the mind.

It is within our hearts and spirits that we can accept this awesome gift. Almighty God listens! Almighty God pays attention to each of us, when we come forth openly confessing to You our sins of commission and our sins of omission.

You not only listen KINDLY to our prayers, Father, but You listen with LOVE! We have seen parents looking lovingly at their child when the child asked for a favor. It is such a blessing to see the loving look exchanged between the parent and the child! We can only try to imagine the loving look You beam down on us here, dear Father God!

Thank You for the answers to our prayers that You have granted to us in the past…Thank You for the prayers that You hold in Your heart waiting for the right moment to answer! And dear Lord, thank You also for the prayers that we asked You to grant us, which You DID NOT answer! You, as our loving Father, know the request should not have been given - for You knew the consequences of it...Thank You for the loving wisdom which You show to help us grow, dear Father...

You love to hear Praises from us, too! Let them continue to rise from our lips and float up to Your ears and Your heart...However You answer our prayer requests, may we continue to PRAISE YOU!

YOU ALONE ARE WORTHY – YOU ALONE ARE WORTHY – YOU ALONE ARE WORTHY TO BE PRAISED, ADORED, AND WORSHIPED... ... ...

...To Enter In   Nov. 5

Hebrews 10:19,20
And so, dear brothers, now we may walk right into the very Holy of Holies where God is, because of the blood of Jesus. This is the fresh, new, life-giving way which Christ has opened up for us by tearing the curtain – his human body – to let us into the holy presence of God.

Oh gracious Father, how can we ever thank You enough! How can we ever thank You enough for dying for us – for me...

When You died so painfully for us, You allowed us to enter in – to enter into Your Heavenly Home! There is nothing about any of us that is worthy to do this! It truly baffles the mind!!

When we look deeply inside ourselves we KNOW that we are short, so very short, of being worthy. We look back at the times we know we failed You, our Savior...

But then, You remind us that You never said we had to be perfect to enter in! Oh gracious, kind, wonderful Lord, You are so good to each of us! We give You our thanks and gratitude. It is so difficult to put into words, but we feel deep relief, for Your acceptance of it...It's often hard for us to realize that YOU LOVE US! YOU LOVE ME! WOW, LORD!!!

Sometimes we have the blessing of meeting a truly wonderful person. When that person shows us favor in their sight, it makes us feel so good! So, when we realize You, Almighty God, Creator of

ALL, LOVE US, we are sometimes at a loss to tell You how our hearts feel...Thankfully, dear Lord, You can look into our hearts without us saying one word and then You know...

How we look forward to the moment when we can see You clearly! Then we'll know that once there with You, we will never have to leave You! Oh, precious Lord, may the remainder of our lives show You, as best we can, our love and gratitude toward You...

You, dear Savior, died for us, for me...Thank You for allowing us to enter into Your Presence...Dear Sweet Jesus, there are no words to express our deep appreciation... ... ...

Lord, I Wonder...   Nov. 6

Isaiah 53:2

In God's eyes he was like a tender green shoot, sprouting from a root in dry and sterile ground. But in our eyes there was no attractiveness at all, nothing to make us want him.

Lord Jesus, I wonder what You look like...I look at pictures of You painted by numerous artists...Right now I'm looking, very intently, at a picture of You...Do You look anything like this picture?

It is a very beautiful rendition of what the artist thought You'd look like...Your eyes—they are deep and penetrating...Your countenance is so peaceful...I love looking at this picture...

But, it is only a piece of paper...It is only someone's version of You...Beautiful though it is, one must never give adoration to a piece of paper...It is only there to remind one of You, Jesus...It is only to bring You closer to our minds and spirits...

It doesn't really make any difference as to what you really look like, Lord Jesus...When we see You, whatever You look like, we who love, adore, praise, and honor You, we will be drawn to You...We will never want to let You out of our sight once we truly see you!

In the New Testament, not much is said as to what You looked like, Lord Jesus. However, Your apostles must have been drawn to You for some reason...They loved You deeply, all but one...And so it is today, some are drawn to love You without ever having seen You— or even a picture of You...Others still reject You, may continue to reject You...

We, who love You, don't really care what You look like; it truly makes no difference…When one loves, truly loves, the appearance of the loved one satisfies the heart of the one who loves.

Thank You, Lord Jesus, for the gift of Yourself for us to love…Thank You also, for a heart that can love…There are those in this world who do not love, who choose not to love…

How grateful we are, Lord, that we found You and Your unconditional LOVE…We look forward with renewed JOY and anticipation to the moment when we will look into Your face, Your precious face…

Come, Lord Jesus, Come… … …

God's Perfect Truth   Nov. 7

John 8:31,32

Jesus said to them, "You are truly my disciples if you live as I tell you to, and you will know the truth, and the truth will set you free."

Father God, some of my loved ones are searching. They try this religion, that church, perhaps even a cult - searching, searching for they know not what, although some say "Truth"…

There is so much in the world now to learn, and also much which confuses. Which is the truth? Whose truth? Yes Lord, that is the bottom line. Whose truth? Do I want my loved ones to follow me? Do I want them to choose the denomination that I now belong to?

Did I not change along the way myself, Lord? You know that I did. Sometimes we are born into a certain religion because of our parents. Perhaps only one of our parents puts pressure on us to follow them. Years pass by, then for some reason or other, we decide to change churches.

Oh, this new church offers something the past one didn't. Perhaps the last one changed leadership and we didn't feel comfortable anymore. Sometimes, Lord, even money enters into the picture. That church was always asking for money. Maybe this one will have more social events. Different reasons cause us sometimes to church-shop.

What are we to do dear God?

"I am Your Creator. I have perfect truth for each of you. You must search it out. Perfect truth from and about Me awaits you. Pray to Me and I will enlighten you. Come to Me in prayer."

Yes Lord God that's it! We don't need my version of truth, or anyone else's version of truth. Your truth is perfect, God! Only Your truth is perfect!

That must be my prayer for myself and my loved ones! I want only Your perfect truth, Almighty God, my Creator! That is and will always be, my prayer for my loved ones: Your Perfect Truth!

Thank You, Heavenly Creator, Almighty God! Thank You... ... ...

Pieces Of The Puzzle   Nov. 8

Philippians 1:6
And I am sure that God who began the good work within you will keep right on helping you grow in his grace until his task within you is finally finished on that day when Jesus Christ returns.

You knew Lord God, several years ago, how one "little" experience would lead to another...Then that "little" experience would lead to another...Now, looking back, a pattern is coming forth...The pieces of the puzzle are falling into place...

Oh, dear Lord Jesus, all of these "little" experiences are pieces of a puzzle that represents LIFE. This puzzle is the LIFE of one of Your creations...

In a sense, Lord, each of us is a puzzle as we go through LIFE...We add a piece here and then another one there. Sometimes we put together several pieces in a very short time...Then there may be a lull...We are not adding any pieces to the puzzle. Suddenly several pieces fit together so beautifully that we are content to leave the puzzle alone...

No need to finish it now, there is plenty of time...But is there? Is there "plenty of time"? How do we know this? Can we know this?

No - there is a blank for each one of us regarding our future...We don't know if we'll even be allowed to finish our puzzle! But each one of us who loves LIFE wants to finish...We each have our own ideas

349

as to what we want to happen in our lives...We make choices, decisions...

Some work out beautifully, these choices, these decisions of ours...But, because YOU are who You are, God, You allow things to enter our lives that we may not want to happen...

Whether we like it or not, another piece has been added to our puzzle - our personal puzzle of LIFE...One thing is certain, Lord...When we ask You to take charge of our lives, all the pieces of our puzzle will fall into place...

Thank You for the way You bring things together, Lord...You watch over the pieces of each of our puzzles as we continue on in our experiences of LIFE...

Thank You Lord, for the way You are working out all the pieces in our lives...My heart is gratified at Your Hand in the exciting puzzle of LIFE...Many, many thanks, dear Jesus, for the way You are completing this work of Yours... ... ...

Dear Little Friend...   Nov. 9

Hebrews 12:2
Keep your eyes on Jesus, our leader and instructor. He was willing to die a shameful death on the cross because of the joy he knew would be his afterwards; and now he sits in the place of honor by the throne of God.

Oh Almighty God, thank You! Thank You for taking my dear little friend to Heaven today! Oh, how she loved You! Oh how she showed in her beautiful eyes the love she had for You...

We won't see those beautiful blue eyes here on earth again...But oh, when we greet her in Heaven one day, how they will sparkle as she greets each of us who loved her here on earth...

She was a rare flower in Your garden here on earth, Lord – one of the rarest ever. Everyone who came in her path had the opportunity to be a blessing to her or to be blessed by her.

When friendship blossomed with her it was so special! Yes, Lord God, she was a very rare flower here. Yet it seemed that she had every right to be an angry person, even angry with You!! This sounds harsh, Father, but only You know how much she suffered here in her relatively short life.

She suffered pain, frustration, and humiliation. She lost so much of all that You blessed her with, when she was just bursting forth on the road of life.

Why did this terrible tragedy happen to her, Lord? We wonder why...But out of the tragedy she slowly came. Little by little she took charge of her life and showed us such fortitude – such strength in her weakness...

In a way Lord, she experienced some of the pain, rejection, and humiliation You did...And as You said, "Father, forgive them for they not what they do," so she reflected this to all those who really did not understand her.

The love, which sparkled forth from her eyes, so bright and so blue, amazed those around her. Oh, how she loved You and continues to love You, Heavenly Father. Oh, how she loves You!

Oh happy day, she is sparkling with You in Heaven, Father God! She is in the Glory of Your Home, Lord - her home now! Oh thank You, thank You Jesus, she will have no more pain, no more heartache. How we who loved her thank You for bringing her Home... ... ...

Food For The Soul   Nov. 10

Isaiah 55:2 (NIV)
Why spend money on what is not bread, and your labor on what does not satisfy? Listen, listen to me, and eat what is good, and your soul will delight in the richest of fare.

"You, Lord Jesus, are food for the soul; You are all that I need to nourish my soul..."

The above words came just as I was about to sleep, so I quickly wrote them down. Now, the following day, I feel You, Lord, want me to continue...

We can live only so long without food and without water...But strangely, dear Savior, we can "live" day after day, week after week, month after month, year after year without spiritual food...

There is a difference between living and existing...We can exist without You, dearest One... Oh, unfortunately, we can...But again,

351

the difference is vast...It is like living here on earth without the sunshine; it is living always in the dark.

There seem to be no flowers, no real beauty to see...Oh there is light, but it is not the same as the sunlight that You created! You, Son of God, are the real LIGHT! You are the Son-shine to our souls...You are food for our souls!

You dear, dear Jesus, make all the difference between existence here on earth and real LIVING...Living means receiving all the fullness from LIFE that can be had! Real living has LOVE, JOY and PEACE because of the knowledge of YOU!

Oh Father how blessed are we who feed upon all that You desire to give us...You are our substance, our nourishment...We have only to draw close to You and be nourished again...

What a dreadful place this would be without You, Lord! Dreariness would plague us night and day! Depression would govern our lives! The real LOVE, JOY and PEACE of soul would not be available to us...Without Your Presence we would all become as animals in our relationships with others. We see in our society that it is happening already...How sad this must make You, Lord...

The world needs to know that because of You and Your death on the Cross no one needs to lack food for their souls. Because of You alone, there is more than enough food for all the souls existing here on earth! And, dear Jesus, we deeply thank You for nourishing us... ... ...

Repent!　　　　Nov. 11

1st John 1:9,10

But if we confess our sins to him, he can be depended on to forgive us and to cleanse us from every wrong. (And it is perfectly proper for God to do this for us because Christ died to wash away our sins.) If we claim we have not sinned, we are lying and calling God a liar, *for he says we have sinned.*

Acts 3:19 (NIV)

Repent, then, and turn to God, so that your sins may be wiped out, that times of refreshing may come from the Lord,...

Lord! Repent – that's a very sobering thought! We hear of John the Baptist in the Scriptures screaming out "Repent!" But what does that mean to us? What does repent really mean? The dictionary states: "repent – to feel such sorrow for sin as leads to amendment of one's ways..."

We think, "I'm a pretty good person – what need do I have to repent?" We try to dismiss the thought of repentance...Now the difficulty begins. That word nags at us in the quiet moments - Repent, Repent, Repent...

"Almighty God, I'll give it some thought, but not right now. You know how much I have on my mind these days," we say.

Time passes and we are quite content to file that word "Repent" back in the farthest place of our minds. Somehow we can't seem to feel as comfortable as we used to. There seems to be a dullness as we go about our lives.

Suddenly, that word REPENT rises up again and we are faced with a decision! We must try to forget that word, or make a decision to face it!

Oh Father God, we are now ready to look deep within our souls! Reveal to each of us, what we need to bring out into the openness of Your Forgiving Light! Reveal to us what has been hiding there, causing conviction within our spirits, which needs to be faced.

Whether it is commission or omission, Father, please bring it all forth so that a deep cleansing can take place. You, Jesus, know each of our hearts...We now deeply desire to bring "all" to the surface so that it can be dealt with by Your Loving Attention...

As we repent, a spirit of comfort seeps into our souls...As we empty out what we've been carrying (consciously or unconsciously), peace is also entering us. Your peace fills the void of what has been emptied in Your Presence.

Oh Father thank You for not letting us continue to carry that heavy burden! It's such a relief to feel the freshness surge into us and breathe new life into our bodies, minds and spirits!

Thank You for Your patience with us...You Father God, always know best...Thank You for Your unconditional LOVE! And Lord, thank You especially for Your FORGIVENESS, when we are obedient to Repent... ... ...

"...Thy Will Be Done"   Nov. 12

Matthew 6:9-13 (KJV)

After this manner therefore pray ye: Our Father which art in heaven, Hallowed be thy name. Thy kingdom come. Thy will be done in earth, as *it is* in heaven. Give us this day our daily bread. And forgive us our debts, as we forgive our debtors. And lead us not into temptation, but deliver us from evil: For thine is the kingdom, and the power, and the glory, for ever. Amen.

Dear Savior, Jesus Christ, You gave Your disciples, what today we refer to as "The Lord's Prayer". As so many of us know, it says: "Our Father, which art in heaven, Hallowed be thy name. Thy Kingdom come. Thy will be done..."

"Thy will be done?" But Lord, why isn't Your Will being done? Why are there relatively few doing "Thy Will" here and now? Why, Lord Jesus, why?

"It isn't easy, My child, it isn't easy. But it isn't that hard either. If you truly want to do My Will, if anyone really desires to do My Will, I will be the strength to be counted on. I will be there always to be the helping hand to do My Will."

Oh dear Jesus, of course! You have promised countless times in the Scriptures that You will never abandon us, when there is a genuine desire in our hearts to do Your bidding. Once we have digested these Scriptures and have buried them deep in our spirits, we can truly do what Your Will desires each of us to do.

How amazing it is to realize that in the many billions of Your people, You call each one to do specific things! As we are each different, no two exactly alike, so You have an individual plan for us, for our lives. When we say: "Here I am, Lord, use me" then we submit to Your using us in whatever way You best know.

Lord Jesus, when You asked Your disciples to go out into the world to bring the Good News about You, You were telling them that You wanted Your Will to be done. May we bring these words to fruition, dear Lord, may we bring action to Your words...

There are so many who don't know You as their personal Savior, dear Jesus. If each of us who know You as our Savior and Lord, touched one or more souls a year, we would make a difference in spreading Your kingdom. Then Your WILL would be done on earth – Your Kingdom would come... ... ...

Your Team   Nov. 13

Ephesians 6:10-12
Last of all I want to remind you that your strength must come from the Lord's mighty power within you. Put on all of God's armor so that you will be able to stand safe against all strategies and tricks of Satan. For we are not fighting against people made of flesh and blood, but against persons without bodies – the evil rulers of the unseen world, those mighty satanic beings and great evil princes of darkness who rule this world; and against huge numbers of wicked spirits in the spirit world.

Yes, my dear Lord Jesus, I am on Your Team! I would be a fool not to be on Your Team! Your Team is victorious! You were and are the Victor!

One can wonder who is on the other team? Some don't even realize that there is another team against Your Team, dear Savior!

War has been declared by satan on You, Jesus, and all those who choose You, over sin...He represents every type of sin that has ever been committed. Evilness emanates from satan and his followers...

Each of us here on earth HAS to choose a side...You, God the Father, Your Son Jesus Christ, and Your Holy Spirit lead one team, which includes countless legions of angels! The other team includes satan and all his many, many evil spirits.

Oh Lord, how hard they all work to try to drag down Your children...And, Father, how unknowing so many of Your followers are to the wiles and snares of the devil. He lurks about EACH of us, always looking for an entrance through our weaknesses. We need to become so aware of our weaknesses that we can protect ourselves against the onslaught from the enemy, don't we, Lord?

Deciding to be on Your Team, dear Lord Jesus, is the first step in protecting ourselves. Learning about You, through Your Bible brings us into an intimate relationship with You. As we feel more comfortable with the knowledge of You, it begins to fill our hearts as well as our minds.

Then Lord, as You already know, we become stronger and stronger so that we can become a servant for You to use, in whatever manner You choose...

We become Team Players, each with our own responsibilities.

To be able to hear Your instructions as the Coach of our Team, we must have some quiet time to listen to You. It is in quieting ourselves that we will be able to hear You...

And, Lord, thank You for the refreshment and directions we receive when we do spend time with You. Father God, thank You for whispering Your precious words into our hearts as we wait with You in the stillness. We are secure in the knowledge that we are on the WINNING TEAM... ... ...

Salvation, Salvation, Salvation   Nov. 14

Acts 4:12
"There is salvation in no one else! Under all heaven there is no other name (but Jesus) for men to call upon to save them."

Yes, my precious Savior, I pray Salvation for all my loved ones! In this whole world, dear Jesus, nothing is more important than Salvation!

We only have one life on this earth. Even if we should live to a ripe old age, how brief our earthly lives are compared to Eternity...Still, so many of us, even Christians, get caught up in accumulating the temporary things of this world...

In this age of materialism the wants of people go on and on...Self has taken over so many of Your people. "Give me this! I want that!" In no time, the list gets longer and longer...Salvation seems to be the last thing that some have on their minds...

Is the heart satisfied after all of the "wants" are received? Perhaps it is for awhile...Then the eyes find another sight to behold and the wanting continues...If only their eyes could be opened to recognize that only You, Lord Jesus, can fully satisfy their hearts! Only You can fill the deepest needs. Salvation should be the only lasting need we desire...Only Faith in You, Lord, can insure Eternal life...

Becoming a Christian is the very best insurance policy! For you, Jesus Christ, are our dear Savior! YOU gave Your life for me, for us all! YOU paid the price, the premium, for our insurance to go to Heaven for all Eternity!

Oh, dear Jesus, help our loved ones to understand this wonderful gift of Salvation, which You made possible! Thank You too, for creating the precious gift of prayer...Let us continue to pray for our loved ones. As we pray, Your Power is released to reach them with the message of Salvation...

May we be faithful, not only to pray, but to share the Good News of Salvation through Jesus Christ. For knowing You, dear Jesus, as Lord and Savior, meets all our needs for now and for all Eternity!

Yes, dear, dear Jesus – SALVATION, SALVATION, SALVATION... ... ...

What A Difference A Day Makes...   Nov. 15

Acts 2:22-24,38

"O men of Israel, listen! God publicly endorsed Jesus of Nazareth by doing tremendous miracles through him, as you well know. But God, following his prearranged plan, let you use the Roman government to nail him to the cross and murder him. Then God released him from the horrors of death and brought him back to life again, for death could not keep this man within its grip."

And Peter replied, "Each one of you must turn from sin, return to God, and be baptized in the name of Jesus Christ for the forgiveness of your sins; then you also shall receive this gift, the Holy Spirit."

Remember dear Lord, when recently the old song "What a Difference a Day Makes" was playing? Yes, sweet Jesus, what a difference a day makes! You made the difference the day You went to the Cross for everyone on this planet!

You make a difference to each one who recognizes You as our Loving Savior. Sadly, there are so many who have not recognized this tremendous gift You so lovingly gave us.

Some may ask, "What difference does it make to me that someone called Jesus died on a cross? I didn't have anything to do with his dying – why does anyone want to blame me?"

Oh Lord, help us to share Your story with others who do not yet understand. Your Life sounds like a "story," but in reality it did happen!

You came as a Babe here willingly and You lived a simple, short life. Even the work Your Father sent You to do was short, as we count time, but it turned the world upside down!

In those short years so much was revealed to all those who would listen to You. Some men followed You, some women too. Only a few though, stayed until the end.

Yes, it is a beautiful story, dear Lord Jesus...But we who read Your words from the Bible take them to be Truth. As we allow ourselves to let all your precious words sink into our spirits, our faith in You grows and grows.

Thank You, dear Father God, for graciously sharing Your Son, Jesus, with us. And thank You, dear Savior, for being willing to come here to teach us what we need to know. But most of all, dear Jesus, thank You for Loving us unconditionally, when You willingly died for us...

Yes, what a difference a day did make many long years ago... ... ...

Children   Nov. 16

Ephesians 6:4
And now a word to you parents. Don't keep on scolding and nagging your children, making them angry and resentful. Rather, bring them up with the loving discipline the Lord himself approves, with suggestions and godly advice.

Father, I trust You with my loved ones: my children...Some time ago You loaned them to me...Little did I know then what You would have me learn...

Oh Father, You taught me so much, but it took me such a long time to learn! For so long I thought their father and I were the only ones to have responsibility for them...I thought we were the only ones to decide what was best for them as they were growing up...

If only I knew then that in every decision it was to You I should have turned. If only we, as parents, had realized that it is You and You alone who should guide us. We would have, perhaps, acted differently so many, many times...

But Lord, no matter what mistakes were made then, it is never too late! We realize that with You in the center of our lives now, all things can be better, so much better!

It's wonderful to realize too, that by trusting You with our loved ones, it is so much easier than struggling by ourselves! Once we turn them over to You, truly turn them over to You, we can enjoy our lives so much more! Father, I return them willingly to You, even at this late date...

You and You alone make the difference in our lives, dear Jesus...We have only to PRAISE You, thank You, give You all the Glory and all the Honor that is for You and You alone! Though the mystery of the Trinity is there, we know when we PRAISE You, Jesus, we PRAISE God our Father, God our Creator! When we PRAISE the Holy Spirit working in our lives, we PRAISE God our Father and Jesus, His Son!

Father, today is the birthday of one of my children as You well know...I ask You to guide this child in a special way to Your pure Truth...I ask You to bring this loved one into the fullness of what You have planned.

If I could give one gift, it would be the gift of Salvation...Without that, none of us can enter into our Heavenly Home with You for all Eternity...

Dear Jesus, draw this dear one to You. Have mercy, dear Lord, have mercy...Thank You, dear Father God, thank You from the bottom of my heart... ... ...

No Expectations   Nov. 17

Luke 6:30, 31, 35,36

"Give what you have to anyone who asks you for it; and when things are taken away from you, don't worry about getting them back. Treat others as you want them to treat you."

"Love your *enemies*! Do good to *them*! Lend to *them*! And don't be concerned about the fact that they won't repay. Then your reward from heaven will be very great, and you will truly be acting as sons of God: for he is kind to the *unthankful* and to those who are *very wicked*. Try to show as much compassion as your Father does."

Father, I was just thinking about something nice I had done for someone. It wasn't the first time and there was, seemingly, no appreciation shown me. A feeling of annoyance crept over me, I found myself murmuring as I wondered why they acted as they did. Then You, Father, started speaking to me:

"My child, if you are doing something to please someone, isn't that enough? Why do you feel that they should heap thanks upon you if you did it to please them? I have said in My Scriptures that you will receive your thanks from Me when we meet in the Heaven we will share. That will be time to receive your appreciation."

I should have realized that, dear Lord. Somehow we feel that any good we do to others should be followed by their appreciation.

What appreciation did You receive, my Lord, when You were here? You did not get the appreciation You should have received, considering all the many miracles and healings You brought forth. Why do we not learn from You more quickly than we do, Lord? When we realize how petty we have been it makes us feel so ashamed of ourselves...

Help us, dear Jesus, to have no expectations from anyone. You are the greatest blessing that we could ever experience, so why should our egos have to be fed and fed to make us feel good?

Please help us to view the times when we feel "generous" through Your eyes...Help us to have a true spirit of generosity, then if we are thanked it truly won't be necessary.

How much we can learn from You, dear Lord God, when we allow ourselves to understand what You did when You sent Your Son, Jesus, here. He came to teach us what WE must learn...Please create in us a sincere desire to become true followers of You... ... ...

Have We Boxed You In, Lord?   Nov. 18

Exodus 15:11
Who else is like the Lord among the gods? Who is glorious in holiness like him? Who is so awesome in splendor, a wonder-working God?

1st Chronicles 17:20a
O Lord, there is no one like you – there is no other God.

Dear Heavenly Father God, have we boxed You in? Have we, in our littleness, not allowed the awesomeness of You to soar?

Each of us here on earth has different concepts of You, Almighty God. When we attempt to demonstrate OUR ideas about You, Your abilities, Your Power, we are sizing You up...

There are those who are on the outside, looking at Christian churches, schools, and homes. They sometimes question what they see...That could be Lord, because of our very own attitudes and actions.

Some have placed You in a small box...As consciousness of You grows, You are allowed a larger box. You can do SOME things, but there's a limit...Unfortunately, not only are You put into boxes, but the covers are pushed down so that You have to stay there...We only call upon You to do the little things... Sometimes a child puts You into a huge box and not only puts You in, but leaves the cover off!

Could it be that the reason we put You into a box is because of the smallness of our minds? Could it be that You are so great and awesome that all Creation cannot contain You? WOW, what a revelation Father, this can be!

Often times, dear God, we lose sight of Your greatness! We become so used to You being in our lives we allow ourselves to let You diminish...We lessen You because we forget who, what, why, and where You are! You are EVERYWHERE! You are our Almighty God; please, Lord, may we never forget that...

Oh, Heavenly Father, the awesomeness of You simply cannot be contained in any shape or form! The mightiness of Your Power is without equal! One only has to study about You and desire to make a commitment of friendship with You, to learn that You cannot be contained!

As we get to know the fullness of Yourself and realize the depth of You, then we look upon You with the rightful respect, admiration, adoration, and exaltation which belong to You alone!

Yes, Almighty God, You are an awesome God! You are the source of all Goodness, all Love, all Mercy, all Forgiveness...There is no other in the Universe to compare with You...Thank You, Father God, for looking down upon us as Your children. Yes, You ARE an awesome God... ... ...

Every Drop...   Nov. 19

Ephesians 1:7
So overflowing is his kindness towards us that he took away all our sins through the blood of his Son, by whom we are saved; ...

Jesus, Jesus, Jesus – every drop of blood in Your precious Body was spilled out for mankind...What more could You give?

Your gift, Your precious gift, is still covering the sins of mankind...The world itself is innocent of sin; it is we humans, who alone are capable of sin, and sin we do...

With so much blood spilled out in the movies, television, newspapers, and books of fiction, we have become jaded. We are no longer innocent because of what is thrown out at us on a daily basis. We are saturated by all this bloodshed...

So when we hear about You, having shed Your blood, every single drop of it, we sadly, are no longer sensitive to that amazing event...How can we bring ourselves to stop and ponder that act of perfect LOVE? The Bible shows us the depth of that great LOVE...Your Holy Spirit, dear Lord God, can teach us what we need to understand about this Loving act.

It was the most Loving act in all of history, because You, dear Savior, were and are PERFECT...Your Father, Almighty God, Creator of all the Universe, asked You, Jesus, to sacrifice Yourself...You willingly laid down Your life for me, for us all. Why? Because it was and is the only way WE can have an opportunity to spend our eternity in Heaven!

There will be a place for each one who professes that You, Jesus, shed Your Blood for us...YOU are the only Son of God! YOU became our Savior! YOU are the One who makes the difference between Heaven or hell...

We must make the choice; we either accept YOU or reject YOU...We must choose...No one can ever say that they have been treated unfairly when it comes to making that decision.

Jesus told us in Luke 11:23a
"Anyone who is not for me is against me;..."

Are you for Jesus? - - - - - or - - - - - Are you against Jesus?

Life's Storms   **Nov. 20**

Psalm 118:27a (NIV)
The LORD is God, and he has made his light shine upon us.

Dear Lord Jesus, I was reflecting on today. When I first awakened, Your sun was shining in the clear blue sky. The air was cold and fresh. Then later as the day blossomed, the sky suddenly filled with dark clouds. It became very cold and snow began to fall. The wind blew its cold blasts and the beautiful day changed so quickly.

Then Lord, I began to see...Life is like that...Everything seems to be going so well! There is nothing to weigh us down. Suddenly a storm darkens our life. What are we to do? Where do we turn for help? Why has this happened?

We can spin about not knowing which way to turn! We can stumble on through the darkness of our circumstances, seemingly making no progress...

The Sun of Righteousness (Malachi 4:2) - not the sun of earth, but the Son of Almighty God is there for us! Where the earthly sun had temporarily brightened the day, now the Son of God, Jesus Christ is available! The Light of Jesus is willing and able to help us through our storms of life.

Thank You, Heavenly Father for giving us Your Only Son, Jesus, for our needs! Thank You Jesus, for Your Loving help and care for each of us. You are always there waiting to help. But, we need to remember to call upon You so that You know we do put our trust in You.

You are the answer to life's ups and downs, dear Savior! You are always waiting for each of us to come to You, to desire Your friendship. Yes, what a friend we have in You, Jesus, just as the beautiful song relates.

Hopefully we realize this great treasure we have in You, dear Master. May we look forward to spending our Eternity with You, forever, and ever and ever... ... ...

Mail Person   Nov. 21

1st Timothy 2:1

Here are my directions: Pray much for others; plead for God's mercy upon them; give thanks for all he is going to do for them.

Dear Lord, I was praying for those You have put on my heart to pray for. When I finished, the thought came to me that, in a way, I am like a person who delivers mail!

Someone needs prayer – I take their names and their needs…In a sense, I put this information lovingly into an envelope and send it up to You, Father God. I am like a "deliverer" carrying out a service.

You, precious Lord, put on my heart many years ago the need to be a prayer person on others' behalf. During this time I have seen so many prayer requests answered! Thank You, dear precious Savior, for taking such loving care of Your followers, and of those who do not claim You as their God yet…

As we grow older and are not as active as we used to be, praying for others is a wonderful way of serving our brothers and sisters in this world.

There is such a need for people to pray…One has only to read the newspaper, listen to the radio or watch television to realize that there are total strangers who are in need of our prayers. We may never know here on earth the good our prayers may do…

Thank You again, dear Jesus, for the compassion You put in our hearts as we mature spiritually. Thank You for blessing our prayers with Your Loving-kindness. May more and more of Your followers realize the mighty power of prayer!

We cannot understand here on earth what goes on in Heaven when we raise our voices to You in prayer, dear Father! But what a privilege it is for us to be able to pray to our God, our Creator!

Praying one for another is like giving a wonderful gift to each other…How blessed are we to have someone praying for us! Please Lord, open all our hearts to the realization of this…

While we are still here, Lord, let us bless others with our prayers for them to You, our Father God. Prayer doesn't cost a single cent! It is a free gift from one's heart to our Savior…

Yes, let us each become a "mail person" delivering prayers to our gracious Lord God... ... ...

You Are My Love...   Nov. 22

John 15:13

"And here is how to measure it – the greatest love is shown when a person lays down his life for his friends; ..."

Romans 5:8

But God showed his great love for us by sending Christ to die for us while we were still sinners.

You are my Love, dear Jesus, my true Love...Oh yes Jesus, there are those here that I love, and deeply too, but You are my true Love...

Nothing will ever change that, dear Lord, nothing...The amazing part of this Love is that You return LOVE to me! You LOVE me, along with countless others, but it is as if I were the only one receiving it...Your LOVE completely fills the void in me...Your LOVE completely fills all hearts that are desirous of receiving it...Your LOVE is that special unconditional LOVE which covers us like a warm, cozy blanket...

Love is a strange thing...One cannot touch it or see it...But one can feel it...But then again, one can see it in another's eyes...One can touch another with a hug that exudes love...It is a strange and wonderful thing...

Happy is anyone who can experience real love here...A loving act has saved lives many, many times. A loving word has comforted others time and again. Material aid and finances have lovingly blessed others so often...Real love finds joy in giving to another, in sharing...

But we will not know, not realize, the depth of true LOVE until we meet You, Lord Jesus...You are the epitome of TRUE LOVE, dear Savior...You came into this world expressly to teach us the real meaning of LOVE...

Time after time, the Scriptures tell of experiences where You demonstrated LOVE...It was always an unselfish giving of Yourself for someone else's good...Then when Your time came to leave this place, You, in a truly Loving way, asked Your Father to forgive the very ones who were putting You to death!

365

Your death was the purest act of LOVE, Divine Savior…There is no way we can ever repay You, Lord…In our own way, we accept what You came to teach by showing You, even now, that we love You…We appreciate You, Praise You, Adore You, put You in the highest place in our lives. Then You can see in our hearts that Your divine act of LOVE was not in vain - not wasted…

Your LOVE has touched our lives…You are our LOVE…When Love comes through us it is because of You, only You, dear Lord, for You are TRUE LOVE, UNCONDITIONAL TRUE LOVE… … …

We All Fall Short…   Nov. 23

Jeremiah 17:10
Only the Lord knows! He searches all hearts and examines deepest motives so he can give to each person his right reward, according to his deeds – how he has lived.

Romans 3:23,24
Yes, all have sinned; all fall short of God's glorious ideal; yet now God declares us "not guilty" of offending him if we trust in Jesus Christ, who in his kindness freely takes away our sins.

Dear Father God, it is so painful to look inside our hearts, when we truly examine them. We don't like to see how we've failed You so many times…We want to do better! We hope to do better in our relationship God, but we fall short…We all fall short…There's sadness in our hearts, Lord, when we realize this. We want to look perfect in Your eyes, Lord…

We try to shine ourselves up, to make You think better of us…We sometimes brag or tell about our good deeds to others; we want to impress them. In our impressing them, we hope You will look down on us and smile indulgently…But, the reality sinks in and we know that we can never fool You, Lord - for You are Perfect Truth. You know our hearts; You know ALL…

How can we impress You, Lord? How can we make points with You? Tell us Lord Jesus, please tell us…

"You can't make points with Me, Your Creator… I have seen you since you took your first breath and even before while you were being formed in your mother's womb. When you learn humility you will

begin to see with pure eyes what is pleasing to Me. Then you will become what I have created you for..."

Oh Father God, how foolish we are so often in our lives! We don't need to strive...We don't need to be above our brothers and sisters...We don't need to impress You or those around us. Your humility is the greatest lesson we can learn.

As we learn humility, You will continue to share with us other lessons to help us become true imitators of Your Son, Jesus Christ of Nazareth. Though we do fall short, Lord, we desire to do better, much better as time passes...

That wonderful expression "Where there is life, there is HOPE" encourages us to continue on. In spite of our imperfections, thank You Lord, for giving us the opportunity to go on...We have HOPE in our hearts - because of YOU!

Remove Self   Nov. 24

Philippians 2:3-8

Don't be selfish; don't live to make a good impression on others. Be humble, thinking of others as better than yourself. Don't just think about your own affairs, but be interested in others, too, and in what they are doing.

Your attitude should be the kind that was shown us by Jesus Christ, who, though he was God, did not demand and cling to his rights as God, but laid aside his mighty power and glory, taking the disguise of a slave and becoming like men. And he humbled himself even further, going so far as actually to die a criminal's death on a cross.

Good morning, dear Lord Jesus...Here I am hoping to hear from You...You are Inspiration to me...You pour forth thoughts You want me to express on paper...Thank You, dear Savior, for being so generous, so constant...

Whenever I take the time to listen to You, You are always there with me, waiting to share with me...How grateful I am, dear Father...

As I meditate on some thoughts, the words "remove self" come...Oh dear Lord, how very important and necessary it is for us to remember these words...We must not only remember, but we must put them into action...

How easy it is to slip into our memories and recall all the "good deeds" WE have accomplished…Accomplished? We have accomplished??? Oh Lord, see how easy it is to fall into taking the credit for what we've done for others…We have forgotten that it was through You!

It is Your Grace, Your Inspiration, which guides us into the lives of others…Because of Your using us, lives are changed! When we remove "self" and only act as Your willing servant, then we can see the awesomeness of You at work!

How exciting it is to observe! It is true we partake in the actions necessary to accomplish what needs to be done. But we MUST recognize always that it is You, and You alone, who are orchestrating Your Plan!

You look down from Your Heavenly Home, and see a particular need for one of Your Family…When we are in tune with You, we can readily see what You want accomplished. Then, hopefully, we are ready to be Your Hands, Your Heart, Your everything…What a privilege it is to be used by You…

Oh Father God, the wonder of it all! We can see lives changed, circumstances altered, and hearts relieved of heaviness. This happens when we "remove self" and are faithful to You…Thank You, gracious Father, for Your trust in us…Thank You, thank You, thank You… … …

"To Do Or Not To Do?…"　　　Nov. 25

Psalm 143:10
Help me to do your will, for you are my God. Lead me in good paths, for your Spirit is good.

We are all searching in this world of ours…Each one of us is seeking to find our way. Do we go this way or that way???

It's so hard Lord…There is so very much to learn. Do we really want to learn about You, Jesus? Or do we want to ignore You and go our own way?

Decisions, decisions - life is full of decisions. Shakespeare once said, "To be or not to be; that is the question." We, now in this generation, might easily think or say: "To do or not do; that's our question!"

Each of us is constantly faced with choices. If we choose to become a Christian, even then we must make a choice...Which group will we choose? Shall we become a nominal Christian, or one who wants to find out all there is to know about the Creator of this Universe, and all mankind... ... ...

How far shall we go to follow this man, Jesus, called the Son of God? Again each of us, because we have been given the gift of making choices, will have to decide...

Thankfully we do have a choice! No one has the right to make us become puppets. We can exercise this gift of choosing, understanding that we should use it wisely...

Should we search the Book of Rules, the Bible, we shall find many answers to the questions we have stored up. The answers are there for us to find. As we search, we begin to mature so we can grasp the depth of the Scriptures.

"To do or not to do" – these words have deep meanings. Shall we do the work that Jesus left undone because of His early death? Or shall we leave it to be done by others? Shall we become a person who gives freely of ourselves or shall we not...These are our choices.

Hopefully, Father God, as You look down upon this earth, You see countless children of Yours who choose to do Your Will... ... ...

Into Each Life Some Rain Must Fall...   Nov. 26

James 1:2- 4
Dear brothers, is your life full of difficulties and temptations? Then be happy, for when the way is rough, your patience has a chance to grow. So let it grow, and don't try to squirm out of your problems. For when your patience is finally in full bloom, then you will be ready for anything, strong in character, full and complete.

These words, dear Lord, entered my thoughts as I meditated about my life...As I remembered, I recalled some very hurtful and difficult times...

I immediately thought of You, dear Jesus...I remembered how some of those closest to You hurt You the most...You suffered emotionally and physically…You suffered every kind of hurt, dear Lord…

When I again thought of the past, I realized how much those times have helped me to grow. Instead of being angry and resentful toward those who were responsible, I could now see that into each life some rain must fall…Thank You, Heavenly Father, for allowing us to go through these negative situations. These experiences have helped us to grow and hopefully to mature…

If we were to have only positive experiences, everybody treating us with "kid gloves," we would become immature, selfish, spoiled individuals. We would always want to be in the center of everything!

Thank You Lord, for letting us see the necessary steps we must take to grow into the person You know we can be…This is not an easy task. Each day we must look at ourselves with a critical eye.

Please dear Savior, help us to look deeply within ourselves to see what needs to be changed…Help us to remove those characteristics, which need to be dealt with… With Your Loving forgiveness and encouragement, dear Jesus, we CAN change into new creatures!

Now we can see as You want us to see…Following Your precepts we can accept whatever may come, both pleasant and difficult things…Yes Lord, into each life some rain must fall, but You are our umbrella. As we remain under Your care, You sustain and teach us when the rains come…

Thank You, dear Lord, for the rain which helps us grow closer to You…May we Praise and Glorify You, Father God, for the beautiful rainbows You then bring forth into our lives… … …

Lord, What Do You See?   Nov. 27

Psalm 139: 1,17,18

O LORD, you have examined my heart and know everything about me.

How precious it is, Lord, to realize that you are thinking about me constantly! I can't even count how many times a day your thoughts turn towards me. And when I waken in the morning, you are still thinking of me!

Lord, what do You see when You see me…As I was thinking and meditating about You, I wonder what You see when You look at me…

What are Your thoughts about me? I think about You and wonder about You...I have my special thoughts about You...I think things about You only because I cannot see You...

But You can see me, watch me, and hear me whenever You want to...You have thoughts about me...I wonder what they are...I wonder what You would tell me about myself if You were here sitting in the chair near me...

You have the ability to tell the truth without hurting...I want to know the truth about myself...Perhaps I have been deluding myself in my relationship with You...

Dear Jesus, You gave us the story about the Samaritan in Luke 10:27-37. It was about a Jewish man being robbed, beaten and left half dead on the roadside. Later a Jewish priest saw his body lying there and crossed the road so as to avoid helping him. Next along came a Temple assistant, a Levite, who actually looked down upon his body. But then he crossed the road to avoid helping the victim.

Now a Samaritan, who was traveling saw the man lying there. He felt deep pity and did what he could to help him. Then he put the man on his own donkey and brought him to an inn and nursed him through the night. Before leaving he paid the innkeeper and said if it cost any more he would repay it on his return journey...

We can easily see that the Samaritan was the only one of the three who acted with compassion, with LOVE for another human, can't we Lord...

Yet the first two who found the man were "religious" men...We who think of ourselves as people of God, must search ourselves deeply...Are we any different from the first two people on the scene? Who would You say that we were most likened to, Lord Jesus?

Oh, Father, let us truly examine our hearts, our motives, our actions, our words...Let us reflect on what You came here to teach us...It is absolutely necessary that we care for one another, LOVE one another as You LOVE each of us...

Lord, what do You see when You see me???

Soft Crown   Nov. 28

Matthew 27:27-31
But first they took him into the armory and called out the entire contingent. They stripped him and put a scarlet robe on him, and made a crown from

long thorns and put it on his head, and placed a stick in his right hand as a scepter and knelt before him in mockery. "Hail, King of the Jews," they yelled. And they spat on him and grabbed the stick and beat him on the head with it.

After the mockery, they took off the robe and put his own garment on him again, and took him out to crucify him.

Dear Jesus, oh dear, dear Jesus – a crown of very, very sharp thorns was thrust upon Your head...It was not gently laid upon Your head, but pushed down, hammered into Your flesh until drops of Your precious blood spilled down upon Your face...Oh, the agony of what was done to You crushes my spirit...The thought of what You suffered for me, and all mankind, causes my heart to ache...

Hundreds of years later, we Christians of today think that some of the burdens we have are too much to bear. We sometimes feel that we are wearing a crown of thorns upon our heads...

We even feel at times that we are being a martyr for You, because of the burdens we bear. But the only crown we are willing to accept is a soft one...We are willing to wear one, but we expect to have those extremely sharp points filed down until that crown sits lightly upon our heads...

What? I am expected to wear a crown like You, Lord Jesus? But the pain would be too intense! I couldn't stand that kind of pain! I am willing to wear one, but only a soft crown...

"I will give you the strength to carry whatever burdens come your way. Whatever the pain of the crown you wear, will be shared by Me... We will share all that goes with wearing it. That crown will be exchanged, for one especially made for you when you enter into My Kingdom."

Oh, dear Savior, our hope is in YOU...We can go on, because of Your example, Your encouragement, Your LOVE for us...Please keep reminding us through Your Scriptures of all the promises You made to us, that You WILL keep... We have not seen You, as Thomas the apostle did, but our Faith in You is firm...It is steadfast, not because of anything in us, but only because of You and Your Faithfulness...

Thank You, dear Savior, for wearing that torturous Crown for each of us... ... ...

Blessed Assurance   Nov. 29

1ˢᵗ John 5:11-13

And what is it that God has said? That he has given us eternal life, and that this life is in his Son. So whoever has God's Son has life; whoever does not have his Son, does not have life.

I have written this to you who believe in the Son of God so that you may know you have eternal life.

Oh Lord, one of the many mysteries of LIFE is not knowing when we'll leave this earth - when our last breath is taken…We do not know how we will die, either…

But, dear Lord God, there are countless numbers who KNOW WHERE THEY ARE GOING! Yes Lord, so many truly know where they are going - HEAVEN! What a blessing! As one beautiful hymn quotes:

> "Blessed assurance, Jesus is mine!
> Oh, what a foretaste of glory divine!
> Heir of salvation, purchase of God,
> Born of His Spirit, wash'd in His blood.
> This is my story, this is my song,
> Praising my Saviour all the day long"…

That assurance is from You, dear Savior Jesus! Oh, truly what a blessing it is!

The number of days or years remaining of our lives really is meaningless once that assurance is discovered…How and why we will depart, again, is really unimportant…IT'S WHERE, WHERE we are going, which is meaningful!

There is so much striving to climb the ladder of success. There is so much concentration on how fit and trim our bodies are…There is so little devoted to understanding the spiritual part of ourselves in this race to achieve success…The spiritual part is so often neglected…The expression which seems to fit here is an old one, but suitable. "We must stop and smell the roses" as we juggle our responsibilities…

On the day we leave this world what will be of eternal value? Jesus said in Matthew 7:24,25

"All who listen to my instructions and follow them are wise, like a man who builds his house on solid rock. Though the rain comes in torrents, and the floods rise and the strong winds beat against his house, it won't collapse, for it is built on rock."

Jesus is the Rock upon which we must build our lives.

Are you building on "the" SOLID ROCK? Each of us must make the time to learn what is necessary to assure us a place in Heaven. Yes, Lord Jesus, You are our Blessed Assurance; You are our Savior, our Light in this darkened world...

Oh, thank You dear Master, dear Teacher, thank You for how richly You assure us of Your LOVE... ... ...

If I Could Only Understand...   Nov. 30

1st Corinthians 13:12

In the same way, we can see and understand only a little about God now, as if we were peering at his reflection in a poor mirror; but some day we are going to see him in his completeness, face to face. Now all that I know is hazy and blurred, but then I will see everything clearly, just as clearly as God sees into my heart right now.

Oh Lord God, if only I could understand...If only I could understand the great mystery of You...I try so hard to peek beyond the curtain which separates You from me. I try so hard to comprehend the magnitude of You, the magnificence of You, the awesomeness of You!

So often we humans make reference to You...We hear from different sources around us the words - "Oh God". Sometimes it is said in anger, fear, or impatience...Other times it is said in despair, surprise, or ignorance...

In these times You are not being given the proper recognition of WHO YOU ARE...You are THE God of the Universe! Even those who understand this don't seem to have the feeling of AWE that should emanate from them...We all need to realize WHO YOU ARE!

Yes Lord God, Almighty God, if only I could understand You...Sometimes it seems as if I can, to a tiny degree. This fills me with such wonder, such awe, and such excitement! But then it fades away...

Your Bible tells that now we only know in part, while here on this earth...Oh how I wish we could know fully and see You more clearly! Dear Father God! Thankfully, we have a blessed future to look forward to...You, Jesus, lovingly went before us to prepare a place for each of us who believes in You...

Oh, Almighty God, Father of All, please draw all our loved ones to You...Because You are the Pearl of Great Value, we want all our loved ones to join us with You, for all Eternity...

Thank You, dear Jesus, for giving us Hope to carry us through the ups and downs of LIFE here on earth. Thank You for the gift of Faith so that we can be assured of joining You, when that special of all special moments comes.. When we breathe our last breath here, we will understand...For then we will start our real LIFE with You forever and ever and ever and ever... ... ...

December

Made A Difference   Dec. 1

Ephesians 4:22-24

...then throw off your old evil nature – the old you that was a partner in your evil ways – rotten through and through, full of lust and sham.

Now your attitudes and thoughts must all be constantly changing for the better. Yes, you must be a new and different person, holy and good. Clothe yourself with this new nature.

Oh dear Jesus, thank You for coming to earth...By Your coming You made a difference here...Oh, sometimes it isn't readily apparent, but Your coming HAS made a difference...

Your coming has made a difference in my life...Your coming has made a difference in countless lives ever since You came here as a tiny babe...

In a few weeks Christmas will be celebrated by many all around our world...Yet in all the celebrations of Your Birth, which we call Christmas, how many really celebrate Christmas because of You? Your Birth, Your coming to earth changed this world... ... ...

Man's knowledge of real LOVE would be unknown without Your coming...Your coming MADE a difference! You taught us about real, perfect, unconditional LOVE, when You willingly died for each of us...Even today, hundreds upon hundreds of years later, we still hear about You. We hear of Your LOVE for all mankind, and how You went to that wooden cross without complaint...

Yes, dear Savior, You were slain to set us all free from our sins...This is such a complicated thought, yet it is a simple fact...You were sent by our Almighty Father God to make a difference here...Your LIFE reflects simplicity, honesty, tenderness, dedication, and pure LOVE...

Yet You were strong when You needed to be strong...Though You often stood alone, many were fearful of You...They couldn't understand You; they were judging You by their own selfish standards...They didn't want to understand You, because You were different...You were making a difference in the lives of others and they were afraid of You...

Oh, dear Savior, thank You for coming here to earth…Thank You for truly making a difference in our lives…Thank You for teaching us compassion, tenderness, honesty, loyalty, LOVE, and so much more…

By Your coming, Precious Jesus, You truly made a difference… … …

Diamonds In The Rough   Dec. 2

2nd Corinthians 4:16,17 (NIV)

Therefore we do not lose heart. Though outwardly we are wasting away, yet inwardly we are being renewed day by day. For our light and momentary troubles are achieving for us an eternal glory that far outweighs them all.

Father, the above words came to me recently…We are Your diamonds in the rough, aren't we? When diamonds are taken out of the earth, they don't appear to have any beauty. They seem like a lump of something without any worth…

There it is, a lump of something…It is only by cleaning the lump that it begins to have some worth…Then comes the hard part…That piece of matter has to be cut and shaped. It has to be polished…It has to go through many different steps to bring forth its final beauty – its full value.

The similarity between a rough diamond, Lord, and us is amazing! Each time we go through a cutting, a shaping by life, and its problems and burdens as we submit to You, we are being made more valuable to You, Lord God…

In researching diamonds we learn that the "cut" affects the brilliance of the diamond…You and You alone can cut and shape us to be made into a gem, which brings forth a brilliance for You…

We look around at those outstanding Christians who represent You so sincerely…We see that each one of them has been cleaned up, cut, shaped, and polished for You and Your services.

Am I willing to submit myself to Your refining, Lord? Are You asking me, Lord? Well, Lord, there's a price to pay…Let me examine my heart…As I meditate and examine myself, I must consider what it means to become a diamond for You, dear Jesus…

Yes, dear Savior, I am willing...No matter what the pain, what the price, what I need to go through, it is worth the price! Nothing is too great to pay!

I am ready, Lord...Cut and shape me, Lord...Clean and polish me, please...Lord, I am ready... ... ...

Why Did You Come?   Dec. 3

Ephesians 1:7,8

So overflowing is his kindness towards us that he took away all our sins through the blood of his Son, by whom we are saved; and he has showered down upon us the richness of his grace – for how well he understands us and knows what is best for us at all times.

Why did You come, Lord? You must have been so very happy in Heaven there with Your Heavenly Father, Almighty God...Why? Why did You have to be sent down to earth? You knew what Your fate would be...You knew what was going to happen to You all along!

It's so very difficult to comprehend this mystery...It seems there could have been another way where You, dear Jesus, wouldn't have had to experience such terrible treatment from so many...It is so hard to understand that a father would send his child, his only son, into a battlefield. For surely this world was a battlefield for You, dear Lord Jesus...

As we follow Your life through the teachings from the Bible, we learn so much about You. Yet, there is much we do not know. You were rejected...When that happened You moved on to another place. Some along the way received Your messages...But, how few out of so many received You, dear Savior.

The few years of Your ministry passed quickly, too quickly for us to realize. Why only a few short years? As they came to a close, rejection was not enough to satisfy the ugliness of mankind! Hatred of You filled their souls; anger and resentment burned within them!

The cries scream forth: "Crucify Him! Crucify Him!" Then You are laid down upon that cross of death...Your Hands, Your Feet are nailed fast...You are then raised up, with a cruel crown of sharp thorns pounded into Your Blessed Head...Now You are raised up for all to see...Then the sword is thrust into Your side so that all blood, all fluids drain from Your Body. Oh, Jesus...Oh, my Lord, my Savior, why did You come?

Luke 23:24a
"Father forgive them; for they know not what they do."

FORGIVENESS! You came to forgive us from all our sins! Oh precious Savior, thank You! Thank You for coming down from Heaven to give Your life for us...Thank You for Your unconditional Love, which You have for us...You willingly died for us and as You died, You asked Your Father to forgive us!

Thank You, dear Sacrificial Lamb of God...But, my Lord, – how little is "thank You" for such a magnificent and priceless gift... ... ...

Return On Your Investment   Dec. 4

Psalm 86:12,13
With all my heart I will praise You. I will give glory to your name forever, for You love me so much! You are constantly so kind! You have rescued me from deepest hell.

Dear Father God, You didn't get much of a return on Your investment from Your creations, Your children...Reading through Your Scriptures points out the failings of Your chosen ones so many times. These chosen ones, in whom You had such hope, disappointed You time after time.

In the New Testament, how could the apostles who were around You, Jesus, day and night, disappoint You so often? One would think that if the opportunity were possible to be there with You, one would become a perfect example of what a Christian should be!

Alas, the Scriptures indicate that none of Your followers were perfect...Father, as You looked down from Heaven and witnessed their shortcomings we wonder how You must have felt...

We, in this present time, wonder how we possibly can become pleasing in Your sight, Lord. We haven't had the blessing, the privilege of seeing You, dear Jesus. We must take on Faith what Your followers were able to witness with their own eyes...

Ah-h-h...Now we remember what You said to Thomas, dear Jesus...He was so stubborn! He would not believe his brethren who said that You returned from the dead and appeared in their midst...You showed Thomas Your wounds and he fell to his knees at Your feet. He gasped out "My Lord, and my God!"

We today can receive a tremendous blessing directly from Jesus because of Thomas!

John 20:29

"Then Jesus told him, (Thomas) "You believe because you have seen me. But blessed are those who haven't seen me and believe anyway."

WE ARE THOSE!

Hopefully dear Father, we will become more aware of what a tremendous blessing You gave us, when You gave us the gift of Life itself. May we realize that because of this gift! Now we can give You a return on Your investment...We appreciate and love You so much...Let us give You all the Glory!

We hope Your investment in each of us will be a blessing and that Your heart will feel our gratitude...Thank You for Loving us, forgiving us and seeing the best in us, because of Your unconditional LOVE... ... ...

So Many, So Many   Dec. 5

1ˢᵗ John 5:14(NIV)

This is the assurance we have in approaching God: that if we ask anything according to his will, he hears us.

Dear Precious Lord, there are so many, so many...I keep coming with more names of people who are in need of You...The years are passing by and I am still bringing before You those who are in need...Yet, looking back over the years there have been so many blessings of healings and answered prayers for all sorts of circumstances and situations! You have been so very faithful, Father. You have never made me feel that I have taken advantage of our loving relationship! I am very grateful for that, Lord...

I don't think I realized the power we, as Christians, had been given...We have the privilege and power of praying for people who may not yet have Faith in You, Lord…This Power comes through praying to YOU! When we send up our prayers to You, You open the door of Your Heart and receive them…

We, as Your children, can come into Your Presence through our prayers…We don't need an appointment or a reservation. We don't have to stand in line, or take a number. So often we get a busy signal when we try to use our telephones, but Your line is NEVER busy! Your giant computer is never, never down! You are open to listening to us twenty-four hours a day!!! Thank You, Lord, for being so gracious to us…What would we ever do without YOU???

Name after name, year after year - so many Lord, have been brought to You in prayer…It is an overwhelming thought to realize that if each believer were sending requests, Heaven would soon be saturated with petitions to You! But still there is room for as many as we are obedient to send up to You!

Some people say "I don't bother God with the little things – I only go to Him for the big needs." Children don't decide to ask their parents only to fix their big toys! They go and ask for EVERYTHING to be fixed, no matter how small! And You, Lord, have told us to come as little children…

How wonderful to realize that we have the privilege of going in prayer to our Father for any and every care of those in need, as well as for ourselves…Let us be obedient to ask according to Your will as 1st John 5:14 above, reminds us.

The windows of Heaven are open! Our dear Lord is always listening for us to share our lives with Him. Thank You Father, for always hearing our prayers and for answering them according to Your Will… … …

From A to Z   Dec. 6

Revelation 1:8

"I am the A and the Z, the Beginning and the Ending of all things," says God, who is the Lord, the All Powerful One who is, and was, and is coming again!"

From A to Z, throughout all Eternity, You will always be...Yes dear Creator, God of all, You are the beginning and the end...There is no other like You...

You are Supreme...You are alone, yet three, in the Trinity...You are the greatest mystery in life...There is no knowing You in the fullness of Yourself...Our minds simply cannot grasp You, will never fully grasp You while in our human form...

Thankfully Master, Teacher, Savior, You made arrangements for each of us to reside with You in our new life! Yes, each of us who responds to Your beckoning, and believes in You as our Lord and Savior, has a free entry into Heaven!

We cannot understand Eternity! Everything we seem to understand has a beginning and an end...Eternity has no end! How can we comprehend such an awesome thought – we cannot...

It is only with our trust in You, dear Father God, that we can accept this thought. We will be able to stay with Almighty God forever - on and on and on with no end! It is simply amazing!

What a gift, Heavenly Father! What a gift You have made available for such a small sacrifice on our part...If You, Lord, were to give each of us a life span of even 125 years, what a small sacrifice it is to dedicate ourselves to You...

Yet You know we all are imperfect...We fail time and again, but You are always there to encourage us to try once again to continue on our path towards You...How You LOVE us, dear Jesus! Your unconditional LOVE for us is always there, pouring out to cover each of us as we are in need. How blessed we are to have such a Loving and forgiving Creator...

Please Father, as we come to You, wherever we are, guide us along the way. And when that last breath of ours is taken, may we hear Your precious voice welcoming us to our everlasting Heavenly Home...As we enter the threshold of Heaven, which has no end, our spirits will be filled with gratitude...

From A to Z, throughout all Eternity, You will always be... ... ...

Stepping Stones   Dec. 7

Matthew 10:8b
"Give as freely as you have received!"

Life is a continuing path from the day we are born until the last day of our lives. My dear Lord, as I look back on my walk toward and with You, I see that You placed so many loving people in my path. I see them now as stepping stones to help me along my path toward You...

Dear Jesus, so many stand out in my past. These loving people gently helped me along so I could become stronger for You, Lord. How grateful I am, Lord, how very grateful!

There comes a time when we are given the opportunity to become a stepping stone for others. The thought, dear Jesus, of becoming a stepping stone perhaps leaves one with the feeling of discomfort. It sounds like someone wanting to use us and You know, Lord, how unpleasant that could become! Are we willing? Will it cost us something to become a stepping stone? What does it require?

"Give, My child... Give of yourself. Allow yourself to be what another requires at the moment. Put others ahead of yourself as I call you to do."

Yes, the cost – in life there is always a cost. The cost is giving of ourselves, but the blessings come also...Sometimes Lord, when You call upon us to help others, a feeling, a special feeling begins to surround us. There comes a peacefulness when we answer Your call to help another, as others have helped us...

Only You, Lord, as You look down upon Your children see those loving steps which have been given one for another. Dear Savior, continue to allow those who are willing, to become stepping stones to bless others.

You, dear Master, were the perfect example of a stepping stone. We read in the Bible how You taught us to be imitators of You. Your apostles carried out Your teachings so that we can, over 2000 years later, become stepping stones!

Are we willing to become stepping stones for others?

Some One Appears   Dec. 8

Luke 1:28-31,34,35,38 (NIV)
The angel went to her and said, "Greetings, you who are highly favored! The Lord is with you." Mary was greatly troubled at his words and wondered

what kind of greeting this might be. But the angel said to her, "Do not be afraid, Mary, you have found favor with God. You will be with child and give birth to a son, and you are to give him the name Jesus.

"How will this be," Mary asked the angel, "since I am a virgin?" The angel answered, "The Holy Spirit will come upon you, and the power of the Most High will overshadow you. So the holy one to be born will be called the Son of God."

"I am the Lord's servant," Mary answered. "May it be to me as you have said." Then the angel left her.

A sweet maiden stands there alone...
Some one appears, speaking in a special tone.
"Who is this that appears to me?"
"Listen to me and you will see –
in time, the mother of a Babe you'll be..."
"But I have known no man, not one..."
"Truth you speak, for this is God's Own Son..."
The Angel looked down upon this girl
And knew she was chosen from all the world,
To birth this Precious Babe in a lowly place...
He should have had cashmere, down pillows, lace...
But into this world He came – for you, for me...
And now thankfully, He holds the Heavenly Gate's Key.

GNL

Your Way   Dec. 9

2nd Samuel 22:31-33 (NIV)

"As for God, his way is perfect; the word of the LORD is flawless. He is a shield for all who take refuge in him. For who is God besides the LORD? And who is the Rock except our God? It is God who arms me with strength and makes my way perfect."

Dear Father God, I was just thinking about You and I found myself saying to You "Father, help me find my way to You"...In moments You let me know that I should have said, "Father, help me find YOUR way to You"...

My way, dear Lord, might bring me through places and circumstances, which would separate me from You...My way could possibly waste many months or years...Please, dear Creator, have

Mercy on me and show me the way to a closer relationship with You...

Our hearts are willing, Lord Jesus, so willing to follow You...Yet as time passes we have found that we still want to do things that lead us astray from You...As we have heard so often, "My spirit is willing, but my flesh is weak."

Please, dear Lord, point out to us our failures and anything, that needs changing...It is so easy to gloss over them when we have to examine ourselves. In the past when You have wanted to get our attention You have used several different means to do this...Always though, dear Lord, You have been successful in getting our attention...I know that You must deeply LOVE us when You take the time to help us - if we are willing...

In reflection, how can we ever want to go our own way when You have told us in the Scriptures, how much You desire us to come to You...As we come YOUR way, Your many wonderful promises are ours! You are faithful to Your promises... For You alone are the most trustworthy of all!

Many of our loved ones have disappointed us, at one time or another and it was so heartbreaking...But we are assured that YOU will never abandon or desert us...You are faithful to Your Word, as we abide in You, and You abide in us.

Yes Lord, yes Father, help us find YOUR way to You - Only YOUR Way... ... ...

Insensitive   Dec. 10

John 15:9-14

"I have loved you even as the Father has loved me. Live within my love. When you obey me you are living in my love, just as I obey my Father and live in his love. I have told you this so that you will be filled with my joy. Yes, your cup of joy will overflow! I demand that you love each other as much as I love you. And here is how to measure it – the greatest love is shown when a person lays down his life for his friends; and you are my friends if you obey me."

Forgive us, dear Savior, for being so insensitive to You at times...We tell You, over and over again, how much we love You...Yet there are times, so many times, that You are left far behind in our thoughts, words and actions. Yes, dear Jesus, when we become insensitive to You, what we think, say, and do can carry us far away from You...

When these times occur, dear sweet Jesus, let us recall in our minds what You did for each of us...Your last days here on earth were filled with lies, hatred, anger, physical abuse and rejection...Did all of these experiences cause You to become bitter toward those who were responsible? No...You became our Sacrificial Lamb...You accepted Your role of being our Savior, our Messiah...

As You were hoisted up upon Your sacred Cross, You looked down upon those who were responsible for Your physical death...Did You scream obscenities at them? Did You shout down to them and ask for Mercy? No...You spoke to Your Heavenly Father and asked Him to forgive Your persecutors...

What an example You were to all who witnessed those horrible hours on the day of Your death...What a powerful example You are for all the world...When You, dear Savior, went to that horrifying cross You demonstrated the greatest LOVE for all mankind...For those who have not yet accepted You as their Savior, what a wonderful gift of LOVE awaits them...

Oh, Praise You, Glorious Savior, Jesus Christ! Oh dear Lamb of God, please whisper into our ears which thoughts you want us to reflect to all those around us...Please Lord, reveal to us not only thoughts, but words and actions also...

Let us take the word "insensitive" and take two little letters off, changing it to SENSITIVE. Then please, Master, remind us again of what You did for us here on earth...Help us to become sensitive to the reality of Your UNCONDITIONAL LOVE for each of us... ... ...

How Can I?   Dec. 11

1st John 4:19 (Amp)
We love *Him,* because He first loved us.

How can we love You so much, Lord, when we have never seen You? Dear Lord, it's a mystery to us! Yes, we've heard about You, read about You, thought about You, prayed to You and talked to You...But we want to know You in a deeper way...

When one hears about a special person, there is a desire to get to know about that person. Then as more is learned about them, one wants to have that person pointed out to them.

Ah-h-h, then a face-to-face meeting is desired! That's the way we feel now! We desire to see You face-to-face, dear Jesus! We desire to sit at Your Feet and visit with You, to hear Your Voice, to see Your Smile, to hear Your Laughter!

Here we are, loving You with all our hearts and souls, never having seen You...We content ourselves with the awesome thought that we will be meeting You face-to-face some time in the future...We will sit at Your Feet...We will hear Your Voice and see Your Smile...We will hear Your Laughter!

Oh thank You, dear Savior, for teaching us about Faith, about Trust – even when we cannot see You...Your Holy Spirit teaches us through Your Scriptures the reality of WHO You are! Then we, Your children, can have Faith even though we have not seen You with our eyes. We must learn to Trust in You as our spirits see You.

The strange thing, dear Jesus, is that we can be at peace with You and within ourselves...Loving You creates that inner peace which is beyond our understanding...What a gift we have from You, dear Lord, the gift of Yourself to each of us!

We all can feel as if we are Your only child! There need be no jealousy among Your children, no matter how many there are of us! We can each love You and know that You LOVE us as an only child! And Your LOVE for us is an unconditional LOVE!

How can we love You so much, Lord, when we have never seen You face-to-face? It's easy, Lord, for You first LOVED us...It is Your LOVE in us which we can give back to You...

Dear Jesus, thank You for Your LOVE, which is so incredible!

Will You Have Time For That, Lord?   Dec. 12

Revelation 21:3b (Amp)
See! The abode of God is with men, and He will live (encamp, tent) among them, and they shall be His people and God shall personally be with them and be their God.

Here I sit, Lord, thinking of You…I've just pictured myself arriving in Heaven and seeing You! As fast as I can, I run and jump into Your arms! They are strong and I become as a child to be cuddled and loved by You…

Then, dear Jesus, after some time, You put me down and I'll sit at Your feet. I'll look at Your beautiful face and listen to Your voice…Oh, will You have time for that, Lord? Will You have all the time that each of us wants and hopes for, to spend with us individually?

One believes that it will be so! After experiencing our journey here on earth, we so look forward to having special times with You as Mary, Martha's sister, did. In Luke 10:38-42, You told Martha that Mary had chosen well when she sat at Your feet instead of hustling and bustling about.

Oh yes, dear Savior, our time with You will have arrived! All our struggles, burdens, problems will have been left behind! Our real life begins when we pass over into our Heavenly Home!

What a time that will be! What glory we have waiting for us! Thank You, dear Jesus, for going before us to prepare this special place for each of us…

I want no crown; I do not long for streets of gold. My only desire is to see You, to be with You, to get to know You as I have never been able to imagine while here on earth! Excitement surges through my spirit as I try harder and harder to picture that first experience as I enter Heaven!

But, back to earth I come knowing that You still have plans for me here, Lord. There is work to be done here while I still have breath in my body.

I am reminded of the beautiful song "Soon and very soon, we're going to see the King! Soon and very soon, we're going to see the King!" Lord, it will happen because You have told us so. Dear Jesus, as a child asks its father "Will you have time for that?" I ask You, "Precious Jesus, will You have time for me to sit at Your feet for as long as my heart desires?"

Oil in Our Lamps   Dec. 13

Dear Jesus, You clearly tell each one of us how extremely important it is to always be ready for Your coming. In Matthew 25:1-13, You Lord, plainly illustrate through this parable the consequence of not making a decision for You...

Matthew 25:1-13

"The Kingdom of Heaven can be illustrated by the story of ten bridesmaids who took their lamps and went to meet the bridegroom. But only five of them were wise enough to fill their lamps with oil, while the other five were foolish and forgot.

"So, when the bridegroom was delayed, they lay down to rest until midnight, when they were roused by the shout, 'The bridegroom is coming! Come out and welcome him!'

"All the girls jumped up and trimmed their lamps. Then the five who hadn't any oil begged the others to share with them, for their lamps were going out.

"But the others replied, 'We haven't enough. Go instead to the shops and buy some for yourselves.'

"But while they were gone, the bridegroom came, and those who were ready went in with him to the marriage feast, and the door was locked.

"Later, when the other five returned, they stood outside, calling, 'Sir, open the door for us!'

"But he called back, 'Go away! It is too late!'

"So stay awake and be prepared, for you do not know the date or moment of my return."

The last words You said to the five bridesmaids seemed so very harsh. "Go away! It is too late!"

"It is too late!" Any one of us who has ever been late to an appointment or a meeting and been turned away knows how very disappointing that was. But You, Jesus, are telling us that we must also be ready to hear Your call!

"Go away! It is too late!" How many people will be like the five bridesmaids, who fell asleep without making sure they were all prepared to enter into the marriage feast with Jesus, the bridegroom.

While they slept, He came and locked the door after Him. Are we one of those who entered in with Jesus or are we one of those who will be locked out?

It's time to evaluate our situations. Are we ready? Are we putting off until a more convenient time the trimming of our wicks and filling of our lamps?

Dear Savior, You are the most perfect one ever born. Some think because You are a generous and Loving God, that You will overlook what they want overlooked. But because You are perfect, You are also a very just God.

You see the heart of each of us and we will be judged by You in a just way! Thank You for being just, dear Lord. May we realize the responsibility is OURS...Will we hear:

"Enter in my good and faithful servant" or "GO AWAY! IT IS TOO LATE!"

Revival   Dec. 14

Isaiah 64:1-4

Oh, that you would burst forth from the skies and come down! How the mountains would quake in your presence! The consuming fire of your glory would burn down the forests and boil the oceans dry. The nations would tremble before you; then your enemies would learn the reason for your fame! So it was before when you came down, for you did awesome things beyond our highest expectations, and how the mountains quaked! For since the world began no one has seen or heard of such a God as ours, who works for those who wait for him!

Oh Father God, your people need to be revived! They need to become revitalized! They need to be brought back to Life again as Webster's dictionary defines the word "revival". They need to have their vitality restored.

Who are "they", Lord?

We are "they", dear Lord. We, who call ourselves Christians – we need to be revitalized, energized, refreshed, renewed!

Lord, conditions in the world have gotten so terribly sad. Murder, rape, abortions, and evil of all kinds are commonplace now. Government officials, whom we once were able to look up to with respect, have fallen from grace, as have many religious leaders. If there ever was a time of spiritual need it is now, Father!

But how do we ignite people? How do we get revival into the hearts of your people, Lord"?

"... then if my people will humble themselves and pray,
and search for me, and turn from their wicked ways,
I will hear them from Heaven and forgive their sins
and heal their land. I will listen, wide awake,
to every prayer made in this place."
2ⁿᵈ Chronicles 7:14,15

Yes dear Lord God, please give us a heart for revival! We must desire revival so much that it will burst out like the atomic mushroom many years ago! That mushroom was a cause of much destruction. Let Your Holy Spirit burst upon us with Your Almighty Reviving!

Let the Power of Your Holy Spirit permeate through each of Your children who call themselves Christians. Let it flow out into our churches and communities, until revival spreads across our nation like a heavenly vapor!

Oh, Spirit of the Living God, Spirit of our Redeemer Jesus Christ, fall afresh upon us. The world is so in need of refreshment, renewing, and reviving. Revive us, Holy Spirit; revive us as we come to You seeking a fresh anointing... ... ...

Those Eyes   Dec. 15

Matthew 25:37-40

"Then these righteous ones will reply, 'Sir, when did we ever see you hungry and feed you? Or thirsty and give you anything to drink? Or a stranger, and help you? Or naked, and clothe you? When did we ever see you sick or in prison, and visit you?'

"And I, the King, will tell them, 'When you did it to these my brothers you were doing it to me!' "

Haunting eyes stare out of swollen bodies...
Those eyes, created by our God, our loving Father -
Are we to look at them, and look away?
And turn the page so we don't have to bother?

Bother to be the hands, the feet, the instrument
To change their world, their lives, their place,
As we, perhaps, sit in comfort and are served
Ample lunches on trays of silver covered with lace...

Oh brother, sister, you out there, and also me,
Let us wake up to what is happening to our earth!
Let us care to such a depth that those eyes
Can be changed to see new hope, a great rebirth...

Places that have little water can now have more.
Trees that have been felled and land now bare
Can have little ones to grow very tall and flourish.
Yes, caring on our part can turn that haunting stare

Into eyes filled with laughter, joy and peace...
For we know working with our Father, all together
Makes such a difference, a world of difference.
Now all mankind together can make things better... GNL

A Little Cut...   Dec. 16

Isaiah 53:4-6 (NIV)

Surely he took up our infirmities and carried our sorrows, yet we considered him stricken by God, smitten by him, and afflicted. But he was pierced for our transgressions, he was crushed for our iniquities; the punishment that brought us peace was upon him, and by his wounds we are healed. We all, like sheep, have gone astray, each of us has turned to his own way and the LORD has laid on him the iniquity of us all.

A little cut – it was a little cut on my finger shaped like an upside down "U". It was so small, dear Lord, but it hurt. It was constantly reminding me of itself. As the days passed the little flap of torn flesh would get caught on whatever I touched...

As I look at it tonight I am reminded of the tears on Your precious Body. When You were beaten by that terrible instrument with barbs at the end of it, Your flesh was cruelly torn.

Thank You, Lord, for this little cut. It has brought me back through the ages as if I were witnessing Your scourging. Thank You for reminding us of what You willingly suffered for us, for me.

It seems there are times, Lord, when we should all be reminded of what You suffered for us. We can get so complacent, so caught up in the busyness of our everyday lives, we can forget the sacrifice You made for us.

Your Word says that there is a time for many things. Life itself brings us through many of these "times". Tonight is a sad time for me reflecting about Your pain...

A thought has just come to me, Father. When we get to Heaven, will we be able to see the past? Will we be able to relive as a spectator those parts of history we would most desire to experience?

For me Lord, for many of us, there are times when we would like to experience Your life. We would like to be able to see first hand, so many wonderful times described in the Bible!

Would any of us want to relive the horror of the last days of Your life? That would be a hard decision to make... Thankfully, dear Jesus, Your Father called You to experience it just once and You were willing to become our sacrificial Lamb. Keep reminding us so that we will not forget what You did for us. Thank You dear Jesus, for a little cut – a little reminder... ... ...

Ring! Ring-g-g-g!   Dec. 17

Hebrews 3:7a
And since Christ is so much superior, the Holy Spirit warns us to listen to him, to be careful to hear his voice today...

Ring! Buzz! Ding-a-ling! Dong!!! Isn't it amazing, Lord, how we have programmed ourselves to stop what we are doing and quickly answer those particular sounds!

They get our immediate attention! Though one is busy with a particular duty or speaking to someone, we have tuned ourselves to listen to those sounds! We interrupt what we are doing and answer the buzzer, beeper, doorbell, telephone, or fax machine...

Wouldn't it be wonderful, Lord, if You had a special sound! It might be a sweet sounding, tinkling bell to call us to answer You, dear Jesus, to get our attention...

We are so prompt to answer the bells of society. Yet we allow these sounds to interrupt You, when we take time to meditate with You...It's so strange, Lord...What we need to do is to program ourselves to listen to Your Voice. We need to make that special time of meditation top priority instead of trying to fit these precious moments into OUR schedule...

Life seems to get busier and busier. Yet through You, Lord, we can have the strength to make changes if we desire it...We don't have to give in to the demands and distractions of the world. Thank You, dear Lord God, that You allow us to make choices for ourselves. How blessed we are to be able to make choices...

We seem to manage fitting into our lives all the pleasures, which appeal to us. Yet, You are so often forgotten or put aside until a more convenient time...Strangely, it seems the more we put off spending time with You, the harder it is to get back to You...

Time seems to play tricks on us...Yet each day has the same amount of time in it...How we use that time is one of the choices You give us...What choice will we make today?

Ting-a-ling! Ting-a-ling! Is that You, dear Savior???

Our Ticket   Dec. 18

John 17:3
"And this is the way to have eternal life – by knowing you, the only true God, and Jesus Christ, the one you sent to earth!"

In a sense, dear God, You gave us a ticket when we were born as we entered this world...It's a ticket into the school of LIFE. As Life progresses, much like a school, we have lessons to learn - lessons to experience...

One of the hardest lessons to learn is to have a healthy attitude about Life. In the Bible, You speak about us having Joy...You want us to learn how to be joyful! How can one be joyful when "things" turn our lives upside down – when suddenly terrible things are thrust upon us? We cannot understand how this could have happened...We are good people! Why should something like this happen to good people?

Joy? We should become joyful? How, oh Lord, how?

"Get to know Me... I am your Creator. All things pass through My hands... When you become close to Me, very close, I will share with you the secrets of My Heart. Joy is one of them. Come close to Me..."

Oh Lord, how do we get to know You? There is so much in life to learn!!! Perhaps some of our education has been lacking. Subjects like history, math, spelling, science, and computers are all very necessary – BUT we need to learn about the spiritual part of ourselves!

Because we come into this world with a body, a mind, and a spirit, we need to understand that all three need to be educated! We go to school to educate our minds...We feed and exercise our bodies, but what about our spirits? Where do we go – what must we do to learn about educating our spirits?

Without learning what the Bible teaches with the Holy Spirit's guidance, we are only partially educated. We need to be educated about what our options are after we leave this world!

A one-way ticket to Heaven or a one-way ticket to Hell awaits each of us...Getting to know You, Father and Your Son, Jesus, as our Lord and Savior is the way to Heaven. Choosing not to know You, going our own way, leads in the opposite direction...Only we can made that decision for our eternal future. Thankfully, Lord God, we have that choice! Thank You, thank You, thank You!

Reader, have YOU made your decision yet?

Possible God   Dec. 19

Jeremiah 32:17

"O Lord God! You have made the heavens and earth by your great power; nothing is too hard for you!"

Luke 18:27 (NIV)

Jesus replied, "What is impossible with men is possible with God."

Oh God, thankfully You are God of the impossible! You are the Possible God! Oh how we praise You and glorify You for being who You are!

How exciting it is, dear Father God, to witness the many, many times You have stepped into impossible situations and brought about positive results!

Gracious Father, Almighty God, let us as Your children share these exciting testimonies time after time with others...Please give us the courage to step out in Faith and speak out. We have been privileged to witness these special miracles! We need to help build up others in their experience with You. We need to share the positive happenings, which touch our lives. Sometimes it takes only one testimony to change a person's life!

Yes dear Father, we thank You again for being so Loving to us by continuing to be our God of impossible situations! How often You have taken some of the darkest circumstances and turned them into the most glorious!

Hopefully each of us can look back and see how You did make a difference in our lives. Some of us have had deeper problems than others, but whatever we have been through, in sharing we can grow into stronger Christians. Then we can also help our brothers and sisters.

We Praise You, Heavenly Father, for all those times when we were desperately in need...Thank You for always being there, ready to save the situation for us!

You, thankfully, are our Father! An earthly father is ready to help his children - he tries his best. But our earthly fathers cannot be with us 24 hours a day, every day of our lives. How blessed we are that we can call on You in a split second...WE BELIEVE YOU ARE THERE, AND WE ARE IN YOUR LOVING HANDS...

May many more of Your children come to realize that You are the Possible God of the most impossible situations! Thank You again, Father God... ... ...

Appreciation   Dec. 20

Proverbs 28:20a (NIV)
A faithful man will be richly blessed, ...

Colossians 2:7b
Let your lives overflow with joy and thanksgiving for all he has done.

Dear Jesus, the word "appreciation" should point to You...There is no one or nothing in this whole world that could ever come close to You...

We are so conditioned to receiving blessings from You that we often take them for granted! Just opening our eyes each morning and being able to rise out of bed is a gift from You...Walking about as we start the day is another blessing. Hearing the sounds all around us is also a blessing. Speaking to a loved one, and so much more, are privileges from You, Lord.

And Lord, that's just the beginning, isn't it? Having cold and hot running water, stoves, refrigerators, bathroom facilities are more…Electricity is a blessing too! Being able to hear a loved one's voice from thousands of miles away is another! Cars, airplanes, pleasure boats, great ships at sea, all are blessings from You, Heavenly Lord…

Looking at the spectacular sights of Nature causes us to hold our breath at times! What a joy! Seeing the beauty of Your many varieties of flowers with their Heavenly colors and fragrances is another gift…

Spring comes after a dreary winter and precious little shoots of greenery appear everywhere! The sun, Your sun, brings forth these lovely creations. You shower down the much-needed rain to cause all these growing things to flourish. Then in the Fall the trees turn from green to beautiful shades of crimson, gold, orange and everything in between! All these are blessings that we see in Nature…

Oh Mighty God, there are so many more reasons for us to thank You, for us to show You our appreciation…The beauty of Your Moon when it is full, shines down and makes lacy patterns on Your earth. Stars stud Your skies appearing as little diamonds sparkling up there!

Yes, God our Father, Jesus, Son of our Father and Dear Holy Spirit, thank You for all Your countless blessings!

Let us, Your children, begin anew to lift up to You, our deepest APPRECIATION… … …

Lost Reverence?   Dec. 21

Nehemiah 1:11a (NIV)
O Lord, let your ear be attentive to the prayer of this your servant and to the prayer of your servants who delight in revering your name.

Psalm 33:8
Let everyone in all the world – men, women and children – fear the Lord and stand in awe of him.

Dear Lord Jesus, have we lost our reverence toward You? Have we become used to thinking of You in a casual way?

"Oh yes, we'll pray when we get a chance to...After all, God is always 'up there'. Time is not that important to Him..." Do we realize that without the wonderful privilege of prayer, we would have absolutely no way to communicate with Him?

Do we put You in a little place until it's convenient, then take You out and spend a few minutes with You?

Oh Father, Almighty God, Creator of All, how sad it must be for You to look down upon us and realize how very immature and irreverent we are...In the Old Testament, there were those who showed such reverence toward You...

In this modern day of another millennium, You see the shallowness of Your people. We have lost the excitement of experiencing You in a fresh new way! You have become diminished in the eyes of those around us. We, as Christians, have allowed this...

In so many of our churches as one enters, there is no sign of respect that they are in Your House, dear Lord. Socializing seems to predominate. Gum chewing abounds among the children and adults, even those who sing in the choirs!

Reverence means to love, to be in awe of You, to show You deep respect, to honor You, to worship You. These are some of the ways we can try to regain our reverence for You, Heavenly Father...

There are those in this world who love to look up to royalty throughout the nations. All sorts of honors and displays of homage are given to them. Newspapers send their reporters and photographers all over the world to catch a glimpse of them!

Yet You, God Almighty, Lord of all this Universe, have to play the waiting game...Oh Father, please forgive us, Your children. Whether we have accepted You or not, we have All been created by You...How sad that so many do not understand this...

You are our merciful God. How thankful and grateful we are Lord, for Your Mercy, when we realize how badly we have treated You...

Please forgive us, dear Father...Please forgive us... ... ...

Gift of Prayer   Dec. 22

Psalm 17:6 (NIV)
I call on you, O God, for you will answer me; give ear to me and hear my prayer.

Oh Almighty God, a thought came as I was listening for Your voice. It was that Prayer is a gift to us! This gift of Prayer always has an answer too! This gift of Prayer also has another important part to it and that is it's God's timing, not ours...As we wing up our prayers to You, dear Father, You in Your omnipotence, know exactly how the prayer will be answered! You also know how long it will take for an answer to be forthcoming...

As Your children, all our needs and desires are tender to Your heart...How wonderful we feel many times when our deeply desired prayer requests are answered quickly! What joy spills out of our souls as we rejoice! When we hear of an answered prayer, Lord God, especially a miraculous one, we are flooded with joy and happiness!

But then too, dear Lord, there is waiting, and waiting, and waiting...Sometimes days, weeks, months, or even years pass...What is wrong? Lord, is there such a thing as a "bad" prayer? Is there a prayer that never gets an answer?

"No, My child, only I know how the prayer that you offered up to Me will be answered. So many times the answer is 'Yes'... But there are times when I know that it will take many years for your prayer to bear fruit... Then too I may never answer your prayer, and remember, that it is answered by not being answered."

Oh Father, again we thank You for this precious gift! Sometimes it takes us so long to realize how wonderful this gift of Prayer is! Suddenly we realize that the gift of Prayer is a privilege from You!

There is no waiting for an appointment to send our prayer to You! You are constantly available to each of us. There is no standing in line and taking a number! There is no long distance expense to call You! You are there waiting for us day and night, twenty-four hours a day!

May we take advantage of this gift of Prayer, to share our big needs and the very, very little ones as well...Thank You again, dear Creator God, for the precious gift of Prayer... ... ...

In Heaven There'll Be...   Dec. 23

2nd Corinthians 5:1,2

For we know that when this tent we live in now is taken down – when we die and leave these bodies – we will have wonderful new bodies in heaven, homes that will be ours forevermore, made for us by God himself, and not by human hands. How weary we grow of our present bodies. That is why we look forward eagerly to the day when we shall have heavenly bodies which we shall put on like new clothes.

In Heaven there'll be no loose ends, dear Lord, will there? As I was snipping off loose threads from a garment, I was thinking how I always cut them off when I see them…Then I thought "There'll be no loose ends in Heaven!"

Suddenly my spirit brought me into the whole concept of Heaven! Nothing will be a halfway measure! No repairs will be necessary! There will be no huge bills to be paid, because of something needing to be fixed.

Here on earth we are delighted with something new. The excitement lasts for a period of time and then the novelty wears off…Then as the years go by dullness sets in; drabness covers the attractiveness of the once new item.

We are accustomed to these facts of life. "That's the way it is," we tell ourselves. In a way, that is how it is with our human life.

Most of us are born with all our body parts in perfect order. Our parents and those in the delivery room proclaim "The baby is perfect!" Life brings this child through different stages of growth and adulthood blossoms. We have a body in fine condition, a sound mind ready to meet the challenges of life, a spirit ready to fully develop.

Years pass on and then more…Suddenly parts of this perfect body begin to show wear. Time continues. The body is having more and more problems. One hears "Try this – try that!" There are medications, surgeries, and replacement parts for some. Sadly, for many the once perfect mind begins to diminish. Memory has lost its sharpness…Recognition of loved ones fails…

There'll be no need to try this doctor and that doctor in Heaven! There'll be no loose ends to be concerned about! Thank You, dear Father, that all of the loose ends of LIFE will be brought into the perfection, the fullness of Heaven!

Yes, dear Lord Jesus, we thank You and our Heavenly Creator, Almighty God, for creating Heaven for us! There we shall spend our Eternity with You and all our loved ones! What more can anyone ask of LIFE itself! What a gift You have given us, Father God! With grateful hearts we are in awe of YOU… … …

Creator Of All Creation!   Dec. 24

Genesis 1:1,2 (NIV)
In the beginning God created the heavens and the earth. Now the earth was formless and empty, darkness was over the surface of the deep, and the Spirit of God was hovering over the waters.

Heavenly God, You are the Creator of all Creation! No matter how many galaxies, meteors, planets, or comets are newly discovered, You know about them already - for You created them! No big bang! You, Creator of All Creation, put what has been created in perfect order. You need not explain in detail how this wonderment came about.

We hear on occasion that something new in the heavenlies has been discovered. Large headlines appear! Something new has come to the attention of the world! Some of us smile knowingly because we believe there is so much more to our Universe that has yet to be discovered!

When You, Creator of all Creation, formed Your Master Plan, man was not invited to watch! We, who love You, know that whatever the fullness of this Plan was, it was and is perfect!

This earth was created by You and it WAS good in Your sight...Man was created and next a companion was brought forth - woman. How it must have grieved Your Spirit to watch as these two broke Your rule not to eat of the tree of knowledge of good and evil.

As generation after generation passes, man learns little by little what You, Creator of all Creation, brought forth! Was the earth flat or round? Question after question came...Answers came more slowly. But here we are in the 21st century and questions are still being asked about what You, God, created...

Wise men have come and gone dear Lord God. Hopefully in all the studying of creation man will come to the realization that the most important thing to seek is Salvation in Jesus Christ! Each of us has a certain life span here on earth, whether long or short, only God our Creator knows. But it is essential that however long or short each of us has, we must find the key to our real home after we leave this earth...

Earth is just a temporary place for us. It is a school to learn what is important to our growth. Blessed is the person who learns the lesson early! This lesson is found in John 3:16,

"For God loved the world so much that he gave his only Son so that anyone who believes in him shall not perish but have eternal life."

Believing in the Son, of whom this Scripture speaks, allows us to enter into our Heavenly Home! For the discovery of Heaven awaits all those who believe in You, dear Author of Creation... ... ...

Blessed Babe   Dec. 25

Luke 2:6-7(KJV)
And so it was, that, while they were there, the days were accomplished that she should be delivered. And she brought forth her first born son, and wrapped him in swaddling clothes, and laid him in a manger; because there was no room for them in the inn.

Blessed Babe...Did You raise Your tiny hands to all this world? Did You fill Your eyes with all the faces of mankind? Did Your little ears hear the screams and yells of those who would persecute You? Oh, Blessed Babe, Blessed Babe, You were a tiny bundle of Divine Love...

That night so many years ago, was the significant night of all nights...So quietly did You enter this mad world of ours...Only the soft braying, cooing, mewing noises of Your creatures filled the air, as You entered as our sacrificial Lamb. Those little fingers, those tiny toes were to grow into the man who was to heave the heavy burden of His very own Cross upon His back. Those tiny fingers had to grasp that instrument of death; those tiny toes and tender feet had to climb that hill of gloom...

Blessed Babe, Blessed Babe...You saw the love within Your mother's eyes. You saw the tenderness of Joseph as he cared for You and Your mother...Did You know what fate had in store for You as You lay there so peacefully in the manger? Will anyone ever know what took place that most special of all nights?

How brave and trusting was our God to allow You to come to us...Could we ever do what Your Father did? He gave us His only

Son, knowing what was to come...Blessed Babe, You are the example for all this world...

Blessed Babe, come wrap Your little fingers around our hearts! Come coo into our ears with words of love...Come smile at us and melt our indifference and coldness...Teach us the ways of simple love, the love that has no strings attached, Your kind of LOVE...

Tiny Hope for the whole Universe, remind the world of the purpose of Your coming. Remind us that Your day, Your birthday, is the celebration of Your gift to us! Without Your coming what would things be like now? As bad as this world is now, how much worse it would be without You! For such a little while, words like "Peace" and "Joy" are talked about, written about. For such a little while, giving and sharing happens because of You...

Blessed Babe, remind us that it is Your birthday we celebrate! Turn back the clock if need be, to ways of celebrating Your birthday in a truly spiritual way...With Your tiny innocent Body wrapped in simple clothes, remind us it is the simple giving of ourselves, as You gave to us, which can be the most beautiful of all gifts...

Yes, Blessed Babe, as You hold up Your tiny arms to all of us, to every man, woman and child born into this world, You give Yourself to us without any hesitation. Each one of us can claim You as his own! Each one of us can have all of Your LOVE, all of Your promises, which You made while here during Your short stay...

Silent night, holy night, our Blessed Babe is born this night... ... ...

The "LOVE" Chapter   Dec. 26

1st John 4:7,11

Dear friends, let us practice loving each other, for love comes from God and those who are loving and kind show that they are the children of God, and that they are getting to know him better.

Dear friends, since God loved us as much as that, we surely ought to love each other too.

Father God, are You testing us? When we come upon a very difficult situation concerning us, who call ourselves Christians, are

You watching us? Are You hoping that we will see it as a lesson You want us to learn?

Tonight Your children were gathered to pray and seek Your Face. We needed Your direction – we needed to set our sights on Your goal for us...Someone entered the group and Your flow seemed to be interrupted. Some felt that confusion started to invade the gathering...Yet that person is a Christian who simply seemed to be misguided...What to do, dear Lord God?

"Dear children, what message did I come to teach you? Was it not LOVE? LOVE overlooks the misguided. LOVE overlooks what seems to be interruption of the moment... LOVE needs to soften the problem. LOVE needs to be spread about, permeating all there... Your love can make a difference in that person's life – in each of your lives..."

Oh Lord – how disappointed we feel when we see Your children acting in an unloving way to other Christians...We, who call ourselves "Christians" must realize that the world is looking at us to see if we practice what we are taught...How many lessons do we need to learn, dear Father, before we truly understand the fullness of Your teachings...How many people do we "hurt" as we practice our Christianity...

Heavenly Father, we must be more careful of each situation we are involved in...We must seek You.. We must quickly ask You what to do - what to say. WE MUST GROW UP! No matter what age we are, we must grow in Christian maturity so that we can carry out Your will...

We do not have a choice. Your Word, dear Lord, COMMANDS us to LOVE...But we have to grasp the true understanding of this word...It is found in the "Love Chapter"- 1st Corinthians Chapter 13...Reading this Chapter is easy, isn't it, Lord? Putting it into daily, hourly practice is one of the hardest things to do...But when we invoke You, dear Jesus, to help carry out our desires to truly LOVE with Your understanding, we will succeed...

"Dear children what message did I come to teach you?"

No Distractions   Dec. 27

Hebrews 12:2

Keep your eyes on Jesus, our leader and instructor. He was willing to die a shameful death on the cross because of the joy he knew would be his afterwards; and now he sits in the place of honor by the throne of God.

Dear Lord Jesus, I came to say my prayers quietly here in Your Presence. I was sincere, but my mind kept drifting to one thought after another.

Then I thought how wonderful it will be when we arrive in Heaven! There'll be no distractions to keep us from giving You our undivided attention! No matter the circumstances, all our attention will be focused on You, our sweet Lord and Savior…

Oh how hard it is to imagine that, here and now! But because of our faith in You, we know this will come about sometime in our future! What excitement there will be; yet all will be in perfect order! Nothing will be too loud, or out of order; everything will be beyond our dreams!

Some ask, "What will we do there?" We will do whatever You, Lord Jesus, decide! This will be a wonderment to us, because in our human state, we always want to be in control. We want to get the best seat, to be the leader and so on…

All of those concerns do not exist there…LOVE will be the password! Each of us will want the best for each other! No pushing or shoving! No distractions to keep us from Adoring You, Praising You, Glorifying You!

Heavenly music will surround us…Angels will be attending to You, our Heavenly Father and Son, Jesus Christ. As we meditate here and now about these things, it seems as if we shall be constantly in awe! The majesty of You, King of Kings, will have us in awe! Our minds simply cannot comprehend this!

As each moment brings us closer to our entrance into our Heavenly Home, let us keep our eyes upon You, dear Lamb of God. Let us shake off the thoughts, which keep distracting us from You! Our spirits long for a precious time of Praising You, Worshiping You, Adoring You as we come into Your Presence!

Teach us, Father, how to deepen our prayer concentration on You until that moment in time when we meet You face-to-face… … …

One Little Sparrow   Dec. 28

Matthew 6:26

"Look at the birds! They don't worry about what to eat – they don't need to sow or reap or store up food – for your heavenly Father feeds them. And you are far more valuable to him than they are."

Silently, the little bird flew off into the dusk. As I gazed into the distance following its flight, I marveled at the bravery of this little creature existing in a harsh world. Yet, Your Word says You feed them. My thoughts then turned inward as I reviewed how You have taken care of me all my life.

Oh Father God, we can learn so much when we quiet ourselves and look around, all around…When we are in sync with You and spend quiet time with You, You open our eyes to things we have taken for granted. Our eyes suddenly see so much more and our hearts and spirits are uplifted as we Praise You for the wonders of our Universe!

As I continued to sit, night crept upon the scene. The sky became black velvet with small diamonds scattered here and there in the heavenlies. How glorious! How awesome to realize that we are on the outer edge of our planet and able to discern other planets and stars scattered apparently at random…

Yet in the vastness of Your creation You care for that little bird who was so tiny…It was so vulnerable to all the negative factors in its little life, yet it flew away with little concern.

Dear Jesus, there are no words in my vocabulary which can ever thank You enough for Your Loving kindness to me, to us…Just as You care about each little bird with LOVE, which seems amazing, You care about us…You care about each and every human being who has been birthed here! How mind-boggling that thought is! When we realize the care You extend to us, it causes us to understand that we must be more caring of others.

That little bird delighted me while I watched it feed and hop around seeking its supper. Then it flew away to a hidden nest…May we be as that little bird in our efforts to delight and draw others to

You, Father God. Let us look for opportunities to bring a sweet surprise to others as that little bird blessed me.

Thank You, our Glorious Creator God, for all the beauty in this world. May we learn to appreciate Your workmanship in even the simplest things more and more each day... ... ...

The Name Of The Game Is Trust   Dec. 29

Proverbs 3:5,6 (NIV)
Trust in the LORD with all your heart and lean not on your own understanding; in all your ways acknowledge him, and he will make your paths straight.

Yes, dear Lord, the name of the game is TRUST. For that's what LIFE really is: a game...To each game there are rules, aren't there, dear Lord?

The game of LIFE has specific rules which help us become winners. We all want to win at any game we play. No one wants to be second or third, only the winner!

Rules, Lord, where are the rules? Oh, in that book lying on the shelf? Look at all the dust on it, Lord...Whoever owns it must not review the rules of the game very often. They must not be very interested in being a winner after all!

Let us come closer to that book of rules...Oh, it's called a Bible. As the pages flip open and we glance at some of the words in it, TRUST jumps out at us...TRUST: what has that got to do with winning the game of LIFE?

Oh Lord, You want me to TRUST You? But why should I do that? What's the percentage in that for me? Oh, maybe I can win? You mean I will be SURE TO WIN, if I follow the rule – to TRUST You?

How is that possible, Lord? Oh, You have already gone before me and know the answer...YOU will teach me, step by step, so that at the end of the game of LIFE - I WILL BE A WINNER!

WOW! That doesn't seem so bad; I can do that on my own! I don't think I need You, now that You have shown me the ropes...But it's not quite that easy? I need You to teach me? You need to be around me each and every day of my life, almost like a coach? All right Lord, be my coach...

As we listen to the Coach we learn about TRUST by learning about YOU, the Savior of the world... The more we get to know You the deeper we grow in TRUSTING You...Once we reach the deepest degree of TRUST, we are able to feel completely at peace within ourselves.

No matter what comes, our TRUST is now in You, dear God. You, Mighty God, Creator of All, are in control and so I rest myself in Your Everlasting Arms...Oh, the JOY of knowing, truly knowing and experiencing the TRUST, which only You can give! It overwhelms us! Thank You for being so faithful to Your children, dear Father God...Thank You that our TRUST in You makes us winners for all Eternity... ... ...

Emptying Out...   Dec. 30

Psalm 68:19
What a glorious Lord! He who daily bears our burdens also gives us our salvation.

Oh, Lord, look at the junk we carry around in us...Day after day, week after week, month after month, year after year, we continue to carry it.

Hurts, misunderstandings, sins of commission and of omission, unforgiveness all jumble up inside us...Guilt hangs on and on...

Oh, Lord Jesus, how can we bear all of this???

"You can't, My child, you can't... Haven't I become the Burden Bearer for you, for all mankind? You offend Me when you continue to carry these burdens..."

Yes Lord, I see now that it is an offense to You to keep holding to these things within us...You already paid the price to set us free! You took upon Yourself our sins, to set us free! Oh, Lord, please forgive us for hurting You so...You have sensitive feelings, Lord...We hurt You when we insist on trying to work out our problems by ourselves...

No one in this whole Universe has more LOVE for each one of us, than You, Lord God...If only we can grasp this amazing gift - You truly LOVE us! You want only to help us untangle the messes we have made, undo our mistakes.

Lord Jesus, may we give up all the "junk" so that we are ready to start afresh on our walk with You. When we learn to picture You walking along with us, then we fully understand You ARE our burden bearer…In this picture we look so free of our burdens!

Oh, Jesus, how can we ever thank You for this wonderful gift?

"You can praise Me, adore Me, worship Me. You can give Me all the glory! For I am Your Lord God, your Creator… I am the Alpha and the Omega, the Author and the Finisher…"

Oh yes Lord, You alone are worthy to be praised, adored and worshiped! Yes, YOU are the only One who is worthy… … …

After We've Gone…   Dec. 31

Psalm 112:6 (NIV)
Surely he will never be shaken; a righteous man will be remembered forever.

After we've gone and left this world, dear Jesus, what will there be for those who are still here to remember?

Will we leave joy, love, patience, happiness, generosity, and laughter? Or will we have left a bitter memory in the lives we lived among?

Oh Father that's a sobering thought…It causes one to reflect, this very moment of what comes quickly to our minds. What will the ones closest to us remember about us?

They have been observing us, listening to what has been coming out of our mouths. Are there conflicts between what we say and what we do? Will they have seen us with two different personalities, one for the home and one for the outside world?

Oh dear Savior, help us here and now to consider our values…Help us to communicate to our loved ones who may be out of harmony with us. Let us do, let us say, let us be what would be pleasing to You…

Perhaps we've been negative to others in our lives. Sweet Jesus, please help us to change! Oh, it won't happen overnight, we realize

Lord...Each day, each minute, help us to make the effort to be what You want us to be - gentle, loving, compassionate, forgiving, patient.

After we've gone, there are no more chances to change the memories, which will remain long after...Let those who knew us remember that we did try to brighten this world from the small place of our existence. We have read that some who have gone before left a legacy of many different characteristics...They range from generosity, heroism, compassion, and love to bitterness, jealousy, hatred, anger, and unforgiveness...

Please, Father God, open up our minds and our hearts, to make a promise to You, which will make a positive difference...May we have left some seeds of love, to be remembered after we've gone...

Let us, hopefully, leave this world not with thoughts of pride, but with a grateful heart, because You have allowed us to be a vessel for You... ... ...

Index Of Special Days

A New Year

Philippians 1:20,21

For I live in eager expectation and hope that I will never do anything that will cause me to be ashamed of myself but that I will always be ready to speak out boldly for Christ while I am going through all these trials here, just as I have in the past; and that I will always be an honor to Christ, whether I live or whether I must die. For to me, living means opportunities for Christ, and dying – well, that's better yet!

Happy New Year! Happy New Year!

These words ring out as the bells peal, as the clocks chime 12 o'clock midnight around the world! Firecrackers fill the air; sirens pierce the night...Another year has begun...

Another year - what will it bring? To some it will bring joy, happiness, love, marriage, births of tiny babes taking their first breath...For others there will be heartache, sorrow, ill health, death...

Each year we all start out and no one knows who will still be here at the end of this new year...That can be a frightening thought for many...For those who truly believe in You, Lord God, there is no worry, no fear, and no anxiety. When we have put our trust in You, Lord Jesus, Lord God, there is no reason to worry!

No matter what happens, no matter what, we are completely in Your care! If we are not here to celebrate another new year on this earth, it will mean we have already started the celebration of our new life in Heaven!

If we are still here for the commencement of another new year, we will have more opportunities! We can continue to be Your hands, Your feet, Your heart, Your LOVE, Lord, for those who are in need...

So as we reflect on this day, this first day of a new year, let us gather our thoughts together to make decisions for this new year...

Each of us has our own responsibility toward LIFE, to those we are responsible for and to ourselves. Each of us owes LIFE something...LIFE is a gift and because of that we must, we are obliged to, return something to this LIFE, to this world we live in...

A new year is a time to reflect...Hopefully it is a time to change...May this year become the best year of each of our lives to date and may each year become better as we celebrate the gift of LIFE itself... ... ...

413

Your Eyes

Hebrews 4:13

He knows about everyone, everywhere. Everything about us is bare and wide open to the all-seeing eyes of our living God; nothing can be hidden from him to whom we must explain all that we have done.

Lord, some day I will be looking into Your eyes…Your eyes are filled with TRUTH, perfect TRUTH and LOVE, perfect LOVE…

You are filled with Perfection for You are Perfect…When that time comes, when each of us has to face You and look into Your eyes, suddenly all that we have ever wanted to know will be revealed to us…

All knowledge will fill us; all mysteries will be unfolded…Your eyes will speak to us, Lord Jesus…They will tell us immediately what we need to know about our future…

We will be able to see it all there in Your eyes…Without a word spoken, as our eyes meet Yours, we will know our fate, our future…

For only TRUTH can be reflected in Your eyes, Lord Jesus…When You look at each one of us, You will be seeing our whole lives, every moment with no exceptions. There will be times in our lives that we would rather hide from You, but that will be impossible, is impossible…Your eyes are all seeing - all knowing…There is not a single soul ever created who can hide a detail from You…

So Lord Jesus, this is the first day of a new year. It is a new chance for us to start with a clean slate. May we each try to visualize Your eyes so that we will resolve to make amends…

Let us ask forgiveness of You, for all we have done to offend You. Let us ask forgiveness of those we have been out of harmony with. Let us forgive those who have hurt us…Let us begin this new year with a fresh start, a truly new beginning…

When that moment comes, Lord Jesus, when our eyes meet with Your eyes, may we read in them "Well done, good and trustworthy heir of Heaven, enter in…"

Another Year

2nd Corinthians 3:18(NIV)

And we, who with unveiled faces all reflect the Lord's glory, are being transformed into his likeness with ever-increasing glory, which comes from the Lord, who is the Spirit.

It is another year, another opportunity - an opportunity, dear Lord, to better ourselves...This does not mean materially...But it is an opportunity to grow into the person You intended us to be...

Each of us has an opportunity to become a changed person...I must allow You to change me, Lord...When we think about change, sometimes we'd like to change "that person" who seems to antagonize us so frequently...But we cannot change someone else...

Yes, Lord, I know that I must leave everything in Your Hands and work on myself...I must look deeply into myself...I must not try to hide my imperfections from myself with all sorts of excuses for them...

It's hard, dear Father God, it's hard...Yes, this is the day for resolutions. I resolve to _____; I resolve not to _____... ... ...But didn't I make those same resolutions last year, and even the year before?

I see now that resolutions are nothing but words unless I truly allow You to change me...As I meditate upon the realization that January first is here again, I wonder how many more January firsts I have left...They seem to fly by!

Lord, I need Your help...I need You to encourage me; to guide me; to chasten me...I need You every step of the way...Only You know what the future holds...Only You can help us through the ups and downs of this new year...

It's so easy to say to all around us "Happy New Year! Happy New Year!" The excitement of the coming year may turn out to be a disappointment or heartache for some...But we must leave the future to You, Lord Jesus, and put our trust in You...

Thank You, dear Savior for all Your many blessings...May this year draw us closer to You... ... ...

Another Year Gone By...

John 15:4,5 (RSV)

Abide in me, and I in you. As the branch cannot bear fruit by itself, unless it abides in the vine, neither can you, unless you abide in me. I am the vine, you are the branches. He who abides in me, and I in him, he it is that bears much fruit, for apart from me you can do nothing.

Dear Lord Jesus, another year has gone by...The Christmas excitement has passed...The trees and their trimmings have lost their charm...

As we stop to look and reflect on this past year, we remember certain experiences and events. Some were joyful and some were sad...We are reminded of those who will no longer see another year...We also rejoice at the thought of little ones who are experiencing their first year of life!

Yes, another year has gone by – what does this new year hold in store for us? None of us really knows what is to come...But some of us do make resolutions, which we hope will make things better in the year ahead.

Some speak openly of these; others keep them buried inside. Hopefully each one, whether they spoke their resolutions or not, will keep them. Some good can come from these resolutions for our bodies, minds, and spirits.

One resolution we should all make and keep, is to be prepared for the time when we will have no more "new" years on earth...Each year is drawing us closer to the time when we will enter Eternity - Heaven or Hell! Whether we come to the end of our life here, or You, Lord Jesus return, we still need to be prepared...

Knowing and accepting You as Savior and Lord, is the most important preparation! We also need to learn to know more about You and grow in our relationship with You...As we draw nearer to You, You may use us to become extensions of Yourself. Then we can truly become Your Hands, Your Eyes, Your Feet, and Your Heart. And Lord, let us not forget our wallets, which we should open to You...

May this year bring an increase in our resolutions to know You better, and to do more of whatever You tell us...As we abide in You and You abide in us, You will help us to be prepared for whatever the new year may hold... ... ...

The Year Two Thousand!!

Genesis 1: 1,2 (KJV)
In the beginning God created the heaven and the earth. And the earth was without form, and void; and darkness *was* upon the face of the deep. And the spirit of God moved upon the face of the waters.

And so the year 2000 was ushered in as You, Almighty God, looked down upon your earth. You've watched down upon this earth since the beginning of time, for You created it...How much You have seen since the very beginning!

Last night, New Year's Eve, by our standards, must have caused You to experience many different thoughts in regard to the human race...

Some were fighting ongoing wars, year after year. Some were celebrating the new millennium with all sorts of noise...Fireworks were flying upwards into the sky! Music blasted out!

Yet, in some of Your countries children were continuing to die from lack of food and medicine...They were totally unaware of celebrating the year 2000.

Father God, what right do we have to celebrate the new millennium? What good have we accomplished on a large scale? What difference do we make in the scheme of things...

Though much has been invented to make life easier, morality has dropped to an all time low in this century...

How disheartened You must become at times, dear God - knowing that Your desire to have a people set apart for Yourself, cost You so much...Your Plan was to send Your Son Jesus. Oh, Father God, how we thank You for allowing Your Precious Son to come here...He came to teach us Your thoughts to live by...It grieves us that He died such a horrible death...But by His death, He saved us from having to pay for our sins...

And in learning these lessons which Jesus taught, we find that there is great satisfaction to our inner selves, our souls. Just as we need food and water to keep us healthy, so we need to satisfy our souls by learning YOUR ways...

Yes, 2000 has come…The earth's inhabitants are given another chance to better the past…Dear Father God, help us to see the importance of this new opportunity!

Help us to see the need to stop putting ourselves first…Help us, please, to understand that money and all that we have been blessed with, is to be shared and not stored up.

Yes, Father God, You are giving us another chance – may we change our hearts so the future can improve on our past… … …

My Lord's Feet   Palm Sunday

John 13:14-17

And since I, the Lord and Teacher, have washed your feet, you ought to wash each other's feet. I have given you an example to follow: do as I have done to you. How true it is that a servant is not greater than his master. Nor is the messenger more important than the one who sends him. You know these things—now do them! That is the path of blessing.

Dear Lord, as I meditate about You at this moment, I keep seeing Your feet. So many thoughts keep running through my mind when I picture them…Are they the feet, the only feet in this whole world that I would wash? Most certainly, dear Lord, I would wash Yours! Feet are such odd and often unattractive parts of our bodies and some are so much worse than others! But Your feet would be soft to the touch, without a blemish on them! I would like to have the privilege of washing Your feet!

First, Lord, let me unbuckle Your sandal. I'll do one foot at a time. What sturdy sandals - they look like someone took many hours of patient care in making them for You…Now then, let me take Your foot. It is soft! Wow Lord, You are letting me do this special task! I am truly privileged! Now that the first one is bathed, let me rub it with these special lotions which I have! They will refresh and cool Your foot. There Lord, doesn't that feel good?

Now for the other one - this foot is just as soft, just as special as I knew it would be! Thank goodness for this heavy towel I have…It is worthy of being used to tenderly wipe and dry Your feet! There, it is all dry and ready for the lotions. Doesn't that lotion make Your feet feel great?

Well, sweet Jesus, that was indeed a great pleasure and an honor! How blessed I am that You allowed me to be the one to bathe Your feet! I'm glad You didn't want me to wash someone else's feet instead!

What Lord? You want me to wash those dirty and ugly feet over there? But they belong to a person I don't like! I never liked that person, Lord, from the very first time we encountered each other. Surely You don't want me to wash those feet? I only wanted to wash Yours, Lord Jesus. Only Your feet were worthy of being washed by me. And look at those sandals, they're not sturdy like Yours are. They will never be able to wear them as long as You will wear Yours!

When did You get those beautiful sandals, Lord? For Your 33rd birthday? They will last many years! Blessed is the man with such sandals...

Oh, Jesus, I was hoping You'd forget about having me wash those feet! All right I will, but only because I love You and You want me to...Oh, You'll let me walk in those beautiful sandals next week? But won't You be wearing them, dear Jesus?

My Lord's Hands   Monday

Mark 8:25 (NIV)

Once more Jesus put his hands on the man's eyes. Then his eyes were opened, his sight was restored, and he saw everything clearly.

Mark 10:16

Then he took the children into his arms and placed his hands on their heads and he blessed them.

Dear Lord, how precious Your hands must have been...How many times You used them for such important roles in history! Your hands, Your innocent hands, took the bread and broke it and divided it among Your apostles. Your just hands took the wine and poured it for Your apostles. These hands took the symbols of Your precious Body and Blood and divided them among all who were present at Your last supper...You knew how Your own flesh would be bruised and Your precious skin torn... Your Blood was spilled as that wine was poured out! You knew Lord, what was to happen and yet Your hands were as steady then as they ever were...

419

Those hands, sweet Jesus, were the hands, which were so chubby and kissable as a baby too. How Your blessed mother, Mary, must have loved to squeeze them and kiss the hurts when You injured them as a child...

Those were the hands, dear Sweet Jesus, that ran through the curls of the children who sat on Your lap when You called them to You. How gentle those hands were...

Those were the hands, which touched the bodies of countless men, women and children for special blessings of healing and Love, my Lord...

Those were the hands, which picked up the ear of the soldier who carried a sword against You. Those were the hands, which Lovingly replaced that ear! Lord, what a generous thing to do...

Why then, dear Jesus, did they have to take these precious, innocent hands and bind them so until they were white from lack of blood! No, that didn't satisfy them. They had to lay You out on that terrible cross and take those precious hands, those pure hands, and deliberately, slowly take a spike and hammer it into You...With no emotion they steadied the spike...Down went the hammer, but another heavy stroke was needed. Down went the hammer again until Your fingers curled up in excruciating pain! Oh my dear God, dear Savior, Jesus, how could they do this to You? Once more, those men went through the some ghastly ritual, until Your hands were covered with blood..." Father, forgive them for they know not what they do."

Dear Jesus, is it possible? Do I see Your finger beckoning?

My Lord's Face   Tuesday

1st Chronicles 16:11

Seek the Lord; yes, seek his strength and seek his face untiringly.

Dear Jesus, tell me what to say as I sit here meditating and praying. I feel You have something very special for me to say today about Your beautiful face...But Lord, I feel so inadequate! How can I put on paper with mere words anything that can describe Your face? It's true Lord...Where can I start? What am I to say? Tell me, Lord Jesus, what You want to be said...

I'm speechless, Lord; the words won't come...Holy Spirit help me; fall afresh on me. Guide me. Use me please, Lord Jesus, as I am powerless without You...

If only I could have had one moment to look at Your face, dear Jesus, it would have been etched there forever! So many saw Your face, Lord. So many saw Your face and would not, did not, accept it! That seems inconceivable!

In Isaiah 53:2, it says that in our eyes there was no attractiveness at all, nothing to make us want You.. Yet, look at the apostles; they followed You for the remainder of their lives after You called them...What did they see in Your face? Was it Your eyes? Did Your eyes hold a promise in them only You could offer? Did they see that? What was it that made them follow You...

Once hearing Your voice, looking into Your face, and seeing all the goodness which was there, many were drawn to follow You...Even children followed You. They knew in their little hearts You offered the secret of life! How many mothers called their children back, not understanding who You were, who You are...

How blessed their children were to have been near You or to have touched Your hand or robe...What blessed little children they were to have looked up into Your face from Your lap and to have seen Your pure Love looking down on them! Oh, Lord, how we would love to have been one of these children! What beautiful memories they must have grown up with...Seeing Your face once was enough to last them a lifetime...

Now, Jesus, we are forced to remember when Your face was streaked with tears. You are in the Garden praying to Your Heavenly Father to remove the burden You are about to face...Your face, the face we long to see, was in anguish. You Loved mankind so much; You promised Your Father You would carry out His decision, His Plan...

Your face, the face of pure innocence, is now dotted with drops of Blood. Your Loving eyes are closed as You hang there on Your cross...Silent tears, mingled with Your Blood, spill down Your face. It is Blood shed for us - tears of pure LOVE... ... ...

My Lord's Body   Wednesday

Mark 14:22

As they were eating, Jesus took bread and asked God's blessing on it and broke it in pieces and gave it to them and said, "Eat it—this is my body."

"Eat it - this is my body." Dear Lord Jesus, to someone who doesn't understand that very powerful statement, it must sound very mysterious...You took a lowly loaf of bread and tore it apart and shared it among Your apostles telling them those mystifying words...

You wanted them to know at that moment, You were willing to be shared by men. Not only were You willing, but it was also Your Father's Will, Your Father's Plan...

Your Body was subjected to so much those last few days of Your life here on earth, Lord...You sweated actual blood through Your pores in anguish. You suffered in the Garden where You knelt to pray to Your Heavenly Father. That agony would seem enough for any one man to suffer! But for You, the cross was just hours away...

Men tore the flesh on Your Body with nails. They tore Your head with thorns. They tore Your feet with spikes. That still didn't satisfy them. They tore open a gaping hole in Your side until every last drop spilled from it...

They took the Son of Man and tore this Body in any way they could to vent their anger at You! Why? Because You were an evil man? Because You were bringing into their lives, wrong-doing and evilness and they had to rid themselves of You? No, my dear innocent Lord, it was because of Your goodness! It was because of jealousy, fear, envy, anger, and suspicion on their part, not Yours! It was the imperfections in themselves that brought out these hostilities when they saw Your purity and goodness! They could not bear to let You live, to keep reminding themselves of their evil natures. So You had to die...Your Body was the sacrifice offered up to Your Heavenly Father, for the world, for each one of us... ... ...

They did not understand that only You could have suffered for the sins of mankind. You, the supreme offering of all time, would be the very one to ask Your Father to forgive them – and all of us! Only You, dear just Master, would think of a thing like that to do, with the very last breath in Your crushed and torn Body...

Lord today, this minute, draw us all closer to the realization of what You did through Your Body...For You lovingly freed us from damnation and allowed us the privilege of Eternity with You... ... ...

My Lord's Blood   Thursday

Matthew 26:27,28

And he took a cup of wine and gave thanks for it and gave it to them and said, "Each one drink from it, for this is my blood, sealing the New Covenant. It is poured out to forgive the sins of multitudes."

My Lord, my Master, let me drink from Your cup. Let us all drink from Your cup for it is an everlasting cup...Your cup never runs dry. It constantly keeps filling so that all of us can share in Your divine request in asking us to drink from Your cup...

Again, sweet Jesus, this is the mystery of Your LOVE. It is the mystery of the wine You offered us to drink, but is Your very own Blood! Lord, this must have been so difficult for Your apostles to hear...They were simple men and You had so much to teach them, in so little time...

Each one of us has felt the pressure at one time or another of trying to absorb some things quickly. These things had to be learned, but there just didn't seem enough time to grasp them.. We were panicking inside. We were hoping no one near us would realize what an effort we had to make, in order to comprehend the whole picture!

Father, we can relate with Your apostles so well that night. What panic they must have felt! You were saying such mysterious things to them...You were telling them You had to leave them...You said this was the last time You would share supper with them. How absolutely sad they must have been...

You also told them Your Blood would be shed for many so they could have freedom...Dear Jesus, when we think of blood, it usually is an uncomfortable thought...No one wants to think about blood...You told the apostles You would give them Your Body! Lord Jesus, that would seem like a complete sacrifice right there! Yet, every drop of Your Blood You also offered...And lovingly, You gave this same sacrifice for us...

423

Holy Jesus, You are the only one who gave a total gift to all mankind...You held nothing back...First You gave us Your LOVE, Your unconditional Divine LOVE. Then You offered us Your Body, Your innocent Body. Finally You offered us Your Blood, every single drop until there was no more...You gave Your ALL for us...

When we meditate on this, we realize one human being does not contain very much blood...But Your Blood, Jesus, Savior and Lord, was enough to cover this whole earth and cleanse all who live on it! Here is the mystery again...This is what You will explain to us some day, dear loving Savior...

"Each one drink from it, for this is my blood..."

Our Crucified Lord   Good Friday

John 1:29
The next day John saw Jesus coming toward him and said, "Look! There is the Lamb of God who takes away the world's sin!"

"Look! There is the Lamb of God who takes away the world's sin!" Yes dear Savior, let us all look at You as You hang there on the Cross...When John the Baptist uttered those words when he first saw You, he probably didn't realize how appropriate they would be...How fitting they are today on Good Friday, as You hang there, crucified.

Let us really look at You as You hang there...Can any of us look at You without feeling remorse, guilt, utter despair, disgust, deepest sadness, tremendous love, grateful thanksgiving? All these emotions well up in our breasts as we gaze upon Your defiled Body. You are our sacrificial Lamb!

Yes, dear Jesus, You were the ultimate sacrifice...You were slaughtered for one and all. As gentle as a lamb, You submitted to this barbaric end for all of mankind! It was Your Father's Plan, and You willingly paid the price for our Salvation.

Many, many words have been written about this last day of Yours, sweet Lamb. What more can be said today? What words, mere words, can capture it?

If You were to have to judge men by their actions on that last day, sweet Christ, how would You judge those who were with You on that

424

eventful day? Many screamed for Your death; "Crucify Him! Crucify Him!" Many wept openly as they watched You silently struggle with that burdensome cross...Some spit on You! Others shouted terrible things at You!

One man helped You carry Your Cross. Only he and You know what was in his heart as he hoisted it up on his shoulders in Your place. Did he hold resentment inside himself as he carried it against his will? Was he forced to do it, or did he willingly pick it up in deep compassion for You? He, Simon, has a questionable role in history doesn't he? You know what was in his heart though, as You know what is in all our hearts. How would You judge us, dear Lord, if we were in Simon's place? Only You know that too, Lord...

Perhaps a little child came forward and kissed Your cheek tenderly. Maybe this young one placed a wild flower in Your hand as You laid there when You fell...Perhaps this innocent child was the symbol of the only complete act of love You experienced that last day. Did this child come forward with the kind of love You want from all of us?

Your Love is so trusting, nothing in all this world could or can compare to it...Perhaps this little child had to pull away from the security of a safe and cautious position. You fell there before hundreds of eyes watching this cruel scene. Is this what You want from us also? Do You want us to run out from all our securities and make a commitment of our love and compassion for You?

There were so many, many that day who wanted to watch another man be crucified... They looked at You hanging there, Your Body draining itself of its last signs of life. They waited for the thrill of excitement to surge through their depraved bodies...None came - only uncontrollable shuddering. These shudders were felt in every household around the world, as the earth turned black with horror at what was done to You, dear Lamb of God!

Now all have left this terrible place...Light begins to filter back into the sky, Your sky...

What blows there gently in the breeze at the foot of Your cross? Is it the wild flower: the same little flower, which was clutched in the small hand filled with love for You? Is it the same broken little flower that You carried along Your final walk.

Can we go closer to see it? Does Your judgment hinge on this flower; a symbol of a little child's love? Will it be renewed, fresh and whole again as before it was picked, or will it be lost forever? Is the judgment made on Your last day, not of You, but made of each and every one of us who walk this earth?

Was that flower a symbol of ourselves? Was the child a symbol of our faith? With a child's faith, we, the flower, broken and imperfect from the crushing walk of life, can be made fresh...We can be made whole again to bloom as never before!

Thank You, thank You, Lamb of God, for helping us flower again by Your Blood spilled at the foot of Your Cross... ... ...

Rest In Peace, Lord   Saturday

Luke 23:50-56

Then a man named Joseph, a member of the Jewish Supreme Court, from the city of Arimathea in Judea, went to Pilate and asked for the body of Jesus. He was a godly man who had been expecting the Messiah's coming and had not agreed with the decision and actions of the other Jewish leaders. So he took down Jesus' body and wrapped it in a long linen cloth and laid it in a new, unused tomb hewn into the rock (at the side of a hill). This was done late on Friday afternoon, the day of preparation for the Sabbath.

As the body was taken away, the women from Galilee followed and saw it carried into the tomb. Then they went home and prepared spices and ointments to embalm him; but by the time they were finished it was the Sabbath, so they rested all that day as required by the Jewish law.

My Jesus, it is finished...Your agony is over. You are in Your sleep of death...Your torn and battered Body has been wrapped in a pure white linen cloth saturated with herbs and spices. Thank you, fellow Christians of long ago, for caring so sweetly and tenderly for our dear Lord, our loving Savior...Gently your hands wiped our Lord's Body clean...Gently your hands oiled His Body with fragrant scents...

Though You slept in real death, dear Jesus, Your soul must have been comforted by those gentle and loving hands caring for Your lifeless Body. They laid Your Body with the greatest of love in that quiet tomb so generously given to You...

With a great thud the rock was put in place for what was thought to be Your final resting place. Then all was silent as You laid there...

We would prefer You slept quietly, Jesus, as Your Body rested in the tomb, but only You and Your Father really know what You experienced for us...

As Your Body lay there in death, it was a day of quiet also in the town in which You died, Jesus...It was the Sabbath. It was a day of setting aside the ordinary duties of life, a day devoted to prayer and meditation. How many in that town, dear Lord, on the day after Your death, saw You in their minds? Did they try and blot out Your memory? Did they finally come to the realization that You, and You alone, were their Redeemer? Blessed were those who did come to that conclusion, dear Jesus...

As You laid in Your silent tomb, what joy and great preparations were being made up in Heaven awaiting Your arrival! If the fatted calf was used to celebrate the return of the prodigal son by his happy father, what a glorious celebration all Heaven was preparing for Your arrival! The thought of it is beyond our comprehension, Jesus!

Just dwelling on that thought fills our hearts with wonder! What was the celebration going to be like? Would there be a parade of angels waiting for Your first moment of entry and then a great fanfare of trumpets and all the heavenly musical instruments? Wow, Lord! Just thinking of what was perhaps being prepared for You is so exciting it makes us long for the day when we will make that journey too!

So, dear Savior, Son of God, Your time of glory is on the morrow.

Forever after You and Your Heavenly Father will reign... ... ...

Glory to You, Lord God, King of Heavenly hosts... ... ...

Glory, Alleluia!   Easter

Luke 24:34
"The Lord has really risen! He appeared to Peter!"

"The Lord has really risen!" These words, this exclamation or whatever words were blurted out, or shouted out have been the difference between wishful thinking and reality! Dear Jesus, Your apostles wanted so much to believe You were not dead forever to them! They wanted to believe You were the Messiah - are the Messiah! However, death has always been so final...They saw You die on Your cross...They saw You buried in that tomb...They fell into deep despair at the loss of their dear Lord and Rabboni...They had to face the fact You were dead...

Then the word was spread around: "The Lord has really risen!" What wonderful joy must have filled their hearts! What a tremendous burden was lifted from them when they found out they were no longer alone! They did not have to go on without You and Your tremendous strength, wisdom and courage! They had their leader back, their Savior, their Lord and Master!!!

Yes, Lord, we can just imagine how excited they were that first Easter day! We can imagine so easily, because we know about that joy too! Even though all those years have passed between us, we share in that joy today, Easter Sunday, knowing You fulfilled Your promise to return from the dead!

Thank You, dear Jesus, for allowing us to return from the dead too...If we do not have You in our lives every day, we are just as if we are dead, spiritually dead...We go through the motions of life, but inside, death has claimed us...There is no inner joy, no peace, no friendship with You, Jesus...So for all appearances we look and act dead to You...Perhaps to others also we look dead...

How many faces do You look into every day, Lord, and see this emptiness. How many have this look of hollowness, almost like zombies...Lord, it is so sad to see them because they haven't found out yet, that they don't have to go through life this way...

You returned from the stillness of death that morning so long ago. You returned radiant with life! Now let the good news be shouted to all, through the joy of those who have found You! Let each and every Christian over this entire earth spread the word, spread the glorious message: "The Lord has really risen!"

Yes dear Savior, we know in our hearts You have risen! We know by the love and compassion we see in another's eyes...We see Your LOVE, Your JOY! We know only You have the power to renew this feeling all through the ages! Glory, Glory, Alleluia! Our Lord is alive and well!!!

Your Lasting Supper

Matthew 26:26-28

As they were eating, Jesus took a small loaf of bread and blessed it and broke it apart and gave it to the disciples and said, "Take it and eat it, for this is my body." And he took a cup of wine and gave thanks for it and gave it to them and said, "Each one drink from it, for this is my blood, sealing the New Covenant. It is poured out to forgive the sins of multitudes."

Dear Lord Jesus Christ, I picture You sitting at the table with all Your apostles around You eating Your last meal together. So many pictures have been painted of this scene since men finally realized what Your Last Supper was all about! With all that has been written, Lord, and painted, it makes us long to know what that evening was really like! How I wish I could visualize what that Last Supper meant to Your loving followers...Did they know what was about to happen? Did they understand at all how significant this last meal with You would be? Did they hope that the evening would pass by very slowly so as not to have it end? Was it a joyous evening with some sadness or was it a sad evening with some joy? How many hours were you all together, Jesus?

Lord, You were really flesh and blood like all of us...You enjoyed eating and drinking. You enjoyed the fellowship of Your apostles; You Loved them very much. It must have been so difficult for You to be there in the midst of all of them knowing what was to be...You knew that there was one among you who was to hand You over to Your enemies.

Sweet Jesus, we try to relate to this scene. It is hard for us to realize how someone could share this loving and meaningful evening with You, knowing in his heart that he was to betray You...

Oh, holy Savior, please make us conscious of the significance of this Last Supper! Let us know why You are still willing to share this Last Supper with us so many years later! The same time You gave Your Body and Your Blood to Your apostles, You gave Your Body and Your Blood to us...One Last Supper has been feeding millions of people since that one eventful night!

You were so generous that last evening...You arranged for us all to share in this one Lasting Supper! What Love You had for us! What Love You still continue to show us and give us! You are constantly feeding us, dear Jesus! Your Body and Blood continue to renew us, each and every one of us, who claims You as their Savior and Lord! Please let us always hunger for You, as You continue to help us recognize - only You can satisfy this hunger... ... ...

Your Precious Wounds

Isaiah 53:5
But he was wounded and bruised for *our* sins. He was chastised that we might have peace; he was lashed - and we were healed!

Dear Lord Jesus, I have been thinking about the many, many wounds that Your Precious Body received during the time before Your Crucifixion...

Just a few days after Easter, I accidentally cut my thumb with a serrated knife...You know how small that cut was. As each day passed countless times this little cut throbbed with much pain. I was constantly surprised at how much pain could come from such a small deep cut...

Each time the pain drew my attention, all I could think of was Your Precious Body...You were whipped with that cruel instrument which tore Your flesh in countless places on Your Body...I was made freshly aware of the pain You experienced because of my little insignificant cut.

Now, days later, I continue to reflect on the pain You suffered for me – for all mankind, even as my cut slowly heals. Your dear Body had no time to heal...

Thank You, dear Sacrificial Lamb, for allowing me to suffer this extremely small wound. For this deeply reminded me of what You suffered so many, many years ago for me, for us...

As I reflected, I remembered I was cut while preparing food for a dear one. My little loving act of kindness ended up by my having cut myself...As that thought turned in my mind, I suddenly correlated Your Loving Act for me and for all humanity! You, Bread of Life, allowed your Body to be sacrificed for us...

You Lovingly accepted the brutal cuts on many parts of Your Precious Body...The thought of it, dear Savior, crushes my spirit and brings tears to my eyes.

Remind us, dear Savior, when we become complacent about what You did for us...You did this out of unconditional LOVE for each of us...You did not die just for "certain people". There are those who may be more outstanding than others, but You suffered and died for each and every one who has come into this world, no matter who they might be...

Dear reader, do YOU believe this?

No Greater LOVE... ... ...

John 3:16
"...For God so loved the world so much
that he gave his only Son so that
anyone who believes in him shall
not perish but have eternal life."

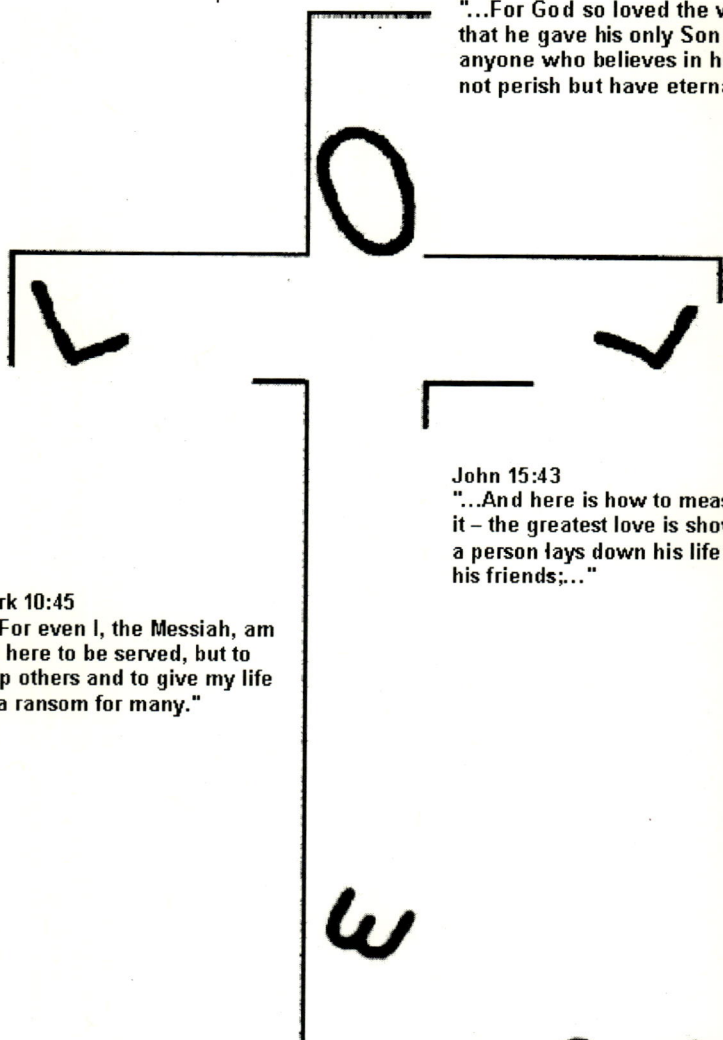

John 15:43
"...And here is how to measure
it – the greatest love is shown when
a person lays down his life for
his friends;..."

Mark 10:45
"...For even I, the Messiah, am
not here to be served, but to
help others and to give my life
as a ransom for many."

LOVE

GNL

Good Friday

John 19:28,30

Jesus knew that everything was now finished, and to fulfill the Scriptures said, "I'm thirsty."

When Jesus had tasted it, he said, "It is finished," and bowed his head and dismissed his spirit.

This day, oh Lord, this day - my spirit grieves this day, Good Friday...My heart is heavy with the knowledge that You, Perfect You, went to the Cross for me...

Each time my thoughts picture You at different stages of Your Agony, I cringe inside...My spirit, my mind, and my body are weighed down by these thoughts...

The day goes on and on, minute by minute, hour by hour...Your dying on the cross took place between 9:00 in the morning and 3:00 in the afternoon. Then finally, it is done. It is finished...

A quietness settles in... ... ...Where are You Lord, as You sleep in death? Where are we, Your followers, in our understanding of this?

Are we uncertain of whom You are? Are we uncertain of why You went to the Cross for each one of us? Is it just a historical piece of information handed down through the centuries?

Oh Jesus - oh Jesus... ... ...Draw us to Your Perfect Truth of this perfect example of pure LOVE...Show the world that You are the only one who loved us all, so very much...You were WILLING to die for each one of us! You were and are the only perfect human being...You are the ALMIGHTY GOD!

This is a mystery to us, Lord...You ARE Father, Son, and Holy Spirit revealed as three in One! But though the mystery is there, FAITH CAN MAKE IT REAL TO EACH OF US!

And so, dear Jesus, as tears fill my spirit and roll down my cheeks, my heart aches for the suffering You went through for me, for all of us. We thank You from the very depth of our souls for what You did that day - centuries long ago... ... ...

Blessed Day, Lord

Luke 23:33

There all three were crucified - Jesus on the center cross, and the two criminals on either side.

Luke 23:34a (KJV)

Then said Jesus, Father, forgive them; for they know not what they do.

Today Lord, commemorates the day You were crucified...It is a blessed day, Lord – it is a sad day...

In many places around the world, people are remembering Your unconditional act of LOVE which You gave to each and every one of us...

Calendars are marked with this day...Yet Lord, how many really care that You went to the Cross for them?

Services are held for those who do seem to sincerely care...Oh Lord Jesus, touch the hearts of all those who go there...Let it not be out of duty that they go, but out of deep compassion and gratitude... Others quiet themselves and stop their busyness...They take time to recall and ponder...

Yet Lord, there are so very many who do not realize what the day represents...They are oblivious to it...How can they act as if they are immune to what You did for them, for me?

Oh, Lord Jesus, as the years draw closer to Your Coming back, break the hardness of the hearts that overlook You...Draw those to You who pass You by without any recognition...Yes, the years are diminishing between now and Your Coming back, Lord...

Allow the scales to drop off the eyes of all those who, sometimes without their realizing, ignore You. Yours is the most pure Act of LOVE, which has ever happened here on earth...

How wonderful it is that You still wait for each one to come to You – You, Precious Savior, with Your open arms and forgiving heart! You, the one and true Son of Almighty God are desirous of a personal relationship! May millions and millions and millions of Your children turn to You as never before! May there be such an outpouring of genuine acceptance of You that all of Heaven will resound with Joy!

Oh Lord Jesus, thank You again for what You did… You suffered rejection…You went to that infamous Cross… Thank You for all that you suffered…

Only You, being Perfect, could lift Your dying head to Your Father God, and say "Father, forgive them, for they know not what they do."… … …

The Long Road

Acts 13:38,39a
"Brothers! Listen! In this man Jesus, there is forgiveness for your sins! Everyone who trusts in him is freed from all guilt and declared righteous…"

It was a long road that You willingly went on, dear Jesus, that day many, many years ago…Yet, we today were part of those for whom You went down that road, which ended at Your Cross…

Oh yes Lord, we would like to forget that! None of us today wants to take any responsibility for what happened to You that day…

None of us wants to remember what actually happened to You…You suffered rejection, scourging, humiliation… The agony from the crown of thorns should cry out to us this day… The pain You felt was excruciating when huge nails were driven into Your limbs…Then came the final shock! Your side was ripped open allowing the last of Your Precious Blood to pour forth for us!

Yes, we can deny our part in what happened to You that day…Denial is sometimes the only way out of a stressful confrontation with others, and also with ourselves…Deny all we want we must accept our role in what You suffered that day of all days in the history of mankind, because we too are sinners.

But thankfully, Lord God, when You created us You gave us a conscience…This conscience also allows us to feel remorse, deep sorrow for having offended You, others, and even ourselves…

Yes dear Savior, it causes us to look back and realize what You did for mankind, what You did for me, for us…By going to the Cross willingly for me, You opened the gates of Heaven!

Your final words: "FATHER, FORGIVE THEM FOR THEY KNOW NOT WHAT THEY DO" again shows us the deep LOVE

You have for us…You even used Your last breath to ask forgiveness from Your Father God, for us, for me…

Oh, Jesus, Son of our Almighty God, sacrificial Lamb, we pray that more and more will come to accept Your death as a payment for our sins…This is such a mystery Lord -You being Perfect and we so imperfect…Gratefully may we repent and thank You for that sacrificial act of LOVE… … …

Horrifying Friday

Matthew 27:22,23

"Then what shall I do with Jesus, your Messiah?" Pilate asked. And they shouted, "Crucify him!" "Why?" Pilate demanded. "What has he done wrong?" But they kept shouting, "Crucify! Crucify!"

My dear, dear Savior - today is called "Good Friday"…Why call this day good? It was a horrific Friday for You, dear sweet Jesus…It is a horrifying day for me.

As I read the four accounts of the Gospels describing Your last hours on this earth, I am appalled at the cruelty of the people…They acted like animals waiting for a kill - and kill You they did…

What kind of satisfaction did they receive? As they looked at Your Body, Your earthly Body, what went through their minds? It is so very hard for me to understand this barbaric act of theirs.

Sometimes I wonder what I would have done had I been there as part of the crowd. What would my response have been as You were being nailed to Your Cross, when You were hoisted up?

As You looked out into the faces of those who were there, what were You thinking of them? Did you know what was hidden in each heart regarding the decision to crucify You? If I had been there, would You have known what was in my heart concerning You?

Would I have had the courage to break forth from the crowd and tell You that I loved You, that it was not me who wanted You to suffer and die so painfully? Or would I have hidden myself from Your eyes so that You could not see me and my sinfulness?

Oh, it's so easy now, hundreds of years later to think that we would have had the courage to stand out there in public and worship You as the Messiah, as King of the Jews, King of Kings.

Even now at this very moment, You know what's in our hearts...You are the great Judge. You are pure justice. Oh, dear Savior, may we purify ourselves by confessing our shortcomings, our sins to You, so that we may truly become one of Your followers. May we be willing to face persecution for You, our Master, our Loving Savior...

As You have forgiven us, may we be generous and forgive others who have offended us...May we have grateful hearts filled with compassion for those You put in our lives...

Oh, gracious Savior, Jesus Christ, we gratefully thank You! We adore You! We love You with all our hearts for what You suffered for each of us... ... ...

The Plan

Acts 2:22-24

"O men of Israel, listen! God publicly endorsed Jesus of Nazareth by doing tremendous miracles through him, as you well know. But God, following his prearranged plan, let you use the Roman government to nail him to the cross and murder him. Then God released him from the horrors of death and brought him back to life again, for death could not keep this man within its grip."

Dearest Jesus...Yes, Lord Jesus, You are the dearest of all! Today is Good Friday, which symbolizes the day of your Death, so many years ago...This day each year causes my spirit to deeply grieve...I want to shout to the world that You should not have had to die...You, the only Perfect One, should have been treated as the King of the whole world!

Yet the ones living in those days screamed for Your Death. And so it came to pass...The unfairness of Your trial declared to history what happened that day. Part of me still aches at the unfairness of it all...

Why, God, why did You let Your Precious Only Son go through all that pain, humiliation, and rejection? Why, why, why???

Oh, The Plan - Your Plan, Father God - You knew it was the only way that WE could be redeemed! It was Your ultimate Plan for all mankind! By Your Plan to save us, Your Precious Son Jesus, would have to stand in for each of us sinners...You sacrificed Your Only

Son, Your precious child, grown to manhood...Amazingly, Your Son Jesus accepted this Plan for Him to die for us! His death was a debt that we, each of us, should have paid, but could not.

How would we have reacted if we were there that awful day...Would we have been indifferent to His difficult walk? He had to carry the heavy cross that He would be laid upon to be crucified...Would we have been horrified at what was happening to Him?

Perhaps today is the moment for each of us to look into ourselves. How WOULD we have acted???

Now he has been hoisted up and silhouetted against the sky as the earth darkened...Did anger pour out of His parched lips to one and all standing and watching? Did He scream at those who were taunting Him?

No...No...As a hush fell on the scene, all became quiet...His voice, the voice of our Savior, raised up to You, Father God, and called out, "Father, forgive them for they know not what they do"...

Dear Jesus, were You speaking about us also?

Five Liters

Ephesians 2:13

But now you belong to Christ Jesus, and though you once were far away from God, now you have been brought very near to him because of what Jesus Christ has done for you with his blood.

1st John 1:7

But if we are living in the light of God's presence, just as Christ does, then we have wonderful fellowship and joy with each other, and the blood of Jesus his son cleanses us from every sin.

Oh Precious Lord Jesus, You gave every drop of Blood from Your Body for me, for us...You shed Your Blood for each one who was ever born...

When we were created, Father God, You ordained that each one of us would contain five liters of blood in our bodies. Because You, Jesus, were born as a human, Your Body also contained the same amount – five liters of blood. That doesn't seem like a great deal of blood to travel throughout our bodies...When we suffer a cut or wound of some kind, we see some of our blood appear...To some it is difficult to see their blood dripping from themselves...This is a subject which most of us prefer to shy away from, Lord...

Yet You, dear Savior, willingly gave every single drop of Your Precious Blood for us...As that extremely sharp crown of thorns was hammered into Your Head, Your Blood was spilled...As You were nailed to the Cross Your Blood dripped from Your Hands and Your Feet...

That wasn't enough though, was it Jesus? Those who were torturing You, then ripped open the side of Your Body until every drop of Your Blood spilled down at the foot of Your Cross...These five liters of blood were enough to cover the sins of every man, woman and child who entered this world...Your physical Blood entered the earth at the foot of the Cross...This Precious Blood then, through Your mystery, was able to pour out over the entire earth, covering each of us who wanted to be saved from sin...

Would I, or any of us, willingly do this for even one other person? Would we be willing to give every drop of our blood unselfishly? This is a question only each of us can answer...

Oh Father God, You allowed Your Son to shed all His Blood for us. Since His Death centuries ago You have called countless others to die for Your Cause...You gave Your Blood, Your Life, willingly for us...Your Precious Blood mysteriously released, and still releases the Power to heal, to forgive, to bring forth Salvation...

Oh thank You, thank You dear Jesus, for those five liters of Your Precious Blood... ... ...

Early Easter Morn

Matthew 28:5,6
Then the angel spoke to the women. "Don't be frightened!" he said. "I know you are looking for Jesus, who was crucified, but he isn't here! For he has come back to life again, just as he said he would. Come in and see where his body was lying..."

Father, You are the Light of this dark world...You alone shine like a beacon of pure Light drawing all to You who want to get out of the darkness...

We praise You, Jesus, for being there for all to see - a free gift to all! Oh Jesus, we love You so much! Once having found You, we can see how You affect mankind...You change hearts! You change lives!

How we long to see You face to face! No one can ever take Your place; nothing can ever satisfy hearts once exposed to Your Divine LOVE. Oh Jesus, how we love You!

You rose from the dark tomb many long years ago...We can only imagine how You opened Your eyes and looked about You, as Your body stirred with Life and Light. Oh Jesus, how we rejoice with You! How we thank God for granting You eternal Life so that You can continue to be the Light of the world!

Only a risen Christ could leave the grave clothes undisturbed, as if shed by a butterfly leaving its cocoon...It is proof that Your precious Body laid there after being taken down from Your Cross...

We can only imagine that it was dark when You rose from Your still position. We can only imagine that as You left, a tiny glimmer of light was rising from the horizon. You silently went Your way...Oh what rejoicing the angels were experiencing! Their Lord, our Lord, was alive again! How they must have sung their praises of thanksgiving for having You alive and with them once again! How we rejoice again today!

Nothing has changed in the heart of man since that morn...He still needs a Savior. He still needs to ask You into his life. As You put Your Light into the Apostles, we can see how You changed them from simple men to fishers of men! They shed Your Light, which shines upon us even today...The Light which started to shine in the dark tomb that early Easter morn still shines because of You, Jesus...Alleluia! Jesus Christ has risen from the dead! Alleluia!!!

No Words Spoken

Acts 2:24
Then God released him from the horrors of death and brought him back to life again, for death could not keep this man within its grip.

It's quiet, Lord Jesus...It's so quiet...Here it is in the middle of the night, so quiet - so peaceful...What would You have me think about, Lord? What would You have me meditate about, Lord?

Into my mind comes a scene of You, early Easter morn, leaving behind Your grave clothes...You are now so alive, so vital! So full of Life!!! Oh Praise You, Heavenly Father, for raising Jesus back to Life! You fulfilled the Scriptures! Thank You, Almighty God!

And You, Jesus, look so strong and are already starting on Your journey...It all happened so quickly!

Where did You go first? Oh, if I could only know, or have been able to watch, when You started Your resurrected life here on earth! If only I could have been there in the background watching You; following You; listening to You. You spoke to those You met along the way...I can almost picture You smiling as You go about Your business...You, perhaps are already picturing meeting those You Love. You are cherishing the moments that are to take place...Oh, to have been with You that day...

But now, in the silence of this night, You are in Your Heavenly Home while I am here...The night is all darkness, but there is a coziness here in this place as I reflect on You...No words have been spoken, yet I feel the closeness of You about me...You, in Your Heavenly home, are joined with me...

Thank You Lord God, Savior, and Redeemer, for bringing about this sweet experience. Though I am alone, I am not lonely...Though no words were spoken, I have felt the comfort of Your Presence Lord, and Your LOVE... ... ...

The Lord Is Risen!

Matthew 28:5-7

Then the angels spoke to the women. "Don't be frightened!" he said. "I know you are looking for Jesus, who was crucified, but he isn't here! For he has come back to life again, just as he said he would. Come in and see where his body was lying...And now, go quickly and tell his disciples that he has risen from the dead, and that he is going to Galilee to meet them there. That is my message to them."

When the angel guarding the tomb of Jesus called to the two women who had come, we can only imagine their shock...

"Where is He? Where is my Lord Jesus?" they might have asked.

441

The angels might have replied: "ALLELUIA! THE LORD IS RISEN!"

Yes, the Lord Jesus is risen! How we thank You, Almighty God, for bringing Your Son Jesus, back to LIFE again! For if You had not accomplished this, our lives here today would be much different...Yes, dear Jesus, our lives today would be so very different...

We, perhaps, would have heard about Your LIFE and the MIRACLES You performed...We might have heard about Your horrible death on the Cross too, dear Jesus...But, that would have been the end of it - Your death...

Thankfully, gratefully, You Lord Jesus, sacrificial Lamb, came back to LIFE again! "THE LORD IS RISEN! JESUS CHRIST LIVES AGAIN!" How the women and Your followers must have responded to this news! Oh the JOY that must have filled their hearts and minds!

Now the reality of what actually happened to You, dear Master, hits them...YOU ARE WHO YOU SAID YOU WERE! THE SON OF ALMIGHTY GOD! The magnitude of this must have dazzled their thoughts! Oh, Lord God, Your Master Plan has been revealed...Little by little, reality unfolds to those there...What an experience follows as You, JESUS, fellowship with them...Oh, to have been there ourselves...

Dear Lord, we, who love You this day, many hundreds of years later, will also have the JOY of seeing You! We will fellowship with You and praise You when we see You in our afterlife! Oh the JOY that will flood our beings!

And now today, Easter, the day You rose from the dead, from the tomb, we can experience a portion of that JOY! The reality is here for us too! You, the Lord of Hosts, rose from death itself! You sit on the right side of our Father God! OH, ALLELUIA!

GLORY TO THE FATHER!
GLORY TO THE SON!
GLORY TO THE HOLY SPIRIT!

Spring

Psalm 65:10-12

He waters the furrows with abundant rain. Showers soften the earth, melting the clods and causing seeds to sprout across the land. Then he crowns it all with green, lush pastures in the wilderness; hillsides blossom with joy.

Oh Lord, Spring is coming...Looking out and quietly observing, I see Your beautiful Nature coming alive again! What is here today, was not yesterday...Oh Lord, You are the very breath of life! You cause the buds to swell and the leaves to burst forth overnight!

The colors, Lord, are all so refreshing! How many shades of green there are, dear God...How exciting it must have been for You to decide long, long ago what each tree, bush, plant, flower would be dressed in! Today, many years more than we know, we can still see Your handiwork – Your miracles!

Thank You God, for making this such a glorious world! Some of Your beauty is so awesome that it absolutely takes our breath away! Yet with all this beauty here on earth, what must it be like in Heaven! You were such a Loving Father to give us so much beauty here...You must have such glory in Heaven that we cannot even come close to visualizing it!

The little creatures, Lord, they also know it's Spring! The birds are singing; their bright feathers are so beautiful amidst the greens...How can we not praise You for this delightful time of year, Father...Yes, there is so much to praise You for.

As the showers come and the skies darken, we know through the raindrops, tomorrow's blossoms will be tenderly opening...As the marvel of the sun does its shining down after the rain, we know that it is all part of this beautiful Springtime...Glory to You, Almighty Father, for this beautiful creation!

The majesty of Your trees as they sway back and forth seem to say, "Thank You Father, for creating me." The poet Joyce Kilmer said, "Only God can make a tree." All hail to You, Mighty Creator, for giving us this delight! Please make us more conscious of this gift from You, Father...Let us be sensitive to all that You have created for us - for You created this beauty! Let us all become more sensitive to protecting and appreciating Your wonderful gifts... ... ...

Raindrops!

Song Of Solomon 2:11-13

"'For the winter is past, the rain is over and gone. The flowers are springing up and the time of the singing of birds has come. Yes, spring is here. The leaves are coming out and the grapevines are in blossom. How delicious they smell! Arise, my love, my fair one, and come away.'"

Clouds, rain, mist - raindrops pitter, patter...
The ground drinks up this precious matter...
Earth blooms as grasses begin to grow...
Flower bulbs swell from down below,
Ready to burst forth with radiant glory!
So how can we, watching out, feel sorry...
For God has His Plan to bring Spring here...
So rain today! Perhaps tomorrow will clear!
Then we'll see green grass and flowers galore!
Dear God, looks like You've opened Heaven's Door!

GNL

A Breath Of A Breeze

2nd Corinthians 1:21a (NIV)

Now it is God who makes both us and you stand firm in Christ.

Dear Lord, I'm sitting here this beautiful day looking out the window and seeing the beautiful new Spring growth on Your trees! They are so very beautiful, Lord. Thank You!

These new leaves dance in the sunlight. They flutter with giddiness, as if excited by themselves! Then, very slowly, they stop. Then they become still - still as if in contemplation...Then a breath of a breeze comes along and they begin to flutter back to life again...

As the breeze enlarges itself, the branches now also begin to swing and sway...Nature, Your Nature Lord God, is dancing with the gift of Life! The leaves, the branches, the trees themselves, seem to allow Your breeze, Your wind, to flow through them with no apparent annoyance...

Is that what we must do in Life, Lord, when winds of adversity come into our lives? Are we supposed to bend in certain circumstances and not stand rigid? It seems it is the small things, which annoy us...Is that the time to bend and let those annoyances roll off us as the branches bend to let the breeze have its way?

But yet, Lord, there are those limbs which stand so rigid - the strongest wind does not even allow the slightest bend...

Oh now I see Lord...In the areas of our Faith, we are to stand strong, unbending, unyielding to sin. We are to stand firm for the principles that You came to teach us, Jesus. That's when we know without a doubt that it is Your strength within each of us which carries us through, no matter how hard the winds of adversity blow.

Gentle and strong Jesus, Teacher of all good, continue to teach us how to deal with all areas of our personal growth...Show us, when we need to bend and when we need to stand strong and unmovable.

We appreciate Your gentle ways of showing us through the beauty of the trees, the seasons, the breezes...Thank You Lord God, for blessing us with all this beauty, and Your Wisdom... ... ...

Satisfaction For My Soul

1st Corinthians 2:9

That is what is meant by the Scriptures which say that no mere man has ever seen, heard or even imagined what wonderful things God has ready for those who love the Lord.

Your little birds are singing, chirping, Lord; what a delightful sound they make! They seem so happy, so full of Joy! They flit through the trees from one to another with such ease!

It causes me to think when I hear them...If they bring such pleasure to me here on earth, what must the birds in Heaven be like? What real Joy they must experience there!

Thinking of Heaven, Lord Jesus, I began to wonder about other delights that must be there - the flowers...Oh, the flowers must be so very beautiful that we will be in awe of them! Even here on earth, Lord God, You have created such beautiful flowers they can almost take one's breath away!

Last night the air all around was filled with a perfume of such sweet fragrance that it caused me again to wonder about Heaven…What must it be like!

Outside the sun is shining; the white fluffy clouds are so clearly defined against the blue of Your sky, Lord…Yet all the beauty of this earth, cannot compare to what is in Heaven…

If You so Lovingly have given us just the few wonderful things I have mentioned, Heaven must be Heavenly, dear Jesus! But the best part of Heaven, will be seeing You, dear Savior…Yes, even if there be nothing there but You, Jesus, that is the only place we should want for all Eternity…

For You, dear Lord, are the "Pearl of Great Value"! You are our heart's desire! You alone are the only satisfaction for our souls… … …

Earth's Joy

Song of Solomon 2:11-13a (NIV)
See! The winter is past; the rains are over and gone. Flowers appear on the earth; the season of singing has come, the cooing of doves is heard in our land. The fig tree forms its early fruit; the blossoming vines spread their fragrance.

Oh Lord, what JOY there is for me as I watch the beauty of Spring arriving! The lushness of the fresh green clothing the trees is so restful. The bareness of Winter falls away…

Even the birds sense the newness of the season. Spring is breaking forth again! Weariness, grayness passes and gives up to the newness of Spring…

Would that we could follow over all the earth to see the wonders of Your creations, Lord God…Would that we could gaze upon each flower as it lifts its face to You…Would that we could gather up all the perfume of Your magnificent flowers and bottle it. We would like to share it with those who are bedridden or lonely, Lord. Would that we could…

Yes Lord, earth's Joys are so beautifully reflected in Nature - in the splendor of fields filled with wild flowers bursting forth in color! The splendor of color is another of the Joys of the earth, Lord!

Only You, the great Artist, could ever capture the expanse of color, the magnificence of color...There are flowers which You have created that man has yet to see. They are hidden deep within the jungles or scattered upon the mountains of the world...Yet, You created them for the pleasure they give to You Lord, as You look down upon them and enjoy them...

The grasses turn from brown to many shades of green—the skies seem bluer, the clouds whiter! Oh Lord, such JOY comes from appreciating the earth You created for our pleasure!

May each one of us look at some special part of Nature and let our spirits become blessed...As we gaze upon it, we realize what a gift it is from You to each of us...

The Spring rains come, washing away the soil and dust from Your trees, plants, bushes and all that has life in it. Fresh new life bursts forth!

Oh, Father God, thank You for earth's JOY! This JOY comes from knowing it is a free gift! We have only to open our eyes and feast ourselves on the beauty of Your Nature...Let us see it with a new freshness, a new appreciation, a new JOY... ... ...

Spring Forward

Psalm 39:4,5
Lord, help me to realize how brief my time on earth will be. Help me to know that I am here but for a moment more. My life is no longer than my hand! My whole lifetime is but a moment to you.

Minutes ago, it was time again to change the clocks - to change time...Yet we cannot change time, Lord Jesus, we cannot...

Time will continue to run on second by second, minute by minute, hour by hour...Each of us is moving forward...From the time we are born, the clock is ticking off the seconds, the minutes, and the hours. Each of us has a set number of days, weeks, months and years...

Each of us has a different amount of time here on earth...We read or hear of those who have lived over 100 years. We also hear of the ones whose lives have been cut short, almost before they have learned what Life is all about...

447

Only You, God Almighty, know how much time each of us will have...It's one of the mysteries of Life for us...Some hang on to Life as if that is all there is...They cannot fathom that there could be another Life waiting for them when they leave this Life...They are afraid of death...

Yet death is the gateway to our eternal Life! We must pass through death's doorway to experience what You, dear Jesus, died to give us! Death is necessary for each one of us to experience so that we can begin our real Life with You, Lord, for all ETERNITY!

Lord, may each one of us realize the tremendous sacrifice You made for us by dying on the Cross...May we, who have already accepted You and embraced You, tell others about this wonderful act of unconditional LOVE...May we not hold back for any reason.

Time - how much time do I have? How much time do you have? Let us realize that the clocks continue to pass the seconds, the minutes, the hours...Time will reveal the difference between everlasting Heaven or everlasting Hell... ... ...

Farewell Jesus...

Acts 1:4,5,9

In one of these meetings he told them not to leave Jerusalem until the Holy Spirit came upon them in fulfillment of the Father's promise, a matter he had previously discussed with them. "John baptized you with water," he reminded them, "but you shall be baptized with the Holy Spirit in just a few days."

It was not long afterwards that he rose into the sky and disappeared into a cloud, leaving them staring after him.

What an amazing sight that must have been, dear Lord! The excitement the apostles must have experienced was almost enough to burst their chests! Yet for all they saw, there must have been a deep sadness to watch You disappear from their sight...

After such a momentous time, there perhaps, was a letdown...That is how they probably felt after all the ups and downs experienced during that last week: the Last Supper, Good Friday, Your resurrection on Easter morn. Then, forty days later You, Lord, ascended into Heaven and they were left with a range of emotions...

Lord, they must have been so filled with mixed feelings at that time! The apostles still loved You with their whole hearts, but were somewhat mystified by it all...They had not yet experienced Pentecost...

Jesus, it's much like having a large wedding. The preparations are made and emotions are running high. Then comes the ceremony with all the joy and tears of happiness! But when the final moment comes to say "Farewell" we are filled with such sadness. We have to give up our loved one to another for the remainder of our lives...We are happy for them because we love them, but we are sad because we have to lose them in a sense...Lord, it must have been somewhat that way with the apostles...They were happy for You because You were alive and well again! They were happy You were going to join Your Heavenly Father. But they were sad at the thought of losing Your physical presence...

Lord, you were their security blanket! You were their everything! When You left You promised them You would send them something very special! You asked them to be patient and You would send Your Holy Spirit, the Comforter. Your Holy Spirit would fill them with power from Heaven!

That promise must have been a ray of hope to them, dear Jesus. They returned to the upper room and talked about You for many days, prayed, and waited...

And so today, our Lord Jesus Christ, we must remember the same promise. You have sent Your Holy Spirit! He IS here and He IS ours for the asking! We don't have to wait for the days to pass as the apostles did. Your Holy Spirit is here, present and ever ready for us to call upon Him!

Spirit of the Living God, come and stay close to us...Spirit of the Living Christ, please fill our hearts with joy... ... ...

Your Magnificent Ascension!

Acts 1:9-11

It was not long afterwards that he rose into the sky and disappeared into a cloud, leaving them staring after him. As they were straining their eyes for another glimpse, suddenly two white-robed men were standing there among them, and said, "Men of Galilee, why are you standing here staring at the sky? Jesus has gone away to heaven, and some day, just as he went, he will return!"

"Do you believe that Jesus Christ is the Son of God?" Those around us sometimes ask this question, Lord. They say they believe in God, but what they have heard or read, confuses them.

How could You, Jesus Christ, be recorded through over 2,000 years of history as only "a good man," when the most celebrated holidays in our world attest to Your birth, death and resurrection?

Who else's birth and death have been celebrated for even 1,000 years? Yes, my dear Lord Jesus, only You have left Your lasting stamp on this earth. Only You, Jesus Christ, died without sin, for all of us, from the beginning of time…Only You ascended on a cloud with the promise of returning to us in the same way!

Lord, what a day that will be! What a glorious celebration for all Your Loved ones! What excitement there will be on this earth and in Heaven! Our hearts race with joy at the very thought of it!

For those who believe Your Bible is just a "storybook" or set of fables, or whatever else they want to call it, please, Heavenly Jesus, reveal to them who You really are! You are the Son of God! You are Jesus Christ, our Creator! Show them they don't have to understand the mystery of Your Divine Trinity…They must just believe it is so…You said it ALL in Your Holy Scriptures!

What could Your apostles have been thinking of as they watched You rising from them into the sky, higher, higher and higher until they could see You no more…What a magnificent sight!

Their hearts must have been filled with so many mixed emotions, dear Lord Jesus…They must have been perplexed, joyful, excited and awed to witness one of the greatest events in this whole world! We praise You, dear Lord Jesus, Savior of this world! We glorify YOU! We await Your most welcome return!

May it be soon, Savior of this earth, may it be soon… … …

Birthday Gift

Psalm 139:13-15

You made all the delicate, inner parts of my body, and knit them together in my mother's womb. Thank you for making me so wonderfully complex! It is amazing to think about. Your workmanship is marvelous—and how well I know it. You were there while I was being formed in utter seclusion!

Oh Father, Father, Father, how can I ever thank You enough for the precious gift of Life? It is the greatest gift You could ever have given me...Today is the anniversary of my birth...Today is the day that I can especially celebrate the gift of Life, which You have given me...

Yes, it's true Lord, that my mother physically gave birth to me. Yet it was You who gave the gift of Life inside her womb as I was knitted together as it says in these verses above, from Psalm 139.

You breathed the breath of Life into me as I came into this world! Without You and Your gift of Life, I would never be able to see the glory which You have prepared for me in my Eternal Life after I leave this world...Oh thank You, Lord God, thank You!

Lord, for so many years I did not appreciate this wonderful gift of Life, which You gave me...I felt burdened by Life. It was a struggle that seemed more than I could bear...Oh Lord, how many years I wasted in denying myself the real purpose of my being created...Forgive me, dear Lord, forgive me...

Oh Lord, You don't want me to feel guilty? You don't want me to feel sad? You say it took time to learn? Oh Father God, You are always so kind and Loving to me, so patient with me...You don't want me to feel anything negative about myself. You only want me to see myself as a student of Life and most of all, Your child...

Yes, Father, for that is what Life is all about; it is a learning process. We are here to learn about the many wonders and facets of Life itself...We are here to learn about the purpose of Life. We are to know and to learn about YOU! Oh dear Jesus, thank You again for the gift of Life! Help us all to truly understand this precious gift. We must learn to live our lives in a way, which makes You happy to have shared this gift of Life with us...Thank You again, precious Lord for this special gift... ... ...

Joseph

Matthew 1:20,21

As he lay awake considering this, he fell into a dream, and saw an angel standing beside him. "Joseph, son of David," the angel said, "Don't hesitate to take Mary as your wife! For the child within her has been conceived by the Holy Spirit. And she will have a Son, and you shall name him Jesus (meaning 'Savior'), for he will save his people from their sins."

Dear Jesus, sometimes we wonder about Joseph. We know so little about him! He must have been such a special man, dear Lord, for Your Heavenly Father to select him for such an honorable position.

How we would love to sit at Your feet and visit with You. Then we could ask You about so many things that You experienced while living on this earth. You could tell us more about Joseph. He seemed to be a very quiet strong man. He must have had all the qualities, which would make him the right earthly father for You, and the right husband for Your mother, Mary.

I can imagine You playing as a child with the shavings from his carpentry work. You doubtless came under his feet and caused him to be distracted in his measurements from time to time. I feel that he was very patient with You being there, his heart filled with silent joy knowing You were with him. As You grew, we can visualize him teaching You how to use his tools!

What wonderful stories he could tell us, dear Jesus! There must have been a time or two when he had to stifle a little smile at Your childish attempts to make Your first hand-crafted bowl for Your mother!

Joseph seems to fit the expression "the strong silent type of man." You must have been so content knowing Your Heavenly Father, Almighty God, appointed him. He also must have been a very simple person, getting pleasure in the satisfaction of taking a piece of wood and turning it into a useful item.

Joseph had the unique responsibility of answering to Your Heavenly Father. He had to take You, a small innocent baby, and teach You to become a man in the surroundings of his world. He had the responsibility of taking You and guiding You into a son to be grateful for. His role, dear Jesus, must have been so much harder than any other man's in all of history…

Lord so many times Joseph seems to be forgotten, but we know, dear Son of God, that he holds a very special place in Your Heart. Dear Lord, please instill the desire in more men to truly emulate Joseph.

Please, dear Jesus, tell him for us how much we appreciate his loving tender care of You... ... ...

A Son Talks To His Father

John 17:1-26

When Jesus had finished saying all these things he looked up to heaven and said, "Father, the time has come. Reveal the glory of your Son so that he can give the glory back to you. For you have given him authority over every man and woman in all the earth. He gives eternal life to each one you have given him. And this is the way to have eternal life—by knowing you, the only true God, and Jesus Christ, the one you sent to earth! I brought glory to you here on earth by doing everything you told me to. And now, Father, reveal my glory as I stand in your presence, the glory we shared before the world began."

"I have told these men all about you. They were in the world, but then you gave them to me. Actually, they were always yours, and you gave them to me; and they have obeyed you. Now they know that everything I have is a gift from you, for I have passed on to them the commands you gave me; and they accepted them and know of a certainty that I came down to earth from you, and they believe you sent me."

"My plea is not for the world but for those you have given me because they belong to you. And all of them, since they are mine, belong to you; and you have given them back to me with everything else of yours, and so *they are my glory!* Now I am leaving the world, and leaving them behind, and coming to you. Holy Father, keep them in your own care—all those you have given me—so that they will be united just as we are, with none missing. During my time here I have kept safe within your family all of these you gave me. I guarded them so that not one perished, except the son of hell, as the Scriptures foretold."

"And now I am coming to you. I have told them many things while I was with them so that they would be filled with my joy. I have given them your commands. And the world hates them because they don't fit in with it, just as I don't. I'm not asking you to take them out of the world, but to keep them safe from Satan's power. They are not part of this world any more than I am. Make them pure and holy through teaching them your words of truth. As you sent me into the world, I am sending them into the world, and I consecrate myself to meet their need for growth in truth and holiness."

"I am not praying for these alone but also for the future believers who will come to me because of the testimony of these. My prayer for all of them is that they will be of one heart and mind, just as you and I are, Father—that just as you are in me and I am in you, so they will be in us, and the world will believe you sent me."

"I have given them the glory you gave me—the glorious unity of being one, as we are—I in them and you in me, all being perfected into one—so that the world will know you sent me and will understand that you love them as much as you love me. Father, I want them with me—these you've given me—so that they can see my glory. You gave me the glory because you loved me before the world began!"

"O righteous Father, the world doesn't know you, but I do; and these disciples know you sent me. And I have revealed you to them, and will keep on revealing you so that the mighty love you have for me may be in them, and I in them."

WOW, Lord! I feel so privileged to have been able to read the words, which You spoke to Your Father! How You Loved Your apostles! How You Loved and Love Your Father, our Father! How He Loves You! How He Loves us! How You LOVE us and want us to share in this unending LOVE as we are the "future believers" whom You told Your Father about!

Thank You, dear Jesus! Thank You for Your prayers—that we will all be of one heart and mind, just as You and Your Father are! What an ideal to set before us! It is irresistible! Teach us to be of one mind and one heart. It is what we want so much deep down in our very own inner beings...

We praise You for Your undying LOVE for us—Your faithfulness to us...We never deserve Your LOVE, Lord Jesus, but we will be eternally grateful for this truly Divine gift to us of pure LOVE...

Almighty God, Creator of All, please thank Your Blessed Son, Jesus Christ, for His beautiful example of true brotherly LOVE for each one of us...Without His LOVE we would be doomed... ... ...

Father

Matthew 18:2-4

Jesus called a small child over to him and set the little fellow down among them, and said, "Unless you turn to God from your sins and become as little children, you will never get into the Kingdom of Heaven. Therefore anyone who humbles himself as this little child, is the greatest in the Kingdom of Heaven."

Show me the way, Lord. Show me the way...I want to do Your Will, Father, but sometimes I feel lost and confused...

"Put your trust in Me, child. Put your trust in Me. Only when you do this will I reveal Myself to you... Take My hand and I will lead you. Yes, I will lead you, like a child taking its father's hand. That's what I want from you, a childlike trust in Me."

Oh, Lord, You know that's what I want to do, what I really want to do, but it's so hard! I want to give up my way of doing things...What you tell me to do should really be so easy - just trust You! To really believe, and not just say the words, is what You want, Father, isn't it?

All right, Lord, that's what I'm going to do...I'm going to put my trust in You - completely...I'm going to believe You are right here now standing beside me, with Your hand reaching out for mine...Thank You, Father, for being here...Thank You for assuring me that You are always here, whether I be awake or asleep...

But Lord, can this go on and on and on? Will You truly be here always? I want to believe so very much...The words sink in, but my flesh steps in and tries to get me to think as the world does. "Believe in God - well, nice thought but it's just for kids." I can't really believe that You God, are standing by with Your hand reaching out all the time just for me, can I? What kind of a fool am I anyway!

See Lord, what I mean? See how foolish it sounds to those around me? How can I live in this complicated world, so full of unbelievers, without looking like I'm some kind of a religious fanatic!

"Believe in Me. Trust in Me. Love Me. I will protect you from the world just as a father protects his child... I will protect you."

Thank You Father, for You ARE my Father. No matter how old I am or will ever be, You are and will always be my Father. I know

now without any doubt You care for me! You will protect me and guide me! What more can one ask from a father! Thank You too, Father, for Your LOVE, which is always here surrounding me, comforting me when I most need it…Truly You are the perfect Father of all mankind… … …

Thanksgiving Day

Psalm 136:1,26

Oh, give thanks to the Lord, for he is good; his lovingkindness continues forever.

Oh, give thanks to the God of heaven, for his lovingkindness continues forever.

Oh, Lord God, how very grateful we are to You...You have given us this earth we live upon! You have blessed us with great beauty! The colors of Your creations are magnificent!

Yes Lord, this is the one day in the year that we refer to as Thanksgiving Day...Yet, after we let our minds wander and realize the many, many blessings we have all year, we should be calling each day – Thanksgiving Day!

Thanksgiving means giving thanks...Many on this earth have not yet discovered that it is You we are to give thanks to...How sad this is...For You, the Great Giver, should be thanked every moment somewhere on this earth...

It is so very little for us to do...Yet, so many find it difficult to give You, the Creator of ALL, thanks for the countless blessings we receive...Oh, Lord, unfortunately many equate money, power, prestige, material things, as the most sought after, in order to feel they have been blessed...

Oh no, oh no, precious Lord, You are the greatest blessing of all! Peace of mind, a happy heart, the love and affection of one's family and friends are the real blessings along with good health! Appreciation of those around us, caring for us, loving us are also blessings.

On this special day, Thanksgiving, let us truly look into our hearts and give thanks to You Lord, and to all those in our lives who contribute to our reasons for giving thanks... ... ...

Being Thankful

Psalm 100:1-5

Shout with joy before the Lord, O earth! Obey him gladly; come before him, singing with joy.

Try to realize what this means — the Lord is God! He made us — we are his people, the sheep of his pasture.

Go through his open gates with great thanksgiving; enter his courts with praise. Give thanks to him and bless his name. For the Lord is always good. He is always loving and kind, and his faithfulness goes on and on to each succeeding generation.

Dear Lord God, You are the Great Creator of all that exists! When we stop and look around this world of ours, we are often overwhelmed with the grandeur of Your Creation! What a beautiful world You have blessed us with!

Your generosity to us is apparent when we realize Your goodness to us. We each have so very much to be thankful for…As we pause to look back, we become aware of our own special blessings to be grateful for…

We, who have a loving family, are especially blessed. There are so many people alone today with no one to care for them…Thank You, dear God, for our families…But Lord, You also want us to touch others' lives with Your Love and Compassion. As we grow, may each of us be more loving, more caring to all those whom we come in contact with…It doesn't cost anything to be kind and caring. A helping hand, a kind word, a hug CAN make a difference to another!

May those who have families reach out to those who are alone. Then more of us could share in this special experience called Thanksgiving Day…

Thank You, Lord God, for the Gift of LIFE itself. It truly is a gift though we may not realize it at times in our lives. Let us use this gift of LIFE and show You how grateful we are for creating us…May we choose to be obedient to whatever You tell us to do…Then we will become what YOU want us to be…

Dear Lord, when we think about being thankful, it would take countless pages to list all Your many blessings…You are the Great

Giver in this life of ours! There is no one as generous as You in all the Universe!

Hopefully, each of us will be brought to a deeper understanding of giving thanks, on this special day of Thanksgiving... ... ...

Giving God Thanks...

Psalm 136:1
Oh, give thanks to the Lord, for he is good; his loving kindness continues forever.

Father God, Creator of all the Universe and more, we come today to give You thanks... Why we only set aside one day in all the year to do this is very strange, when You have continued to bless us day after day! Lord, we have only to look around us with keen eyes to see the many blessings You have provided for us...

On this special day, loved ones are united together. Fellowship is enjoyed and a happy feeling surrounds the hearts gathered around.

Yet in the midst of all this, many are suffering from the lack of the very blessings we are enjoying...May we stop to think of others who are not as blessed as we might be...

Not only should we think of them, but Lord, place a burden upon our hearts. Let us reach out and help those whom You bring to our attention.

Thanksgiving Day – may each of us look inside ourselves and truly count our blessings. And, most importantly, may we give You all the thanks for them...

Dear Father God, there really are no words in any of the world's languages to thank You! You have done so much for us here on this wonderful earth with all its beauty... ... ...

Please, Dear Savior, look deep within our hearts and see the unspoken gratitude there... ... ...

Christmas

Happy Birthday, Dear Jesus!

Isaiah 9:6,7a

For unto us a Child is born; unto to us a Son is given; and the government shall be upon his shoulder. These will be his royal titles: "Wonderful," "Counselor," "The Mighty God," "The Everlasting Father," "The Prince of Peace." His ever-expanding, peaceful government will never end.

Once upon a time many years ago, there lay in a manger a precious Babe...No one remembers what He looked like, but His Birth gave hope to the World...

No one remembers what His first words were, but His later Words still fill this World...

No one remembers what He did in the first part of His life, but the World remembers His many acts of brotherly LOVE in His later Life...

This little Babe, how His mother adored Him! Her husband, Joseph, must have wondered in amazement about Him!

No fine clothes awaited this infant when He was born. A simple cloth wrapped Him gently. No fine furniture filled His place of birth, only the barest walls and roof surrounded Him...

Yet a King was born! Yes, a King was born! The King of Kings was born that day! Oh the Glory of it all, yet the simplicity of it all - still amazes us today!

How many days did He lay there resting so calmly and peacefully? How many birds and animals came to visit Him as He lay there in that stable? So few men knew of the Glory of what was happening! So few knew their Lord and Savior was born amidst them so simply, so innocently...

The story has been told over and over again...Songs have been written, but never can the beauty of His Birth and those precious days ever be known in all their perfection! We can only imagine what took place that very special of all days...

No matter what the Babe looked like, He was Perfection! No matter what He was dressed in, He was King! No matter who His subjects were, He was the Savior of the World!

Oh, happy day of Your Birth, dear Jesus - we Rejoice! We Rejoice, for into this world came our Hope, our Peace, our Joy, our Salvation!

Happy Birthday, dear Jesus, Happy Birthday to You...May the word Christmas be renewed in our hearts as the Birthday of You... ... ...

The Young Shepherd

Luke 2:16-18

They ran to the village and found their way to Mary and Joseph. And there was the baby, lying in the manger. The shepherds told everyone what had happened and what the angel had said to them about this child. All who heard the shepherds' story expressed astonishment,...

It was lonely in the field that night...The young shepherd lay down his staff as he sat on the hill tending his flock.

What light was that, shining so brightly, high in the sky? Quietly he watched as the brightness filled the sweet night air...Night sounds filtered through, made by special creatures which God brought forth...How quiet the rest of the world was...

"That light...where does it come from? Why does it come? Come, little flock, follow me; I must find out where it comes from...I will play my flute as we go forth this beautiful night for something tells me this is a special night!"

"Look, little flock; look over the hill! There lies a stable bathed in glorious Light! Let us go down to see what can be there!"

Slowly, so slowly comes the young shepherd down from the hill...There is a special quietness as he approaches the stable...A glow shines forth from the openness there. What could it be? Curiously he comes now, crouching down low. There in a manger lies a newborn Babe...

What light shines round the Babe's head—what purity shines from the Babe's eyes! What JOY is seen in that beautiful face! Oh God in Heaven, only You could send forth such a child!

Suddenly the loneliness that the young shepherd felt a short time ago was lifted and gone...Suddenly he felt filled with a rapture he's never known before!

What could he do to show this beautiful Babe how happy he was to find him? What could he do…

"I will play a sweet tune, one especially for Him, yes, a sweet tune."

As he drew forth his flute to honor this glorious Babe, he knew in his heart that this special night would forever be praised!

Glory to You, dear Precious Babe, for coming to this earth!!!
All honor and glory are for You alone, King of Kings!!!

Christmas

John 1:14

And Christ became a human being and lived here on earth among us and was full of loving forgiveness and truth. And some of us have seen his glory—the glory of the only Son of the heavenly Father!

A cry breaks the stillness of the night as the breath of GOD breathes into this tiny infant…GOD BECAME MAN through the birth of this infant…

Can we ever comprehend the magnitude of such a thing!!! GOD came to us here on earth as man!!! GOD dwelt among us in our own likeness!!!

Though centuries have passed, though millions of people have come and gone, the mystery of GOD MADE FLESH still draws man into it…

As GOD breathed that first breath into JESUS, as His first cry entered this world, all men were drawn into this Plan of GOD. All men would have an opportunity to accept this GOD-MAN-BABE into their hearts, to save their souls…

CHRISTMAS – it is the opportunity for our rebirth, if we are uncertain as to why we celebrate this precious day…CHRISTMAS… It is the opportunity for us to grow in His LOVE as we deepen ourselves, to fully understand why JESUS CHRIST was born this day…

May we deepen our thoughts and our spirits to recognize Him, accept Him, and thank Him for coming into this world for us…

As mankind celebrates this 25th day of December, this day called "CHRISTMAS," may they know the Plan of our Heavenly Father,

GOD! He sent His Son, JESUS, as a tiny babe to become our Savior, our Key to LIFE Eternal...Truly this IS a day of Rejoicing!

The cry that broke the stillness of the night now turns into the sweet sound of love and mercy as the Babe, JESUS, looks into our hearts... ... ...

Celebration!

Colossians 3:12-15

Since you have been chosen by God who has given you this new kind of life, and because of his deep love and concern for you, you should practice tenderhearted mercy and kindness to others. Don't worry about making a good impression on them but be ready to suffer quietly and patiently. Be gentle and ready to forgive; never hold grudges. Remember, the Lord forgave you so you must forgive others.

Most of all, let love guide your life, for then the whole church will stay together in perfect harmony. Let the peace of heart which comes from Christ be always present in your hearts and lives, for this is your responsibility and privilege as members of his body. And always be thankful.

CELEBRATION! Today is a day of Celebration! Bells are ringing, songs are being sung! It is a day to be celebrated above all days, Lord Jesus!

Today we celebrate Your Birth! Throughout the world today is the day we stop our normal activities and turn our attention to You...Hearts are gladdened this day...Warmth and LOVE are shared this day...

Friendships are renewed; greetings are exchanged from all over this earth, Lord...That seems so wonderful...But why can't we, who celebrate Your special day, continue to share these warm friendships, this affection, during the other days throughout the year?

Why do we reserve these special feelings, these acts of kindness, to a short period of time during the year? Wouldn't it be wonderful if these special feelings permeated the whole year?

Kindness doesn't hurt us; it blesses our nature, our personalities...Thoughtfulness doesn't necessarily cost one penny! Giving of one's self can make one feel good...

Lord Jesus, You were the perfect example of what we should be...You were - You are the epitome of true LOVE...Why can't we make a conscious decision this day, to continue these feelings, which come because of Christmas...Christmas is a time of sharing, a time of caring, a time of giving of ourselves to bless another...

CELEBRATION! CHRISTMAS! Yes, let us celebrate this day, dear Lord Jesus, for You came here to this earth...Let us celebrate Your Birth as a human, though You are GOD ALMIGHTY! Let us celebrate Your Birth, because You came to teach us about LOVE - pure LOVE! Let us celebrate Your Birth, because each of us becomes more humane...Because of You we can call a stranger, brother or sister...

Yes, Lord Jesus, let us CELEBRATE this special day, which we call CHRISTMAS, especially because of YOU...

May this time of year, because of Jesus' birth, bless you and your loved ones... ... ...

Christmas Love

1st Corinthians 13:4-7

Love is very patient and kind, never jealous or envious, never boastful or proud, never haughty or selfish or rude. Love does not demand its own way. It is not irritable or touchy. It does not hold grudges and will hardly even notice when others do it wrong. It is never glad about injustice, but rejoices whenever truth wins out. If you love someone you will be loyal to him no matter what the cost. You will always believe in him, always expect the best of him, and always stand your ground in defending him.

1st John 4:16

We know how much God loves us because we have felt his love and because we believe him when he tells us that he loves us dearly. God is love, and anyone who lives in love is living with God and God is living in him.

What is LOVE? LOVE is a tiny newborn Babe lying in a place of lowest esteem...LOVE was sent down to earth from our Creator above, over 2000 years ago...

Today we call the day of LOVE'S Birth - Christmas...This is a day that is looked forward to for many weeks. This is a day when so much worldly activity stops...This is a day to remind us that our understanding of love CAN make a difference...

But does our understanding of love make a difference? Sometimes it does...But that little Babe covered in swaddling clothes knows a different kind of LOVE – unconditional LOVE...

Our love sometimes lasts such a short time. The Precious Babe came to teach us REAL LOVE – LOVE that is patient, LOVE that forgives and LOVE that forgets our faults. His LOVE builds up and does not tear down. His LOVE is lasting and kind. His unconditional LOVE covers every situation and circumstance...

May we each desire to give this kind of LOVE to all those whose paths we cross, wherever we may be…This would be the greatest gift of all that we could *give* for Christmas. This would be the greatest gift we could *receive* for Christmas!

This IS the greatest gift our Creator has given to us here on earth…If we were all obedient to share God's unconditional LOVE, then Christmas, this special time of LOVE, could happen 365 days a year! Dear Baby Jesus, what a wonderful birthday gift this would be to You IF we all understood Your gift of unconditional LOVE… … …

Wise Men Saw The Star…

Matthew 2:2
"Where is the new-born King of the Jews? for we have seen his star in far-off eastern lands, and have come to worship him."

Silent night…Holy night…You, Jesus, are born this night…Angels preceded Your coming! Shepherds heard them tell of Your place of birth…Wise men came bearing You gifts…

If we were there that night of all nights, what gifts would we bring? That is thought provoking… Each of us may wonder what we would bring – but perhaps there are those who would bring nothing…

More than two thousand years have passed since that blessed night…

A babe was innocently born into this world. We're told this babe grew into a man who was and is remembered throughout history…

Each of us has an opportunity to accept this man as something more than a figure in history - or not…Was He just a good man? Was He a prophet? Is He the Son of Almighty God?

Christmas – a time to stop our busyness – a time to gather with loved ones…It is a time to share love, joy and peace.

Silent night…Holy night…You Jesus, were born this night, many centuries ago… … …

(Sing) Happy Birthday to You,
Happy Birthday to You,
Happy Birthday, dear Jesus!
Happy Birthday to You… … …

Message about Salvation

God the Father and His Son, Jesus Christ, created the Universe. In Genesis 1:26 it says:

Then God said, "Let us make a man – someone like ourselves, to be the master of all life upon earth and in the skies and in the seas."

God created Adam and then Eve. God told them not to do a certain thing, but they disobeyed Him. Therefore they had to leave the beautiful garden that God created for them. Through them the earth multiplied.

God needed a Plan to save us, for we were all tainted with the sin of Adam and Eve. This Plan was to ask His Son, Jesus Christ, to go to earth and live as a human. Then God's Plan required Jesus to be willing to die for you and for me. Jesus prayed until drops of His Blood oozed out of His Body. He then agreed to die for us. Many people, opposed to His Goodness, wanted to crucify Him.

Jesus' death on a cross many, many years ago opened the door for us to enter into Heaven when we leave this earth. When the Holy Spirit of God draws us, we must come to Him with a truly repentant heart. We must be sorry for our sins, both of commission and of omission. When we openly tell others about our acceptance of Jesus Christ, as our Savior and Lord, we are confirming our salvation...

For it is by believing in his heart that a man becomes right with God; and with his mouth he tells others of his faith, confirming his salvation. (Romans 10:10)

When God knows our hearts are truly sorry for our sins, and we sincerely hope to stay free of sin, He graciously opens the Door to Heaven. There we will live for Eternity with God, the Father and Jesus Christ, His Only Son... ... ...

About the Author

Grace Newheart Love is a pen name. She was born in Connecticut and has lived in several states. Grace has been a Christian all her life and has attended different denominations as the Holy Spirit led. She was baptized in the Holy Spirit in the early 70s. She is a widow who has four children and three grandchildren.